STELLA NANA-FABU

Woes of Womanhood

An African Experience

M-A-P
Kansas City, MO

Woes of Womanhood: An African Experience
Stella Nana-Fabu

First published by

Miraclaire Academic Publications (M-A-P)
Kansas City, (MO) USA
Website: www.miraclairepublishing.com
Email: info@miraclairepublishing.com

ISBN-13: 978-0692295717
ISBN-10: 0692295712

Printed in the United States of America

In Loving Memory of

My Parents, Jacob Sunday and Therese Nana-Fabu, who recently passed on;

All the unemployed persons of the world; Women in particular;

and

The "Grand Maître" in Sociology, Professor Jean Marc Ela whose disciple I am

ACKNOWLEDGEMENTS

My hearty thanks go to the Minister of Higher Education, Professor Fame Ndongo, for his sagacious management of universities in Cameroon, and to my colleagues at the Universities of Douala and Yaounde - Cameroon and the Department of Sociology in particular for their moral support and their insightful comments and suggestions: The Pro-chancellor, Pr. Ngando Mpondo, the Vice Chancellor, Pr. Oyono D., the Deputy Vice Chancellors, Pr. Dontsi, Pr. Mol Nang, Pr. Ntone H., the Secretary General: Pr. Tang A., the Conseiller Technique- Pr. Bouelet R., Pr. Efoua Mbozo'o, Pr. Mpoche K., Pr. Misse Misse, Pr. Ekomo Engolo C., the Dean and Vice Deans of the Faculty of Letters and Social Sciences, respectively; Pr. Bidja R., Pr. Um Ngouem, Pr. Ntone H., Pr. Bikoi C., Pr. Assako Assako R., Pr. Elong G., Pr. Ebobisse K., Pr. Mono Djana, Pr. Djongwane Dipoko, the late Pr. Ngwasiri, Pr. Njikam S. M., Pr. Balepa A., and in particular Pr. Ndongko T. of blessed memory, Pr. Bekolo Ebe, Pr. Same Kolle, Pr. Kelzock, Pr. Dikoumè F., Dr. Ade C., Pr. Boyomo Assala, Pr. Nga Ndongo, Pr. Mbangwana P., Pr. Ngatsi., Pr. Zambo B., Pr. Biyon, Pr. Jua R., Pr. Mbonji E., Pr. Pondi, Pr. Nze Anvela, Pr. Maurice Kamto, Pr. Forgwe Z., Pr. Abbe C., Pr. Owona Nguini, Pr. Kamdem E., Pr. Fouda M., Pr. Atangana M., Pr. Massoma C., Pr. Ambiamina F., Pr. Nguepi G. , Pr. Chindji-Kouleu, Pr. Assoumou J., Pr. Fomani T, Pr. Malolo Dissake., Pr. Nkakleu R., Pr. Tumde M., Pr. Yanou M. Pr. Fonyam J., Pr. Vounda Etoa, Hon. Nitcheu, Hon. Ossi J. and of course the "Grand Maître" in the Social Sciences and Egyptologist, Pr. Grégoire Biyogo for his great contribution in academia worldwide; Dr. Bot, Dr. Akoko, Dr.Tassang C, Dr. Njoh Kome F., Dr. Houli D.

Dr. Ngadjifna C. and Mr. Damaigue D. for their constant and unwavering support and encouragement; other colleagues at the Department of Sociology: Dr. Nkoyock, Dr. Tefe, Dr. Yomb, Mr. Mballa E. E., Mr. Harouna, Mme Ngossengue Moukouri L. and other collaborators, Mrs Ngo Kana E., Mr. Segnou, Mr. Sidjui, Mr. Kouotou Mama, Mr. Ndinga, Mr. Nsoe, Dr. Edjua, and Dr. Atangana.

Dr. Ba'ana M.L., Dr. Vera Bouleys, Dr. Tchoumtchoua, Dr. Tchiadeu G., Dr. Fouda, Dr. Fotso J., Dr. Njoya, Dr. Balana Y., Dr. Banindjel, Dr. Kemayou L. R., Dr. Metote C., Dr. Nnanga M., Dr. Ngoaba, Dr. Attoh, Dr. Moba, Dr. Ngalla, Dr. Fonkpu C., Dr. Dika, Dr. Minjo, Dr. Mamoudou, Dr.Bondo, Dr. Baha M., Dr. Dashako V., Dr. Songue G., Mrs Ndzie M. R. L.., Mr. Nkounda V., Mrs. Fougue, Mr. Meka A. L., Mrs Noumbissi, Mrs. Aboya A., M., Abel Ze C., Dr. Ngo Nlend N.L., Mrs. Aissetou D., Mrs Ebegne C., Mr. Tchakossi, Mrs. Nzie, Mme Abissi, Dr. Bassilikin, Dr.Mbufong P., Dr. Mbaha P., Dr. Leka Essomba, Dr. Atenga T., Dr. Madiba G., Dr. Ikele R., Dr. Angoua A., Dr. Mbome A., Dr. Fingoue C., Dr. Manga M., Dr. Ntjam M.C., Dr. Medjo Elimbi S., Mr. Bruno Bekolo, Mr. Boteteme, Mr. Bandjokotok, Mr. Mbepi, Dr. Mpake, Dr. Pegha, Dr. Bikoko, Mr. Bapes Bapes, Mr. Ondo, Mr. Ewusa L., Mr. Belinga Belibi, Mrs. Wako, Mr. Mbarga, Mr. Nantche R. Mrs Kafack, Mr. Etindele J., Mr. Mekongo, Mrs. Mbouelet, Dr. Nug B.T., Mr. Ewane, Dr. Ekorong, Mrs. Mague Kamdem J.D., Dr. Tohnain N., "Le notable" Mr. Wemba S., Mr. Boris of the Central African Printing Agency (ESSEC).

I also wish to thank my dear brother Nana-Fabu Charles Nyinke who has always stood by me; Dr. Scot; Mr. Guebou Tadjuidje F. and Doris, My late friend and sister, Matilda Besong, Mr. Solomon Kemzo and wife, Pa and Ma Fusi, Mr. and Mrs Mouyombon of Douala, Richard Ole and Wife, Mrs Bondji R., Mrs. Birmo Theresia, George, the journalist, my visually impaired godchild and friend for his inspiration to me, and the many people who supported and encouraged me in the writing of this book. I express my special word of gratitude to all my sociology students and especially those of the "Cercle de Pensée Sociologique" at the University of Douala who participated in data collections of this work and for their encouragements; Ndondock A. C., and Tokam W. in particular, who typed this work with such painstaking care and devotion; Ndongmo M., for his technical assistance for the layout of this book; Mama Bell, the mother of the famous Cameroon Musician Dina Bell, for her kindness. I also thank some seasoned journalists in Douala, Kouamo E., Bica V. and his group- Bebe Muna, Le Bailleur Abou, Gros Bras, Pa'a Bo, Tendance and Aribel; Mbatchou C.

and team, Njasso, Coulibally, Patrice D., Bitter Kola, Ngoyok, and Aribell; Eto'o R. and company – Ngebou M. L. etc; Ben, Matop F., and Fotso E., Fangoua D., Yemelong C., Kouetcha C., Fongang C., Olinga G., Akong R., Ngantsop M., Nekachessi, Nyamga S., Fanga M., Nana I.C., Nufele C., Ndimu L., Etoundi H., Chris Tobie, Nfor H., Tchango W, Penda Serge, Tchokodo R., Onana A., Flo Tanko B., "L'Empereur Léonard le Pichichi", for his program on Tuesdays which reminds us of the importance to communicate in our ethnic languages or our dialects; Yannick E., Tanyi K. and the dynamic and diligent General Manager of Equinox Radio and Television, Tchunkeu S. and Team, Motassi J.G. etc. for their insightful programs on social issues in the country. Special thanks also go to Bertrand Bonzini, D.J. Shardin and H. Cool or Hervé Nana, Nziwa C. etc., who helped me discover the many great female musicians in Cameroon.

My deep gratitude also goes to "His Royal Highness" the chief of Bangoulap, "Sa Majesté Yonkeu" for his support and kindness to the Nana-Fabu family.

I wish to acknowledge my debt to Pr. Nga Ndongo Valentin, the renowned professor and top sociologist in Cameroon who generously consented to review, edit, and write the Foreword of this book.

Finally, I sincerely thank everybody especially the women and men who graciously took valuable time off their very tight schedules to answer questions and provide me with very useful, up-to-date and first-hand information on unemployment and Poverty in the City of Douala.

PREFACE

Le mouvement pour la libération de la femme comme minorité sociale remonte, tout au moins dans le monde occidental, à la fin de la Grande Guerre. On peut rétrospectivement observer, depuis, lors, qu'il s'est orienté vers deux directions dominantes. La première direction est tout à fait classique : idéologique, combative et revendicative, elle s'est traduite par des actions et manifestations pacifiques, symboliques, parfois violente mais toujours visibles et marquante comme les mouvements féministes aux Etats-Unis et ailleurs. C'est au début des années 70 qu'émerge la seconde direction que je qualifierais d'épistémique. Sans nullement renoncer au combat contre la soi-disant phallocratie infériorisante pour la femme, cette direction du mouvement féministe entend mener son travail sur le terrain de l'«heuresis », de la défense scientifique, pourrait-on dire, de la condition de la femme. Elle s'est ainsi illustée par de nombreux travaux de recherche et publications sur le genre, spécifiquement sur le statut de la femme, la différence ou l'opposition masculin /féminin (Françoise Heritier). Mais il convient de le reconnaitre, cette tendance épistémique du mouvement féministe n'est ni monolithique, ni unidimensionnelle. On peut y distinguer, d'abord, une approche engagée, dans la pure tradition de la direction originelle et idéologique. La science n'étant, d'ailleurs, pas nécessairement antinomique à l'idéologie, cette approche plonge ses racines dans le modèle théorique du féminisme radical qui n'est pas sans rappeler les thèses de Simone de Beauvoir, philosophe française du courant existentialiste, lequel pose que « l'existence précède l'essence » et que, par conséquent, « on ne nait pas femme (ou homme) mais qu'on le devient » par ses valeurs, son action et ses conséquences. La féminité, et la masculinité, ne se résulterait donc pas d'un quelconque déterminisme biologique mais d'une construction sociale assumée.

On peut distinguer, en suite, dans le féminisme systémique, une approche que je considèrerais comme positiviste. Elle repose, en effet, non sur des déclarations brutales, tonitruantes et échevelées, mais sur des faits, des études de cas concrets, des démonstrations et argumentations, des données et réalités froidement analysées.

A mon humble avis, c'est d'une direction scientifique positiviste que tentent d'épouser les travaux de madame professeur Stella NANA-FABU. dans ses multiples réflexions antérieures, en particulier des articles scientifiques et surtout l'ouvrage The *Feminization of Poverty in Cameroon*(Yaoundé, Clé, 2009), cette brillante sociologue a gratifié la communauté scientifique de remarquables analyses sur la nécessité de la réduction, à défaut de l'éradication, de la pauvreté chez les femmes camerounaises dont les besoins socioéconomiques sont, sinon identiques du moins parallèles à ceux de tous les êtres humains.

Le présent ouvrage, *Woes of Womanhood*, qu'on pourrait traduire par *Malheurs du monde des femmes*, s'inscrit dans le droit fil des précédentes réflexions de madame NANA-FABU. Il est évident que, depuis 2009, sa pensée a acquis maturité, consistance et solidité. Adoptant cette fois-ci une approche interdisciplinaire, la sociologue livre au lecteur une analyse globalisante sur les rapports, essentiellement conflictuels, de la femme africaine au monde et aux autres. On retrouve ainsi cette dernière au Cameroun ou aux Etats-Unis, à l'école ou à l'université, dans la rue ou sur le lieu de travail, en ville comme au village, où Dr YONKEU, figure féminine emblématique, est, comme disent les philosophes, mise en situation, permanemment confrontée qu'elle est, à toutes sortes de discriminations sociales tels que le chômage, colonialisme, racisme, le tribalisme les intrigues, la discrimination sexuelle, etc… Mais Dr YONKEU, femme de conviction, d'endurance et de volonté, finira par susciter la fierté de ses parents en surmontant tous les obstacles et en allant jusqu'au bout de son rêve d'être utile à sa société.

Comme on peut le constater, le present ouvrage présente des qualités fondamentales dont les deux principales sont les suivantes:

a) L'évidente originalité de l'approche la condition de la femme.

Professeur NANA-FABU adosse son analyse non à une lecture classique du phénomène mais à un récit, une histoire individuelle et singulière qui permet à l'auteur d'aborder des problématiques aussi variées et diverses que l'urbanisation, l'école et le racisme, la sexualité, la pauvreté, les dynamismes démographiques ; le statut de la femme devient ainsi, sous l'analyse critique de la sociologue NANA-FABU, un « phénomène social total », selon la savoureuse formule de MARCEL MAUSS;

b) L'incontestable scientificité de l'ouvrage.
Reposant non seulement sur une positiviste mais encore sur le recours à ces nouvelles méthodes en sociologie qui constituent les biographies, les récits ou histoires de vies, les études de cas ; le texte de NANA-FABU s'en trouve, de la sorte, résolument ancré dans la pensée et l'approche sociologiques contemporaines ; il est donc d'une saisissante actualité scientifique.

Comme aîné dans « le métier de sociologue », selon le pertinent propos de Pierre Bourdieu, il ne me reste plus qu'à inviter professeur NANA-FABU à se maintenir, voire à aller de l'avant dans cette lumineuse conception de son champ de recherche sociologique, pour continuer à offrir à l'espace public camerounais, africain et mondial, des travaux toujours aussi substantiels que celui-ci. Me référant donc à la célèbre devise des compétiteurs romains, je voudrais lui lancer à mon tour : « Altius et fortius ! » (toujours plus haut et plus fort)

Yaoundé, le 07 Août 2014

Valentin NGA NDONGO
Sociologue
Professeur des Universités

PREFACE

Themovement for the promotion of women, as a social minority group, in the western world at least, goes as far back as the end of the Great War. Retrospectively, one could observe that since that time, the movement had been oriented toward two dominant directions. The first direction is the classic one: ideological, combative and demanding women's rights. This is translated into actions and often peaceful demonstrations, which may be symbolic, sometimes violent but always visible, clear and noticeable; like the feminist movements in the United States and elsewhere. It is during the 1970s that the second direction which I call "epistemique" scientific discourse, without in any way renouncing the struggle against male superiority, emerged. This direction of the feminist movement was determined to move on to "l'heuriss"; which is scientific debunking of the heretofore stance on what one would call women's condition. This could be seen in the numerous research and publications on gender, specifically, on the status of women, the difference between masculine and feminine (François Héritier). However, it is worth noting that this scientific discourse on the feminist movement is neither monolithic nor unidirectional. One could therefore distinguish the first approach, the engaged approach; the pure traditional approach which is original and ideological. Considering that science is not necessarily anti- ideology, this approach is rooted in the radical theoretical feminist model which is the thesis of Simone de Beauvoir, the French philosopher; the existentialist view, which states that: "existence precedes the essence" and that consequently, "one is not born woman (or man) but that one becomes" by one's values, one's actions and one's competences. Femininity or masculinity does not therefore result from any biological determinism but by an assumed social construction.

Thus one could also distinguish in the feminist scientific discourse, an approach which I consider positivist. This is constructed not on brutal "tonutruantes" and "achivelées" or loud and illogical declarations but on facts, concrete case studies, demonstrations and arguments, data and the reality, analysed as is.

In my humble opinion, it is this scientific and positivist direction that "Madame Professeur" Stella NANA-FABU adopts in this study. In her other multiple works, scientific articles in particular, and above all in her book "The Feminization of Poverty in Cameroon", (Yaoundé Clé, 2009); this brilliant sociologist gratified the scientific community with her salient analyses on the necessity to reduce or to eradicate poverty that is currently plaguing women in Cameroon; women whose socio-economic needs are as a matter of fact identical to or at least parallel to those of all human beings.

This book, "Woes of womanhood", that one could translate as "Malheur du monde des femmes" is in the same line of thought as the other work of madam NANA-FABU. It is evident that since 2009, her thought process has acquired maturity, consistency and solidity. This time around, adopting an interdisciplinary approach, the sociologist gives the reader a globalized analysis on the essentially conflictual relations of the African woman with the world and with others. This is seen in her experiences in Cameroon and the United States ;at school and at university; on the street and at work ; in urban and rural areas; where Dr. YONKEU, the emblematic feminist; and as the philosophers would put it is: "mise en situation" or finds herself in the situation where she is permanently confronted with all sorts of social discriminations , such as unemployment, colonialism tribalism intrigues, sexual discrimination etc.... However, Dr. YONKEU, a woman of conviction, endurance and willingness ends up being the pride of her parents, and surmounts all the obstacles; as well as realizes her dream of being useful to her society. As one can see, this book presents fundamental qualities of which the principal two are:

a) **Original Approach on the Condition of Women**.

Professor NANA-FABU focuses her analysis not on the classic approach of the phenomenon but on a story; an individual and singular history which permits the author to examine varied and diverse "problematics" such as urbanization, education, racism, sexuality, poverty, demographic dynamics. Thus with the critical analysis of the status of women by the sociologist NANA-FABU; it becomes a "phénomène social total", an all-encompassing social phenomenon; according to the "savoureuse formule de Marcel MAUSS" or Marcel Mauss' savoury formular.

b) The Uncontestable Scientific Nature of the Book.

This is seen not only on the positivist approach but also on the new sociological methods consisting of biographies, stories or life histories and case studies. NANA-FABU's text is resolutely anchored in the contemporary sociological thought and approach. Scientifically, it is therefore timely and pertinent. Paraphrasing and quoting the renowned sociologist Pierre Bourdieu: "comme aîné dans le métier de sociologie" or as an experienced and respected scholar in the "metier de sociologie", I can only say to professor NANA-FABU to keep up the good work and carry on with this enlightening conception of sociological research as well as to continue to offer Cameroonians, Africans and the world such substantial works as this one. Thus quoting the famous advise to the Roman competitors, I would also say this to her: "Alteius et forties" or ever "higher and stronger".

Yaoundé the 7th of August 2014.

Valentin NGA NDONGO
Sociologist,
University Professor

CONTENTS

CHAPTER ONE

INTRODUCTION

It was one of those awful nights when it was raining cats and dogs, incessantly, with plenty of lightning and thunder in the sky. Slightly leaning forward at the window pane, in her second floor apartment, her curtains half drawn, and from a vantage view point, Dr. Yonkeu stirred out on the street. Nothing interesting she thought to herself "just rain, rain, rain." Heavy rain drops fell on her window. The sky was over cast, pitch black with not a single star in sight; and the street was almost deserted, but for some lights of cars speeding off to avoid the heavy tropical downpour as many of the roads in the city of Douala were steadily transformed into small lakes. The drains in this city are constantly blocked or inadequate. Then at the spur of the moment her mind wandered to those poor persons who live in the swampy areas of the city; such as Bonaberi, Bepanda, Malangue, Makepe Missoke, Ngangue, Nkolmitang, Feu-rouge Bessengue, Mabanda, etc. those risk areas which are constantly flooded even when there is just a little rainfall. She imagined the hell, the distress those families in these areas must be going through now with such heavy rains; obviously struggling to get the often nasty and smelly flood waters full of dirt and rubbish as well as plastics of all sorts and even excrement from overflowed pit latrines, from their houses; others tying strings to beds and other valuables to hang up in their rooms to avoid the flood waters; and still, others crying their hearts out in such pain, such total helplessness after one or two little children have been swept away by the merciless flood waters. Oh the vicissitudes of nature fuelled by human greed, negligence and poor governance! All these quite literarily sent chills down her spine. "Mai What misery, what it means to be poor in these parts of the world where poverty and inequality are institutionalized! Terrible"; such a "paradox of poverty amid plenty"! She murmured to herself (see, Lewis M., 1973, Kamdem E., 1999).

Indeed the challenges facing this country are daunting. Take the urban problems for example. The Cameroon government and many governments in Sub-Saharan Africa seem to have neglected their "Mission régalienne" or their very important role of instituting order especially in urban areas or cities. As a quick reminder, urbanization in Cameroon remains a huge social problem. There is still so much disorder involved in urban development in Cameroon. This has been particularly so after World War II, the post-independence years; marked by an accelerated, often unplanned urban growth. In fact, in most urban areas in Cameroon, buildings are constructed in a haphazard fashion, the streets are unplanned, dirty nameless and without street lighting. For example, the construction of many urban socio-economic and leisure infrastructures such as roads, warehouses, extractive industries mainly, schools, hospitals, cinemas, night clubs, bars etc., in the city of Douala attracted and continues to attract a massive influx of rural people, especially the rural poor into the city in search of work or a "better life". This massive rural/urban exodus or social migration has simply overwhelmed urban authorities in the socioeconomic and political domains. The demographic boom and its attendant ills (such as insufficient healthcare, roads, schools and housing), in many cities and towns in Cameroon seem to have taken urban authorities by surprise. The disorder in urban development in Cameroon ends up as a serious threat to urban life, especially for the urban poor. For instance, when there is urban clearance or when the ugly urban sprawls are destroyed, many of the urban poor become homeless and poorer with little or no compensation whatsoever. The urban government authorities seem to have forgotten that to govern is to anticipate; or like the French put it: "gouverner, c'est prévoir". Urban authorities should always anticipate the factors that may impact on urban development, such as a high demographic growth rate, and take the necessary measures to ensure that the appropriate infrastructures are put in place. For example, the creation of new neighbourhoods should be anticipated and good plans drawn up that will include construction of all-weather roads or streets, the provision of good drainage, affordable safe clean water, electricity, green spaces or parks, and other services such as schools, markets, hospitals or health centres etc., before the population starts moving into the area. This will help a great deal in the proper functioning of our cities and towns. At the moment, it is a big mess.

Also, the highest proportion of Cameroonians lives in extreme poverty as the economic growth in the country is at a "vitesse de torture" or tortoise pace (see Fangoua D., Ottou D., Esseme G., Nyope, Tachouang J.N., Ndongo F., 2014 Equinox Radio). The wealth gap in Cameroon is indeed huge and so visible as the few rich live a lavish lifestyle in their "sumptuous" neighbourhoods while the majority poor live in their dingy shanty towns where the government's service delivery record leaves very little to be desired. People here are unable to have the necessaries of life[1]. This is a country where basic human dignity is somehow neglected. For example the provision of public toilets, clean water and disability friendly public environments such as at markets, schools and even universities, remain a huge problem despite the fact that there is a 2010 law (Ministry of Social Welfare Cameroon, 2013) to ease the integration of handicapped persons in all domains of life in the country. Multiculturalism and credentialism are fast disappearing from our mores with often serious consequences on national development. Ensuring environmental sustainability is also necessary in this country because many Cameroonians, especially the poor depend on natural resources for a healthy diet, clean water, shelter, energy and medicines (see Nana-Fabu S., 2009). The poor are also most vulnerable to disasters, hazards such as flooding, landslides as was recently (November 2013) in Nyala Parizo

---

[1] For instance, of the total Cameroon population of about 20 million, recent statistics show that there are only 2 medical doctors for 10.000 Cameroonians and that only 38% of households have electricity. Only 50% households in Cameroon and 42.7% households in the city of Douala have clean safe drinking water. (Cameroon Government paper on "Growth and Employment Strategy" 2009), National Institute of Statistics (2013-2014) Cameroon.

Douala where a whole family perished and pollution brought about or exacerbated by environmental degradation (UNICEF, 2011). Persistent poverty in Cameroon is a real challenge for policy makers and the citizens alike. The almost total collapse of moral traditions, incivility, unprofessional conduct and abuse of power of some government officials and workers, the lack of a real independent judiciary; tax evasion or non-payment of required taxes by some of the very rich, the relative loss of self-esteem, the relative decline of family or community spirit, the brutal resurgence of the ethnic factor, which determines opportunities open to one, poor governance, general lack of improved and effective technology in production, political patronage, cronyism, poor sanitation, the prevalence of prejudices against social groups with different cultures and ways of life, the delay and sometimes non-payment of pensions to retired persons, the relative neglect of the aged, the general rise in insecurity, full scale banditry at banks and microfinance institutions in particular and petty crime, very high interest rates for the few available bank loans, over-burdened courts, HIV/AIDS, early marriages, single parenthood, unmarried people living as married couples or "concubinages", premature motherhood, polygamy, prostitution (male/female),unaccountability of many government officials and the chronic economic crisis since the late 1980-1990 period till presently, made worse by political instability, mainly by terrorist groups and civil wars in neighbouring countries like Nigeria and the Central Africa Republic respectively with often negative impact on the country's development efforts, administrative bottlenecks, in setting up business, poor work condition; the worsening pupil/teacher and student /teacher ratio in schools and state universities respectively resulting in overcrowded classrooms and inadequate guidance for pupils and for students, lower quality of teaching and a growing number of unemployed graduates from our colleges and universities[2]; in other words a

---

[2] For example, in October 2013, the University of Douala and "GICAM" (an organization of business persons), organized a forum to discuss ways in which the unemployment rate of university graduates could be reduced through the employment of graduates by businesses and the adaptation of university programs to the needs of the national and global markets. Certainly, this initiative is laudable but many industries should also be created or built in the country to absorb these young graduates.

decline in quality and infrastructure in the educational system at all levels resulting in the provision of literacy and numeracy rather than industrial skills and adjustment to the changing demand for knowledge, skills and aptitudes the labour market demands (see Okojie C., 2003); impunity, inertia, the culture of bribery and corruption, beer culture, inadequate energy or electricity, and of course gender inequality have all in no small way contributed to inequality and chronic poverty in the country. Severin Cecile Abega (1999:6) summarizes the general socioeconomic and political malaise in the country so well. For a long time now the economy of the nation has suffered from massive debt, indiscriminate exploitation of our natural resources, failure of many development projects, and general misery with poverty in urban areas becoming more pronounced. In the political domain, there has been poor governance. The ruling class has been discredited and there is an opposition doomed to remain in the opposition. Also, in the social domain people are barely surviving with corruption and demagogy paralyzing the whole administration[3] (see research by Nana-Fabu S. and Ndongmo M., 2013). In all, morale in the country is low and many people are disillusioned.

Indeed the disillusionment of many Cameroonians was made worse recently by the abrupt price increases of petrol for cars and cooking gas announced on July 03, 2014.For example a litre of "super" petrol that used to sell for 565 francs CFA, that is a little over a dollar, now sells at 650 francs CFA, an increase of 14%; and cooking gas that sold at 6,000 Francs CFA, now sells at 6,500 Francs CFA. This was really a bitter pill to swallow for many Cameroonians, especially the majority poor. Some top opposition party leaders in the country like Maurice Kamto, Ndam Njoya, Anicet Ekane and Carl Walla quickly lashed out at government's insensitivity to the suffering of the masses. This is because immediately following the announcements of the price increases of petrol and cooking gas, speculators increased prices of foods and other basic goods and services leaving many consumers, with already a very low purchasing power, desperate

---

[3] For instance recently (November 2013) Cameroon Parliament approved a budget that heavily weighted in favour of the functioning of Government than on investments.

and helpless. For instance at the Sandaga market in the city of Douala, prices of foods and other basic commodities were immediately increased. For example, a basket of tomatoes that sold at 8,000 francs CFA, was increased to 11,000 Francs CFA; the price of Irish potatoes was raised from 20,000 Francs CFA to 27,000 Franc CFA a bag; a basket of fruits- pawpaw, that sold for 1,000 Franc CFA was selling at 1,700 Francs CFA; a basket of charcoal was also increased from 5,500 CFA to 8,000 Francs CFA etc. etc.

The opposition leader Marice Kamto attributed the price hikes to the general poor governance in the country that resulted in billions and billions of Francs CFA being spent each year on the socioeconomic well-being and comfort of top government officials, what the French called "dépenses de prestige"; rather than on social and economic investments that could be beneficial to the ordinary Cameroonian and the development of the country as a whole.

Ndam Njoya on his part focused on the Cameroon government's improvisation in resolving critical socioeconomic problems which end up having serious implications and consequences on the wellbeing of the already suffering masses; such as inflated prices on food and basic goods and services. He found this deplorable and short-sighted on the part of government.

Similarly, Anicet Ekane and Claude Abe the Political Sociologist saw this problem as a real provocation on the part of the government on people undergoing tremendous hardships; that is the ordinary Cameroon woman and man. (Equinox Radio News, 04/07/2014).

Of course the Cameroon Government has not been really insensitive to the people's sufferings as the opposition leaders insinuated for on the 7th of July 2014 there was a presidential decree that increased the pay of civil servants and the army by 5% and halved the taxes paid by motorcycle taximen. Also, on July 17, 2014, the Cameroon Government raised the minimum wage to 36,270 francs CFA.

Of course, these changes were welcomed by some Cameroonians but others rejected them outright as being insignificant to resolve the massive problems of inflation and poverty in Cameroon. For example they insisted that civil servants and the army constitute a very small minority of the Cameroonian population; and that it will make very little difference on the lives of the suffering masses who struggle day in day out to make ends meet (Equinox Radio News, 07/07/2014).

Other trade unionists like Bikoko G.M. found this move by government very insignificant to help Cameroonian scope with the high cost of living in the country. In fact to the economist Alaka Alaka, these government measures were irrelevant and reflected the confused state of governance in Cameroon. Similarly the political sociologist Abe C. feels the whole situation makes a total mockery of Cameroonians and that it could actually ignite socio-political strife in the country (Equinox Radio News, 06/07/2014). The economist Bassilikin on his part sees the 5% pay increase of civil servants and the army as a policy that will only benefit about 3% of the entire Cameroon population leaving the rest of the population wallowing in poverty. Indeed, he went on that Cameroon is like a country in a war situation where the majority of the population remains poor while only a handful of persons are rich (Equinox Radio, 13/07/2014).

Also the gap between the rich and the poor Cameroonians has widened tremendously in recent years, (institutionalized inequality); with young people somewhat marginalized in the socio-economic and political structures. The crude and unrestrained capitalism in the country characterized by greed, selfishness, corruption and monopolistic companies with very little or no ethical considerations whatsoever, has led to such inequality, grinding poverty and mass suffering. Companies such as the lone electricity and water companies do not know that when they make such massive profits, they should at least reduce "considerably" the prize of electricity and water for consumers, especially for the poor in order to reduce inequality in society. Although the cost of electricity was reduced in 2012 for the poorest in society, it was not reduced enough to have a real impact on the poor. Many households still encounter tremendous difficulty to make the monthly payment of electricity and water bills for that matter. Also there are many households especially in rural areas that still use bush lamps, and "trucans" -a sort of locally made candle light[4]. In fact the high cost of electricity has led to fraudulent connections which have resulted in many fires and deaths, especially of children in big cities and towns such as Douala, Yaounde, Limbe, Kumba, Bafoussam, Ngaoundere, etc. in recent times. One need not mention the poor quality of water many Cameroonians still consume leading to water borne diseases such as diarrhoea for children especially, dysentery and even cholera. In fact, recently, in November 2013, it was reported that, about 1000 people died within ten months of malaria[5] in the Extreme Northern Region caused by the floods that washed away their mud huts and the dirty water that they consumed. Also, in July 2014, many people were reported dead of cholera in the Extreme Northern Region. (Equinox Radio News, November 2013, July 2014). It is a shame, Dr. Yonkeu thought.

For other companies operating in the country, they should not only maximize profits for themselves, but they should also think of their employees. When they have made excessive profits they should for example increase the pay of their employees. This would go a long way to reduce inequality in society. Wealth creation or capitalism is not a bad thing when it is done responsibly and ethically (Adapted from Debate on capitalism on: The British Broadcasting Company, 20th April, 2013). In fact, increase in workers' pay would lead to increase of purchasing power of Cameroonians, increase in consumption and increase in production culminating in development.

Similarly, to resolve the perennial problem of integrating young people in the socio-economic and political structures, government must focus on two great concerns of development

---

[4] Trucans are made out of empty "peak" milk sized tins and a long piece of string of cloth. Each milk tin has a hole made at the top through which the kerosene is poured in the tin; and the long piece of string meticulously put inside of the tin until just a little piece is left hanging at the top. This is where the trucan is lit to provide light for the room.

[5] To combat the high incidence of malaria and other illnesses in the country, the Cameroon Government plans on opening three referral hospitals in Douala, Yaounde and Sangmelima in the South Region in the near future; which is commendable? However, this policy would have a more positive impact on the health situation in Cameroon if the hospitals were built first in regions where the healthcare situation is dire, such as the Extreme Northern and East Regions (see End of year speech. Biya Paul 2013).

namely human development (Biya P., 1986) and the protection of the planet and their inevitable interdependence. This will guarantee people a good quality of life at all times, socially, economically, politically, culturally, environmentally and health-wise. In other words, this will lead to sustainable development which entails continuous accumulation of wealth and economic power as well as sustained growth and improvements in the general standard of living (see Slim, 1995); or like Brundtland (1987) puts it, development that meets the needs of the present without compromising the ability of future generations to meet their own needs.

At the moment youth unemployment and underemployment are on the increase in Cameroon; a country with no safety nets for the unemployed such as unemployment benefits or food stamps as in developed countries such as the United States, France, England, etc. There are not enough industries to absorb the many job seekers in the country. Often they have to fall back on their parents or family members who on most instances are also struggling to survive. This increase of unemployed youths is seen in the many idle young persons at the street junctions and others who often congregate at bars and eating places to drink, converse or smoke marijuana. For example, Valsero a leading rap artist in Cameroon sings that in Cameroon there is peace but there are no jobs for the unemployed, especially unemployed youths.

Such places encourage the development of street gangs and other deviant or criminal activities. Many street youths in Cameroon who have for a long time, been denied the legitimate means of livelihood, have developed a culture of crime and violence. They usually survive by engaging in activities that range from petty trading, casual work such as "car washing" porters in markets, borrowing to stealing, pick-pocketing such as at Rond-Point Dakar, Bépenda Tonnère, Marché Mboppi and Marché Central, prostitution, drug peddling and other illegal activities (see Okojie C., 2003).In fact crime has spiralled out of control in these areas and other neighbourhoods in the city of Douala. For example, our research in the city of Douala shows that many of the street gangs and many criminal and deviant activities are often carried out by young persons between the ages

15 to 29 years old; sometimes, even persons below 15 years old. In fact recently in Ngodi Bakoko in the city of Douala a gang of young persons between the ages 13 to 27 years were arrested by the police for burglary in shops and in houses as well as in motorcycle taxis and taxis generally. These young people often stole valuable household items such as fridges, cell phones, lap tops, money, jewellery, etc. (Equinox Radio News, 23 rd. April 2014). Thus, we see that without the hope of finding decent work, many young people become disillusioned, feel marginalized and frustrated as they are trapped in a cycle of working poor, usually in the informal sector of the economy; or they may detach from the labour market altogether. This represents a vast waste of economic potential. (International Labour Organization, 2011).

In a similar way, youth frustration and anger from their relative exclusion in the socio-economic and political domains could be seen in their dress code which many Cameroonian adults consider as provocative, deviant, immoral and indecent. In fact, recently (November 2013) this was a burning issue of debate in the country when four ministers of state (the Ministers of the Promotion of Women and the Family, Culture, Communication and Territorial Administration) came on National Television and Radio denouncing the way many young people (both male and female) and even some adults dress. For example young women were accused of wearing "DVD's" and miniskirts; that is clothes that expose their thighs, breasts, bellies, buttocks and backs; and young men wearing the "taille-basse" trousers that exposed their buttocks. The morality and values of these young people were seriously questioned as the Ministers felt they deviated from the norms of society; and that they would be legally sanctioned.

It is a truism that many Cameroonians would want people to dress decently but the question remains as to what decent dressing entails.

To answer this question it is vital to find out why some adults and these young Cameroonians in particular dress the way they do at this particular point in time. From a sociological view point and from our research finding in the city of Douala in particular, there are many reasons why people generally dress the way they do.

One of the reasons is cultural or ethnic pride. Many adults and even some young people in Douala said they dressed the way they did to reflect the fact that they are Africans to begin with and as members of a particular ethnic group in Cameroon. This is similar to the perception or feelings of the Great African hero Kwame Nkrumah who had gone to the United Nations wearing his native Ghanaian attire (a piece of special cloth tied around his chest and body), which was a way of saying he was Black and proud of being an African; and more particularly a Ghanaian. Another great African hero of recent times, 'the Giant of Africa' was Nelson Mandela who is often seen wearing simple shirtsto show his pride as an African and the simple man he was. There is also the late President of Cameroon, Ahmadou Ahidjo; and the present President of the National Assembly of Cameroon, Cavaye Yeguie Djibril, who also often wear the "Agwada"; which is a long flowing gown over trousers Cameroonian men from the Northern Regions of Cameroon and even Nigeria and other sub-Saharan countries often wear; and Fru Ndi, the current most powerful opposition leader in the Cameroonian political landscape, who often wears his native attire; which is also in the form of an "Agwada", the long flowing gown over trousers; but which is very colourful with rich embroider and a very distinguished colourful headwear. This is a typical traditional dress of people in the north-West and West regions of Cameroon. For all the above persons, wearing their ethnic or traditional outfits is a manifestation of their pride in their "Africanness", their ethnicity.

Others may also dress to make socio-political statements or as a deliberate revolt against the socio-political status quo in a given society at a particular point in time. The example that comes to mind is Mahatma Gandhi who was often seen with a piece of cloth tied around his body. This was to show his strong disapproval of the social injustice and British Colonial rule in the Indian society at that point in time in the country's history.

Not to downplay the very important role Ghandi played in bringing about social justice and freedom in India and the world; one can say many Cameroonians dress the way they do, so carelessly, to show their disgust and frustration at social injustice and their relative exclusion in the Cameroon society. It is like they are crying out for help, to be noticed by the authorities that be; to take notice of their plight in society and do something about it. Gangs and other sub-groups in society also dress in a particular way to show their sense of belonging to a particular gang or sub-group in society.

People also dress the way they do to emulate the stars they see in the Mass Media, TV, Internet, Films etc.; they all want to be fashionable to keep up with the fashion of the times. These stars have become their role models. The youths in particular want to be like these stars in every way. It is like an escape from reality from all the indignities and suffering they encounter daily in their lives in society. It gives them some hope of what they imagine they could be some day. This brings some solace in them.

Others, especially those suffering from some form of "middle age crisis" may want to dress in fashionable ways that make them feel younger and beautiful too. It makes them feel good. Still others adopt a particular dress code because of climatic conditions. People living in hot and humid climatic conditions such as in the city of Douala usually dress somewhat "scantily" in light fabrics and light coloured clothes, while those in very cold climatic conditions would often wear thick, heavy and dark coloured clothing.

Some people also dress for material reasons to show how rich they are, how affluent they are, a sort of status symbol. They usually dress in expensive fabric or expensive imported clothing and jewellery from Europe and America; while the poor make do with cheap clothing-here in Cameroon; this is usually cheap Chinese clothes or shoes or "okrika", used clothes from Europe and the United states.

Other people dress to stand out in society, drawing attention to themselves. This range from people like prostitutes to people who do not want to look ordinary or look like the rest of society; such as movie, music and TV stars. There are others, somewhat artistic people, who simply enjoy the art of dressing differently from others in society. Sometimes, one's dressing also reflects whether one is free spirited, or easy going or conservative, uptight and closed in; or even whether one lives in a democratic capitalistic or communistic or dictatorial society.

However, with the world becoming a global village with relatively similar tastes in clothes, foods and values this may be difficult to discern today.

Also one's religious beliefs and moral values also have significant influence in one's dress code. For example here in the city of Douala, many deeply religiously minded people would dress in clothing that covers up most of their bodies unlike non religions or ordinary people.

One's occupation and one's lifestyle also impacts on one's dressing or the type of clothes and shoes one wears. For example whereas many sex workers like wearing clothes that are tight fitting, that show off their body parts, the curves and bumps and high-heeled shoes to attract male clients; many people in the "buyam sellam" business or in the petty trade business here in Douala wear loose clothes and shoes that they are comfortable in them all day long, bending, sitting, standing, running up and down the market to get change to reimburse customers and; which they can move freely in when selling food stuff to people. In fact, people who want to feel at ease and be comfortable would most likely wear clothes and shoes that are either loose or not tight fitting.

Thus we see that the clothes people wear or people's dress code have various representations and meanings to various groups of people in any given society. In most instances they reflect people's lifestyles. Similarly, while some people consider what they wear as their human rights to do so; others want to impose their ways and morality on others.

Still, other Cameroonians even see a link between indecent dressings of females especially and the recent high incidence of rape in the country. Indecent dressing should never be associated with rape. They are two different things. It is true that some men may be aroused sexually when they see some parts of the female body such as half exposed breasts; but for God's sake, this does not give these men the right to rape these women. We are not animals that we cannot control ourselves, our feelings and emotions. Self-control is what separates us from animals. As a matter of fact, there is no justification whatsoever of rape. Human beings must learn to respect one another.

"Think of how boring, how monotonous and unexciting society or the Cameroon society would be if everybody was similar, wore similar clothes and did the same things etc. Society would really be unbearable to live in. There is such beauty in differences. In fact, God our Father in Heaven had wanted that people, animals and things generally in the world be different but equal. That is why he created people with different skin colours and different physical traits, different bird and animal species etc. There is such unity, such dignity in differences as long as we all respect one another. There should never be any legislation to force people to live, dress and behave in a certain way. These are such personal things to legislate upon in a certain way. If this happens there would be no fun in living. We all need one another, with all the differences in race, culture, ethnicity and species to make this world go round so to speak and to make life worth living in this our world. So "all hands on deck" to make this world a better place. All humans have to guard against never to become extremists, fanatical or exaggerate whatever they do such as the way they dress; and there would be fewer problems in this world than we currently have.

Again, the Cameroon Government should never legislate what people do in their personal life, such as what people wear on their bodies. These are very personal things. Cameroonians too should do all in their power to dress decently even when they are keeping up with fashion or as they say in the city of Douala "tendances" (see Tendance Kengne and Vivian K., Equinox Radio 2013).

It is true, it is the role of government to ensure the common good, to ensure that everybody's human rights are respected, that there is social justice in society, that society is inclusive, and that any form of extremism is unacceptable in society, including extremism in the clothes people wear, which could be offensive to many people in society; but by all means there should not be legislations to regulate the personal life of people. It is obsolete to do so in the 21st Century where increasingly we are living in a "global village". People should only be educated to respect the sensibility of other people by not behaving in extreme ways that would be repulsive to others. This is so because when government starts legislating on how people live their personal life, the government automatically becomes dictatorial causing so much pain and suffering to people.

In fact, if the state is to legislate what one wears, where would it draw the line? What would be their definition of decent dressing? Similarly on what basis would one be imprisoned and asked to pay a fine for dressing indecently as the four Ministers inducted?

Thus, it is clear that it would not be an easy task to establish whether one is decently dressed or not. Also the Government would have to censor the media to ensure that only decently dressed women and men should be shown on TV, movie houses and in magazines. Government should also have to ensure that only decent clothes are sold in markets and shops. On the whole, Government should also have to make sure that parents are responsible enough and that they raise their children properly or in strict accordance with the norms and "morality" of the Cameroonian society, so that they dress decently. (See Nga Ndongo, 1993)

As one can see, all these things are not easy to define and legislate; and as earlier pointed out they would infringe on people's human rights. Again we all agree that Cameroonians should dress decently, but it should not be legislated. Instead Cameroonians should be educated and sensitized to dress decently. With time, many Cameroonians would come to understand and appreciate why it is necessary to dress decently.

For young persons in particular, sustained improvements on nutrition, medical and appropriate educational facilities are a sine qua non for their success, socio-economic empowerment and integration in society. For example, Cameroon needs a healthy and well trained population for a sustainable development. Currently the Cameroon government carries the burden of being the main employer of young people. For example, in 2011, the Cameroon government employed 25,000 young people. However, if these young people are well educated, most of them would certainly develop the technologies, capacities and skills to create wealth and employment for themselves. They would then become independent adults rather than solely depend on government for employment; a government that barely holds its own financially. The education reform that is in progress in the country such as the introduction of technical education programs in secondary and high schools as well as the Bachelor, Masters, Doctorate (BMD) program at the university level are all in a bid to make education in the country to be more professionally oriented, focused on science and technology and respond to the needs of both the Cameroon economy and the global labour market which is less hospitable to young people especially now with the current economic crisis. Like Agih I. (2007: 92-93) makes clear:

> *Self-reliance and sustainable development of any nation are dependent on the level of resourcefulness of its people, which in turn is a direct reflection of the quality of training and the development of education of that country. Among the major constraints to sustainable development, of 'many sub-Saharan African countries such as Cameroon' is that of human resources which are not skillful and creative enough.*

Furthermore, Agih quotes Asawe, 2007:8 that:

> *Competition global today is not about abundance of natural resources but creativity. For instance, the top wealthiest nations in the world did not make their wealth from the oil materials; it is from knowledge and ideas. To get knowledge and empower a nation is to build a strong knowledge base institution.*

Surely, the above education reform would go a very long way to reduce the massive youth unemployment and general unemployment in the country. However, a lot more has to be done to make this education reform a success in terms of the provision of appropriate and adequate infrastructure such as good libraries amphitheatres and classrooms for the ever growing student population, well equipped laboratories for productive scientific research, finance and expertise (human capital). The country obviously needs support from both local and international donors to make this happen. Of course the Cameroon government also has to provide the enabling environment for this to be possible by ensuring good governance and equal opportunity for all Cameroonians, irrespective of one's ethnicity or gender. This is so because as (Eliou 1973: 36, in: Robertson C. 1986: 109) explains, often "the road which leads girls to school is in fact only a detour, which leads them back to the house;" which means that, generally girls and women usually receive training or education that prepare them to return to the home as "good" household managers. Dr. Yonkeu concluded.

As far as gender inequality is concerned, it is incumbent on the government to create pro-women policies that would reduce or why not do away with it altogether. African governments have been slack in doing so. Male control could be seen in all aspects and sectors of life in Cameroon. Male participation and authority and even the relative exclusion of women in top decision-making still to the large extent characterize major social, economic, political and cultural institutions of the Cameroon society. Most families for example are patrilineal and overwhelmingly virilocal. In fact, a typical Cameroon wife has a multiplicity of tasks. She has to care for her home, cook food, raise crops, for the use of her family as she is still largely responsible for feeding the family; as well as sell part of the food to have some money for the purchase of household and her own personal needs. This is usually the case whether her husband is employed or not, incapacitated or not; or whether she is a widow or not. Even when she is not a farmer, feeding the family largely remains the role of the woman. Also, in many households, especially in poor households without running water; or in "normal" households with running water, when the water company for one reason or another cuts the supply of water, women and children of course have to fetch water and firewood. Women also have to supervise their children. Wives and women in general have to be somewhat servile and acceptable to the censure of men; not only for their own possible failings as wives or women but also for their apocryphal sins of womankind. Often the behaviour of women who drink, neglect their children, commit adultery and engage in prostitution is vehemently condemned by men and the laws. However, when it is men who do all these things, it is to a large extent accepted by men and even women and considered as natural things that men do; "gender-appropriate" behaviours.

Of course there are many socioeconomic, cultural and religious based justifications for women to be obedient to men. For example, Christianity and Islam insist on wifely obedience and male superiority. In the cultural domain, examples of "male superiority" and therefore women's obligations to be obedient to men are legion. For example, breast ironing, clitoridectomy or "female genital mutilation" is a clear manifestation of men's domination of women and the desire to control and lord it over women and women's bodies in particular. Women are not allowed to be in control of their sexuality. The practice of clitoridectomy is still practiced in the Northern Region, the East and the South West Regions of Cameroon.

There is also the payment of bride-price, which is a common practice of ethnic groups all over Cameroon. It has been so misinterpreted and so misconceived in contemporary society so much so that it is currently perceived by most Cameroonians as a commoditization of women.

In fact, with the chronic economic crisis today in Cameroon, many families use the payment of bride-price to make money. As such, it is not uncommon to find family members bargaining for the payment of the bride-price for their daughter as if she was a commodity in the market. In fact, among many ethnic groups in Cameroon, in the West, Centre and Northern regions brideprice has been so commoditized that there are even differential payments (goods and money) for women of slave ancestry, women from the nobility and ordinary women. Usually women of slave ancestry are less valued and less costly than women of the other groups respectively (interview with Ndondock Samba M. woman from Mbang Nkondjock, Littoral Region, 2013).How terrible! How pathetic! We are back in the days of slavery all over again. No wonder some husbands actually treat their wives as "slaves" because they have paid bride-price for them. It is a pity! These women are forced to do whatever their husbands want; even sometimes; putting their lives at risk, such as having unprotected sex with their husbands suffering from AIDS. It is so inhumane indeed.

This is unlike in pre-colonial, pre-capitalist times when the use of money in the economy was not en vogue; or when most ethnic groups in Cameroon lived outside the money economy and when the payment of bride-price was purely symbolic and a way of cementing ties or relationships between kinship and ethnic groups. Like Nana-Fabu S. (1987), puts it, a woman's services during pre-colonial times in Cameroon were highly valued since the wife's contribution to her husband's kin was worth far more than the value of goods and services given as bridewealth in her name. What is happening today is erroneous. It is a misrepresentation of the African past or more precisely the Cameroonian culture.

In fact, during pre-colonial times, women were well respected in both private and public domains. Most societies in Cameroon were mainly subsistence agrarian societies based on the household economy. The dominant production sector was the cultivation of food crops dominated by women. In sum, skills women learnt during pre-colonial period provided them with the basic necessities of life. Their products and property remained largely under their control and were disposed of as they pleased apart from clearly specified marital obligations. Husbands had no claims on their wives' resources (see Keller and Bay, 1977; Geschiere, 1982; Forde, 1954). The fact that women had a multiplicity of tasks within and outside the household was a mixed blessing. Their workload was usually enormous and arduous; but this made it possible for women to exercise considerable autonomy and influence on issues within and outside the households in Cameroon (see Nana-Fabu S., 1987).Thus it is clear that it is not the practice of the payment of bride-price that has debased women's status but the new changes involved in the payment of bride-price in Cameroon today. Indeed, Leacook (1981:241) In: Stamp (1986) illuminates the importance of bride price, during the pre-colonial times in Cameroon and many other African societies so well:

> In some societies women move back and forth as valued people, creating, recreating and cementing networks and reciprocal relations through their moves which are recompensed with bride price.

"Similarly, Nana-Fabu S., (1987) quoting (Keller and Bay 1977) states that the concept of bridewealth or brideservice in both patrilineal and matrilineal societies is today, often misconstrued by both outside observers and Cameroonians as "buying" a wife and with all the degradation that comes with it. However, during precolonial times in Cameroon, brideprice was not an economic transaction. It was rather, a token of friendship between families and long lasting love for the husband and wife. The bridewealth during this period could also be seen as a partial compensation to the woman's lineage for the loss of her services while she is gone with her husband and bears children for his lineage. In addition payments of bridewealth did not compel the woman to stay married to her husband at all cost. Rather it was seen in terms of protecting a woman from excessively harsh treatment at the hands of her husband and kin.

However, today in Cameroon, the payment of bridewealth or dowry has taken a real U-turn. It has been so misconceived, so unethical that, recently on July 2014 in Dschang in the west Region in Cameroon, a man's throat was slit by his son-in-law because he was unable to reimburse the dowry paid to him by the son-in-law after his wife, that is the man's daughter, had divorced him. One really wonders aloud if this son-in-law had to carry out such a monstrous act on his father-in-law because he could not reimburse the dowry he had paid for the man's daughter. Moreover who said a woman had to stay married to a man at all cost simply because the man had paid a brideprice for the woman? It is so inhumane, so cruel! What materialism in the Cameroon society today! It's shocking (Equinox Radio News, 3rdJuly 2014)

The misconception of the issue of bride-price today is similar to the issue of polygamy today in Cameroon. Polygamy is in some ways similar to serial monogamy (usually in Western countries); which is a cultural pattern that permits a person to have more than one spouse but not all at the same time as in polygamy. The problem of polygyny today is that it is practiced very differently than it was the case during pre-colonial, pre-capitalist times in Cameroon. Women find themselves in polygamous marriages nowadays mainly for material selfish reasons or 'mariage par intérêt'; cold calculation (see Max Weber 1922/1947). They refuse to understand the workings of polygyny as was practiced during pre-colonial times. This explains why many people in Cameroon today are against polygyny. This is so because the general consensus is that it oppresses and exploits women and that it causes frictions and fights among cowives leading to "witchcraft" and poisonings among wives and children who are struggling to gain the father's love and favour. This also poses a serious problem when the husband dies and does not leave a will. Sometimes even when the man leaves a will there are still many challenges to this will by the wives and children as they struggle to get the maximum of the man's property or why not to be in control of the property. This is often the negative picture many Cameroonians have of polygamous marriages. However, note should be taken that these same squabbles among family members over the acquisition of property of deceased husbands is nowadays, also very common in monogamous marriages. This notwithstanding, women could really gain both socially and economically in polygamous marriages (marriage of a man to two or more women). Stamp P. (1986) explains this well;

> *Contrary to the received truth that polygyny always oppresses women; the polygynous household may offer women a basis for solidarity and task sharing. At the level of the household, cowives cooperate to organize production, consumption and child care. Although friction between cowives is widely reported, many studies also stress the economic and political advantages of polygamy including the autonomy made possible by shared responsibility (*See Mullings, 1976:254; Obbo, 1980: 34-35; Boserup 1970-43*).*

So in all we have to examine both sides of a social phenomenon to make responsible rational appreciations. For instance, the example of the "Reine Blanche" in Bangangté – Cameroon is a case in point. This white French lady who was married to a Bangangté chief, tells of the peaceful, cooperative and productive atmosphere that reigned at the King's Palace when she was there as one of the many wives of the chief or king. There was so much cooperation among the wives that when some of them had babies and had to go to the farms to work, they sometimes kept their babies with her to take care of them and vice versa. So there were times she breastfed these babies left at her care, and the other women did the same to her babies when she was not around.

From these examples, we see that the cowives gained a lot socially and economically from polygamy and that it is not all negative as many scholars and other citizens explain.

Thus, from the above findings, it is clear that there must be some reworking, some reviewing or some deconstructions of the relatively sexist socio-political, economic and cultural setup and mind-set in Cameroon today which seek to justify the relative lack of women in top decision-making positions in major institutions in Cameroon based on the natural inferiority of women or the natural superiority of men; and the expectations that wives and women should be obedient and subjugated to men. For example, to asset their control and dominance over their wives, husbands in Cameroon often tell their wives this: "I married you, you did not marry me". This shows that he has to have the final say in whatever goes on in their lives. Therefore, wives should be obedient to husbands. This should not be the case, for both sexes equally work for the creation of wealth and prestige of each other and the nation as a whole.

It is apparent that today in Cameroon men and women still, to a large extent, occupy separate social categories in the social organization. The assignment of differential rights and roles to women and men in the socioeconomic, cultural and political domains is a manifestation of this distinction. This certainly continues to undermine the Cameroon woman's self-confidence and assertiveness (see Kettel B. 1986: 50-51).Cameroonians have to learn a thing or two from the social organization of pre-colonial, precapitalist Cameroonian societies which were more inclusive and in which women had considerable power in all domains of society, socially, economically, politically and culturally; and exercised relatively more control of their lives and bodies. Indeed, as pointed out earlier, during pre-colonial times in Cameroon like in most societies in Africa during this period, subsistence agrarian societies, based on the household economy in which women dominated were prevalent. Through their economic power, women were able to exert considerable influence on issues within and outside the household. As such, the degree of inequality between the sexes during this period was tempered by the more equal power of distribution among the sexes inherent in the simple production system – subsistence agriculture pervasive in most societies in Cameroon and in other parts of Africa (See Nana-Fabu, 1987).

Being a society bedevilled by patriarchy, Cameroonians and their Government tend to be more acceptable of complementarity of men and women than equality of the sexes. This, even after the scientific debunking of the "natural inferiority of women" or the "natural superiority of men" perspective by feminist scholars such as De Beauvoir(1953), Romanie S. (1994); Robertson and Berger I. (1986), Mascia–Lees (1984), Boserup E. (1970), Afonja S. (1981, 1983) etc. It is true recently (2013) the Cameroon Government has been trying to reduce gender inequality especially in the political domain. For example, in the senatorial, parliamentary and mayoral elections in 2013, the government insisted that all lists of political parties for these elections must have female candidates; for example for every three males on the list there had to be one female; in keeping with the Maputo convention. This is a very welcoming policy for people campaigning for gender parity in the country. However it still falls short of the mark. For instance, why not equal candidates of both sexes in every list? After all, 52 per cent of the population in Cameroon is women. Nevertheless, for a society known for being so deeply conservative as far as gender equality is concerned, this is a step in the right direction and the government deserves a pat on the back for allowing at least some female representation on these lists. This is so, while hoping for the better of course, in the very near future.

This notwithstanding it is worth noting that this Law by the Government that every list during these elections must have female candidates did produce some positive results as the number of female parliamentarians increased from 25 in 2012, to 51 (31%) out of the 180 members in October 2013. Similarly, in the newly created Senate, 20% are females). One only hopes that these women are qualified and capable, and that they would be more vocal or articulate enough on issues dealing with gender equality in Parliament and in the Senate.

Similarly, the Ministry of Women's Affairs and the Family recently published a sort of hand book to inform Cameroon women of all they need to know on women's political participation in Cameroon. This was particularly so for Muslim women who are still relatively reluctant to join the band-wagon and participate fully in politics and other social activities of the nation because of cultural reasons. By writing this book, the Minister of Women's Affairs hopes to sensitize Cameroon women of the crucial role they have to play in nation-building and as such, to encourage women to massively participate in the just ended municipal and parliamentary elections in September 2013.

The minister is commended for encouraging women to participate in the politics of the country, to develop the political culture among Cameroon women (Eteki Otabella, 9th March 2014 interview at Equinox Radio) and in a way, make their voices heard in the decision-making of the nation. However, this begs the question as to the effectiveness of her strategy of using a book to do so when we know that there is such a disparity in the literacy rates between men and women, and that because of the socio-economic constraints as seen in their multiple tasks many women do not have the time to read books (see Nana-Fabu S., 2009), especially women at the grassroots, rural women; who as a matter of fact constitute the majority of women in Cameroon. Therefore alternative strategies such as door to door sensitization campaigns by NGO's and women's associations, the insistence of the education of the girl child, the application of the new "Family Code" etc., including the book of course, must be sought to reach the vast majority of Cameroon women if the noble goal of female participation in politics is to be achieved in the country. This is so since the empowerment of women emphasizes gender equality as well as improvements in women's social, political, health and economic status, as well as their general autonomy; all factors which are important in themselves and very necessary in achieving sustainable development (Nana-Fabu S., 2007, 2009).

Men and women deserve equal opportunity. For example, generally today in Cameroon, married women are still treated as indentured servants especially when there is the payment of the bride price. Women must be helped to overcome their oppression by building their capacities and self-esteem. The "culture of machismo" too has to go. In fact, the Cameroon government and Cameroonians must be re-educated that gender equality is a sine qua non for the full enjoyment of human rights by women and men[6]. Therefore women's rights must be promoted and defended. Also, there must be an esprit de corps among women for this to happen. For example, they could successfully challenge the sexist traditional beliefs and male institutions that are resistant to change if they work hand in hand irrespective of their ethnic background, political affiliation, social "class" or group, educational level etc. For instance, motherhood is often used as a pretext to keep women in their traditional roles in the household (private domain) which are often debased and devalued; with often serious consequences on their employment status outside the household. For example with little realistic basis, many women are markedly underrepresented in many occupations for which they might be personally and intellectually qualified due to sex discrimination in employment. For example, these women are not usually allowed to go away for a long period of time to seminars which could help improve upon their business skills; or create partnerships with other business persons, especially male business people, so as to expand their businesses. In short, there should be some deconstruction of sex and culture to show that the difference between men and women is relative, not absolute in many aspects such as competence, that is, if one has access to the required socio-economic and cultural resources and skills. Violence against women, gendered poverty, or the relative exclusion of women from decision-making in the cultural, political and economic life are examples of issues which must be resolved if gender equality is to be achieved. For example women who are capable, qualified, authoritative, and brave and dedicated to women's issues must be given the opportunity to represent women's interests at all levels of power.

Some examples of influential or exemplary women in Cameroon today are Biya C., the elegant, courageous and generous First Lady, known for her material support for disadvantaged women and children as well as persons with

---

[6] See the U.N. 1995 Fourth World Conference on women in Beijing which was on Peace, Women's Rights and Social Development.

HIV/AIDS; Obama M. T., the very intelligent, dignified, simple but very effective minister of Women's Affairs and the Family; Foning F., the dynamic, brave, shrewd, prominent business woman who was president of the organization of businesswomen worldwide in 2012 and astute politician, mayor of Douala 5, who is so sure of herself and never falters even when faced with hostile criticisms from her opponents and critics, both male and female; Ketcha C. the extraordinary, and capable mayor of Bagangte who has won the price for the cleanest town in Cameroon several times and who happens to be the first successful female president of a popular football team- Panthère de Bagangté; Kah Wallah, political analyst and the only female president of a political party; Kala Lobe S., Anne Nsang N., Glory Nbagwana, Ndingue C., Nseke O., Etoa B., Zachiatou Boubakari, Inna Djenabou, Atogo J., Mvotto A.M., Essoka P.; Mbala Atangana A., Kebbi E., Sally Messio Abediong, all renowned journalists, Late Lyonga R., female parliamentarian who was known for her brave campaigns for the empowerment of women petty traders in Limbe, the South West region of Cameroon, that earned her the nick name "Mammy Buyam sellam"; Fampou D., soft spoken but determined mayor of Douala 2, who is not afraid to make her views heard by often hostile male colleagues and opponents; Tankeu E. former Cabinet Minister and Ambassador to the African parliament in South Africa, Ekwe H., prominent journalist, committed to her ideals, undaunted political analyst, whose bravery and campaigns for women's rights and human rights generally cannot be fully underscored within and outside Cameroon; as could be seen in 2012 when she was one of the women worldwide who won the price of bravery from the United States of America; Baka Mbock C., Youssouf Adidja, Muna Tutu A., Tchuinté M., female ministers of state, Afitie, distinguished civil society leader, Kemogne N., the Savvy activist and environmentalist, Mbom Munjo A., brave journalist known for her tireless campaigns for social justice; Tamanjong E., top female politician whose struggle for gender parity and justice in society cannot be fully underscored; the brave female parliamentarian of Noun, West Region Mrs Njoya P.T., known for her forceful and constant denouncing of fraud during elections in Cameroon; Bidja R., Um

Ngouen M. T., Ntone H., Ndongko T. of blessed memory, all distinguished university professors known for their commitment in fostering gender equality in the academic domain; Njeuma L.D., the first female vice chancellor in Cameroon, Ambami Olama P., Ngaska P., Yaka R.,Abunaw Nana M., some of the top female officials of the forces of law and order, Zongo née Nyambono A., first female Senior Divisional Officer, Akono née Ngazang R., first female Regional Secretary General, Marie-Claire Nanna, Director General of Cameroon Printing Press, Maître Weledji, one of the first top female lawyers in Cameroon, Kom A., prominent female lawyer and activist, Haman Adama M., coordinator of an Ngo in the Extreme Northern Region of Cameroon, - "CROPSEC"- based in the regional capital Maroua, which has as its main goal to combat poverty in the region; Mongue Din E., a determined lady who created her own association of which she is president known as "plate-forme Ensemble pour la parité" dedicated to bringing about gender equality in Cameroon; Kambiwa C., vice president of female socialists who is also working hard for women's rights worldwide and in Cameroon in particular; the courageous president of the association- "Widow's Outreach Cameroon"- Mary Taka Tanni; Dikoume D., President of the association "Dames de Coeur" de Yaoundé a sort of self-help and banking Association for women; Calixte Beyala, a prolific author who has contributed greatly in fostering women's rights in Cameroon; Biloa M. R., Epopte D., Edwards V., Nyatcha L., Wakam N. all seasoned, no nonsense journalists working abroad who have greatly fostered a very positive image of the Cameroon woman worldwide; three great sportswomen Mbango F., Etonge S. and Ngwana Y.;Chatue C., the Director of the Television Station Canal 2 International; some distinguished female musicians Anne Marie Nzie, Ngaska O. Dinaly, the only woman who owns and runs a TV. Station, Ayissi C., Zambo M., Katino, Fotso C., Lady Ponce, Grace Decca, Nono F., Coco Ateba,Stella Stella, Dipanda C., Beko Sade, Narhodia, Sabimatou, Nicole Mara, late Charlotte Bango andBebe Manga, Bebe Black, Nguea La Route, Dikosso C. Annie Anzouer, Ange Mbanya, Mia Guiamba, Princess Khadja, Yanmad, Amina Poulho, Nguea la Route, Lizza T. Nono F. Ewande N., Ruth Kotto, Marole Chamber, Mbianda, Manoe;

two renowned artists, Ndagnou J. and Nana S.;Kombou Ngongang J.A.; a successful and an exemplary self-made business woman with an MBA Degree, worth emulating by struggling Cameroon business women to lift themselves out of poverty; Mouyombon O., top business woman in Douala; Ma Foncha A., Ma Endeley G., Ma Chilla, Ma Burnley G., Ma Muna, Ma Atabong, Ma Ahidjo G., wife of the first President of Cameroon- Ahmadou Ahidjo; Ma Jeanne Irene Biya, former First Lady; Ma Manga Bell, wife of the king Douala Manga Bell, from the 1960s to 2013; Ma Tchanga D., Ma Keutcha J., Ma Kala Lobe; all top female politicians of the former West Cameroon and the Republic of Cameroon respectively.

There are also prominent lawyers like Wandja, Ntanfah, Bille and Njoke known for their determination to bring about gender parity in all domains of society through their work in various female associations; Ngo Eheg A., an audacious crusader of women's rights who will go to all lengths to make her voice heard in her struggle for gender equality at all associations and meetings for the promotion of women's' rights; Makedjo A., trade unionist; Dr. Eteki Otabela, politician and militant feminist for many years now; Libom Likeng M., an exceptional lady with managerial skills that could be seen in the tremendous increase in custom revenues since her appointment as Director General of custom; which amply demonstrates that women could be good, and if not better managers of top businesses and government institutions, if they are given the opportunity to do so, Donfack J.F. and Mbiakop C., two extremely knowledgeable and conscientious Bankers; Monjowa Lifaka E., the only female vice President of the Cameroon National Assembly, 2014; the Rev. Sister Atabong J. and Rev. Sister Belinga S. for their Charity works; Diffo Tchunkam J., the brilliant university professor and jurist who manages the NGO "More Women in Politics" to help bring about gender parity in politics in Cameroon; Djibrilla Sidiki, a top female economist who manages an NGO- "COMPRESSA"- in the Extreme Northern Region of Cameroon that has as its main goal to reduce poverty, especially female poverty in the region; Beyala S. K., a popular talk show host on radio and television prepared to defend women's rights at all times ; Manga Bell M.R., female parliamentarian of Wouri known for her fight against extremism in the country; the brave religious leader Khadija, with her "Khadija Foundation", an advocacy group for religious tolerance in the country, a crucial value for a true democracy; and these brave ladies and patriots, Ma Moumie, Ma Um Nyobe, Ma Ouwandie, Ma Afana, Ma Ngosso Din etc.

All these women and many others I have not named in this book, are very influential or as the French would say, "femmes qui s'imposent" in the very male dominated socio-political and economic landscape of Cameroon in various ways. Granted, sometimes some of the female politicians may exaggerate their support for their various political parties more than they do for women's empowerment. In addition, some of these women may be elitist in their vision and in seeking solutions to women's problems. For example some of these women are not often out to change the current unequal organization of society in terms of gender relations that ascribes stereotype roles for the sexes within the family and the society. This restricts women's access to valued socio economic resources. For instance more often we find that women's needs are identified by "professionals", even female professionals or top women in society without the participation or consultation of ordinary women themselves. As the French would say: "Souvent, les offres politiques de ces femmes professionnelles et des 'femmes bourgeoises' ne respectent pas les desirata des femmes ordinaires, femmes pauvres ou bien des femmes d'en bas".For example, like the young musician, Petit Montagnard sings in one of his songs, during election time generally, to solicit votes from the mainly female electorate, usually those of the lower socio-economic groups, some male and even some female politicians are known to offer bags of rice, boxes of tins of sardines and the very popular cheap imported fish from Morocco known here in Cameroon as "Maquero" or even some negligible sums of money to these often desperately poor female voters. Preposterously, these politicians assume that these bags of rice etc. are what these poor women need to resolve their poverty and health problems, or better their lives; without even asking them what their priority needs are. Often quite a number of these politicians or top women and men in the Cameroon society generally continue to treat women and even men in the lower socio-economic categories as sheep, "betails politiques". This is unfortunate and sad. Other times some of these women insist on preserving the pervasive ideology and anti-feminist discourse of male superiority; and argue that Cameroon women should at all-times be obedient and submissive to men just like the legendary African Jazz musician, Fela Ransome Kuti sings of the "African women". All these only go to reinforce the existing status quo and the strict gender division of labour in Cameroon. This leaves many women in Cameroon with a low self-esteem leading to feelings of incompetence and lack of confidence in their ability to achieve. A person with low self-esteem sets lower goals and still feels incapable of achieving them. Nevertheless, we cannot really blame these influential women for these shortcomings for they only mirror the egocentric nature of the Cameroon society today. In fact, credit must be given to these Cameroon women and others in other walks of life who in one way or another have dared to venture into heretofore all male domains, made their voices heard and sometimes, have even brought about worthwhile changes on some pertinent socio-political and economic issues in the country. However, much remains to be done to achieve gender equality in the country. For instance March 8th, the International Women's Day should be a day set aside to reflect on women issues and ways sought to promote gender equality rather than as it is currently the case in Cameroon. Here the acquisition and the importance accorded to the fabric or cloth or "wrapper" designed for Women's Day, and the self-destructive ways many Cameroon women commemorate this day in terms of very high consumption of alcoholic beverage, beer especially on this day, leading to high rates of adultery, like they say in Douala "soulevez les Kaba" or lift up your dress; and other deviant behaviours have by far superseded the very noble goals of this day.

It is a truism that Africans generally and Cameroonians in particular like to celebrate events, even death. Here, a certain day or days are set aside to celebrate the death of someone (see the Bamileke tradition in particular). For example, fabulous sums of money are usually spent for death celebrations among the Bamileke of Cameroon. Other ethnic groups are also catching up with this "tradition". However, some order must be brought to the March 8th celebration in Cameroon for it is really exaggerated. Often in poor families where the man of the house or the woman's partner does not have money to buy this march 8th "wrapper" for his partner, this has led to so much discord and even divorces. This is because the wife usually feels let down by her husband. She even feels less loved and even neglected by her husband. She becomes traumatized. Other times, some of these women go as far as prostituting themselves to have money to have this fabric. They feel their husbands are incompetents and somewhat "lesser men" who cannot provide for their wives. Still others even suffer from the post traumatic syndrome after Women's Day has passed as a result of their husbands' inability to buy the fabric for them. Unnecessary quarrels, mental, verbal and even physical abuse (violence) become recurrent in these families. In the face of this situation many men become so confused and feel emasculated in this very patriarchal society. They develop such deep resentment for their female companions who simply want to be like their female peers in Cameroon. Who can really blame them?

This is so unfortunate for this is not what the International Women's Day is all about. Many Cameroon women have certainly lost track of the essence of women's day. With such distortions concerning this day and women's subsequent alienation of the men folk from the commemoration of Women's Day, gender equality in Cameroon risks becoming a lost cause.

Therefore some order needs to be brought to the commemoration of International Women's Day in Cameroon. There must be active campaigns by civil society, women groups such as female jurists, female entrepreneurs, female journalists, the mass media and of course the government aimed at raising awareness of the dangers of such negative and self-negating behaviours of women on Women's Day. There must be some consciousness-raising on the socioeconomic and cultural importance of the International Women's Day to the general well-being of Cameroon women and the achievement of gender equality in the country. The situation cannot be left to degenerate.

As a matter of fact there is no harm in celebrating Women's Day, but by all means, enjoying oneself should not in any way be self-abuse or deviant as many Cameroon women are currently doing. After all we all know that Cameroonians or Africans generally are intrinsically buoyant people, full of the festive spirit and that some celebration on Women's Day would not hurt. However we must be careful not to forget the original purpose of this day.

Also the Women's Day cloth or "ashouabi" is not really a bad idea, but considering the chronic economic downturn in the country resulting in so many impoverished households, the Cameroon Government should try to bring some order here too. It could do so by first reducing the price of this particular fabric. The textile manufacturing company in Cameroon is making huge profits on the backs of the masses, poor women in particular. This has to stop. For example, the Cameroon government should ensure that the design of this Women's Day cloth changes after every five years for example rather than annually as it is now the case. Thus women could be able to use the same fabric for at least five years successively before it is changed. This will help women save some money. It will also help bring some sanity and order in this domain. Also the textile manufacturing company should think of investing some of its profits in helping finance some projects for the empowerment of women such as remedial education and training projects for both males and females, the provision of decent markets and stalls for female petty traders or "buyam sellams"; and the provision of refuge or shelters to women and children escaping from domestic violence or victims of domestic violence.

It is true African women usually use specially designed "wrappers" or fabrics as a form of identity and belonging to a particular social group ("Njangi", development, religions, or an ethnic association) or for a certain event such as a marriage or death ceremony. For instance when there is birth or marriage celebration, you need to see these Douala or "Sawa" women well-dressed in their "ashouabi", their well-tailored "kabas"; that is, the majestic gowns or "wrapper" fabrics, that flow from the chest in gathers down to their ankles. It is so colourful, so beautiful to see these women dance or match rhythmically to the tunes of their traditional "sawa" music accompanied by traditional drums, a brass band and of course singing some of those melodic tunes that have withstood the test of time.

As a matter of fact, the Doualas are well known for their musical talent as seen in the "Makossa" music made famous worldwide by illustrious musicians like Manu Dibango, Francis Bébé, Eboa Lottin, Ekambi Brilliant, Madenge J.D. Ebanda Manfred, Salé John, Toto Guillaume, Sam Bende, Nkoti François and the "black style group", Emile Kangue, Eko Roosevelt, some of the godfathers of the "makossa" music. Other famous "makossa" musicians are Ben Decca, Ndedi Dibango, Tom Yoms, Diaz S., Pierre Wilson, Joe Boule, Axel Muna, Moni Eka, Henri Njoh, Dina Bell, Petit Pays, Longue Longue, Douleur, Hugo Nyame, Koto Bass, Jeni Njento, Sergio Polo, Hogen E., Njohreur, Papillon, Jackie Ndumbe, Ndedi Eyango, Joe Masso, Essome J.P., Mathematik, the great Misse Ngoh F., Epé et Koum, Tim and Forty and many others.

Back to the women's groups, or "Njangi" groups, (financial associations); each of them could be identified by a distinct fabric sewn in a particular style with beautiful head gear called "heaties" to match. Sometimes, each association, is accompanied by its menfolk dressed in the traditional gear, the "sandja", that is the same colour fabric or "wrapper" as the women's, tied from the waist down to the ankle with a shirt to match; and sometimes clutching on to a handkerchief or a traditional broom which they manipulate in specific ways following the traditional dance rhythm. It is often so extremely colourful, so impressive to watch, such a picture-postcard view. In fact, for a little while, it sure helps take off the minds of Cameroonians from the very high unemployment and inflation rates that have been so mind-boggling to the majority poor especially. But again, this custom should not be abused. We cannot focus all our attention to the "wrapper" or fabric than on the "raison d'être" or purpose of the event we are celebrating or commemorating. It is absurd!

Going back to our discussion on influential women in Cameroon, we cannot also forget our homemakers or home managers, popularly known here in Cameroon as "ministers of the interior", housewives, non- housewives, mothers, non-

47

mothers and sisters; the "buyam sellams", the female petty traders, the women known as the "mammy makala" the "mammy koki", the "mammy roasted fish", the "mammy roasted corn/plantain and plums" and so on and so forth, all over the national territory, whose massive role in national development cannot be fully underscored.

It is therefore incumbent upon government to provide the enabling environment for these women to excel in their fight for gender parity; and for many other women to emulate them and why not, even do better to improve gender relations in Cameroon. They could also do so by promoting some fruitful campaigns for the actual implementation of gender equality in this predominantly patriarchal society; a society where women are still largely portrayed and treated in stereotypical ways as inferiors to men.

· Personal security of women should be guaranteed. After all, they are the givers of life. More emphasis should be placed on the health and the education of the girl child so that women would be empowered for positive socio-economic outcomes. For example efforts by NGOs, Non-Governmental-Organizations, such as COPRESSA- "Centre Optionnel pour la Promotion et la Regeneration", to educate inhabitants of the Extreme Northern Region in Cameroon, especially women, (e.g.: Bororo women), should be reinforced given that this region generally has a very high rate of illiteracy with only 46.7% of the population in 2007 who had received some education (see research by Nana Fabu S. and Dauoudou M., 2013). The recent creation of a State University in this region -the University of Maroua- is a welcomed move. However, there is still a lot more to be done to reduce illiteracy in this region that suffers from regular terrorist attacks from neighbouring Nigeria. For instance the provision of human resources (teachers) and school infrastructure such as classrooms and benches in some primary schools in this region leaves very little to be desired. Moreover, some ethnic groups in this area such as the "Bororos", a largely nomadic people, have not really integrated into the mainstream of society. They generally feel marginalized and they are actually exploited by other ethnic groups in the neighbouring areas. Sometimes their children are even kidnapped.

Therefore they do not consider education or sending their children, especially girl children to school as a priority. They feel the urgent priority in their area is the provision of water as some "bororo" people interviewed said. As far as they are concerned, education for them and their children could very well wait. So they are reluctant and they are not in fact motivated by the authorities that be to send their children to school; even when primary education in Cameroon happens to be "free". How could they, when basic school infrastructure such as benches is not in the few available primary schools; and sometimes children receive lessons under trees?

Men should also be reminded that empowering women will not lead to their disempowerment. Instead, they would have to work hand in hand to make this world a better place. This is so considering that a pluralistic inclusive society is necessary for sustainable economic prosperity.

In short, women should be respected as women and given the opportunity to excel in both public and private domains; for certain "womanly" traits and skills such as being patient and resilient, the ability to listen to what others have to say and the management skills they use to cope with survival under very harsh socio-economic conditions are necessary in all spheres of life. For instance, it is a truism that Cameroon women are increasingly being incorporated into the economy, but, they tend to enter at the lowest level where low wages, no health or pension benefits, insecurity and gender discrimination all undermine the poverty –reducing potential of paid work both in the formal and informal sectors of the economy. This inequality slows the development of the country. Also the country cannot develop in a balanced way. As a matter of fact, in the professions where there is more competition, this "glass ceiling phenomenon" prevents women from getting job positions that are higher in the hierarchy even when they have the accumulated human capital. Therefore it stands to reason that the higher the post in the socio-economic, cultural and political structures in Cameroon, the less likely is one to find a woman occupying it. Gender stereotyping and patriarchy are certainly alive and well in the country. Thus to overcome gender inequality and poverty in Cameroon there must be profound transformations in the political, socio-economic and cultural structures generally and relations between men and women in particular in positive ways that will help in the development and prosperity of the nation. For example, the workplace should be degendered. Come to think of it there must be conditionality on aid by international donors to Cameroon to promote women's rights and help lift women out of poverty. Of course there must be the right legislation, political will and implementation to achieve this.

Then Dr. Yonkeu's eyes drifted back to the street after this pause. She saw the scantily but flashy and flamboyantly dressed ladies, the "oiseaux de nuits", or "belles de nuits", the sex workers, half soaked from the rains and scrambling for some shelter in the many bars, beer parlours and night clubs in this area. "What a tough life" she thought." This business has been going on from time immemorial and there does not seem to be an end to it. Old habits die hard even here in Cameroon where prostitution is supposed to be illegal" she thought shrugging. This is the joke of the times!" she said sarcastically.

As she watched the last prostitute disappear in the dark of night, this thought suddenly came up to Dr. Yonkeu's mind. Unemployment, yes indeed unemployment; the "bête noire" of the Cameroon government that leaves people with a sense of worthlessness, that terribly dehumanizing word, that monster that scares so many young men and women to death, that dreadful word that leaves both young and old vulnerable. Recently international economic observers have been saying Africa is experiencing some economic growth. However, the growth remains a "jobless growth" because there are still many unemployed Africans, especially young people. Similarly, in his very optimistic speech on the 10th of February 2014 for the celebration of "Youth Day" on 11[th]February 2014 the President of the Republic addressing the nation on the unemployment problem, said things were improving. For example, he said in 2013 the Cameroon Government projected that there would be job creation for 2,000 persons especially for youth. However there were 225,000 jobs created in 2013. He concluded that in 2014, the Government hopes to create over 250,000 jobs. This sounds fair enough, but this job creation is yet to have a real impact on the very high unemployment rate in the nation, as so many Cameroonians, particularly youth are still unemployed and it is not also reflected in the Cameroon woman's bread basket. For example, the unemployment rate in Cameroon (2013/2014) stands at 46%. This is a very high unemployment rate for a country that is bracing up to be an emerging nation by 2035 (The Cameroon National Institute of Statistics, 2013/2014). In fact the unemployment problem has resonated with Cameroonians more than any other in recent times.

Granted, the Cameroon Government has been making efforts to combat this high unemployment rate in the country especially among young people; but there still remains a lot more to be done in this domain. For example, there is a whole Ministry of Youths and Sports, the Organization for Small and Medium Size Enterprises, a National Employment Fund and even youth wing organizations of institutions such as political parties, geared toward the socioeconomic empowerment and integration of youths into mainstream society. These together with some Non-Governmental Organizations (NGOs) are organs that usually provide the most needed funds, counselling and training to enable unemployed people and other persons in need to acquire the necessary skills in job creation and other survival skills such as in setting up small and medium size enterprises, which have been proven to be effective in poverty reduction-through the socio-professional insertion of many persons into the mainstream economy. However the effectiveness of these institutions are yet to be felt on the ground as many Cameroonians especially young people, remain unemployed and poor as they struggle to make ends meet at the informal sector of the economy. These and other institutions have been unable to substantially reduce the problems of unemployment and crushing poverty levels because of the high rates of corruption, cronyism, ethnic bias, patronage, fraud, egotism, inertia, poor governance, greed and unprofessionalism among the many other vices in the country. Moreover, funds destined to help small and medium Size businesses to function and compete effectively in the World marketplace are largely insufficient and often embezzled. For example, the late comedian, the very famous Jean Michel Nkankan had told so many jokes on the problems of corruption and unprofessionalism of some government officials in Cameroon, such as the police force. The situation has been worsened by the recent low annual growth rates. For example in 2013, the growth rate was 4.8 per cent as opposed to the 6.1 percent projected for the year 2013 (see End of year Speech by Biya P. 2013).

Unemployment is a situation in which people with appropriate qualifications for jobs and people who are actively seeking employment even at the ongoing wage rate are unable to find work over a specified period of time or without considerable delay. It should be noted that unemployment does not refer to the people who are occupied in some other way and are not seeking work such as students, retired persons and homemakers. These together with the "unemployable" that is the mentally and some physically handicapped who are either "incompetent" or "inacceptable" to employers are classified as being out of work. Usually, unemployed persons generally and young unemployed persons in particular become alienated or disconnected from society and end up with a very low self-esteem. This is because they doubt their worth and capacity to make it in society. To escape from this self-doubt and alienation, many of them take to drug abuse such as heavy beer consumption, marijuana use and other hard drugs. This is just a quick fix to a problem that would not go away that easily (see Nana-Fabu S., 2009).

There is also the working poor, resulting from underemployment. According to the World Bank (2012) more than 70% of the workforce in Cameroon was underemployed and today 2014, other studies show that 80% of the workforce is underemployed (see Ministry of Labour, Yaounde 2014). This is usually caused when unemployment is persistent and job seekers are forced to accept being employed at jobs that are way below their qualifications and capacities; for example the "educated unemployed", usually at the informal sector of the economy, just to keep body and soul together. Like the famous Cameroon musicians Georges Dickson sometimes ago and now Benji Mateke, singing on the very high unemployment rate in the country puts it, "boulot c'est boulot, il n'y a plus de choix"; meaning in English that "work is work, one has not got a choice in the type of work one does because there are no jobs to choose from. Therefore one has to do whatever job at the informal sector of the economy such as car washing, "moto-taximan", petty trade or "sauveteur" in the popular jargon, prostitution etc. just to survive, even if one is a degree holder. This song says it all. It explains why the informal sector is flourishing in Cameroon today; boosted by the laxity of government to regulate the sector. (Also see songs by Longue Longue and the Political Activist, Song Writer and musician Lapiro de Mbanga 1980's, 1990's, 2000's). In fact, the political discourse of many young people (men/women), in the country today, is very unpatriotic as many are prepared to do whatever it takes, even risking their lives in the deserts, seas and oceans to leave the country for "greener pastures" in Europe and America . This situation has also led to massive "brain drain" in Cameroon where many educated and skilled persons have left the country to look for work in Europe and America.

In Cameroon, the informal sector is unregistered, unorganized and characterized by low pay, little or no job security, no health, and retirement benefits. Many jobs in this sector are usually small, individual or family businesses, using simple local technology. Jobs in this area are also classified as low status, low profile and less prestigious. Many people here usually work round the clock but have very little to show in the end in terms of pay. Indeed, life is rough and tough for these persons who include motor cycle taximen, usually known as "benskin", call box or telephone operators, owners of informal restaurants in make-shift structures known as "tourne-dos" who are predominantly females, "buyam sellam" or market women; and not to forget our sex workers with the majority of them working in this sector.

Similarly Ondogo Fouda M. (2009) writes on the enormous difficulties market women or more precisely women who buy fresh foods from rural areas and then sell them mainly in urban areas, popularly known as "buyam-sellams", encounter in accessing funds from banks and even micro-finance establishments that are supposed to help people in this category finance their businesses. This in large part is due to the cultural bias toward women who are seen as less efficient business persons or entrepreneurs (see Nana-Fabu S., 2006). He states further that, women who generally make-up more than 50% of the population in Cameroon and who dominate in the "buyam-sellam" businesses in the informal sector of the economy slightly over 60 percent in the city of Douala (research by Nana-Fabu S. and urban sociology students 2010) are the poorest in the Cameroon society today. They do this business to survive and fully or partially satisfy the needs of their families in order to help to reduce poverty but they remain ever so poor because of lack of or inadequate finances. This problem has become acute with the debilitating economic crisis now plaguing the nation. The Cameroon economy is in dire straits (also see Nana-Fabu S. 2009). In fact, Ondogo Fouda M. states that 75% of urban workers in Cameroon work in the informal sector of the economy; and that 6 out of every 10 urban households derive at least half of their revenues from the informal sector of the economy. Similarly, Ela J. M (1994) writes about the creation of the informal sector of the economy in Africa. He states that the dictatorship of money and its logic in trade has held Africans hostage. Faced with this situation, the poor have not remained "bras croisés" arms crossed or given up. They have resisted by using their imagination and creativity by doing jobs in the informal sector and coming up with alternative strategies for survival. Like the saying goes, "necessity is the mother of invention". As such for many women, the unemployed and young unemployed persons generally, their indigenous ingenuity and creativity have become a force to be reckoned with. Therefore, it is no surprise that we find many unemployed people in Cameroon today doing all sorts of jobs in the informal sector of the economy. Ela J.M. calls these people "le monde d'en-bas", meaning the poorest persons at the lowest end of the stratification ladder.

These persons range from female entrepreneurs or market women "buyam sellam", mobile nail trimmers known as "abokis", mobile hair dressers, shoe repair men, beauticians, truck pushers-"bambes", to mobile restaurants and those in makeshift structures popularly known as "tourne dos"; that is places where food is sold in urban areas with clients sitting on benches with their backs turned from the streets (see Touré A. 1985). Here in Cameroon, most of these restaurants are run by women. These women often sell foods from their various cultures or regions in Cameroon such as rice and groundnut stew, by women from Yaounde, the Central region (Ewondos). "Macabo ndole" is boiled cocoyam, a tuber crop eaten with a bitter vegetable soup. The vegetable is washed clean until most of the bitterness is gone. It is then prepared into a soup using groundnuts, palm oil, crayfish, onion, salt, pepper and other spices. It is a highly popular meal among the "sawa" people in the Littoral Region of Cameroon. We also have "mami ero"; that is women who sell foofoo and ero – a staple food of the Mamfe people in the South West region of Cameroon. The "foofoo" is a sort of cake made out of cassava flour, another tuber plant and the "ero" soup, a leafy vegetable that usually grows wild in the forests of the central, south and south west regions of Cameroon. We also have "mami Koki". These are women who sell a sort of cake made out of ground beans, palm oil, pepper, salt; bundled up in plantain leaves which is usually eaten with boiled cassava, cocoyams or plantains. This is a staple food of the Mbo people in the Littoral region and the Bamileke people of the West region. We also have "mami Achu". This food consisting of pounded, cocoyams eaten with a soup made up of palm oil, salt and native spices is often sold by women from the North West region of Cameroon. Of course there are other women who sell roasted fish and "bobolo" -ground cassava tied in special leaves, roasted corn, plantains and plums etc., along the road side. Other women known as "mami beignet" or mami makala" sell a sort of fried doughnuts, which children especially simply adore, along the roadsides. There are also some men from the Northern region of Cameroon who sell "soya" roasted beef and bread they carry in basins on their heads from one neighbourhood to another; and from one commercial centre to another. Others have semi-permanent structures at strategic locations such as in front or near bars, where they roast beef and even chicken which people buy and eat while drinking their beer.

There are other foods sold on rented verandas of houses under trees and along the roads. Although most of these food vendors may be occupying public space illegally, they play a vital role in our cities by providing the necessary subsistence for many poor or low income city dwellers, bachelors and spinsters, alike, and even well –to-do city dwellers who simply want to go "native" by eating their indigenous or ethnic foods and other foods at affordable prices; about 500 Francs CFA or one dollar for a plate of food. Many city dwellers would go to bed hungry for several days of the week without these mobile and makeshift restaurants. This is hard work for these women who sometimes have to use their meagre earnings to pay truck pushers (bambes) or taxis to transport the foods to various selling sites; such as from Bonaberi, Douala to the seaport in the industrial zone during peak hours such as lunch breaks. Sometimes they have to pay some street children popularly known as "nanga mboko" to serve clients and wash the plates during these peak hours. This notwithstanding, these women on the average can make about 30.000 to 40.000 Francs CFA a day, well above the monthly minimum wage for an ordinary worker (36.270 Francs CFA). In spite of this, female entrepreneurial activities to a large extent, allow for maintenance rather than accumulation (Nana-Fabu S., 2009). However, the above example shows that if these women's management, marketing or entrepreneurial skills and techniques are well developed through crash courses and business seminars in a business friendly and gender neutral environment and if they have access to appropriate capital, this would really enhance their socio-economic status as well as help reduce poverty in Cameroon. Already, they make possible a strategy of survival for these often hungry street children as well as contribute tremendously to the general upkeep of their families. One woman interviewed puts it so well. "I tell you since, I became a widow, it is this food business that pays for the medicines when any of my 7 children are sick, puts food on the table every day and pays school fees for my children. So I don't play with this business. Without it, I am finished". (see Research by Nana-Fabu S., and Moutombi T., 2013; Ekomo C., and Nana-Fabu S., 2008; Ela J. M., 1992, 1994, 1998; Touré A., 1985; Kengne Fodouop F., 1996; Kabeer N., 1994; Kamdem E., 2002; Weber F., 2000; Balandier E., 2008; Charmes J., 1987, 1998; Crozier M. and Friedberg E., 1977; Cocquery-Vidrovitch C., 1991). From this finding, we see that although many people in the informal sector of the economy have relatively low pay, there are also some jobs in this sector that pay relatively well; and thus helping in the socio-economic survival of many groups in society (Kengne

Fodouop 1991, Kengne Fodouop and Metton, 2000; Dubar C. 1991).

Furthermore, Ondogo Fouda M. notes that despite the fact that Cameroon is endowed with abundant natural and agricultural resources, such as bananas, cocoa, coffee, cotton, forests and oil; with a well-developed human capital, (also see Kamdem E. 2002, 1999) and having enjoyed significant economic growth during the 1965 to 1985 period, the country witnessed a dangerous degradation of its economy during the 1985 to 1993 period which, as a matter of fact, continues today. This period of economic slowdown was characterized by a tremendous fall in the gross domestic product (GDP)[7] and a fall of 40% of household consumption. The Cameroon Government was therefore forced to ask the International Monetary Fund and the World Bank for help. The structural adjustment plans proposed by these Bretton Woods institutions insisted that government withdraws progressively from the production sector. This was how institutions that benefitted from government subventions will eventually disappear. Despite efforts to redress the economy such as the "Highly Indebted Poor Country Initiative (HIPC)" that Cameroon completed in October 2006, not much has changed as far as poverty reduction in the country goes. Problems of unemployment, food insecurity, the war against the high cost of living, as well as the war against poverty remain intact. Given this context of events, one cannot overemphasize the importance of market women or "buyam-sellams" in their efforts in the socio-economic domain to combat poverty and ameliorate the standards of living in the country. It is true human beings' wants are insatiable because once our basic needs are fulfilled, we look for variety in the way they are met, such as variety in foods, in housing, in clothing, in entertainment etc. Unfortunately, the available means are limited or scarce relative to people's wants. In fact no society has the necessary resources to produce enough goods and services to fully satisfy the wants and desires of its

---

[7] The primary measure of production is gross domestic product (GDP) which measures the total market values of all final goods and services produced within an economy in a specific time period. To measure how well the economy is doing in a country in satisfying wants and desires of people, it is essential to know the size of the GDP available for consumption as well as the number of people it must be distributed to and how evenly it must be distributed (Grimes et al., 2000).

people. Therefore this leads to poverty. (Grimes et al. 2000) However one cannot just turn a blind eye because poverty is persistent in society. The poverty situation in cities such as Douala and other rural areas is dire and as such, relevant socio-economic measures must be implemented to at least provide the basic needs of people in the country. The current high poverty rates in the country are very dysfunctional for the development of the nation.

In fact, Dr. Yonkeu said to herself, the Cameroon government must by all means subsidize the few counselling, therapy and the few available job training programs such as the National Employment Fund; projects to finance small and medium size enterprises etc., and the right personnel; the right people in the right places, so to speak, to make them more effective so as to enable persons in the informal sector and the unemployed persons generally to have good jobs; especially young women who are usually the "last to be hired and the first to be fired". Also there must be the creation of industries to transform the many raw materials to semi-finished and why not, finished goods before they are sold to other countries so as to increase the value of these raw materials or goods in the world market (Rodney W., 1999). Furthermore, there must be conditionality on these industries and companies to employ young people and help them develop entrepreneurial skills. This will make these young people more innovative. This is necessary if the vicious cycle of poverty is to be avoided. Like Moore (2005) states, chronically poor people may pass poverty on to their children, die prematurely from preventable health problems, and suffer a multidimensional depravation of hunger, under-nutrition, unclean drinking water, illiteracy, social isolation, exploitation, low income and social assets. "In fact", Dr. Yonkeu thought, "with the persistent unemployment in sub-Saharan Africa and even in the world, there should not only be an International Labour Day, but an "International Unemployment Day" that would be a day to create awareness and of reflection on how to resolve the unemployment problem worldwide and in Africa in particular.

Things have really come to a standstill in this country. The Cameroon economy remains largely static. The majority of

Cameroonians still live in direst poverty surviving on less a dollar a day. For example, many families still live in sub-standard housing with overcrowding leading to the transmission of diseases such as tuberculosis, skin rashes, and scabies or "come no go" as they are called here and of course a high rate of stress and child delinquency. This happens when children find the crowded housing so stressful that they cannot even do their homework in them after school hours. So they always find themselves alone playing outside their homes without any adult supervision; even playing football, the Cameroonian most favourite sport, on the streets where they could easily be involved in delinquent activities as they fall prey to drug dealers, child traffickers and engage in other deviant activities such as alcohol consumption and stealing. In fact, our studies in the city of Douala in poor neighbourhoods such as New Bell, Bepanda Missoke and Village show that most people here live in unacceptable housing conditions with the average density in dwellings being 6.1 persons. This is so since an average woman in the city of Douala gives birth to at least 4 to 6 children with other family members more likely to be living in the same house. Like they say here in Douala, "le lit du pauvre est fécond" meaning that poor people often have many children (Nana-Fabu S., 2009).

Even people's access to adequate food that is, in terms of quantity and quality to satisfy their dietary needs remains a serious problem in both rural and urban areas such as in the city of Douala. This has been worsened by the endemic problem of unemployment or lack of enough income in the country in general and in the city of Douala in particular, which has lowered household spending on food. This could be seen in many poor households where families purchase smaller quantities and cheaper, less nutritive foods; such as a very high intake of carbohydrates (foods such as cocoyams and cassava, both tuber crops) and a very low intake of foods containing other important nutrients such as proteins (meat, chicken and fish), minerals and vitamins-vegetables and fruits. Thus, it is not uncommon for people in these households to have only a meal a day. This reduces the energy they need for their often tough and time demanding labour jobs. As a matter of fact, many women and children in urban and rural Cameroon still go to bed hungry. This is so because priority is still given to feeding husbands and male children first, often with the most nutritive and the best foods before female children and women, who ironically prepare the food, eat. The situation is worse for children who need enough nutritive food for their development. For example it has been shown that the first three months of a child's life are crucial for the rapid development of the child's brain. Too little energy, protein and nutrients can lead to lasting deficits in cognitive, social and emotional development of the child (see American Psychological Association, 2012). Thus, we see that the negative effects of poverty, unemployment and underemployment on children and adults in terms of their physical, emotional and mental health are simply overwhelming. One need not mention the lack of access to healthcare, unsafe neighbourhoods, under resourced schools for children where sometimes like in the Extreme Northern regions and even here in the city of Douala some children have to sit on bare floors, sometimes mud floors, at some schools to receive lessons (Equinox Radio News May and September 2013), the lack of clean water and clean toilets as well as general inadequate sanitation, many poor people in the country generally and in the city of Douala in particular have to put up with. These are things that are fundamental human rights, but remain largely inaccessible to the majority of Cameroonians in both urban and rural areas.

The situation has been exacerbated by the chronic economic crisis in the country that has led to the inflation of prices of basic goods and services in the country. Inflation refers to the decrease of currency which means that it takes more money to buy the same items. People on fixed incomes suffer as the same amount of money buys less. For instance, people who are satisfied with their incomes may become poor if their incomes do not increase as fast as the inflation. So we see that recession and inflation have more negative effects on people with fewer resources than the rich; as they weaken the capacity of the economy to create decent jobs. Thus, Isabel et al., (2012) essentially explain that the "precariat" is a class in the making. This is so because a growing number of people across the world are living and working precariously, usually in many short-term jobs or low pay jobs as it is in the informal sector in Cameroon; without recourse to stable occupational identities and social protection or protective regulations. They warn that these people may produce social instabilities in societies all over the world. People in this new class in the making are frustrated and dangerous as they have no voice in the functioning and management of society. Therefore it is not surprising that these people are or would be vulnerable to the calls of extreme political parties, extreme religious groups and other fanatical organizations such as today in the Extreme Northern Region of Cameroon. Indeed, unemployment and underemployment which are major causes of poverty, ill health and deviance, prostitution, etc. must be reduced and why not got rid of. The eradication of bribery, corruption, impunity and some of the disastrous government policies such as very high taxes[8] on small businesses which are mainly owned by women would go a long way to reduce unemployment and poverty.

The reduction of taxes on businesses generally and the import and export businesses in particular, would really help the business climate in the country positively. This is so because; the current high taxes have led to a considerable loss of tax revenues in Cameroon with grave consequences on national development.

Therefore, to resolve the growing problem of feminization of poverty in Cameroon, in particular, it does not suffice to make available opportunities to women to improve their situation. They also need targeted socioeconomic and cultural support as well as protection by the laws of the land, together with clear political actions such as quotas in the socio economic and cultural domains to confront exclusion. Indeed, the Affirmative Action Policy or positive discrimination by employers or even government to redress some wrongs of past discrimination against some groups or citizens of a country is not a bad thing. However, it should be a temporal solution. First there must be efficient and appropriate socio-economic and education

---

[8] For instance, the president of 'GICAM' an important business association (2013), blames the slow take off of Cameroon's economy on to high taxes on businesses, corruption in Cameroon and other ills. Similarly, the French ambassador to Cameroon (August 2013) said the business climate in Cameroon remains mediocre to attract foreign investors to the country.

infrastructure built in every region of the country accessible to all citizens irrespective of sex or ethnic affiliation while the Affirmative Action policy is being implemented. However, as soon as every region has attained a similar level of development in the above areas, and there is the level playing ground so to speak, the recruitment policy and appointments to positions of responsibility for example should solely be based on merit, nothing else. Of course, discrimination of all sorts, ethnic, gender etc., should also be got rid of. It is only then that the country could really develop. In short, more money should be put in human and infrastructural development. The Western developed nations or high income countries could also help in the matter by conceiving and implementing fairer international trading and financial policies. A good business climate in the country would also lead to good businesses that are meritocratic and would employ, promote or appoint people on merit, thus giving equal opportunity to all, irrespective of one's gender, ethnic group, or social group to move up the social ladder. Of course, there must also be some affirmative action activities or policies to ease the integration of the physically and socially disabled into the mainstream of society. In short, there must be more humanizing policies to reduce or resolve these problems. Things must change for the good of all and Sundry.

With this thought Dr. Yonkeu shut the blinds, turned off the parlour lights and slowly walked towards her bedroom. By now, she was feeling a little tired from all the thoughts and could not wait to go to bed. She undressed, put on her pyjamas, knelt by her bedside like she did every night; said her prayers, got up and quickly slipped into bed. Before long with the heavy downpour that sounded like a lullaby in her ears "… tic tac, tic tac…", she fell into a real deep sleep and before long, she started dreaming. This is her dream.

THEORETICAL DISCUSSION, DATA AND METHODS, BRIEF HISTORICAL SETTING

Theoretical Discussion

The debate on patriarchy or male dominance in society has a long history. The 1960's and 1970's were particularly marked by the surge of the issue of sexual inequality as an important topic of scientific and social inquiry among scholars and ordinary citizens alike. Indeed like Kimmel D.C., 1974: 168 puts it:

> *There is hardly a characteristic of an individual that is more apparent or more universally noted by others in social interaction than the individual's gender. Certainly, racial characteristics (such as skin colour), socio-economic status, age, physical disability and flagrant expressions of social or psychological deviance may be equally noticeable; but there is a sense in which these bases of discrimination become less salient as individual personal relationships deepen and other aspects of the individual's uniqueness become more important. However, this does not seem to be the case with gender differences; the salience of the differences between men and women tends not to decrease (and may in some ways increase) with deeper social involvement that is, while increased social contact and integration may decrease the importance of skin colour, age, or physical handicaps, "(or ethnicity as in the case of Cameroon)" integration of the sexes has not made gender a nonsalient dimension of a person. Not only does an individual's gender affect the responses of the persons she casually passes on the street, but also it permeates nearly all interpersonal relationships.*

Both the condition of women's economic dependence on men and its psychological and social consequences remain the focus of renewed debate and conflict. It has also inspired a plethora of theories ranging from the biological to the socioeconomic implications for and against male dominance (see Mascia-lees, F.E. 1984; Randall, 1982). Some of the relevant theories that pertain to the African or Cameroon situation will be briefly reviewed. This is a necessary step in providing a fruitful analysis and a better understanding of the relative decline of

Cameroon women's status in the socio-economic and political domains and general high unemployment rates in the country in recent times.

Biological effects

The biological explanation for the relative inferior status assigned to women in society generally and the Cameroon society in particular is in large part derived from the obvious biological differences between men and women. Arguments on the supposedly "natural inferiority" of women hinges on women's distinctive reproductive role and their physical vulnerability derived from the reproductive function. Women are said to be emotional, unstable in crisis situations because they become helpless (Romanie S., 1994; Nana-Fabu S. 2009).

Another aspect of the argument stresses that men have greater bodily strength as well as "bigger brains"; and are therefore considered to be more intelligent than women. Women on the other hand are weak sickly creatures; they use little judgment and cannot be trusted with money. Thus they can only be employed at the most low pay, low status and routine tasks. In fact, many men and even some women in Cameroon have similar stereotypical notions of women and even consider women as child-like creatures who should be treated as such (see Nana-Fabu S., 2006, 2009; Randall, 1984).

Implicit in the biological explanation of sexual inequality is a division of labour where women have primary responsibility for child rearing and household tasks (see Egerton, 1938; Forde, 1954) for the sexual division of labour in Cameroon). It should be noted that although the above tasks are as honourable, noble, and as vital as can be in the socio-economic domains; they remain to a large extent devalued and at best considered as 'normal female roles' (see Ciancanneli P., 1980). This is reflected in the socialization process in Cameroon and similar societies, anticipatory socialization based on gender, where men are socialized to perform the more important, high pay, high profile and prestigious extra-domestic tasks of society. On the other hand, women are more likely to be schooled or directed to stereotypical feminine subjects where they will excel in low pay; low status and low profile jobs mainly in the informal sector of the economy and in the household. Contrary, men are trained to be in high pay, high prestige jobs outside the household or in the public domain. Thus women's "inferior status" is seen as derivative from their natural obligations and inability to perform the "more important" and prestigious extra-domestic tasks because of limitations tied to their child-bearing and child-rearing functions (see Mascia-Lees F. E., 1984; Nana-Fabu S., 1987, 2006, 2009; Romaine S., 1994; Chodorow N., 1979).

Feminists tend to reject the logic of this theory, the assumed link between women's inferior status and biological differences between the sexes (e.g. see Mitchell, 1982, In: Mascia-Lees 1984, Cutrufelli R., 1983). The biological explanation of female inferiority is treated simply as an expression of cultural prejudice serving to rationalize the oppression of women as sex objects by men. This means that women are confined to the private or domestic sphere and are assigned an inferior status because they have a special responsibility in relation to raising children and performing household tasks. Such biological based arguments enable men to remain dominant and pursue their interests uncontested (see De Beauvoir, 1953; J. S. Mills, 1958).

A related counter-argument is presented by Rosaldo M. and Lamphere L. (1974) who note that male dominance in society has been legitimized by the differentiation between public and private spheres. They note that, women's mothering role in the private sphere is a reflection of the organizational and biological constraints limiting women's participation in politics and economics of the public sphere (see Randall 1984; Chodorow, 1979).

In fact, in a capitalistic set up generally and that of Cameroon in particular, where child rearing is largely considered a woman's job, this further complicates women's full participation in the job market. This is so because, to begin with child rearing is not only a difficult and complex task, but the energy required by the task, leaves little for occupational investment. For instance educated women may begin to worry that they are losing their intellectual abilities while doing routine, repetitive household tasks. In the same way, the mother who is working may feel anxious about not depriving her children, husband and herself of their rightful "feminine" attention. Seldom do these issues pose conflicts with a man's occupational role or his sense of masculinity.

Thus it is clear that child rearing should not be seen as a "natural" inclination of women only. The African social system or the socialization process of the Cameroon society in this matter has to be reviewed, to be made inclusive as more and more Cameroon Women find themselves in the job market. A sort of gender neutral socialization is needed to deal with this problem in Cameroon and similar countries worldwide. As a matter of fact, Cameroon women should not be seen as better suited to cleaning house, cooking food, typing letters and answering phones as well as working in the informal sector of the economy. Many women should also be hired for executive and professional positions. This is so because they may also bring skills in which men typically do not excel into the positions making them even more successful and reducing the gender gap here. Therefore the new skills should be rewarded as highly as the more traditional masculine skills until such times that the gender neutral socialization process is effective.

Right now in Cameroon, women are able to successfully compete in the masculine occupational world to the extent that they can bring "masculine" personality qualities to the role: "Objectivity and not subjectivity, assertion and not passivity, achievement motivation and not fears of success or commitment or ambition and drive." Unfortunately by temperament and socialization, relatively few Cameroon women have these personality qualities. Therefore the socialization process in Cameroon should be made more gender neutral; that is by making the so-called "masculine" and "feminine" skills accessible to both females and males and more women also hired in high-prestige, top-profile executive and professional positions. This will go a long way to reduce the relevance of sex differences to full participation in socio-economic positions as well as enhance the importance and status of socio-economic positions for which women are likely to be more competent than men resulting from the current gender biased socialization process in Cameroon. (See Kimmel D.C. 1974: 168-170). Obbo (1986: 176) also points out that the interaction of people in groups inevitably generates tendencies toward both social integration and social differentiation. In the former, laws, regulations and social practices emphasize implicitly the dependence and compatibility of groups with one another. However in the latter case, biological differences, such as male/female, are elaborated to explain and or mystify social differences.

What is significant in this socially constructed sex-gender system is the superiority and domination of African or Cameroon men in top decision-making positions in both the private and public spheres in most African societies, in spite of the fact that African or Cameroon women have always worked in both spheres. (See Nana-Fabu S.1987, 2009).

The Effects of Capitalism and Dependent Development

Basically, this theory states that capitalism depends on the backwardness of the household which maintains women as a reserve labour force available to join the labour force, usually at the periphery of the economy (Mascia-Lees, F. E., 1984). Women are not only the reserve labour force, but they also maintain and sustain the capitalist economy by reproducing and maintaining the capitalist labour force by child-bearing and rearing as well as nurturing often alienated working husbands and boyfriends –the capitalist labour force. Furthermore capitalism in developing countries such as Cameroon dislodges workers from agriculture faster than they are absorbed in industry (see Eliot, 1977; Edari, 1978). Also according to dependency theory, economic development occurs in the context of an international economic system in which extracted wealth transforms the economies of developing nations while supporting the needs of advanced capitalist systems. Thus an international division of labour is created in which African countries such as Cameroon supply raw materials for industries in Europe and North America.(Rodney W.,1990). This system certainly exploits and impoverishes both men and women in these African countries, but it is women who are most impoverished. This is so because at least Cameroon male labourers and Cameroon male elites are continuously integrated into formal capitalist work relations; with the latter (the small egocentric elite group) usually acting as middleman who exploits fellow male Cameroonians in the form of cheap labour for the profitability of European/American and now Chinese males and their own relative profitability; leaving Cameroon male labourers barely surviving with very low pay, little or no job security and health insurance. Meanwhile most Cameroon women are left out in these capitalist work relations. This explains why the majority of women in Cameroon dominate in the informal sector of the economy characterized by low pay, little or no job security and health insurance. The interaction between European and African biases towards women, further compounds women's problems in and out of the job market. It undermines the Cameroon woman's traditional authority, autonomy and power (Boserup E., 1970; Mascia-Lees F. E., 1984; Nana-Fabu S., 1987, 2006). This discrimination against women was to a large extent, until at least fairly recently when feminist political discourse is beginning to take root in the country, perpetrated by colonial and capitalist institutions such as the "modern" African family and its socialization process, the government and the schools (see Carnoy M., 1974) that trained women in stereotypical feminine roles and careers. Even in these areas, men still dominate the top decision-making positions. Furthermore, women's unpaid labour at home maximizes the capitalist's profits since it keeps the wages mainly of the male labour force low. To make matters worse, these profits are often taken out of the country instead of using the profits to develop the country (Clignet R. A. 1977).

The pertinence of these theories is seen in their interactions with the key actors in the study-unemployed and poor women, the Cameroon Government and civil society, private and public companies/industries, social institutions such as the "modern" African family, schools, hospitals etc., and the "affluent" in society. The interactions of these groups and institutions are shown in their articulations, actions and strategies as solutions to the problem of unemployment and poverty in Cameroon; with particular focus on female unemployment and poverty are sought (see Goffman E., 1973, 2002, 1956; Garfinkel H., 1984, 1967, 2007; Crozier M. and Friedberg E., 1977; Ela J. M., 1983; Ekomo E. C. and Nana-Fabu S., 2007). As society is viewed in terms of the interactions of people who live in it, one cannot ignore the construction of social networks (Kamdem E.,

2002) and interdependence of all the social actors in this study. (Durkheim E., 1966). We want to know whether these interactions are contradictory, conflictual (Marx K. and Engels F., 1967) or complementary (Durkheim E. 1966/1947, Weber Max, 1947/1958) or both, or whether at times, dialogue comes into play and what consequences they have on the problem of poverty and unemployment, especially among Cameroon women. Thus Goffman (1956, 2002) in his "interactionist symbolic" theory, where he talks of the "constructivist paradigm", explains that it is people who construct by confronting social reality. So he focuses on important interactions that are defined by their productive dynamic (also see Abdou T., 1985; Boserup E., 1970; Kengne Fodouop F., 1991; Kamdem E., 2002, 2010, 1986, Bekolo E., 2002.)

Data, Methods and Brief Setting of the City of Douala

The data for this work were collected qualitatively by my students of Demography and Urban Sociology of the University of Douala, Cameroon and myself in the city of Douala and in the United States of America; based on the empirico-inductive logic, the micro to the macro; and using instruments such as interview and observation guides. This research aims at gaining a better or in-depth understanding of the phenomena of unemployment and poverty among Cameroon city and town dwellers, in general and female city inhabitants in particular, through spontaneous objective observation and interviews on the field in the city of Douala. In this work we observed the principal actors as if we were one of them. As such, we could exploit inter-subjective relations in groups without judging the social phenomena from our point of view. Instead we tried to understand the hows and whys of the phenomenon – unemployment and poverty, rationality beneath the actions and attitudes of the actors as well as the social reality in Douala. Like Nga Ndongo (2013) puts it, we are like the 'sorcier'; witchor wizard who can see and understand what ordinary people cannot see or understand ("sens caché"); or we probe beneath the "taken- for – granted" reality (Nga Ndongo, 1999: 18) – ethnomethodology (See Garfinkel H., 1967/ 1984). By using these actors, the unemployed or the poor in the city of Douala as our case study, we sought to understand the sentiments, the interpretations, perceptions and meaning of behaviours of the unemployed and poor persons themselves, especially unemployed women in all aspects of their lives, such as their marital status, educational status, the foods they eat, their moods, their dress code, the type of healthcare they use, leisure activities and the types of houses/lodging and neighbourhoods they live in, as well as their 'survival strategies' (see Aktouf O. 1992; Balandier G. 1971; Berger P. and Luckmann T. 2003; Dubar C. 1991; Garfinkel H. 1967, 1984, 2007; Crozier M., 1971). All these, together with information from significant family members and friends help us to come up with logical and coherent findings which could be generalized to other unemployed and poor persons, women in particular in other major cities and towns in Cameroon. So we observed the particular and then generalized about them.

Information were also found in books, journals, newspaper clippings, radio news, (the mass media, both national and international),(see Nga Ndongo, 1999: 11 on "Recherches documentaires"),Ministries of Labour and Social Security, Finance, Public Health, Youth Affairs, Public Works, Social Affairs and Women and the Family. Government and Non-Governmental Organizations (NGOs) also provided useful information. Data from informal settings came from ordinary citizens at social gatherings such as churches, ethnic development associations, informal financial associations or "njangis", health centres, from school children and teachers during lunch breaks, university students and teachers, people in bars, snack bars, eating houses or restaurants, informal eating houses known as "tourne-dos" and even in peoples' houses. Female associations for the promotion of women's rights such as female entrepreneurs and female jurists also provided relevant up-dated data on the subject. The study population was selected purposefully, from key neighbourhoods in five sub-divisions in Douala; Douala 1, Douala 2, Douala 3, Douala 4, Douala 5 with focus on neighbourhoods such as Akwa, Bonapriso, Makepe, Bali, some supposedly "chic" or "rich" neighbourhoods and other "poor" and "average" neighbourhoods such as Makepe Missoke, Village, Bepanda, Omnisport, Dakar, Brazzaville, New-Bell,

Bilongue, Deido, Bonaberi, Bonamoussadi, Ange Raphael, Cité SIC, Cité CICAM.

In all 650 persons mainly poor and unemployed persons (300 women, 250 men and 150 resource persons) were interviewed for this study. The ages of the respondents ranged from 18 years, the age one is generally considered to be mature and the official voting age in Cameroon to 75 years. The very rich life histories and information as seen through the eyes of the protagonists of the story provided us with first-hand information and a better understanding on how these social actors (unemployed women in particular) lived their situations of unemployment and poverty as well as their daily struggles for survival in the city of Douala. Observation together with the author's personal experiences, face to face interviews and focus group discussions with the actors and resource persons also provided useful, reliable and relevant data for this study. As such, the findings in this study could be generalized to other towns and cities in the country, as well as similar towns and cities all over sub-Saharan Africa (see Boyomo A., 2013).

It should be noted that most of the characters and events in this book are real except the shooting incident and Koffi's school which were only in Dr. Yonkeu's imagination at the time. In fact, this book is a sociological scientific research which has intentionally been written in story form for easy reading and for a better comprehension of the social phenomena of general unemployment and female unemployment and poverty in particular today in the city of Douala, Cameroon. It is also worth pointing out that the poverty used in this study is absolute, material or subsistence poverty based on a multi-dimensional measure. This is seen in terms of low pay or low incomes that cannot provide basic necessities such as decent housing, decent schools, access to basic sanitation, basic healthcare, clean drinking water, daily intake of adequate decent and nutritive food, access to transportation and electricity; all values which happen to be a consensus of Douala inhabitants (See Holborn B. et al.1991).Therefore absolute poverty is when people cannot afford some minimum of food, healthcare, clothing, shelter and other necessities. These people are considered poor regardless of how they compare with other people. Following this approach, everyone in a society could have the minimum necessities and no one has to be poor. In practice unfortunately, that happy, state has never existed, and it seems very unlikely that it will come about in the near future.

In fact, whether poverty is defined as relative or absolute, it can be a temporary condition for an individual but a permanent feature for society. For example while in the U.S. about one-third of the poor rise above poverty each year or experience some upward mobility, they are replaced by others who fall into poverty. Contrary to the situation in the U.S., in Cameroon, in recent times in particular, there is very little movement above the poverty line. The trend seems to be that more and more people are slipping below the poverty level every now and then; with an ever dwindling middle class. With the economic crisis now plaguing the nation, there seems to be very little light at the end of the tunnel for any prospects of the situation getting better in the near future. It is also worth noting that the difference between the poor and the "rich" is more visible, more marked in urban areas such as Yaounde and Douala than in rural areas (Curry T. et al., 2002; Schaefer 1986; Chindji-Kouleu F., 2005; Nana-Fabu S., 2009; see Research by Nana-Fabu S. and Nanche R., 2013).

The definition of poverty in this study is also subjective because we take into consideration one's perception of one's well-being (see Schaefer R.T., 1986; Grimes P. et al., 2000; Nana-Fabu S., 2009).

Brief Historical, Social and Geographical Setting of the City of Douala

Douala the economic capital of Cameroon is located on the Wouri estuary. The city is divided into two parts by the River Wouri; Two thirds of the city is concentrated on the left bank of River Wouri. According to the last census results, 2007, the total population of Douala is 1,926,513 with a gender distribution of 49.67% females and 50.33% males occupying the six-subdivisions that make up the city. Being the country's major metropolis, it has the biggest labour pool, a city of entrepreneurs. Subsistence fishing is also carried out mainly by indigenous Douala people and Nigerians. Migrants from all over the World and within Cameroon continue to flock daily to this still evolving city (see Marie J.et al., 2010) as it happens to have a major seaport and an international airport. Many road networks in the hinterlands of the country also converge here creating a huge exodus from many rural areas to this city. This has been markedly so since the end of the colonial period. Most of the industries, extractive industries in particular in the country are also located here which attracts job seekers. This together with natural increase, resulting from the fact that most city dwellers in Cameroon are usually people of child bearing age (15 to 49 years) and below, has led to overpopulation, creating a formidable problem of managing population settlements, providing decent work and other basic services for these people (see Nana-Fabu S., 2012).

In fact, the supply of job seekers far exceeds demand in the city of Douala. The "youth bulge peak" that is the overrepresentation of people between the ages of 15 and 24 years who are not necessarily "skilled in the city of Douala (see population pyramid) has significantly pushed up the unemployment rate in Douala. Many of these young people work in the informal sector or in small family businesses.

Population Pyramid Showing The Youth Bulge In The City Of Douala 2013

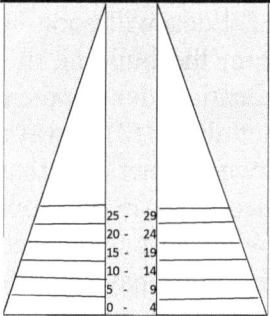

25 -	29
20 -	24
15 -	19
10 -	14
5 -	9
0 -	4

Source: Adapted by Nana-Fabu S., 2013 (see Schaefer R. T., 1986)

Recent estimates of the unemployed in the city of Douala stands at 30%, confirming that unemployment remains a pervasive and persistent problem in the city. (National Institute of Statistics (INS), 2009; Nana-Fabu S, 2012; Sommers M., 2003; Isabel et al., 2012) This has created a massive inequality in the distribution of wealth as could be seen in the ugly sprawl of houses in poor areas of the city in particular.

Also Marie J. et al. (2010) state that the sprawling jerry-built fringe districts with their rutted roads and impoverished inhabitants, in the city of Douala, are hotbeds of ingenuity and informal economic activity ideally suited for the context (see Ela J. M., 1992, 1998; Kamdem E., 2012; Kengne Fodouop F., 1996). Here one finds strings of small markets, crowds of street vendors and a constant flow of traffic consisting of over 2,300 "benskins" (motorcycle taxis); today 2014, over 3000 motorcycle taxis in the city of Douala (Urban Government Douala), which can pass through even the narrowest waterlogged alleyway.

Marie J. et al. (2010) continue that, the old Douala towns (Akwa, Joss and Bell towns) on the bank of the River Wouri have now been turned into harbour facilities and administrative centres. Villages of Douala and other ethnic groups have survived; with names that often begin with the prefix "Bona" meaning the people of Bonaberi, Bonakwamuang, Bonandale etc.

The first new waves of city dwellers, Bamileke, Beti and Bamun from the hinterlands of Cameroon congregated beyond this belt. As the urban sprawl continues, Douala is absorbing far away villages belonging to the Bassa ethnic group which bear the prefix "Ndog" meaning "offspring for" as in Ndogbong, Ndogpassi, etc. In fact, Edea will soon be part of Douala. This sprawl has resulted from the building of residential estates and from unplanned residential developments. As such, Douala according to Marie J. et al. (2010), always look unfinished. As a matter of fact, when town planners or urban delegates try to bring order to these spontaneous urban developments, or to embellish urban areas by destroying vast unplanned settlements, it is the poorest inhabitants who often pay the price as was recently the case in village, Newton Aéroport, Bepanda, Komba Bonaberi, quartier Bamenda, etc. These displaced poor city dwellers more often than not become homeless or squat with family members in very precarious conditions. For instance in April 2014, more than two thousand families were made homeless in Komba-bonaberi by a company that destroyed all the houses in the area claiming that it owns the land. It is unfortunate for this company, like many others in similar situations had no ethical or social considerations for these displaced persons. For example, they could have built temporary shelters for these families somewhere else. (Equinox and KORI F.M. Radio News, April 2014). Sometimes, these people even lose their meagre possessions such as household items and a lot of the time they are not compensated for the land and houses they were evicted from (see the cases of Logbaba, Bepanda and Komba- Bonaberi(2013-2014). This is so even when they had "legally" occupied the land. Other times, middlemen, mainly unscrupulous elites of the area come into the picture and take huge sums of the money that was destined to compensate the evicted population, as was recently the case in Kribi, Ocean Division, South Region, and (2012-2013 Equinox Radio News).

CHAPTER TWO

THE SOCIOECONOMIC AND POLITICAL LANDSCAPE OF CAMEROON: THE CITY OF DOUALA

The morning of the 25th of September was unusually cold and the sun was slowly appearing through the dark clouds that had brought the heavy rains the night before. Time and again, in this city, rain would fall mainly at night time, bringing relief in the form of some coolness to this 'God-forsaken' heat. However, this relief only lasted during the early morning hours. By mid-afternoon, twelve noon to be exact, it was back to normal –; the relentless blistering, roasting and eye-blinding sun worsened by the recent ecological degradation. Terrible!!! And boy! The stench that usually accompanied the heat was just unbearable. One need not mention the mosquitoes that have become synonymous with the name of the city. The city of Douala has no proper sewage system, just a few gutters here and there; which mainly serve as refuse dumps and occasionally as toilets for those miserable city dwellers; you know, the downtrodden, those socially excluded, those "down and outs", of the city, those 'nobodies' those "wretched of the earth" and poor persons whom time seemed to have passed by (see Fanon Frantz, 1963).

Yes poverty, that dreadful word that has become a real problem to many in these parts of the world; these transitional societies of sub-Saharan Africa; as many Cameroonians are stuck in poverty and deprivation while equity and social justice remain only dreams. In fact, the "Growth and Employment Strategy Paper on Cameroon (Cameroon Government 2009:10-13) says it all. It paints a bleak picture for the reduction of poverty in Cameroon. For example evaluating Cameroons' development policies at the macroeconomic level, the report shows a decline in the Gross Domestic Product (GDP) average growth rate from 2000 to 2002 when it was 4.23 per cent. However, from 2003 to 2007 it dropped to 3.32 per cent. During the 2003 to 2007 period, internal demand was the only growth determining factor with an average contributing standing at 3.54 per cent of which 3.12 per cent was exclusively for consumption. Investment expenditure contributed on average 0.44 per cent with a low investment rate of 17.8 per cent on average. Also net exports were extremely low (-0.22 per cent). Therefore, on the whole, economic growth in Cameroon continues to be fragile; 4.8 per cent in 2013 (End of Year Speech Biya P., 2013). As far as prices go, they have been relatively under control with an inflation rate of about 1.9 per cent. The foreign account showed a balance of approximately 44.1 billion CFAF between 2003 and 2008. The balance of trade excluding petroleum showed deficits which widened with time averaging -432 billion CFAF from 2003 to 2008. Currency trends during this period showed opposite counterpart trends of currency circulation marked by a large net accumulation of external assets, combined with a less significant increase of net credits on the economy and a drop in net domestic credits. This was due basically to advances paid to the state. On average, long-term loans stood at less than 3.5 per cent of the total amount of loans granted. This only goes to confirm the fact that the banking sector does not really provide the required funding to support sustainable growth in the country, even today 2014.

As far as public finances go, there was a drop from 4890.3 billion CFAF in 2005 to 1427.6 billion in late 2008. This resulted from debt relief agreements signed after the country attained completion point of the Highly Indebted Poor Country Initiatives (HICPC); a prudent foreign debt policy, in keeping with macroeconomic guidelines as well as respect of the deadlines set for repayment of foreign public debts. During the period running from 2003 to 2008, state financial transactions showed that, in terms of realization; the capital expenditure/total average and donations ratio stood below 25 per cent. There has been no radical change of the situation during the 2013-2014 periods.

On the microeconomic level, the evaluation of the "Millennium Development Goals" on the socioeconomic situation of Cameroon with its main goal of poverty reduction falls way short of the mark. According to the Cameroonian Government this gloomy balance sheet results from the difficulties encountered from the implementation of the strategy as well as from high implementation costs of related actions. Therefore, it comes as no surprise that from 2001 to 2007, extreme poverty and hunger remained intact with the national proportion of people living below the poverty line remaining virtually stable; dropping from 40.2 per cent to 39.9 per cent. Similarly, the rate of illiteracy among the youths 15-24 year olds also remained virtually stable, increasing slightly from 83.1 per cent to 83.3 per cent between 2001 to 2007.

The third goal to promote gender equality and women empowerment noticed some improvements in the education domain between 2001 and 2007. For instance the girls/boys ratio in primary schools rose from 0.83 to 0.89. Also, the eradication of illiteracy from among women aged 15-24 years was stable - 0.88 per cent. So there is hope that this can attain the millennium targets by 2015.

When it comes to reducing child mortality which dropped from 150.7 per thousand to 144 per thousand between 1998 and 2004 with the national target by 2015 set at 75.8 per thousand, it is feared this target may not be reached by 2015 despite efforts made in the health domain. On the other hand, the goal to improve maternal health has improved somewhat. For instance, in 2004, the overall number of deaths among women of childbearing age (15-49 years) was 19 per cent as opposed to 26 per cent from the 1991 to 1997 period. Also the proportion of deliveries with assistance of qualified staff also improved from 78.8 per cent in 1998 to 83.4 per cent in 2004. However, the current rate of maternal mortality has to be reduced to at least single digit to achieve real improvements to women's health[9].

---

[9] The problem of infant and maternal mortality has preoccupied public authorities in Cameroon. Thus, recently, (December 2013), the Minister of Public Health

This will entail training more midwives and encouraging them to stay in the country through decent pay.

In the same way, the fight against HIV/AIDS, malaria and other illnesses has also improved as seen in the 2004 health survey which put the HIV/AIDS prevalence rate at 5.5 per cent nationally; with 6.8 per cent for women as opposed to 4.1 per cent for men aged 15-49 years. Concerning malaria, the prevalence rate stood at 15 per cent in 2004. It is hoped that it will drop to 3 per cent by 2015.

The goal to ensure environmental sustainability has not really worked. For instance, despite the increase in protected areas for the purpose of environmental sustainability (13 per cent in 2000 as against 18.8 per cent in 2008), the goal of reducing the proportion of people using solid fuels to about 42.2 per cent may not be achieved by 2015. In fact, it is currently stabilized at about 82 per cent. Also the proportion of people with access to safe drinking water increased from 40.6 per cent in 2001 to 43.9 per cent in 2007 and it is hoped, it will reach the target of the Millennium Development Program of 72.1 per cent by 2015. However, when we consider that water is synonymous to life, there is still a lot more to be done for the majority of Cameroonians to have access to clean drinking water. The current statistics of accessibility of Cameroonians to clean water are unacceptable in this day and age with the immense technological advancements, immense human capital and immense national resources in the country. Government must do all in its power to resolve this critical problem if we are to be an emerging nation by the year 2035. Besides it is one of the important roles of government to provide clean water to its people.

As far as youth unemployment goes, the statistics showed some improvements with youth unemployment dropping from 14.3 per cent in 2001, to 8.2 per cent in 2007. The government therefore plans to popularize the use of information and communication technology to reduce youth unemployment even further. This is absolutely necessary if Cameroon is to remain a country favourable to foreign investors for this will dramatically

---

signed a decree whereby normal deliveries in public hospitals would henceforth cost 6.000 Francs CFA; and deliveries with operation, 40.000 Francs CFA.

reduce socio-political instability which is often fuelled by unemployed youths.

So, thus far, we see that although there have been considerable improvements in the socio-economic situation of the country, the task of poverty reduction is still immense. For example the low annual growth rate during the 2001-2007 and even today (2014), remains a huge setback to the overall development of the country and the living conditions of households in particular. It is true, income poverty reduced by 13 points between 1996 and 2001 and thereafter stabilized during the 2001-2007 period. In fact, this happens to be the problem in 2013. According to the third national census in 2007, the Cameroon population is about 17.9 million people with 7.71 million people being poor. The spatial dimension of poverty during the 2001-2007 period show that poverty reduced in urban areas by 5 per cent, particularly in Yaounde and Douala, while in rural areas poverty increased by close to 3 per cent especially in the country side of the Northern Region. The third population census also identified some macroeconomic factors that caused poverty in Cameroon which include household size which happen to be large. This is so because an average Cameroon woman gives birth to at least 6 to 8 children. There is also the level of education in the country. The overall illiteracy rate in the country is relatively still high with women suffering more from illiteracy than men. Educational facilities and infrastructures such as classrooms, amphitheatres, and even benches are still in short supply. The socioeconomic group one finds oneself in, also results in poverty. For example, the minimum wage in Cameroon is still relatively low (36,270 CFAF per month) and it is not enough to provide half way decent standard of living especially for urban dwellers who often spend more than half of their monthly pay packets on transportation and rents alone. In fact, the Cameroon minimum wage happens to be the lowest minimum wage in the whole of the Central African Region; for it is only slightly higher than the minimum wage of the Central African Republic which is even a country in war- 35,000 F CFA. When it comes to access to the means of production the situation remains bleak. Few people are able to access loans to set up good businesses. So they remain poor and continue with their hand to month existence as they do one low-paying job or another (see Nana-Fabu, 2009). So we see that not only is poverty associated with low income and low consumption, but that it is also synonymous to low educational achievement, poor health and nutrition, low participation in politics, leisure activities other than drinking in bars and other areas of human development; leading to powerlessness and vulnerability or a poor quality of life. In short, poverty is all encompassing here in Cameroon and in the city of Douala in particular.

In fact, the general living conditions of people in terms of illiteracy rates, access to healthcare and morbidity rates remain dire in 2014. It is true the government is painfully aware of the perpetual problem of poverty in the country which has been exacerbated by the global economic recession; it is also a truism that the Cameroon government has been working toward the reduction, or why not, the eradication of poverty in the country, but there is still a lot more it has to do to win this war against poverty. There are still major human and socio-economic challenges it has to overcome. For example in the health domain children below five years and people aged more than fifty years have a morbidity rate of 32 per cent. For example malaria remains the cause of the overall number of deaths in health facilities, 50 per cent of morbidity among children below the age of five years, 40-45 per cent of medical consultations and 30 per cent of hospitalizations in Cameroon (Cameroon Government, 2009).

Similarly, the main factors of production, physical and human capital have structural deficiencies that have to be fully addressed. For instance, in the road infrastructure sector where 85 per cent of domestic transport activities take place, the available means and strategies introduced to ameliorate conditions in this sector are not adequate to close the wide structural gap between demand and supply. For example, only 10 per cent of the approximately 50,000 km of the domestic road network is tarred; and the proportion of roads in good conditions in 2005 stood at 24 per cent. In addition to this, the low production capacities and dilapidation of energy installations are a setback to the development of home industries and enterprises and do not provide any incentive to investment in the country whose hydroelectric and gas potential is a source of great expectations. Despite the country's significant progress in Information and Communication Technology (ICT), serious problems of access and quality persist, with particularly an optic fibre wire, whose installation and commercialization are not yet fully effective and an access index to the digital estimated at 0.16 in 2002. This makes Cameroon one of the countries which have low access to this technology (Cameroon Government, 2009:14). The provision of good roads and improved ICTs remain huge problems today (2013-2014) in Cameroon

Thus it is also clear that until most of these socio-economic changes, infrastructures and technologies are fully implemented and installed respectively, poverty will never go away. It is true the Cameroon government is doing all in its power to have water supply and power projects such as the Lom Pangar dam it hopes is now functioning (2013); the Kribi gas-fired plant which as a matter of fact, should be now functioning; Memve'ele dam which should be functioning in 2014, Song Mbengue power plant to be functional in 2016, Song-Loulou and Edea power plants etc. to combat poverty. However, poverty[10] is still alive and well in the country. These projects and technologies will certainly go a long way to reduce poverty in Cameroon, but it will be some time before Cameroonians start reaping the fruits of all these investments. These investments are nevertheless a proof of the will of public authorities to focus on the strategy of the generation of wealth and the creation of employment opportunities so as to guarantee a fair distribution of the fruits of growth and poverty reduction (Yang P. 2009/4).However, one can only hope and pray for these projects to become operational; for as things are at the moment, that is, the realpolitik of the country, the road to the reduction or why not the eradication of poverty seems to be still too long and too winding; Dr. Yonkeu concluded.

---

[10] For instance, recently in Cameroon (January 2014), a woman in the South Region of Cameroon sold her baby to a couple from Guinea Equatorial for reasons of economic survival. This is not unique to the South Region. Women have been doing so clandestinely in other regions (Equinox Radio News, January 2014).
Similarly in Limbe in the South-West Region a man was beaten and almost killed as a knife narrowly missed his heart for allegedly stealing a bunch of plantains (research by Nana-Fabu S. February 2014).

Nevertheless, to the inhabitants of this city, I mean the authentic, the real inhabitants of the city of Douala; there is just no other city in the entire world like their city. To them, it is one of a kind. In fact, just ask them how they feel about their city, and listen to their response: 'Our city is great, and we are doing just fine, thank you.' And please, before I forget, one more piece of some vital advice! Do not, I repeat, do not try to complain to them about anything whatsoever you happen not to like about their city; whether it be the dirt, the stench, the heat or the mosquitoes for that matter. Okay, just go ahead and try doing that. But you could be rest assured, you would get exactly what you asked for. First, you would make a complete fool of yourself. These inhabitants, I mean the real Douala city inhabitants, would really think you must have gone out of your mind; and no one would pay any attention to your complaints. They would just simply ignore you. But "woe betides you", should you carry on with your complaining! Then you would really be in trouble.

"How dare you complain about our city, they would ask?" There is absolutely nothing wrong with this city; it is the best city in the world"; at least, so they believe. You know, where ignorance is bliss! Complaining about the stench, the mosquitoes and the unbearable heat, all sounds like Greek to them. The mosquitoes, to begin with, have quite literarily become their "pets". At least, they don't seem to bite them anymore. Ah! The stench! Yes the stench from those gutters and heaps of garbage all over the city. Yes indeed, it would seem the workers in charge of collecting garbage are permanently on strike considering that these mountains of garbage have become a regular sight in the city; except of course when the President of the Republic comes to town. So you see, the people have gotten so used to the stench that it doesn't matter to them anymore. "In fact, is there any such thing?" they would ask? The heat! Yes, the heat indeed. So what about the heat? "There is nothing to it", they would say. In fact, it just helps them consume more of the good old beer, which keeps them in high spirits, help them forget their misery; and of course, keep the beer brewing companies smiling all the way to the bank. You see, beer drinking has almost become the norm in this city; why not even the whole country? It is not unusual to find people consuming beer during the early morning hours till very late at nights; or even the early morning hours the following day. In fact, one wonders where these people get the money from to drink non-stop considering the chronic economic downturn in the country. Beer has even become food to some people who prefer beer to food. Try offering this category of people food instead of beer and watch their reactions. They feel disgusted and wonder where on earth you are from. Indeed why wouldn't they, when every street corner; this is no exaggeration now; every single street is awash with bars and cafés of all sorts.

In fact it seems all other businesses have gone out of business but the brewing industries. You would be there sweating like hell, and you almost feel like taking off all your clothes; but just listen to what they say to that, and please, watch their reactions.

First, they would all stir at you questioningly and surprised for quite some time. Next, they would say: "no doubt about it, he/she must be from out of town, they would say laughing. What the hell is the matter with him/her, they would ask with such astonishment? What does him /she thinks he/she is doing acting up like that? And just look at the amount of sweat pouring down from his/her face! Well, perhaps he/she has an attack of malaria fever. What might one do to help, one of them would ask sarcastically? They would then laugh mockingly. Then goes the popular chorus: "Oh well!" he/she would get over it. It's just a matter of time. They all get over it at some stage." And so it goes on in this city, day in day out. The people are certainly in love with their city.

Come to think of it, why shouldn't they? Of all the cities in the country, this seems to be the only city with relatively a lot more going for it in addition to its relatively more cosmopolitan, dynamic and outgoing population. It also has an international airport and seaport. Chances are that, you would find at least a member of every single country and ethnic group in this city. In fact, it provides a classic example of what Sociologists would call "the centripetal pull of the large city"; forming a real "mosaic of cultures".

As a matter of fact this city has large numbers of people (about 2 million) and remains a huge labour pool, being a hub of industry and commerce in Cameroon. It has a population with a variety of occupations, statuses and backgrounds who live and work there like it is the case in most cities in the world. There are also dense and vertical housing structures everywhere to cater to residential and vocational needs of the people. Of course, there is also the hustle and bustle of normal city life where something is always going on. For instance in these days of high violence and high crime rates in the country and in this city in particular, there are violent scenes in the city all the time. For example there are scenes where a thief is caught here and thereby vigilante groups, judged and sentenced to death by the administration of a snake beating, after which he is burnt to death (jungle justice or mob violence).

Other times, it would be the discovery of a young teenage mother or an unwed young mother or a prostitute who has thrown a new born baby into a pit latrine or trash can because of economic and emotional constraints and huge crowds have gathered to see. Also, there are people who jump into the River Wouri because of familial and other problems, such as owing money to someone they could not pay; or because they have been abandoned by their husbands, boyfriends or fiancées; as was recently the case when a woman tied her child on her back with a piece of cloth known here in Cameroon as "wrapper" and jumped into the River Wouri because her fiancée had abandoned her and the child for another. (Equinox Radio News September 2013). In fact, the city is awash with criminals and deviants of all sorts, both young and old, and all sexes and ethnic groups.

This city also houses huge commercial and some industrial institutions. As one could imagine it is a centre of banking and finance. It is also the centre of communication networks that span the nation and the entire world. In short it is the centre of entertainment. Also like cities all over the world, people here generally live in close proximity but know nothing or they do not seem to want to know their neighbours. Not having each other's biographic information, strangers threaten. They are certainly the "lonely crowd". Here we also find many people with strange tastes, behaviours and lifestyles such as "wizards and witches", homosexuals, alcoholics, drug addicts, prostitutes etc., (see Lewis M.1973: 174-189).

The city of Douala also suffers from insufficient and congested roads. Thus huge traffic jams are common often caused by pedestrians, motorcycle taxis, cars and truck drivers bustling to overtake each other on these narrow badly-maintained roads full of potholes such as at Logbessou, Carrefour St.Michel to Bilongue in the Douala II Area (Equinox Radio News, September 2013). For instance, it has been revealed that these huge traffic jams in the city of Douala account for the loss of about 350 million francs CFA daily by businesses in the city. Many of the streets here are nameless and lack street-lights. Parking spaces are also very hard to come by. As such vehicles are haphazardly parked by the roadsides, often competing for spaces here with roadside vendors and as such reducing the passage way. The massive rural exodus[11] to this city has made a bad situation worse. For example, there is acute housing problem here exacerbated by prohibitive property prices, resulting in uncontrolled urban sprawls where people live in extreme poverty (Marie J. et al., 2010, Nana Fabu S. 2012). One need not mention the inadequate social services in terms of schools, hospitals, etc. Water pollution is also a problem in the city of Douala. For instance, dirt from homes and commercial institutions are thrown in the waters in the city. Industries also throw polluted water into rivers such as the River Wouri and other streams thereby contaminating the water table and endangering the aquatic life, the soil and the air. Heaps of rubbish are found all over the place and debris is thrown on the streets; for example in the New-Bell Aviation neighbourhood, Douala 2, one finds mountains of dirt, and mosquito infested stagnant waters everywhere (Equinox Radio News, 14 September 2013). The cleaning up service (Hysacam) is often overwhelmed by the problem worsened by the demographic boom. Moreover, municipal authorities lack the means and finances to sensitize the population to desist from such unhealthy behaviours (see research by Nana-Fabu S. and Ndondock A. C., 2013). Even the fire brigade is unable to

---

[11]This massive exodus has been triggered by discrimination against women in land ownership in rural areas (see Nana-Fabu S., 2009); the "whirl and bustle that attracts young people to the city of Douala in comparison to the drudgery In the fields, hash discipline, chronic poverty and like K. Little (1974) puts it Douala with its sophistication and bright lights seems to be Eldorado, the place for adventure to many rural poor, especially young people (see Nana-Fabu S. 2012).

function properly because of lack of appropriate equipment and regular supply of water. There is also noise pollution in the city of Douala and other major towns and cities in Cameroon caused by honking of vehicles, loud music from bars, night clubs, cultural and even marriage ceremonies known for their loud drumming, singing and dancing. Recently there are also some churches known for their loud drumming, singing and praying, especially during night time, keeping awake whole neighbourhoods. This noise pollution has been associated with serious mental and health consequences on city dwellers such as, premature deafness, irritation and stress on both children and adults; sometimes even heart attacks of heart patients. This city is certainly suffering from growing pains. Thus urban life remains a major challenge for urban authorities, policy makers and urban dwellers alike as urban areas such as the city of Douala remain very unhealthy places to live in.

However whereas most cities in the country are like "ghost towns", the city of Douala manages to hold its own, both population and business – wise. It is relatively more alive. Things could be even much better here, were it not of the crushing "economic crisis" now plaguing the nation. In all, this city happens to be one of a kind, in the entire country. It seems to have it all; the good, the bad, the poor, the rich; the best and the worst of everything in outsized proportions. The commercial activity of this particular city has brought with it the development of social stratification and inequality that is unimaginable. At the bottom of the stratification ladder are those persons suffering from chronic unemployment, petty traders (mainly women who sell food stuff), call box operators, mainly women too, motorcycle taxi men, servants of all sorts (household and common labourers) and the homeless persons. These persons are often impoverished with little or no education. They are also often mistreated by those they work for, especially in terms of low pay. They often live in slum areas, stigmatized or spontaneous neighbourhoods, usually in improvised housing structures built with scrap, wood or "carrabot" such as New-Bell, Bepanda, Mabanda, Makepe Missoke etc., in such precarious conditions. They are the truly disadvantaged! These neighbourhoods also suffer from high crime rate and mob justice or "autodefense" which is often used to combat crime. The sanitation here is poor and disease is rife as most people in these neighbourhoods do not usually have access to clean water and conventional or modern medicine. In fact, these are similar to ghetto neighbourhoods described by Wacquant L. (2008). According to him, the "ghetto" in the United States, "banlieue" in France, "quartieri périphérici" in Italy, "Favela" in Brazil and "Villa miseria" in Argentina etc. are all terms designating stigmatized neighbourhoods situated at the very bottom of the hierarchical system of places that compose the metropolis. It is the milieu draped in a "sulphurus aura" where social problems gather and fester. It is also where the urban outcasts, people at the bottom of the heap reside, which earn them the disproportionately negative attention of the media, politicians and state managers. They are known to the insiders and outsiders alike as the "lawless zones", the "problem estates" the "no go zones" or the "wild districts" of the city; territories of deprivation and dereliction to be feared, fled from and shunned because they are or such is their reputation; but in these matters perception contributes powerfully to fabricating realities of these neighbourhoods as being hotbeds of violence, vice and social dissolution. In fact, people here often live a hand to mouth existence. They are permanently consigned to the travails and sorrows of poverty. Urban life to these persons is bleak. They suffer defeat as a daily experience. They feel so alienated from society.

At the top of the social ladder are those successful in commerce, the big business persons, the industrialists, the well educated men and women in good paying jobs, the top politicians and top civil servants. These set of people live affluent lifestyles with their luxury cars and houses in "chic" neighbourhoods such as Bonapriso, Bonanjo, etc. They jealously guard their advantaged positions in all aspects of life in this city. Even though they fear the resentment from the poor, they fiercely resist change to the status quo or any attempt to redress the just grievances of the poor. Instead they cling to the privileges they enjoy. With rising crime in the country, these rich people in these well-to-do neighbourhoods use sophisticated strategies such as automatic firearms and they hire guards from expensive private Security companies "societes de gardiennage" to fight crime.

In the middle are a relatively small number of small shop owners, small business people and artisans with skills that allow them maintain their independence through very hard work. They usually live in "average" neighbourhoods such as some areas in Bonaberi, Bonamoussadi, and Ange Raphael etc. Like the very rich, they also use watchmen, security dogs[12] etc., from these expensive security companies to combat crime.

In fact such crude inequality has for long been institutionalized in this city. For a long time now, the rich people have pressed for their claims to wealth, power and prestige as a matter of right; while the majority poor, the urban poor, the downtrodden, the masses have often accepted their life of poverty and misery without challenging the status quo.

However, today in the city of Douala and the country as a whole (see Lewis, 1973: 174-189), things are fast changing and the role of the media in fostering this change has been considerable. More and more persons in the city, especially young persons are becoming "digital natives". They now know how to use the internet, thanks to the many cyber cafés that have been recently opened in this city; and access to "I phones" by some. Many more persons also now have access to television sets. Thanks in large part to the massive trade in second hand goods of all sorts, fridges, cell phones, cars, clothes, mattresses, furniture, etc., from European and Asian countries as well as the United States of America. As a result, many people in the city of Douala are able to see how people live in other parts of the world. This has made them somewhat forceful in demanding their rights to decent living, to speak, publish and assemble or demonstrate peacefully for the respect and guarantee of their human rights generally. More and more people are now beginning to challenge the status quo. They are beginning to believe in the ethos of egalitarian mobility, whereby every person has the right and should be given the opportunities to be all they could be, such as the president, the first lady, the governor, the director general, the minister of state etc., should they have the necessary talents and should they work hard and have some luck. While those at the

---

[12] Recently in one of these neighbourhoods in Bonaberi, a guard dog is known to have slipped out of a half opened gate and literarily eaten or made a meal of a passerby. (Equinox Radio News, October 2013)

top cling to their advantages, and fear the resentment from the poor, those at the bottom are increasingly resenting their poor conditions of living. Not too long ago, in the 1990s this even led to mass hysteria in this city where the military (the "commendement operationnel") was called in to arrest criminals and trouble makers. This led to the death and arrest of many innocent persons; like the case of the "neuf (9) disparus de Bepanda".

The resistance of the rich to change, to ameliorate the living conditions of the poor in the country generally and this city in particular is fast destroying their freedom and freedom of everybody in the city and the country as a whole. For instance there are places in the city the rich cannot go to; and there are times of the day they dare not leave their homes for fear of being robbed, attacked or being killed by criminals. It is ironical that by victimizing the rich persons in this city have become themselves victims or prisoners by the unjust socio-economic system they insist on maintaining. Funny isn't it?

In fact, in February 2008, the anger of the poor was seen in the terribly violent demonstrations in this city and other cities and towns in the country by the masses. This led to the death of many persons and the mass destruction of the properties of these "rich" persons. All these happenings have really destroyed the peace of mind and sense of community normally of these well – to do city dwellers. There is no doubt that the rich persons in this city now more than ever feel threatened by the poor, who increasingly are also challenging their prerogatives. The rich now feel threatened in the streets as well as in the privacy of their homes. It is only predictable that such an unjust system could not remain viable for too long without frictions here and there manifesting themselves in one form of a revolution or another. The recent violent demonstrations were clear indications of a failed social system in this city and the country as whole (see Lewis M.174-189: 1973).

However, for a very long time, no one seemed to be complaining about the mix. If one did so, the popular response was once again: "Our city is great, and we are doing just fine, thank you".

It is just amazing how the poor people live side by side in such squalid conditions with the rich people, the latter, in their often luxury apartment buildings or villas "duplexies" and totally oblivious of the misery surrounding them. For these more often than not "nouveaux riches" or "évolués" their main preoccupation is certainly not whether there would be a next meal, but whether their housemaids would have their French wines or their wines of "haute culture", most likely a "Bordeaux" chilled enough for their next meal. Yes indeed, the stench from the gutters did occasionally rise up to these luxury apartments or condominiums but hey!, that was easy to take care of. All one did, was simply shut the doors and windows, and just a touch of a button on one of those humongous air conditioners, did the trick. Now they could comfortably have their sumptuous lunch, which was usually followed by a good siesta; free from the noise and pollution from passing motor vehicles on the streets; the pitiful cries of often mal-nourished potbellied, running nosed, hungry babies, with feet as thin as twigs, at the nearby mice and roach infested shacks; their only crime – having been born on the wrong side of town; the shouting of drunks on the street; some "poor" wife crying her heart out after having received a thorough beating for no justifiable reason whatsoever from her frustrated husband and as it is often the case, sustained cuts, bruises and broken bones all over her face and body from the beating. Usually the husband must have been taking out his anger and his unemployment problems or frustrations at work, if he works, or his girlfriend or "deuxième bureau" for example, on his wife or more appropriately his "slave" as it is the case in many of these husband/wife relationships here; as it is in some ethnic groups where violence on women by their husbands is somehow legal, where for example husbands show their love to their wives by beating them up; strange indeed; the occasional fights and screams of the often worn-out looking sex workers or ladies in waiting demanding that their "Johns" or male clients pay the right amount of money due them for their services rendered; and still others screaming their hearts out with such joy and excitement : "les Blancs sont là! Les Blancs sont là..." that is of course, whenever a merchant ship, as it is the case nowadays does occasionally arrive at the seaport. For these often impoverished or hungry looking, sex workers, these sex professionals, this means time to make "big money". I mean, we are talking "big" business here now! By all means, it's got to be overtime and sometimes no use of condoms if they are to make these "big monies" from their "rich" clients - the white sailors. And boy, do they really keep these often adventurous – seeking and sex – starved sailors entertained. Poor ladies! Who could really blame them for this improper behaviour, given their terribly limited finances which leave them with no choice than to prostitute themselves? They have got to survive one way or another. They are the "innovator" in Merton's theory of deviance (1957) who accept society's goals but pursue them by "improper" and properly illegitimate means. I tell you, it's really a jungle out there (Merton R. K., 1957).

In fact in this city there are basically two types of workers, those doing the nightshift and those doing the daytime shift. The people doing the daytime shift range from those clad in expensive French made suits and ties, like they say here "cravate", often drenched in sweat, I mean all the way down to their underpants and almost suffocating in the hell-like tropical heat especially during the dry season (really who said the colonial mentality is a thing of the past here?), to the truck pushers (bambes) and other "débrouillards" as they are known here; usually clad in their old raggedy clothes trying to make a living; I mean almost trying to do the impossible in a city where prices of everything-food, housing medicines are prohibitive especially in recent years of the debilitating economic downturn that has been made worse by the structural adjustment plan in the 1980's and 1990's, the devaluation of the Franc CFA by 50 % in 1994 and the Highly Indebted Poor Countries Initiative in 2005/2006, popularly known here as (PPTE). This shift of workers usually starts working at about 6 A.M. and retires very late at night.

Of course, while people at the daytime and evening shifts are sweating it out at work trying to scratch a living, some of those in the second shift are deep asleep in anticipation of the very demanding, very belittling, very exhaustive, and sometimes very unrewarding and very dehumanizing but very "important" all night work. By the way, have you ever really thought of what this world would be without these "nightshift workers"? For instance just think of the number of rapes and violent sex crimes that would be committed in the world every day; and the number of men who will quite literally collapse in anxiety at the sight of their naked wives during the first night of their honeymoon. Again, can you imagine that without these sex workers some men would never know what sexual intercourse is all about; and even some well-meaning handicapped persons would die without ever having the sexual experience, a very normal human experience? How terribly sad! Just think of this. For example Durkheim E. (1893/1960: 139-141) indicated that deviance is not disruptive or evil; but necessary to societal well-being. Therefore to hope to wipe out all sin and waywardness is to ignore the very real functions that deviance plays in maintaining social order. Thus,behaviour that seems irrational, without purpose is not necessarily so. Therefore to Durkheim, crime is a necessary part to all societies for it fulfils an important service by generating social cohesion in opposition to it. As members of a community unite to express outrage and to vent their anger about "criminal" acts, they also develop closer ties to one another. This union in mutual anger creates what Durkheim called "public temper" that is a feeling shared by members of a group that belongs to no one person in particular. Thus through such group consensus, social order is reinforced. This social cohesion in opposition to prostitution is seen in the way Cameroonians generally seemingly "show their disgust and inconsideration for sex work. They usually are very unsympathetic to anything that has to do with prostitution. For example, you dare not talk of anything on the professionalization and legalization of prostitution, no matter how real or profound your arguments. One need not even talk of the tax revenues prostitution would generate, if legalized. Yet, many Cameroonians are often willing to promote activities that usually encourage prostitution such as alcohol consumption in the numerous bars and nightclubs. Indeed, the potentially damaging effects of the portrayal of women in the media in Cameroon are immense. This has been worsened by globalization which has made it easier for many Cameroonians to have access to pornographic channels and books. For instance in Cameroon, we often see half-naked women dancing on Television screens while men are often decently dressed. This contributes in promoting the idea that women are first and foremost sex objects. This encourages female prostitution with often devastating consequences on gender equality in the country. Cameroonians know these different lifestyles such as prostitution and homosexuality are rife in the country, yet, paradoxically, they are always unanimous to condemn and make fun of them. For example this could be seen in the derogatory ways they often unanimously refer to sex work and homosexuality- such as "Ashawo" or "Waka" or "Wolowoss" and "Douala Nkong", "Bilingue" respectively. Yet many Cameroonians use the services provided by these persons with different lifestyles. In fact, for quite a number of married people today in Cameroon, marriage is just a façade for their double lifestyles as homosexuals. How terribly hypocritical! For instance, there are certain night clubs and bars in Akwa and other parts of the city known by many inhabitants of the city of Douala as bars and night clubs for "gays"; yet many Cameroonians remain so homophobic. As a matter of fact, many Cameroonians like many Africans believe homosexuality is behavioural not genetic.

This is not to encourage prostitution or homosexuality for that matter. Rather, it is to sensitize Cameroonians that, whether they like it or not, prostitutes and gays exist in the Cameroon society, and that these prostitutes and gays especially, could be our children, our aunties and uncles, sisters and brothers, cousins, nephews, friends, even our mothers and fathers. Again what do we do with them? Do we kill them because they are gay people? At least, they are human beings and they have the right to live as every human being; and as long as they are not paedophiles. It is true talking about sex or flaunting our sexuality, that is, even among heterosexuals; things such as openly showing affection for one another, hugging and kissing, touching, and simply holding hands in public as they do in Europe and the united States, especially in France, where this is done so openly in public, even in the metro or underground; is certainly not in our mores. Things to do with sex generally remain a taboo in Cameroon. Therefore in order not to shock or offend Cameroonians' sensibilities, prostitution and gay relationships in particular, should be carried out discreetly, at least for now, until such times that it may be tolerated.

Like Durkheim, Hess et al; (1985:139-141) also point out that some deviance is permitted in most societies as a "safety valve" or a way of releasing frustration, tension or anger. For example prostitution which is illegal in most states in the United States continues to exist with only occasional raids and arrests by the police and media crusaders. Why they ask? The answer is; many sociologists argue that prostitution continues to be more or less tolerated -although condemned because it fulfils certain functions for society. The first function is a conservative one in which historically Americans have distinguished two types of women; "good" women whom one marries and "bad" women whom a male sleeps with but does not marry. Prostitution does reinforce this double standard of morality. Secondly, through prostitution sexual outlet is permitted to men but not to women-without threatening family stability. Thirdly, the impersonality and business nature of prostitution also allow men to explore, new or unconventional sexual practices without involvement or anxiety. Lastly, for many men, prostitution is a convenient way to have sexual intercourse under conditions in which they as temporary employer maintain control.

This situation of prostitution in the United States is very similar to what obtains in most patriarchal societies such as Cameroon. Many people especially men, see a positive value in prostitution although official morality opposes it. Given this reality, Dr. Yonkeu feels it should even be legalized until such times that alternative viable lifestyles could be sought for these women. At the moment, the disorder involved in prostitution is enormous. For example, take the case of Baye, who started working as a prostitute in the prime of youth, when she was only 14 years old. She now works at Akwa as a "call-box" or telephone operator during the day and a prostitute at night-time.

When she was only 13 years old, a lady came from Douala, to visit her family in one of the villages in the North West Region of Cameroon. This lady happens to be a "rich" sex worker who owns and runs a bar and a restaurant in the city of Douala. Often this woman would go to remote villages in the North West Region to look for desperate unemployed girls from very poor families whom she will bring along to Douala to work at her bar and restaurant. In fact, this bar and restaurant are a cover for the "brothel" she runs. Often she would convince the parents of these young girls that she would provide training for these girls to enable them have decent work with decent wages in one of the many industries and businesses in the city of Douala. These desperately poor parents often would let their young daughters go with her in the hope that their daughters would be able to find work and send some badly needed money back to them in the village to help them make ends meet.

Little do they know that when the lady takes their daughters to the city of Douala, it is to use them as sex workers for her bar and restaurant male clients; older men who usually like having sex with young girls to make and maximize her profits. The deal is that when these men have sex with these young girls, the payment is made directly to her, the "Madam" instead of the young girls. The "Madam" in turn pays a percentage to these girls for their upkeep. Usually the money paid to these young girls is so negligible that it cannot even pay for their daily needs. So the poverty stricken parents often would wait in vain for money from their young daughters in the city of Douala. During the first few months the "Madam" would send some small amounts of money to the girl's parents back in the village and she will promise them more money in the future, which she never sends. Meanwhile the young girls would continue "slaving" it out as sex workers for the "Madam's" male clients, with payments that permit them to barely survive. When the girls become older and less attractive to these "older" men, they are given some money to start up some small business, usually at the informal sector of the economy because of their very small capital. This happens to be the case with Baye, who now works as a call box operator at Akwa during the day and as prostitute at night-time; with very little money to show for all the many years of hard work as a prostitute for this "Madam".

This case is a clear example of how even women themselves exploit their fellow women to make money and become "rich". It is a real jungle out there. This is the cruellest form of capitalism when young innocent girls are forced to work as prostitutes and exploited as sex objects by mean "Madams" and their mean older male clients, who quite literarily rob these young girls of their youths leaving the girls desperate and helpless, in the end, not knowing what to do with their lives, but to continue in the same degrading sex work business; the only skill they ever learnt. How sad! This is what happens when sex work remains illegal and disorganized.

For instance we also now have prostitution on credit. This usually occurs among males and females who know each other so well. For example, females who rent rooms, apartments and studios in some buildings use sex from time to time as a means of payment to landlords when they do not have money to pay rents. This could also happen between young men and landladies. It is awful seeing women and men using their bodies in this way, as payment for shelter, a real abomination in every way. Other times it is female prostitutes who allow their male clients to have sex with them and pay them later on. This happens whenever the men are broke and are unable to immediately pay for sexual services. Sometimes too, these male clients never come back to pay their debts to these women. Therefore whichever way one tries to make sense of this all, sex on credit and prostitution on the whole remain distasteful. Some order has to be brought to this profession.

Again, Dr. Yonkeu stressed, this is not in any way to encourage or glamorize prostitution. This is so because prostitution is generally so very exploitative and degrading of women as many prostitutes are often subjected to sexual abuse. It exploits women's bodies and it also exploits them financially and emotionally. It is generally a very stressful job as these women often suffers mentally and physically as they are misused and abused by their pimps, male clients and society as well; just like the famous American gospel singer with the smooth and powerful voice, Albertina Walker sings.

In fact, prostitution should only be legalized for the time being until such times that some alternative acceptable and viable income-generating jobs could be made available to the girls and women in the sex industry. This would go a long way to bring order in the industry, protect the sex workers from exploitation and guarantee their sexual health.

Similarly Rwengue (2003), writing on prostitution in Cameroon, states that because many married women usually work at the informal sector of the economy where they receive low pay, they are tempted to have extra-marital sexual partners to make ends meet. Furthermore, parents living poorly, considerably affect their children's sexual behaviours. For instance many poor women petty traders become role models for their daughters who more often than not also become petty traders. Like their mothers, when these young girls cannot make enough money in the informal sector of the economy, they also like their mothers, tend to have sexual relations with older men often referred to as "sugar daddies" or "sponsors" who provide them with money for food, lodging; or school fees uniforms and other school supplies if they also happen to be students (also see Nana-Fabu S., 2009).

Similarly, because of economic hardship and other family problems such as divorce, and child abuse, young boys sometimes, abandon their families to live on the streets. These boys also receive money from older girls, older and married women who clandestinely take care of them in exchange for sex. Boys who are students may also engage in lucrative sexual activities with older wealthy women to achieve their financial goals. Most of the time, these young boys and girls do not even negotiate or insist on the use of condoms; thus exposing themselves to HIV/AIDS and other STDs.

These young boys and girls are unable to negotiate or insist on the use of condoms because of economic constraints. So these older, "rich" men and women benefit from the economic difficulties of these young people to satisfy their sexual desires. The problem of poverty, unemployment and prostitution is also largely linked to single parent households headed by women; which in many ways are dysfunctional family types. This is often the situation when the single mother works at a low paying job, usually in the informal sector or when she is unemployed. When these women cannot make enough money to subsist, they engage in relationships with men who provide them with money in exchange for sex. Also, if the children of these women are not well counselled and trained to enable them acquire relevant skills to be gainfully employed and break the cycle of poverty they have been used to, they may also follow in the footsteps of their mothers by becoming single mothers themselves, leading to a generational transmission of poverty or "culture of poverty" which is really dangerous for a developing country like

Cameroon. The "culture of poverty" is said to be derived from prolonged poverty which leads to the formation of behavioural traits such as the use of drugs and heavy drinking, sexual immorality, violence and fatalism, insecurity, early sex, spontaneity, informal and instable marriages etc., all negative traits for a developing country such as Cameroon (Kottak C., 1991, Lewis O., 1959; Nana-Fabu S., 2009). Thus It is clear that, when all other factors are controlled, such as educational achievement, single parenthood is a powerful predictor of underemployment and poverty as female single parents in particular, struggle with the problem of inadequate income unlike in two-parents households, where at least there are two incomes to meet the needs of families (see Nana-Fabu, 2009).

For example all the above situations of 1) young girls having older men as sex mates for the exchange of money or "sugar daddies" to meet their financial needs 2) intergenerational transmission of poverty through following in the footsteps of mothers who work in the informal sectors 3) single parenthood as a predictor of poverty, are seen in the following life histories in the city of Douala.

The first case is that of young girls doing sex work with older "rich" men for their financial survival as seen in the case study of Samira, a student at the University of Douala.

Samira, aged 25, is a beautiful young lady with wide black sparkling eyes and chiselled facial features. Today, she is wearing tight fitting black stretch trousers, a red "halter neck" top that blends in so well with her long black Brazilian "greffe" hair do, that flows right down to her waist. She was smiling broadly as she welcomed me into her sumptuous one bedroom apartment; not far from the university campus for this face to face, semi structured interview. Her apartment had expensive exquisite furnishings that consisted of 3 leather chairs –a sofa and 2 armchairs. She had the latest digital television set hanging on the wall with a foreign television channel showing one of those popular "soaps" or "série" as the French call them. Her very expensive mobile phone, from the looks of it and a portable computer or lap top were discretely placed on a well-polished wooden desk at the right hand corner of the sitting room. She made me seat on the sofa as she sat directly opposite me on one of the arm chairs. She offered me a sweet beverage and some fried groundnuts on a saucer to eat; took the same for herself and invited me to start the interview.

This apartment could be any apartment in Europe or the United States; real plush I thought to myself as I started with some background information as to how she came to be a student at the University of Douala and lives such an affluent life style that would be the envy of many university students.

"You would not believe this, she said, but I happen to come from a very poor family. My parents are all struggling farmers in a village in the West region. I also come from a large family of 7; 4 boys and 3 girls with me being the eldest. As a matter of fact I happen to be the only child at university. My brother who is about 2 years younger than I am is still struggling to have his G.C.E. A' Levels. He has failed twice now. In fact, because of this, my parents had stopped paying his school fees for he should have been at university now, had he been successful at school as I was. You would not believe this but I am the one paying his fees together with the other siblings at primary and secondary schools.

Financial/ Material Condition

Samira manages to live this affluent lifestyle because she happens to have a "sponsor" or a "rich" man who lodges, feeds, clothes and pays for her healthcare. To tell the truth, when I was admitted to the university of Douala, that is, when, I had my G.C.E. A' Levels, my parents were unable to pay my fees, let alone pay for my daily needs. It was thanks to the money they borrowed from a village 'tontine' or an informal financial association in the village that I found myself here. In fact, the first year was hell for me financially; a real struggle. It was even impossible for me to eat a square meal a day. Little things a young woman needs such as pads, soap for bathing and doing laundry were hard to come by. I was not even doing well with my studies. Poverty was taking its toll on me. Things were so hard that I almost gave up university studies altogether. It was then that one of my friends with a similar background of poverty and deprivation told me how she managed to cope materially at the university. She told me she first started out as a street walking prostitute, when after sometime, luck suddenly came her way. After her classes during the day, she worked as a prostitute at night time to pay for her university and personal needs.

However, she was invited to a party by one of her "hooker" friends one night, when she met this "rich" man who now takes care of her materially. He literarily pays her tuition, lodging, food, healthcare and all her other school needs.

This story got my mind working, Samira said, and with time, I found myself in the prostitution business as well. At first, it was hard for me to combine prostitution and schooling. Moreover, most of my male clients were paying so little for my services. You would not believe it, but I could even earn 500 Francs CFA for a sex work when, things were real bad. With the economic crisis, in the country, things got worse. I was working for long hours with little to show in the end financially. From 6 A.M. to 6 or 7 P.M. were school hours. From 8 P.M. to 5 A.M. were for sex work. The work load was weighing me down. I had very little time to think. I barely satisfied my academic requirements. In fact, I lived in a small studio in a "carrabot" or plank house over there near Makepe Missoke with no indoor toilet or water. I got my water from a well. I lived a hand to mouth lifestyle. In fact, I was about giving up this sex work as well as my schooling altogether and return to the village when luck also came my way. I was walking the street at Rue Mermoz one Saturday night, and feeling really hungry too, having just had only a piece of bread and water for my breakfast; when out of the blue, this "grosse voiture", I mean a black "Prado" stopped right in front of me, and a middle aged man of about 60 started chatting me up. Before long I was in his car as we drove off to one of these fancy restaurants at Akwa that only the "cream of the crop" of society goes to; where we had a sumptuous dinner. I tell you, I ate like someone who had never seen food for days; and I drank the expensive wine that accompanied the food like a real "villageois", gulping down the wine as if I was drinking water. After that night, the rest was history. The middle aged man was a real God sent. He now takes care of all my needs and even those of my family back in the village. When asked whether she did not feel bad or guilty going out with a married man. She just laughed and said to me "you really do not know what it means to be poor, do you? It means you go to bed hungry, for most of the seven days in the week, you lack the basic needs of life such as medical care and as such basic human dignity is more a dream than reality to you. I tell you, it's rough; real rough to be poor, she concluded (translated from French).

The second case is that of Eyenga, a young woman who followed in her mother's footsteps by becoming a petty trader.

It was in the 1990's when my father was laid off his job as a labourer at one of the industries at the industrial zone in Bonaberi. Papa was not making much money doing this job either, about 30.000 Francs CFA monthly. His company was shut down as a result of the economic crisis during this period and the structural adjustment plan etc. Mama has always been a petty trader in food stuff; vegetables, fruits spices and the lot. She was doing this even when papa worked, because like I said earlier, papa's pay was not enough to raise our family of six children as well as three cousins who lived with us. In fact, it is the "buyam sellam" business that mama does that puts food on the table, pay for medicines and even school fees for my younger brothers and sisters, especially after papa was laid off his job. Things have never been easy for the family. Mama and papa have always struggled to make ends meet. Most of the times, we used traditional medicines which are accessible and affordable when we were ill; for conventional medicine is so expensive, so inaccessible (see Mbonji Edjenguèlè, 2009).

I myself happen to be a secondary school dropout. It was always a real struggle for my parents to pay my school fees. Many times, I was sent home from school when I could not pay my school fees. Most of the time, I did not even have the required texts books for my courses. This took a toll on my studies and I was forced to drop out of secondary school. So right now I only have a first school leaving certificate. I had tried to look for work to no avail. So I started helping mama out with the petty trade business. I cannot say we make a lot of money doing this business but at least it helps us make ends meet in the family. It is hard work too but I have grown used to it. If we could raise enough money, the business has the potential of generating more money than we make now. Mama told me how she struggled to start the business from the little money my father gave her, that is when he worked as a labourer, and from our ethnic "njangi" or the informal financial association of our ethnic group, where mama borrowed some money.

I also borrowed money from the same "njangi" since I had no collateral security to pay at the bank where I could access loans. This "buyam sellam" or petty trade business is really hard work, but it is what keeps me going. What can I do?

Daily Routine

You see, I have to wake up very early in the mornings, before it is really day break to go to "Marché Sandaga" where I buy the freshest vegetables and fruits from the North West, West and South West regions at reasonable prices; which I then bring here to the Deido market to sell. I even use to get up very early when it was not yet day light to go to this market to get the best selection of vegetables and fruits at reasonable prices to sell here at Deido market and make some profits. However, after so many "buyam sellam" women were attacked and their money stolen from them on the way to the market, it was then that I now have to wait until there is some day light to venture out of the house in the early morning hours. The risk in doing this job is immense, but what can one do? One has got to survive one way or another. My neighbourhood is full of unemployed, idle young men who have banded up in gangs and steal from people at the very early hours of the morning and very late at nights. The insecurity here has really escalated. There are also many cases of rape here too. I pray, this does not happen to me. I don't know what I will do.

In fact, I am thinking very seriously of moving out of this neighbourhood for another which is somewhat safe. One of my boyfriends, who as a matter of fact, provided the bulk of the money for me to start this "buyam sellam" business, is prepared to give me some additional money which could help me look for a "studio" in another neighbourhood which is somewhat safe.

You see, the "buyam sellam" business especially during these times of the economic crisis cannot provide enough money for all my needs. So I also do some sex work at "Carrefour j'ai raté ma vie" or as it is now called "Carrefour Nelson Mandela" to make ends meet. I really do not like doing this business, but what can I do? I need this money to satisfy my basic needs and help out my parents in raising my little brothers and sisters (Translated from Pidgin English).

The third case is that of Ngo Bikaï, who is a single parent. I became pregnant; she said when I was 18 years old. I must confess I did not know much about sex, becoming pregnant as my parents hardly talked of such things. As a matter of fact there was little dialogue in the family and talking of sex has remained a taboo in the family. Moreover my parents hardly have time for us the children. My mother and father were busy working; papa at his boutique at "Marché central" and mama her hairdressing business, trying to put food on the table every day for us, their 6 children. Where could they have had time to talk about sex and becoming pregnant? In fact, all I knew about sex was from my friends at school and of course from watching television. Actually, when I got pregnant I did not even know I was pregnant for months. It was terrible when I started having morning sickness and the lot. I could not believe it all. I was so scared. When my parents learnt about my pregnancy, they were so angry with me and so reluctant to help me with my financial and other needs. They were so disappointed and felt as ashamed as their friends mocked them. Even boys and girls at school and at the neighbourhood were talking and making fun of me. As a result of all these, I dropped out of school. When I finally had the baby I did not have the courage and desire to go back to school. The author of my pregnancy, a "sauveteur" or petty trader, who went from place to place selling a variety of goods, had also moved to another town and I was left alone to raise the child. My parents who were now reluctant taking care of me and the baby wanted me to go back to school but I rejected the idea. They became so angry with me because I had become a real burden to them financially and otherwise as the baby was another mouth to feed. They were affected psychologically as they blamed themselves for not being good parents to me which had led to me being a single parent. It was all too much for me to handle. I was having sleepless nights just thinking of my situation. With some financial help from my parents, I decided to start the call box or telephone operator business adjacent to the university; a strategic location for the business as many students are often using "call box" or telephone services calling friends and family. With time I also started selling chewables on the side; things such as plantain chips, chewing gums, sweets, fried groundnuts, etc., to students who always like eating these things. In spite of all these, I still did not make enough money for my child and myself; as well as for rents of a "studio"; I had moved out of my parents' house. This is how I got into the sex work business mainly at night time to make ends meet. It is not easy but there is little else I can do with my low educational status. Things are rough and one has got to survive, you know, she "concluded (translated from the French language). Thus with all these life histories it is clear that unemployment or low pay work at the informal sector of the economy and single-parenthood are closely linked to poverty and prostitution in the city of Douala and in other towns and cities in Cameroon.

The fourth case throws light on Douala city dwellers' perceptions, social representations, of sex work and how prostitutes themselves feel about being sex workers. This interview with Azefack, a 33 years old sex worker at Elf Poteau throws light on the subject. She had this to say when asked about her work as a sex worker (see Research by Nana-Fabu S. and Guébou T., 2007).

Madam you think I really like doing this job when you walk the streets all night long and sleep with men you know nothing about? I tell you it is not easy. Often these men have no respect for us, sex workers; they treat us as real sex objects. When they pay their "meagre" sum of money, they expect the world from you. They want you to do almost impossible things, all the gymnastics; for example all sex acts they have seen in pornographic films. They do not care how you feel. All they want is for you to give them the maximum, no matter what it takes to do so. They are not empathetic at all. I tell you, this work is not easy; it is not for the faint hearted. By the time you return home during the wee hours of the morning, you are already so worn out; you can barely work in these high heeled shoes. I tell you, this work is tough. Again before I forget, sometimes these men come to you without having washed. I tell you we are exposed to everything, every smell, every skin or body odour and every sexually transmissible disease you could imagine, every abuse, all the violence. Some of these male clients are so inhumane; they treat you as if you were merchandise they have purchased; a thing, a piece of meat they eat as they like. It's terrible!! So you see, I do this work not really because I want to but because I have to survive. When asked why she could not do some other jobs in the informal sector like petty trade, "call box" or telephone operator, or open a "tourne-dos" or informal restaurant business such as selling roasted fish; she just laughed and said these jobs are so time consuming and so hard to do.

Moreover, you are there all day long and sometimes even during night-time, under the burning sun and the heavy downpour; yet you do not really make much money doing these jobs. It is true, being a sex worker is tough as well, but at least you make a little more money than doing these jobs at the informal sector. For example, you talk about roasting fish or corn, plantains and plums to sell to people. It is true this is a somewhat decent way of making a living; but it is really hard work and like prostitution there are so much health hazards in doing this work.

Women sit all day long on a small stool, in front of a charcoal grill; leaning forward every time to fan the burning charcoal to have fire to roast the corn, plantains or the fish. I tell you this is not easy because not only do you have to be vigilant all the time, to make sure the food does not burn, but you are also exposed to so much smoke from the charcoal grill and the dust from passing vehicles on the road. Thus many of these women in this business end up with acute back pains, eye problems and respiratory diseases. Just imagine yourself sitting on a hard wooden stool day in, day out with nowhere to lean your back on. It is awful. In fact these women start working from about 9 A. M. till very late in the night; with very little money to show at the end of the day; money that cannot take care of all their socio-economic and health needs, let alone those of their families and extended family members as it is usually the case here in Cameroon. I tell you, these women as well as those in the petty trade business, generally suffer tremendously to earn a living. This is why they usually look older than they really are. In fact, you could see the imprint of suffering on their faces. This is unacceptable in this day and age of modernity.

So you see, it is true compared to prostitution you are not denigrated, called all sorts of names "ashawo" "waka" etc., or disrespected; but my sister, we are talking of survival here now. I need the money for my upkeep. Moreover, sometimes one could even get lucky in the prostitution business when occasionally one tumbles on a somewhat "rich" client who can pay you some good money. Sometimes you could even meet a "blanc", a Whiteman who could even take you to "Mbeng", Europe, and America. Really I pray that one day too, I will meet my own "blanc". Meanwhile I will carry on doing this work. I am somewhat used to it, in spite of all the dangers we encounter; "on va faire comment?" or "what can one do?" Things are rough (Translated from French. Interview, with a 33 years old prostitute, at Elf Poteau).

Indeed, Azefack's dream of having a white man is typical of many sex professionals and even ordinary simple girls and in some cases even married women in the city of Douala and other parts of Cameroon for that matter. Many of these persons have for so long watched the soaps on TV that they have come to really, believe that life in the Whiteman's world is all a bed of Roses. In fact many Cameroonians, especially the unemployed and poor have come to believe that life is easy in those countries, and that most whites are so rich that they do not just know what to do with money. Thus many Cameroonians dream of going to work and live in Europe and America. There is absolutely nothing wrong with going to work and live in Europe or America; but they should not think life is so easy there. Like the world-renowned musician "Douleur" sings: Life in Europe, France in particular is not easy. He warns that one has to work round the clock to make ends meet. When whites come to work in Cameroon or Africa, he says, they are generally called expatriates, and are well respected and remunerated. However, when it is the other way round, when Africans or Blacks in particular generally go to work in Paris or France they are known as "travailleurs immigrés" migrant workers and that they often work at very low-pay and tedious jobs. Life is always very hard for them.

Today in Cameroon many of these young people use the internet services to look for white men. They go to all lengths to reassure some of these "mean" white men who insist that these girls send photographs of their half-naked or bare bodies to them through the internet. It is always so sad seeing this on the internet as many of those whitemen often put these photographs on the internet for public viewing. Sometimes one wonders if one could really blame these often desperate poor or sometimes very naive, ignorant young girls for doing what they do. Some of these whitemen really take advantage of these African girls. It is so disgusting and very inadmissible. But what can one do? I guess very little in a world where many are prepared to abuse media freedom in such degrading ways. It is so appalling.

Even here in Cameroon it is not uncommon to see some of these white expatriate men abusing these desperate and vulnerable girls. For example one night in Akwa-Douala, this whiteman and his friends were seen sexually abusing some female prostitutes. It was all so unbelievable. These girls are so desperate to have white men that as soon as they had seen the white men's car drive to a halt near where they were, they all rushed toward the car selling sexual services to the men because it is common knowledge here that white expatriates generally have far more money than an average African. So they are said to pay more for sexual services of prostitutes. It was a real shock as these girls suddenly lowered their skimpy dresses and took off their brassieres. Now they were not only showing their breasts to these white men to show that they were firm and sexy enough but the mean white men were sending out their desperate hands through the window of the car to grasp and feel the girls' breasts, even fondling them to find out which of the breasts were sexy and firm enough to merit selection from among these ten or so prostitutes. The sex workers were also doing everything possible to show off their sex appeal; such obscenity. It was all so sad, so very unbelievable. One could not help but imagine one was in a cow market, not to say a slave market, where one looks for the best cow to buy. Women's bodies have really been transformed into commodities which one purchase and treat as one pleases. Pity!

From this last interview, we see that Douala city dwellers like most Cameroonians are still very reluctant to accept sex work as a way of earning one's livelihood. Ironically though, a considerable number of Cameroonians use the services of sex workers. Thus, we see that although the "oldest profession in the world" remains unacceptable to many Cameroonians, at least on paper, prostitution remains a means of livelihood and survival for many in the city of Douala and in many other areas of the country. The chronic economic downturn in the country continues to make this all the more viable.

Thus, with all these life histories, it is clear that unemployment or low pay work at the informal sector of the economy and single-parenthood are closely linked to poverty and prostitution in the city of Douala and other towns and cities in Cameroon. One also finds even ten year olds, both boys and girls in the prostitution business due to the economic hardship in the country. Child trafficking is also rife nowadays for purposes of prostitution and other ills such as drug trafficking. People use all means to make money. It is not unusual to see some desperate parents sending their young daughter to go and do sex work and earn some badly needed money for the upkeep of the family. Whereas if prostitution were legalized, we would never find such young girls prostituting; and worse still for such little payment; sometimes as low as 200 Francs CFA for sex with a male client. These mainly street walking prostitutes are so poorly paid. HIV/AIDS as well as other sexually transmitted diseases are also prevalent in this group. One need not mention the assault and battery they are often subjected to. At least when legalized this financial exploitation will be less frequent and these women would receive reasonable payments to enable them live somewhat decently. Also, access of these prostitutes to the treatment of HIV/AIDS and other sexually transmitted diseases would be easier and more organized. What is happening right now with these sex workers in Cameroon is criminal and immoral. Some order must be brought to this business; this until she insisted, some alternative lifestyles are found for these women. This exploitation of women must stop. It is true prostitution has helped many families survive especially during these times of the crippling economic downturn in the country; and some women have actually become "rich" from doing this business; but note should be taken that these are the exceptions and not the norm or the rule. Prostitution does indeed have its own status system, from "high class" prostitutes who deal with "rich" men who are well remunerated by these "rich" clients, to the poorly paid streetwalkers who really struggle to make ends meet and who are more exposed to all forms of acts such as theft, rape, beatings, and even murder. Sexual transmissible diseases, drug peddling and drug abuse are also rife among this group. They range from heavy consumption of alcohol to the consumption of hard drugs such as cocaine, heroin and marijuana.

Therefore, we see that although prostitution like deviance of all types creates employment and promotion opportunities for agents of social control such as law enforcement officers, social workers etc., and it happens to be a strategy of socio-economic survival for many in the business, it should by all means, not be encouraged. As a matter of fact what will become of these women when they are older and less attractive or with less sex appeal? Nobody would like to go near them. All their male clients would most likely abandon them for younger women. They will then become poorer than ever especially for those who lived a hand to mouth existence and saved nothing for a rainy day. This is awful, Dr. Yonkeu concluded.

Of course, not to get things all mixed up, the second shift workers, range from these scantily dressed people the sex workers, sometimes almost freezing to death especially during some of those very cold rainy nights with their clients who range from the cream of the crop in society to the "nobodies", the "debrouillards", the "plantons" or the "paysans". And of course there is the dreaded group of burglars, rapists, thieves, often armed to the teeth and almost drugged to death and ready to kill anyone or anything, even a fly that consciously or unconsciously comes their way or; in one way or another is a threat to their barbarous acts. In fact, this is often a replay of violent films from the United States and Europe.

I tell you, this city sure has them all; everyone in his or her own place doing his or her own thing at his or her own time and at his or her own pace. Some city indeed!

As Judge Edu's Renault "VX" drove into the Court premises, the court messenger, Mr. Essomba, a pleasant middle aged man, who looked more like a man in his late sixties because of his grey hair and slightly arched or bent back; walked briskly towards the car, as it came to a complete halt.

"Good morning Your Honour", he greeted the judge as he opened the car door for the Judge, who could not wait to come out of the car after being caught up in a huge traffic jam for hours. The proud judge Edu emerged from his imposing car barely noticing or acknowledging Mr. Essomba's greetings and walked towards his office. Judge Edu was a huge, pot-bellied bespectacled man with a smooth radiant black complexion. Today, he had on a smart grey suit. He was of that special "class" of people in Cameroon those "economic and political aristocrats" who live the "good life". You see living the "good life" in this part of the world meant he lives a lavish lifestyle; lives in an imposing house with all the luxury money can buy. He also has the latest electronic gadgets such as the latest computer set, the digital flat screen television, and the "I" phone even though it may take ages for some of them to learn how to operate these things. He also has more than enough exotic, good food to eat with plenty of wine and champagne "de haute qualité" most likely the "crystal" and other imported expensive drinks to drink. Mind you, the locally brewed beer and other such drinks such as palm wine are for the natives, the "paysans", the "nobodies", and the "villageois". That stuff can never touch his mouth. In short, he owns and uses expensive European and American brand clothes, shoes and goods. This also means he drives an expensive imported car and that more often than not, he has a collection of cars either from good old Europe, America, or more recently from Japan; cars ranging from the luxurious and often prestigious, "4X4's", more likely a Prado, Rolls Royce, the Lincoln continental, the latest Mercedes Benz, and the jaguar, exotic sports cars such as the Ferrari to the simple ones such as the relatively cheap 'Toyota' cars from Japan. I tell you to some of these people, cars have become like play things, toys, one would say, a real display of affluence. One only hoped they have not embezzled public money to buy these cars. Despite the fact that recently (2011-2013) nearly all members of the former government, starting from the former Prime Minister, former Cabinet ministers and some top government officials at the Presidency to General Managers of Public corporations have been put in prison for "embezzling" huge sums of state money, people still continue to steal from public coffers; and colossal sums too; we are talking of billions of francs CFA. The culture of impunity is really alive and well in this country. This is seen in the lyrics of one of the songs of the famous Cameroon, musician, late Eboa Lottin. In one of his songs, he tries to warn the public that stealing public money is really evil; and that people who embezzle public funds and keep them in Swiss and other banks abroad, gain nothing in the end, for when they die they cannot take any money with them. Besides he asks, how much food can they eat at a time? Therefore to him it is all "vanité des vanités" or "vanity of vanities" and that when you die, "tu n'emportes rien, rien" or "you take nothing with you, nothing"

In fact, in spite of Government's efforts to fight bribery, corruption and embezzling of public funds by creating anti-corruption organizations and institutions to dissuade Cameroonians from stealing public money such as "CONAC" as well as the Ministry in Charge of Award of Public Contracts, many public officials carry on stealing. It seems like a curse on these people. When they are appointed to a top position, they feel the budgets are for them to manage as they please. They do not seem to know the difference between state funds and their private money. They feel all the money belongs to them.

The prominent Cameroonian musician Donny Elwood, sings about such behaviours so well: "Mon frère est en haut, ma vie va changer, on va boire on va manger, on va danser, je vais voyager, j'aurais beaucoup de femmes, je vais voyager, visiter les champs –Elysées etc., etc '' In English, this means that, now that they have appointed his brother, to a top post in Government, they will feast like never before, with food and drinks in abundance. Also, he will be able to have all the women he wants in the neighbourhood. Then and again, he would take one of the women to an expensive vacation in Paris, where they will walk hand in hand down the Champs-Elysés, and eat in the most expensive restaurants etc; and simply have a wonderful time. This is typical of a considerable number of people in top posts in Cameroon. When they are appointed to one of these high profile or top posts, (a Minister or Director General) etc; they and their family members feel they could now use the budget of the

Ministry or State Corporation as they please. These top officials forget that they are public servants and that they are there to serve the people. Instead, they use the budgets for selfish ends. 'How terrible! What extravagance, amid such poverty; when the majority of the people could hardly afford even a bicycle. One could not help but wonder how many cars one could possibly drive at a time? It is just like asking, how much steak one could possibly eat at time. To make matters worse one wonders on what roads these more likely "greedy" or "morally bankrupt" people plan on driving these luxury cars on when most of the roads in the country are in such bad shape, bumpy with pot holes here and there and moreover still untarred? The whole thing is just so ridiculous. Really, these people are something else; money crazy and greedy, one would say.

In fact "talking about tarred roads, Dr. Yonkeu thought, they are so rare in Cameroon that a lot of people don't even know what they look like. Fancy this 50 years old guy in the 1990s who for the first time in his life saw tarred roads when he went to visit his brother in the nation's capital and thought they had been painted black ; and when he saw street lights, he thought they were small moons on sticks (see Nyamnjoh, 1994) funny isn't it? Poor fellow! How could he have possibly known what these things look like when they are so rare in Cameroon, especially in remote areas? Can you imagine, it has been ages since electricity was invented, and we are in the twenty first century and it is only not too long ago that this guy had seen street lights and tarred roads? Mai! Are we back in time, way back indeed and so underdeveloped too! Now back to these people living the good life...Naturally, he is married, but of course, has a couple of mistresses who are usually well provided for materially-house, cars, ...Needless to say, he has many house servants at his disposal; and of course, he most likely lives in one of those "chic quartiers" such as Bonapriso, Bonanjo, etc., or exclusive suburbs with expensive living quarters, whose inhabitants are mainly whites, with these few affluent Blacks, like Judge Edu, the évolués; and of course, a couple of shacks here and there occupied by those ..., remember, those "miserable" people, those "nobodies" whom time seemed to have passed by.

One often wonders whether these cities were ever planned. The houses seem so haphazardly built. One couldn't help but wonder aloud what all the guys with big Diplomas on "Town Planning" really do. One would imagine they just sit back in their air-conditioned offices whiling time away; and at noon, they anxiously would switch on to their radios, probably to hear who has been appointed the next "Director General" in one of the public companies or a Director in one of the Ministries, or better still, a Minister of State in one of the Ministries, and so on and so forth, hoping of course, that it would be one of them.

However, the well – constructed and well – covered high fences equipped with cameras and covered with blue or green plastic zinc-like sheets; and the very high iron gates or the well-trimmed or manicured hedge around those mansions; and of course, the "day and night watch men" and the security dogs and the sophisticated alarm systems; these self-built prisons, saved some of those "rich" people from the guilt they might have felt as to why they and even their dogs could have so much to eat and drink, and live in such luxury while just a couple of blocks or so down the road, women, children and men went without either decent food or housing; in fact, living in such squalor and misery. Really you've got to see how the other half, the poor live here! Terrible! I tell you the pitiful housing condition of the poor here, sure makes the "ghetto" in the United States look like "Hollywood" Sad isn't it?

As a matter of fact, the large "trash cans" put outside those mansions are constantly being overturned by impoverished hungry stricken people and skeleton-looking dogs and fowls competing and scavenging for whatever leftover and often stale food there may be there. I tell you, the gap between the "haves" and the "have nots" in this society is just so enormous that, contrary to the views of those Africans who subscribe to the "convergence theory", it would take ages, if at all, for there to be any convergence whatsoever of the classes here. The wealth of the country is so concentrated in the hands of just a privileged few who live in such opulence, while the rest of the citizens suffer from chronic poverty and deprivation. Yet in spite of this, there is something so very special about this city -Douala and the country as a whole-Cameroon for that matter which sooner or later does get to you and you never really seem to want to leave it. You get real hooked. Funny isn't it?

The judge's clerk, Mr. Epoh, a young smart man, in his late twenties, dressed in a well ironed black trousers, a sparkling white shirt and black tie held open the door of the Judge Edu's office that was adjacent to the court house, as he walked into his office and as usual barely responding to the clerks' greetings. He entered his office, quickly unbuttoned his coat, switched on the air conditioner, sat on his expensive Victorian chair and rang the bell summoning his secretary. He was running late because of the traffic jam he ran into on his way to work. "For God's sake where is this woman?" He grumbled to himself

As he was grumbling to himself, his Secretary, Miss Engome walked in. she was a tall, and elegant young lady; very pretty indeed, with big sparkling eyes, prominent cheekbones, an ebony black complexion, and hair straightened out with reddish brown tints here and there. She was impeccably dressed in a white skirt suit. She also had beautiful plump lips painted bright red which she manipulated in ways that said "kiss me darling". A real seductress indeed!

"Good morning sir!" she greeted the Judge.

The Judge probably tired from waiting simply nodded his head nonchalantly; and he was just about to ask Miss Engome what was on the program for the day when the secretary suddenly interrupted him. "Sir", she said anxiously, "I am afraid, the program for the day has been altered. Something serious has just come up. This means Mr. Njomo's court hearing has to be postponed to another day. "What a shame", the judge murmured. After all the hell he's been through so that his case could be heard, today!" he mumbled to himself. The judge decided he was just going to explain to Mr. Njomo that something really urgent had come up and so he would just have to wait for another day for his court hearing. He wondered how Mr. Njomo would take it though. Anyway, he came to the conclusion that in this world of uncertainty, things do not often happen as planned, and he hoped Mr. Njomo would just have to accept this. In fact, there was really nothing he could do about it. "By the way Miss ….eh….. Miss Engome, what is this urgent matter you were talking about", the Judge asked?

"Sir", Miss Engome replied, "it's the case about the young Doctor."

"Which young Doctor" the Judge asked impatiently and frowning?

"Sir" Miss Engome went on "the young Doctor who just came back from, "Mbeng", you know Sir, from the United States of America two years ago, and since then, she has been unable to find work in spite of her qualifications and her world of experience. With such good qualifications, one would have thought finding a good job would just be a piece of cake for her. In fact, one would think, people or companies would be begging her to work for them; but that has not been the case. Instead, most companies feel it would be a drain on their budgets to hire someone with a Doctorate Degree. Besides the big bosses would rather hire someone with a Bachelor's Degree, or better still, someone with a lesser qualification, even though he or she may be unable to deliver the goods; just so that, they may be able to squeeze out as much extra money as possible from funds that had been allocated for certain projects. One may think they may use these extra monies to improve the company's business; but that is not usually the case. Instead, they pocket the extra money for their personal use – perhaps for buying one of those luxury cars most likely the latest Mercedes Benz or a Luxury "4x4" jeep 'Prado' or they may decide to go on vacation Overseas, most likely to Britain or France or "home" as many would like to call it with their young mistresses or girl-friends. In fact, the other day, one of my friends from the United States told me that, there are more of the latest Mercedes Benz cars and latest 4 by 4 jeeps here in Cameroon than there are in the United States. Can you imagine that, when our country is so poor and indebted? It is really something.

Poor Doctor! They really need people like her in this country, but her luck probably ran out. She I guess emm…emm…, she just happens to have been born at the wrong time, perhaps a little too late…Imagine, she completed her own studies and came back home just when there is the notorious "economic crisis". In fact, the intervention of the "International Monetary Fund" and the World Bank etc. has only made matters worse. The Structural Adjustment Plan the Bretton Wood institutions imposes on the Government puts an indefinite hold on recruitment to Government Services, and cut salaries massively. It has led to the shutdown of many industries and businesses, layoffs and massive unemployment generally in the country. Come to think of it, I think this draconian measure should best be referred to as the "Structural Destruction Plan" considering the enormous havoc, sufferings and hardships it brings to bear on people. The Highly Indebted Poor Country Initiative (HIPC) Cameroon completed in 2006 has not helped in anyway. They seem to be more of punitive than remedial measures".

The Chinese invasion too has worsened the unemployment problem in the country. You see Sir, there is an ironic twist to all this. Cheap goods and even manpower from China has really led to the "deindustrialization" of Africa. To begin with, most of these Chinese projects in the country such as road, bridges and dam building, rely heavily on imported labour force especially in top positions with high pay; while the local labour force predominates in low pay manual work.

Second, many Cameroonians are not motivated to create industries to manufacture goods that cannot compete with prices of cheap Chinese goods both at home and abroad. In fact, why all the trouble when one can buy the same goods at a cheaper price from Chinese stores? It makes no sense whatsoever. Our markets have been flooded by cheap goods from China. So because the few locally owned industries that existed could not compete in the open market most of them have shut down and there are very few local persons who would venture into the business. They are so demoralized. This has contributed tremendously to the problem of unemployment in the country.

"Don't you see all the jobless people on the streets," Miss Engome went on? "Most of them are graduates. Others are victims of the closings of public companies such as banks, business and industries said to be unprofitable. Sir, it's bad out there. I am really lucky I still have my job even though I do not even have a big "Diploma", just my GCE O'Levels. Parents spend all the little money they have educating their children, but when the children do come out of school with their big Diplomas, they end up in "Chomecam", you know Sir, ... they end up "chaffing", no job and remain in total dependence on their parents for their livelihood; that is if their parents could afford doing so. I tell you it is a real aberration. Some have even taken to stealing and still some have become big time robbers or bandits. By the way, did you see those guys on TV the other day? I tell you Sir, they were real young, 15 to 24 years old guys who had been arrested for armed robbery; and the other shot dead by the police. It was so sad. One could not possibly help but wonder what these guys would have become have they had jobs. It's such a waste of human resources considering that such intelligent and healthy looking guys have become big time robbers and as such a real menace to the well-being of society. Yet, as much as one finds what these guys do absolutely repulsive and intolerable, one still finds oneself wondering about as to whether society is not in many ways also to be blamed for a lot these things. Indeed sir, like they say "a mind is a terrible thing to waste". Come to think of it, these guys have to survive somehow. They have to survive somehow, you know Sir, although no one accepts their strategy. I tell you things are really rough out there; nothing seems to be going on right, businesses eh …all that stuff. For instance many university graduates today find themselves in the informal sector of the economy, doing one low paying, dead-end job or another. It's terrible Sir … the other day the "benskin", I mean the motor cycle taxi man who brought me to work said he was a graduate from the university with a Bachelor's degree in the sciences. He said he was unable to find work since three years now. It is one of his uncles who managed to lend him money to buy the motor bike he now drives as a taxi. He said he worked day and night just to survive. Imagine … he said he will soon be thirty years old, but he still cannot marry because he would not be able to raise a family on the money he makes as a "motor" taxi man especially now with all the taxes they have to pay. He did not want his wife to be his neighbour's wife as they say here in Cameroon. Sir, times are rough out there. Many young people are unemployed or underemployed as the motor taxi man is. You would not believe this but many young women, even university graduates are "buyam sellams", selling one food stuff or another in the market. Others even sell "okrika" used clothes, bags, shoes, etc., or they are "call box" or telephone operators. I tell you Sir, the situation is terrible!!! There is a climate of general disenchantment in the country in spite of this semblance of peace and happiness among people. In fact sir, were it not of certain social or indigenous solidarity or survival mechanisms in this city and the country as a whole, such as "njangis"- financial associations- where people could have some money to start up or do businesses; and the "born house" phenomenon whereby members of ethnic, financial, church or neighbourhood associations and groups give gifts of baby clothes, foods, toiletries and even money to mothers who have just had babies, the situation would have been dire, impossible.

You find many girls who migrated from the village to the city to look for work but they are unable to find work. Now many of them are in the "Ashawo" business. You know Sir, they have now become prostitutes, sex professionals. Just go to some of the street bars and night clubs in town; to streets, such as "Rue de la joie", "j'ai râté ma vie" etc, the red-light districts. You will find many young girls, even age 10 quite literarily begging to have sexual intercourse with men so as to have some little money for food and other basic necessities of life. Sometimes these women are paid even 200-250 Francs CFA for a sex work... Sir things are bad out there. Only God knows when this suffering will end... it is terrible!

For example, the other day, Sir, this young prostitute together with some street boys popularly known as "Nanga Mboko", got this man well beaten at Akwa during night time (see research by Nana-Fabu S. and Retibe Y., 2013). The man, a client of the young female prostitute of about 20 years old, had had sex with the prostitute; and had not paid the required amount of money for the sex work. The prostitute got real wild "buttoned" the man at the neck with both hands, started kicking him and screaming at the top of her voice at the man to pay all the money due her for the sex work. This attracted some street children, children who could even be as young as 10 years old, who usually roamed the streets late at night looking for some victims to steal from. Sometimes these children who are also usually drugged to the teeth and armed, not only steal money and valuables from people but they also murder some of their unlucky victims; especially those who try to resist their attempts to steal from them. Really Sir, there is terrible insecurity in this city.

Take the numerous cases of ladies whose hand-bags are snatched from them by thieves in broad day light in front of helpless onlookers and some police posts on roadsides and at markets, such as at Marché Central, Marché Mboppi, Marché Ndokoti, Marché Nkololoun Rond-Point Dakar, etc. Lately these bandits have been using a new tactic by snatching ladies' hand-bags in "chic" and poor neighbourhoods alike such as Bonapriso and Bepanda, Grand-Moulin, Ange Raphael etc. during the day and at night time.

In fact generally, because of this high crime rate and violence against women in particular, many inhabitants and women especially, are scared to go out at night time. Even when one does go out during the day for work or for leisure, one makes sure one returns when it is not yet night time for fear of being robbed, raped or murdered by criminals, drug addicts or men of the underworld. Homicides have become common lately in the city of Douala. It is really crazy. One does not know what to do. Even the forces of law and order are simply overwhelmed by it all. For instance sometimes when one is attacked at one's home and one calls the police for help, they ask one if the bandits are armed and if they are many. If it is the case, they would most likely not come to help. Other times the police would tell one who needs help that they do not have fuel or petrol in their car to come and help one. I tell you Sir, things are really becoming impossible in this country. Come to think of it we may be blaming the forces of law and order for their somewhat lukewarm attitude toward crime, but often, these criminals are more armed with sophisticated weapons and firearms than the police. Other times the streets or better still, foot paths, in many of these neighbourhoods, especially poor neighbourhoods such as new-Bell, Mabanda, Bepanda Missoke etc., are inaccessible to vehicles as the houses built haphazardly, have taken up most of the available space with very little space left for roads. These roads are often untarred. Moreover as many of these neighbourhoods are unplanned, the streets are usually nameless and without lighting, making them fertile breeding grounds for crime and other deviant activities. I tell you Sir, the situation is really dreadful. What can one do?

Like I was saying Sir, these street children can play the role of providers of protection to female prostitutes who may be victims of abuse from their male clients as was the case with this young prostitute the other night. However, it is worth noting that these street children's interactions with female prostitutes are very ambivalent or schizophrenic; as sometimes like with this 20 years old sex worker, they protected her from a dishonest male client who wanted to cheat her; but these street children are also known to steal from and even murder female prostitutes when they need money. These children who are often exposed to so much violence and crime end up being traumatized with many mental health problems that make their behaviours very unpredictable. For example, when the street children came to help this young female sex worker, they got her male client well beaten and stabbed with a kitchen knife. As the man lay there bleeding they searched the man and took away all his valuable possessions such as his gold watch, rings, neck chain and all the money he had on him, after which they vanished into the dark of night, in the blind alleys in Akwa at the sight of an approaching police van. These street children have mastered their way around Akwa. When the police arrived they took the young sex worker into custody and rushed the male client to a nearby hospital.

You see Sir; these male clients often refuse paying the little money these female prostitutes demand. One even finds the display of patriarchy in a well-structured situation such as this, when having sex with a prostitute demands that she should be remunerated accordingly. However, men still believe that it is their right to have sex with women when they want to without having to pay for it in one way or another. They just feel women are there just to satisfy their lust whenever they want to; sex objects, and that these women do not deserve any reasonable financial reward even when they are in the sex work business. How psychologically and financially unjust!

No wonder, Majoie Ayi, a popular Cameroonian musician sings in one of her songs that sexual exploitation of women has become almost a norm in Cameroon; where most of the time men see women as sex objects. Usually Cameroon men will sleep with as many women as possible, after which these women are abandoned, "kick and pass" relationships. Ironically, when Cameroon women decide enough is enough and resolve to live their lives as happily as ever with little or no input from men, the men and even some brainwashed women who have internalized male dominance, become angry and panic; "ils ont paniqué à cause de Majoie", she sings. No one puts it better than Majoie in her record. Men often would panic when they see an independent, hardworking, successful, free spirited, intelligent young woman who does not quite literarily believe that, "men are God's gift to women" as Tina Turner sings in one of her songs, and live their lives independently with little or no stress from men.

It is also worth noting that many of these women who become sex workers do not do so because they like it. Most of the time, it is because they have no other choice than to work as prostitutes to survive economically. With the economic crisis in the 1980s and 1990s that hit Cameroon leading to massive salary cuts and lay-offs in public and private enterprises, huge numbers of people became unemployed. This subsequently resulted in a boom of low paying; low status jobs in the informal sector of the economy which mainly helped people survive from day to day (Ela J.M., 1990). Sex work also happened to be a strategy of survival for many unemployed women. The situation worsened in the city of Douala with an unemployment rate estimated at 30% in 2009. Today not much has changed. Douala continues to have a very high unemployment rate and continues to be the most expensive city in Africa.

Most of the time, they also encounter huge socio-economic and health risks doing this job. A streetwalking 30 years old prostitute in a tight mini skirt, a tight fitting blouse, a long flowing black wig, a red high heeled shoes and red bag to match at "rue de la joie" Deido Aïsha had this to say:

"I have been working as a prostitute for the last 10 years now and there does not seem to be anything that can make me want to stop doing this job. What do you expect from a chronically unemployed person like me with only 3 GCE O' Levels including religious knowledge? How do you expect me to find decent work that pays well and work that will sustain me and my small family (one child) in this city of Douala where prices of food and rents of even "carrabot" plank houses are prohibitive? I tried looking for work even as a house servant, but it was difficult to come by. When I did eventually find work as a house servant for an unmarried man, he wanted to sleep with me all the time, for "njoh", you know, paying me no money. Besides my pay was way below the minimum wage 15,000 Francs CFA a month for long hours of hard, hard labour; cooking, washing, cleaning etc, for such a low wage. It was then that I decided to become a prostitute for my economic survival. What could I do? I have to survive, you know? In fact, I don't say I make huge sums of money in this business, but I tell you, it is better than being a house servant where you are constantly exploited economically and sexually too like I was. At least, being a prostitute , I can make even more than 15,000 Frs CFA in a day when the going is good; when I tumble on some rich or generous clients than I made working as a house servant, or if you like house slave in a month. I tell you I am not in this business because I like it, but it is for survival. You would not believe this, but sometimes. I can make even more money when I have sex without condoms. Some men like it like that. People talk about AIDS but what about it? There are risks in every job. So I don't see why sex work should be any different. As a matter of fact who can live forever? If I die it would not be anything new. People will continue to die after me. That is the reality of life. In fact, many of my friends in this business do the same. When the going is rough and we need money badly, we take the risk –"man die, I die", she concluded.

This shows how very few choices are open to women to earn a half way decent livelihood. They are always faced with having to make very difficult and almost impossible choices to survive economically like the 30 years old prostitute. Moreover, they usually do not negotiate or insist on having sex with condoms because of economic constraints (see Rwengue, 2003); thus exposing themselves to such health hazards and diseases such as HIV/AIDS, and other STDs. It is a real jungle out there making these women fatalistic.

"By the way Sir, have you been to the Seaport lately? There used to be a time when ships were all over the place. Those were the good old days when business was booming, quite literarily. In fact, it was often the case that, a lot of ships could hardly find docking space at the Seaport. Today, you will be lucky to find a single ship anchored at the Seaport. Hmm! Thanks to the visit of the British Royal Couple – the late Princess Diana and Prince Charles to Cameroon, years ago; we had a ship anchored at the Seaport for a little while, a grand one at that – the Royal Yacht Britannia. That was something! Pity though the Royal couple did not bring along some charity monies for the suffering, hungry masses of Cameroon. Nevertheless, we could be hopeful, considering that they came, they saw and hopefully, they would think of us when next they are dishing out charity monies to the down trodden of the world and the wildlife reserve of course.

Not to mention the many Foreigners who used to be all over the place doing one business or the other! For example, there used to be a time that when one walked down the city street, one would have thought one was in Texas U.S.A. You need to have seen those Americans in their blue jeans, cowboy boots and hats walking down the streets. Boy!, that was something. Today, you would be really lucky to see one white face on the streets. Most of the Companies that were run by these whites, have all either shut down, or left the country. You know how these companies operate. When they find they cannot make profits anymore, they don't hesitate, they move on to "greener pastures". I tell you Sir, the economy has really taken a nose dive.

The only good thing about this, is that now, we the "little" people with some jobs of course, can afford to live in some half way decent housing. Rents have really somewhat plummeted to the extent that most landlords are now having a lot of trouble trying to make ends meet. Can you imagine that? They would be lucky if tenants even pay their rents at the end of the month. Stories abound of tenants who have lived in villas or apartment buildings for years without paying rents as a result of the economic crisis. It is not an easy business for landlords to evict tenants who have not paid their rents either. Chances are that a landlord may end up spending more money in legal costs to have the tenant thrown out of his house than the rent money due him. It's all so unbelievable considering the fantastic amount of money Landlords used to make when the going was good. Even farmers too have not escaped from the wrath of "Mr. Economic

Crisis". Cocoa and coffee prices, two of the main cash crops of the nation have fallen terribly so much so that many farmers feel it is not worth the trouble to go on cultivating either of the crops.

One cannot help but wonder how Government manages to pay workers every month. In order to meet some of its financial needs, Government passed a law whereby public servants over the age of fifty five should go on retirement. However, the strategy does not seem to have worked. For one reason or another, one still finds people over or beyond the age fifty five still working, not only are some of these people still working, but chances are that they are holding top positions in Government. These old people are literarily stuck up in the upper echelons of most jobs and as such, they are not freeing up opportunities for the young. For instance the average age of Cabinet Ministers today is sixty years. Can you imagine? This has contributed tremendously to high levels of youth unemployment making upward social mobility very rare in Cameroon

It's a shame because just the allowances of some of these people, not to mention their pay, could be used not only to meet some of the peoples' needs such as clean water supplies, but also to employ a great number of young people who are out there on the street jobless and hungry too.

It's amazing how some of these people, these "old cronies" do all in their power to stay looking young. One could hardly see a trace of grey hair on their heads. Thanks to the very popular imported black hair dye from the People's Republic of China. I tell you, that Chinese Company must be doing a hell of a business here in Cameroon. Some other people simply shave their heads so that there are no hairs left on them to show they have grey hair. Others change their ages to a younger age. You will see an old man, some of them with even great grand-children and unable to walk upright but check out the ages they give officially. It will be something like fifty years. How deceitful! I tell you Sir, things are so hard nowadays. Nothing seems to be going on right and everybody seems to be complaining about one thing or the other. However, the complaining seems to be done secretly too for fear of being accused of being subversive by some over-zealous public officials and being thrown into jail. You know how "rotten" those jails are!

However, Sir, Miss Engome went on, what surprises me is that you "big shots" do not seem to be suffering from any economic crisis whatsoever. You do carry on as usual as if nothing serious is going on. You eat and drink well; you still have as many mistresses as possible; your wives still go to "Mbeng" France, Switzerland, England and America every summer: and of course buy some of the most fashionable and most expensive outfits, shoes, and furniture. Your children still attend some of the most exclusive and expensive schools in France and England, Switzerland and even in the United States; some of you still maintain your mansions and chateaux in the outskirts of France and so on and so forth. Ironically, some of your main worries at the moment seem to be how you could arrange to buy some of the most sophisticated satellite dishes and big screen television sets from Japan or the United States and emm...emm..."

The judge, probably having had enough of Miss Engome's stories, rudely interrupted her.

"You just stop running that mouth of yours and tell me what the hell this urgent matter is with the Doctor from the United States and job...etc. etc." the judge demanded?

"Yes Sir", Miss Engome replied, a little frightened now, yes "maître" ...I mean ... your honour, "she just...she just shot her former boss", she stammered.

"What...! The Judge asked, obviously shocked by what he had just heard? Sir, Miss Engome repeated, "she just shot her former boss".

"I will be damned! ..." the judge exclaimed.

"Yes Sir, apparently, there must have been a serious problem between Dr. Yonkeu and her boss. This, I believe, must have led to the shooting. The boss has just been rushed to hospital with serious head injuries. One wonders if he would live! Even if he does live, one cannot help but doubt if he would be able to function normally again. He was being carried away to hospital.

The Judge, probably still in a state of shock at the news of the shooting and all that Miss Engome had been telling him so far, took off his eye glasses, lowered his head and murmured several times, "what a pity! What a pity!"

Meanwhile, Miss Engome just raved on and on.

"Humm Sir, these children who study abroad, especially those from the United States, are really "tough". They often talk of social justice and human rights, and that they would not let anyone "mess around with their human rights". Sir, it seems in that United States, "Human Rights" is such a big thing. Everybody, it seems, is free to think as they like, and speak out about whatever they find improper and demonstrate peacefully. What a country! I wish I could go there someday to see things for myself. It is not every day that you come across a country where people are so free to fight for their rights without fear of punishment, or worse still torture and death in some dark, dirty, rat and cockroach infested prison cell. That must be some country!

The Judge once more rudely interrupted:

"Where the hell is the Doctor …emm…emm…" the Judge asked rudely. "Doctor Yonkeu", Miss Engome replied shivering and said, "she is now in the court premises awaiting trial". "O.K Miss Engome", said the Judge contemptuously: "let's not waste any more time. I am even tired of your raving about so and so…Its time to go to court. We are running late".

The Judge nervously and with all the authority in the world he could muster at that moment, walked into the court room as usual and feeling all important; only this time, he couldn't help not looking a little shaken by the gruesome story he had just heard. "Such a thing had never happened here before. Only in the movies does one come close to seeing such awful things. Moreover, it was a female who did the shooting. That was really unheard of here. Unbelievable! Perhaps these children one sends overseas to study, is not a very good idea after all. They end up knowing too much than they should. All these thoughts ran through the Judge's mind as he walked down the aisle to his seat.

The court was called to order and the proceedings started. The first witness was called to the stand. It was Dr. Yonkeu's father, a retired and very renowned engineer. He was about sixty year old, average height, well-proportioned body, with an aura of wisdom and grace. He looked very healthy indeed. He was obviously someone who had taken good care of himself – ate and drank well, but never in excess. He seemed to have had more than his own fair share of the "good life". However, in spite of all his tremendous achievements in life, he still remained a very down to earth, but very respectable and dignified man; a real gentleman in every sense of the word. He never at any time let his success go to his head. What a man! Rumour has it that, he had provided well for his daughter – gave her the best money could buy. He even occasionally, went as far as bailing out his brothers from very huge debts. This careless lifestyle of this brother of his has indeed caused tremendous pain and suffering to a lot of innocent people. Talk of womanizing. The fellow is a real "skirt chaser" a real Casanova and a stud. I mean, the guy would go after any person in a dress. He just could not keep his pants on for too long strange, isn't it?

Come to think of it, he was so unlike his brother, Dr. Yonkeu's father, who was a perfect gentleman in every way. One would have never thought they were indeed brothers. But believe you me; nature does certainly have its way of doing things.

In any case, today on the stand, Dr. Yonkeu's father looked very well indeed, although he was overwhelmed emotionally by the shooting incident. He was certainly not his normal cheerful self. This has been a painful experience for him. His demeanour certainly showed he was sad. This was how he narrated what happened on that fateful day; the day his daughter "lost her cool" and shot her former boss.

CHAPTER THREE

WOES OF WOMANHOOD

It was around eight o' clock..., Dr. Yonkeu's father Mr. Tchuente, began when it all happened. Dr. Yonkeu had gone into her former boss' office, and I stood by the car chatting with some of my old time friends when suddenly I heard this really loud sound, bang! Bang! ... Boy! I thought, this was not a normal sound around this area. Something serious must have happened. On the spur of the moment, I turned around to see what had happened, when I saw this large crowd rushing toward where Dr. Yonkeu's boss' office was. "Mai, I thought, I hope nothing bad has happened to Dr. Yonkeu. I hope this terrorist business has not reached Cameroon. I also rushed toward that direction, and as I struggled to find my way through the huge crowd that had already gathered there, I saw Dr. Yonkeu lying on the ground unconscious, probably from shock; but still holding onto the gun. "Unbelievable!" I thought. Where did she get the gun from? It was really an awful sight.

Meanwhile, the police had rushed into the boss' office and they had managed to get hold of the ambulance crew on the phone, which arrived a few minutes later; and took the boss who had by then lost a lot of blood from the gunshot wounds, to the nearest hospital. Seeing Dr. Yonkeu lying so helplessly on the ground, the first thought that came to my mind was, "how could such a gentle and peace loving child do such a violent thing? I know she had had it rough since she came back from the United States Of America, but gee!!!, I never thought she could do such an atrocious thing. It is so very unlike her. She valued human life more than anything else in the world. She could not even hurt a fly, let alone a human being. It was more like a dream than reality; a real nightmare; I said.

Wrapped up in such deep thought, I was only awoken by the voices of policemen who were telling the immense crowd to move away from where Dr. Yonkeu was lying unconscious. When the crowd had dispersed, they administered some first aid to Dr. Yonkeu and when she had recovered a little, they carried her into the police van and took her away for questioning; after which she was brought here at the court house for trial.

"Thanks Mr. Tchuente", the Judge said; "but who exactly is this Dr. Yonkeu? What was her upbringing like? What the devil must have driven her to do such an awful thing; so cruel a thing? "Mr. Tchuente started narrating Dr. Yonkeu's life story.

"You see, Dr. Yonkeu who by the way is an only child, was born in a quiet little town in the South West Region of Cameroon. As a child, she was very sweet and loving. However, my wife and I had often wondered about the way our little girl sometimes carried on.

Believe you me, Dr. Yonkeu had not always been what you would call an ordinary child. To begin with, instead of the usual nine months it takes for any baby to stay in its mother's womb before being born, Dr. Yonkeu on the other hand either quite simply resented being born; or she may have enjoyed being in her mother's womb, so much so that it took eleven "good" months for her to finally decide it was time to set eyes on mother earth. And that was not all. You know how babies generally scream the moment they hit mother earth! Well, you can bet on this, Dr. Yonkeu's scream was no usual scream either. Believe you me, she could easily have acquired a very comfortable place in the "Guinness Book of Records" for the all-time loudest and most ear piercing screams ever heard at St. Augustine's Memorial Maternity Ward. It is said her screams were so loud and so sharp that, one could quite literarily hear the walls of the Maternity Ward vibrating as a result of it. Even the Doctors and the nurses helping to deliver her had the misfortune of hearing these screams ringing in their ears long after they had performed their noble duty of helping bring Dr. Yonkeu into this world.

Who knows, perhaps she, Dr. Yonkeu that is, may have foreseen the "woes" she was to undergo in this world, the "woes" of womanhood. That probably may have been why she had screamed her heart out on that fateful day, the day she was born; just so as to show her resentment for what mum and dad had, without her consent or approval, decided to do to her, bring her into this 'god dam' world. This world of sin and woe; this world, in which for the most part, one finds oneself, constantly striving for survival; where one hardly knows whom one's real friends are. What a world! What a world of great contradictions, good and bad, joy and sadness, etc.

You see, in one way, she was like any other little baby. She did all the things little babies do, such as wetting her nappies, crying when hungry, drinking her milk and so on and so forth. On the other hand however, she seemed somewhat awkward. She was too serious for her age, and occasionally, when left alone with her numerous toys, she would just seat there gazing into the air as if she was thinking so deeply; instead of playing with her toys as other children her age would do. We used to wonder what she could be thinking so seriously about at that age. We became worried sick. We wondered whether she would become one of those great philosophers in the future; or some Einstein …who knows, or some sort of a weirdo', some nut case. You know, these things could go either way. One never could tell.

When she had reached schooling age, she was sent to the best primary school in town. Although she had all the luxury money could buy, such as toys in excess, children's books of all sorts, not to mention the pretty colourful little shoes and dresses, she did not seem to be a very cheerful girl. At school, she was not doing well either. At this point, my wife and I became very worried indeed. We hoped and prayed so hard that our greatest fear, Dr. Yonkeu becoming a "weirdo" would not come true after all.

However, in the end, Dr. Yonkeu surprised us all. She did very well in her final year at primary school. We were ever so happy and very thankful to God after all, that our little girl had not only turned out to be a perfectly normal girl, but a very bright one at that. She passed her First School Leaving Certificate and the Common Entrance Examinations with flying colours. She was admitted into a good Secondary School in the North West Region of Cameroon.

While she was in Secondary School, she was of course a boarding student as it usually was the case back then. Her academic performance improved tremendously, but her Professors often wrote to us, complaining about Dr. Yonkeu's aloofness from other students. She did not get along quite well with the other girls especially during her first two years at College. She always kept to herself, and in her spare time, instead of rushing into town as most girls did, she would instead go to the library and read. She was a sort of introvert.

She enjoyed reading History Books, especially the books on the French and American Revolutions, and those on the African Slave Trade. Whenever she had the opportunity, she would often go to her History Professor's office and begin questioning him on certain historical events and facts. She would ask him to explain certain things about the French and American Revolutions. She objected to the whole business of "Colonialism" and of course, exploitation of some human beings by others. She would also demand to know what exactly made people to sell others to complete strangers who would then take them to far off unknown lands to work and live as slaves. Money did not seem a good enough incentive or even a viable justification for such an atrocious, inhumane act. She indeed wondered if there wasn't something else that made people do what they did at that particular point in time, other than money. She could hardly believe that those slave stories were indeed for real because the brutality involved in them was just so terrible, so inhumane...Fancy cutting the leg of a slave who was trying to escape, or severely beating people and hanging them to die; awful! It's so gruesome, so brutal. She could not see any justification in slavery whatsoever. To her, slavery was an abomination in every sense of the word.

In fact, she did learn the song, and read the story of Jim Brown, the great American anti-slavery advocate. As the story goes, he had fought so hard and so bravely for the abolition of slavery in the United States. In the end however, he was caught when he had attempted to steal arms from an arms depot in Virginia, intended for the fight against those who were proslavery. He was then tried, condemned for treason and hung. True, she imagined, "one man's terrorist is really another man's freedom fighter". See what happened to Mandela and the others in Apartheid South Africa; to Um Nyobe, Ernest Ouandié, Roland Moumié, Martin Paul Samba, Ngosso Din, Charles Atangana, Rudolf Douala Manga Bell, Ossende Affana, Bishop Ndongmo, Martin Singat, Chindji – Kouleu, Mboa Massock one of the few freedom fighters still living and the other great men and women who died to bring "independence" to Cameroon. For Dr. Yonkeu, the great American President, Abraham Lincoln, together with men such as Jim Brown, became some of her all time heroes, men of conscience, who would not just sit back and watch their fellow human beings suffer; just like, she thought, was the great William Wilberforce and other ordinary people of high character and sentiment who had so valiantly led the anti-slavery movement in Britain. People of such high calibre, such braveness, such humaneness, she thought, had become such a rarity nowadays. Their strategies may vary, but their goals noble, she thought. "Bless their souls"

She took everything so emotionally and so seriously. Her Professor often explained to her that slavery was indeed a very unfortunate and terrible thing that happened sometimes ago; but that, we should all try not to be so preoccupied by it. Rather, he went on, we should be determined instead to contribute whatever we could to better the condition of mankind, so that, such terrible things, such appalling crimes against humanity; take the case of Hitler and the Jews; the killing of 6 million Jews; would never repeat themselves again, ever. However, no matter what the Professor said, and how he said it, that did not ultimately deter her from being so preoccupied by these things, slavery in particular. She could not just make any sense whatsoever out of it all.

Given the fact that Dr. Yonkeu was so concerned, so preoccupied about past and current events, she seemed to be so way ahead of her time. As such, she could not possibly enjoy doing things girls of her age did. Her friends found her very boring indeed. They felt she was just so mature, so uninteresting, for her age. She in turn often complained about their simple-mindedness and their carefree attitudes toward life amid such suffering in the land.

Why she did wonder, couldn't her friends be just like her? All they seemed to want to do, was to plait or braid or style their hair in the latest styles, and spend all the little money their parents give them for pocket money, on expensive, often imported European and American clothes and shoes, just so that they could attract boys, sometimes, men who could even be their grand- fathers, "Sugar Daddies". All they ever wanted to do was have fun! Fun! Fun! Nothing else ever matters to them. No wonder, she thought, "the other day, Namondo was sent away from school because she had become pregnant. In fact, it was no surprise by any means. All Namondo and many other girls ever did, was to go out with guys and have "fun", whatever that is. I bet she did not know a thing about; neither did she give a damn about the French or the American Revolutions. One could not help but wonder if she even knew a thing about slavery. What a shame! Now, just see what she has done to herself.

Time and again, Mr. Tchuente went on, Dr. Yonkeu's professors would send us reports on her performance in her classes. Often, they said Dr. Yonkeu was doing quite well in her classes. However, they were worried Dr. Yonkeu spent too much of her time reading and very little of her time on extracurricular activities such as sports. They did not think that was very healthy for a student. There had to be a balance of some sort, they would say.

However, during her final year in secondary school, Dr. Yonkeu had changed remarkably, both socially and physically. Physically, she had become so tall and lanky but beautiful in that girlish way; and socially, she had made quite a few girl-friends. She even attended a couple of those school dances, and also developed a great deal of interest in music. She however never gave up her love and quest for historical facts and she had become ever so well informed on world socio-political and economic issues. In spite of all the changes she had undergone, she somewhat remained more of a loner. She kept to herself a lot. There were definitely certain times that she wished to be alone. She said she often needed some peace and quiet, time and again; to reflect on life and that; she could achieve this, only when she was alone, by herself. She was of the opinion that, it was only during such times that she was most creative both physically and mentally. She also did a lot of poetry writing mainly about the sorry state of mankind and about nature –mainly an appreciation of the beautiful and colourful flowers, birds which she quite simply adored. She also wrote on greed and hate in the world; and her inability to change some of these things, left her so frustrated. My wife and I often wrote to her not to take life so seriously. Who knows, perhaps other people would emulate her ways and that the time would come when she would indeed have the opportunity to make her own small contributions to the welfare of mankind. Thus all her life would not have been spent on nothing.

Then graduation day arrived at long last. Once again, Dr. Yonkeu had done so well in her exams that she was awarded the Principal's Price of Excellence on graduation day. She had ten G.C.E. O' Levels with distinctions in History and French. She was admitted at three High Schools but she chose to go to Mokole High School, in the North West Region of Cameroon. Although Dr. Yonkeu had done so well in her exams, she never lost her sense of humility. She was of course happy she did well in her exams, but she never let that go to her head. She was just determined to do even better the next time around and go as high as her brains and of course, as fate would permit her with her schooling. In that way, she hoped to acquire sufficient knowledge about the social, cultural, economic and political matters of the world so as to develop the skills to be able to make a difference in the world someday, no matter how small. She had often said if she could just help change even one person's life from misery to joy, that would make all the difference in the world for her.

Another academic year had started. This time around things were not going to be easy for Dr. Yonkeu both socially and academically. Academically, she knew she had to work twice as hard since most of the students at that particular High School were supposed to be the best, the "cream of the crop", so to speak, academically, who had come from various Secondary Schools all over the country. She imagined the competition among the students academically was going to be real tough and fierce. She resolved she was going to give it her all to be able to make it there.

On the one hand, she had grown so pretty and features of her womanhood, the curves and the bumps, the lot, were becoming more and more visible with each passing day. She was also beginning to become more conscious of men and most men also found her very attractive. It was becoming more and more obvious to her that sooner or later, she would meet a young man whom she would not be able to resist, and this would mean that she would have to combine love and her academic work. The thought of this actually happening, gave her cold feet. In fact this sort of worried her a great deal. She felt that if she did not make it academically, she would be a failure in life for she would be unable to bring about the changes in the world which had been her goal for so long. She decided that she would be real careful whenever she did fall in love, not to let the love take control of her so much so that her academic career would suffer.

As fate would have it though, she had not even made more than six months at High School when she met this really nice looking guy who quite literarily swept her off her feet. Before long they started dating. It was just the ordinary dating stuff of going to picnics and to the movies together, nothing really serious. The farthest they did go, was passionate kissing and other such things, nothing more. As time went by however, Dr. Yonkeu realized that she was becoming very fond of the guy, Wandji, as she later told us his name was. In any case, she always managed to keep things under control.

Besides, she was not going to let this love affair affect her studies in any way negative. She knew she had set her goal and she was so determined to make it in the end. So she tried to imagine nothing had really changed after all and she kept up her hard work at school. She was now going to specialize in History, French, Politics and sociology in order to get into University and study Law and Political Science. As such, she never went on dates except after she had done all her homework and of course after she had done some extra reading on her favourite pastime-History. She was very strict about that. To her, it was always business before pleasure, and never the other way round. She always said one could never mix the two and succeed in life.

"Most failures in life", she would say, "came as a result of people trying to mix business with pleasure. It was like mixing palm oil and water." It often amazed us how at that early age, Dr. Yonkeu had become so much aware about the workings of life, Mr. Tchuente, Dr. Yonkeu's father said. That was something my wife and I, could never understand. She was certainly not reasoning like girls her age would. She seemed to be so much ahead of her time.

As time went by however, her love for Wandji grew stronger and stronger. She also became so preoccupied with Wandji, and the consequences that this may bring to bear upon her – an eventual pregnancy, which would mean the end of her much cherished academic career. This, she thought would be so because in those days, contraceptives were not really "en vogue" and school authorities were very strict about the idea of pregnant girls attending classes. As a matter of fact, pregnant girls were simply not allowed to attend classes because school authorities felt it would be a bad example for other girls. Chances, would be that, some girls might follow suit, and that would not be too good for the reputation and image of the school. As such, even after a girl had given birth, she was still not allowed to resume schooling. In fact, becoming pregnant meant the end of a girl's academic career. Meanwhile, the guy who had got the girl pregnant, if he was a student would carry on with his studies as if nothing had happened. For one reason or another, the regulation for pregnant girls, did not seem to apply to the guys who got the girls pregnant. After all, "It takes two to Tango". Talk of sexism here!

Dr. Yonkeu thought of what had happened to Namondo and the other girls, back at Secondary School; how being pregnant brought an abrupt end to their academic career before it had even started. This brought chills to her spine. She became even more determined never to fall into that same trap. She had her dreams and she would do all in her power to make them come true, she often said. So she kept on seeing Wandji, but she never let the love take the better of her.

As fate would have it, though, time, the great master, took care of everything; and before she knew it, it was already the end of year, yet, another academic year; and another graduation time for Dr. Yonkeu once again. "It's amazing how time simply flies when one is working real hard" Mr. Tchuente said. Dr. Yonkeu did extremely well in her G.C.E. A'Levels examination. She had all her four papers. "Boy! Were we happy with her performance", Mr. Tchuente said. As a matter of fact, she herself was quite happy with her results. She felt she had achieved something but at the back of her mind, she knew that it was just the tip of the iceberg, so to speak. She was aware she still had a long, long way to go as far academia went; and above all, before she could fulfil her goal – to make a difference, no matter how small to the suffering people of the world.

Dr. Yonkeu was admitted at the University of Roses. She had to enrol at law school since the University of Roses had not yet opened a school of Political Science. She did not regret this too much, although according to the National Plan, there would have been a school of Political Science at the University of Roses by that time; but you know how things work in this part of the world – real slow and complicated! All the same, she felt with her Law Degree, she would still be able to defend those poor people who could not afford a lawyer, free of charge, whenever possible. "This was quite a noble thought; Mr. Tchuente went on, especially nowadays when lawyer charges have skyrocketed. In fact, a lawyer friend of his was not too far from the truth, Mr. Tchuente said, when he cold-bloodedly stated that "justice is not for the poor". If such a statement could come from a lawyer's own mouth, one did not need too much brain to figure out what the law profession has become. I mean, there is nothing wrong with trying to make as much money as possible, but when one is out to make money at all cost, even at the expense of innocent people, then one can imagine what an unfair world this has become, Mr. Tchuente explained. Many lawyers like many medical doctors have now become entrepreneurs.

However, it was another academic year once again for Dr. Yonkeu, and she had already had her first experience of what University life was all about. She wrote quite a few letters to us about her new experiences and how she already had to work so hard. In all though, she seemed quite excited about her new life at the University.

Meanwhile, Wandji her High School Sweetheart had been awarded a British scholarship and he had already left for England to study Politics at the London School of Economics. She felt it was best the way things had turned out, because had Wandji been admitted at the University of Roses, she could never tell what might have happened. She felt she wouldn't have been able to cope with her studies and that sooner or later, she would have given into his demands to engage in sexual intercourse and maybe she would have become pregnant, since contraceptives were still not really accessible in those days. This she believed would have negatively affected her academic career. She would have most likely left college. That would have made her really miserable to find all her dreams suddenly brought to an end. Wandji and Dr. Yonkeu did keep in touch with each other through letter writing for some time. However, with time, they did stop communicating with each other. Like the famous adage goes, "out of sight is out of mind". This was so true in their case.

Meanwhile, Dr. Yonkeu got really involved with her studies. She left very little time for fun. She had heard how very difficult it was to make it at the university, and she was not by any means going to be a failure. As usual, she was determined to make it to the very end. Her first shock at the university though was the way in which some female students came to class. Every girl sure tried to look her very best, but some of these girls exaggerated. They came to class all made up, with their hair straightened out and coloured or with expensive extensions or greffe that are waist length. They also had on dresses or trousers and shoes that cost a fortune. Mai, Dr. Yonkeu thought, these girls must have a lot of money, and they must have come from very wealthy families, for they must have spent a fortune on their outfits and their hairdos. Just to go to the "beauty salon" for their sophisticated hairdos cost a fortune, not to mention their expensive outfits. She wondered where the girls got the money from to buy such expensive clothes given that the university allowances, if one was lucky to have them could barely cover one's basic needs, such as food and books; and that most wealthy people often sent their children to overseas universities, France, England, America, Switzerland, etc. This remained a crossword puzzle she could never figure out. However, it would not be too long before she would realize the secret to the girl's exorbitant life-styles.

Dr. Yonkeu had started dating one of the guys at the University, who in fact was ahead of her in class, by one year. She was all so excited about him because, they shared similar interests. He seemed to be genuinely concerned about the injustices in the world; and like Dr. Yonkeu, he was also one of those who believed that with a good education, one could have some opportunity to help those who were less fortunate in the world, in one way or another and make some money for a decent lifestyle. He was also studying Law, and he also hoped that as a Lawyer, he would be able to put justice first before profits. He had come from a very poor family, and unlike Dr. Yonkeu, he knew exactly what it all meant to be poor in this society; I mean real poor, dead poor. In fact, he had lived it most of his life. His greatest ambition, he once said, was never to be poor again. So one could imagine what being poor really did mean to the young man!

He did talk of times when as children they did often go to bed hungry, at least, for five days out of the seven days in a week. This was so, he explained, because, his mother had to sell most of the food stuff she and her father cultivated, in order to pay their school fees and meet other daily household responsibilities, health bills especially. In fact, he did also say fish, chicken and meat were a rarity in their home. He remembered how they only ate chicken on Christmas day. He had said he and his brothers and sisters could not wait to put on their Christmas clothes and   anxiously wait for their mother to call them to come and eat the Christmas rice and chicken stew. He used to say how when they, the children smelt the flavour of onions, garlic, tomatoes and chicken all frying together as his mother was preparing the Christmas meal, this caused the secretion of so much saliva into their mouths. It was all surreal, out of this world! They could not just wait to dig into the bowl of rice with a few spoons of the chicken stew, with the chicken cut into very tiny pieces, scantily spread over it. He said the children were also very careful to ensure that no one ate more pieces of chicken than the others for they all ate from the same bowl. He carried on that it was often a really delicious meal and that it was the only few times they too could have a taste of chicken; even if it meant they only enjoyed the aroma of chicken more than they actually ate chicken. This is because the pieces of chicken were usually so small. Oh! How he missed those few happy moments in their family; he said. He did also say that they also drank water from doubtful sources such as wells and streams. He said as a result of that, they all suffered from chronic stomach illnesses and other water borne diseases, such as diarrhoea, dysentery etc. His parents, he went on, worked ever so hard, round the clock, but they could never make ends meet. In fact, every day, they would leave home even before it was daybreak for the farm, and would only return at night fall. Yet, their miserable conditions of living remained unchanged. It never did improve. They remained ever so poor. As a matter of fact, he said, his mother did die when he was still young, and his father, later on in life. He did find out that his mother did die because she could not afford to buy even the cheapest medicines for her illness. During all her illness, she used traditional medicines rather than modern medicines from the pharmacy because of financial constraints. This has hunted this young man for most of his young life. He also learnt that his parents were buried in coffins made out of "bamboo" because there was no money to buy real wooden coffins for them. This saddened him a lot. "If only they were not so poor", he even used to say, "maybe, just maybe his mother and even his father would have still been alive today. He would have become a good lawyer, made some money, built a good house for them, and made sure they had their three square meals daily and be given the right medicines from the pharmacy and treated in the best hospitals in the country when they fell ill. Oh! What a pity God took them away from him at such an early age".

Nevertheless, the more he thought about all this, the more determined he became to help in the future to ensure that such miserable state of living be wiped out of the face of the earth.

"Poor child", Mr. Tchuente used to say, "How one wished it was so easy to do! Poverty seems to have become part of human existence. It seems to be the case that wherever one goes in the world one finds one form of poverty or another, although relative; in that in some cases, it is all embracing, really deplorable, terrible; and in others somewhat "bearable".

He even used to talk of how they lived in a shack and whenever the rainy season came, it was real misery at their house. Rain simply poured down into their house as if there was no roof at the top. He said he used to pray to God asking that He should not send any more rain; even though he was very well aware of the fact that, without the rains, crops would not grow and they would not be able to even have the little food that kept them going. Their house had no electricity, so they used "trucan" the local candle and one bush lamp. Of course, they used pit latrines. How he absolutely hated to think of those times", he said.

His experiences as a youngster at Primary School were also terrible. He said he vividly remembers how other kids at school used to make fun of his dirty, old "raggedy" clothes, and the way he looked generally. During lunch time, he would go around begging for food from those children whose parents gave them pocket money to buy food at school; or those who brought packed lunches. How, he said he used to envy those children, especially those who came to school in chauffeured driven cars. He used to wonder what it felt like being inside a car for a very long time. He had never been in one before. His imagination went so wild to the extent that sometimes he would actually wonder what awful sins his parents had committed that God made them to be so poor.

However, Koffi, as he said his name was, said he seems to have understood why they were so poor, and that he would do all in his power to avoid being so poor himself in the future. "One sure way of doing this was education, education and education" he used to say.

Koffi like Dr. Yonkeu, often, also could not understand why some of the girls at the University were so vain. These girls couldn't care less about serious socio-economic and political world or home issues. All they seemed to be worried about was how to get their next monies to buy their next dresses, just so that they would be the best dressed in class. What consumerism! It was real competition among these girls. Koffi was having tremendous difficulties trying to save up enough money to buy textbooks. However, they always passed their exams. Some of the girls at the faculty of Law and even the Faculty of Letters and

Social Sciences were typical. One never saw them reading, but they always passed their exams. Koffi often wondered about that for a long time before, like Dr. Yonkeu he finally learnt the secret to their success was underneath their skirts.

For Dr. Yonkeu however, it all came as a shock. She was always working so hard and as such, she spent most of her time in the Library, trying to collect as much information as possible. It seemed most of the Professors had noticed how different Dr. Yonkeu was from the other girls. She was so simple in her outlook. Her hair was always braided and she often wore simple African print dresses. She never looked out of the ordinary, but simply good. She had never wanted to be like the other girls either. She liked the way she was – just plain beautiful and simple. She just wanted to be herself, and go about her work. She was never jealous of anybody either. As a matter of fact, it was because of her simple ways that Koffi said he was first attracted to her.

Dr. Yonkeu often went to see her Professors in their offices whenever she came across something she could not understand, and she would ask for some assistance from them. Remember? She had always done this back at High School whenever she did come across certain things she could not really understand or even figure out.

However, to her greatest disappointment, she discovered that whenever she went to see some of her Professors at their offices, they were very reluctant to receive her. Besides, whenever they did receive her, they often would very quickly change the topic of discussion to something else. For example, they would start asking her about her love life, and she wondered why they should be so concerned about things so personal such as those when there were so many important things to be worried about. On several occasions, some of the Professors even tried to be fresh with her. She could hardly believe what was happening to her. She thought she must be dreaming. This was her first experience of sexual harassment.

This is another constraint of women's access to educational opportunities. Sexual harassment is rife in educational institutions and workplaces in Cameroon. For example, the slogan "Sexually Transmitted Marks (STMs)" is common in schools, colleges and universities in the country. Many students are often asked for sexual favours from mainly male teachers who in turn promise these girls high marks or passes in tests and exams. Failure to respond positively to the teacher's demands, the student is doomed for failure in most tests and exams. Sometimes the teacher even blackmails the student to his colleagues who in one way or another also penalize the student. This is a very serious and recurrent problem in a lot of educational institutions in Cameroon, yet policymakers and law enforcement officers remain relatively lukewarm about the problem. The sharp increase of sexual violence against women in educational institutions is a reflection of a general rise of violence against women in recent years. There are also stories of women who have been refused employment; or who have actually lost their jobs at workplaces because they refused to have sexual intercourse with male bosses. Sexual harassment is not only a serious problem in its own right; but it seriously inhibits women's access to productive education necessary in enhancing their socio-economic status.

In fact, an increasing number of female staff members and students now feel alienated and unsafe on college and school campuses. This directly affects their ability to participate fully in the academic life of various institutions. For example, they find it difficult to participate fully in class and tutorials and attend social functions on campus especially during night time; to go to the library or the computer centre in the evening or at night, and to work late in their offices. The lack of adequate security may even mean that female lecturers are at risk of being sexually harassed or molested when returning from evening classes. On the whole women on many campuses study and live against a background of cat-calls, crude jokes, whistles in class, obscene comments directed at them and worse of all severe beating and rape (Nana-Fabu S., 2009). So you see, sexual harassment is not only in the Faculty of Law but in all the faculties. Thus, the status quo remains intact.

One day however, one of the Professors came out boldly and plainly and first asked her why she looked so plain, so simple? He then wanted to know why she did not dress in the latest fashion, styles from Western Europe and America. He wondered if she did not have enough money to buy the fashionable things like the other girls did? He then offered to give her money to go to the "beauty salon" and do her hair in the latest style, that is, straighten it out and put some colour into it; with hair extension or "greffe" to match and after that, he said he would take her shopping to some of the most fashionable dress stores downtown where she would get some dresses of her choice, all at his expense. He said they would become lovers and she would not have to work as hard as she was currently doing. He was going to take care of that and would see to it that she passed all her exams. Furthermore, he said he had seen her hanging around Koffi, the "poor" student. He asked her what in the world she thought a poor student like Koffi could do for her? Koffi, he went on, could barely hold his own. He then demanded that she should immediately desist from seeing Koffi, and start living like the rest of the girls were doing, or better still, as every girl her age.

Dr. Yonkeu's first reaction was shock, utter shock! She could not believe what she was hearing. She then realized how some of the girls at the University often passed their exams even though they hardly did any work. She was then also able to see how the girls at University were able to afford their ostentatious lifestyles. At this juncture, a thought of resentment for her Professor flashed in her mind. "Damn it!" I won't let the son of a bitch mess around with me; she reassured herself and feeling so angry too. "How could girls allow themselves to be used that way", Dr. Yonkeu wondered? When will women stop thinking of themselves as mere sex objects? And why on earth should Professors encourage such practices? They are supposed to be the ones to enlighten the girls and lead them on the right path. Instead, they are the ones leading the girls astray. They want to perpetrate patriarchy even in the university milieu. What a shame!" She thought.

After thinking about all these, she pulled herself together, summoned up some courage and politely told the Professor that she was indeed grateful for the offer, but that she was afraid she could not possibly accept it. Besides, she was simply not interested in changing her lifestyle. All she said she wanted was to acquire as much knowledge as possible at the University which she could put into some constructive use in the future. At this juncture the Professor was really angry. He asked whom she thought she is? He then said what a silly girl Dr. Yonkeu was and demanded that Dr. Yonkeu would leave his office immediately; adding that Dr. Yonkeu would pay very dearly for what she had just done and said. Dr. Yonkeu was really flabbergasted. She just sighed, shook her head and slowly walked out of the Professor's office, still in disbelief. It would definitely take some time for her to get over this sexual harassment on the University campus ... She thought sadly.

That whole day, she felt so sick in her stomach. She could still not believe what had happened to her. She could not wait for Koffi to come by so that she could tell him what had happened and get it all off her chest. Only after that could she get some relief. You see, these things are still a taboo in Cameroon, so she could not report what had happened to her to the authorities that be or the police for fear of the social stigma that is often associated with such things. Moreover she had no real proof of what had happened, just her words against that of the professor. Nobody will believe her. She thought sadly. During the whole afternoon period, Koffi did not see Dr. Yonkeu around campus as usual. He thought however that Dr. Yonkeu was busy doing something, and hoped that he would probably see her at the Library in the evening. As a matter of fact, he had always been sure of finding Dr. Yonkeu at the Library, whenever he could not find her anywhere else on the University Campus.

In the evening, Koffi rushed to the Library, hoping to find Dr. Yonkeu there, but Dr. Yonkeu was not there. He then went around asking some of Dr. Yonkeu's classmates if they had seen Dr. Yonkeu anywhere on campus. Nobody seemed to have seen Dr. Yonkeu anywhere on campus. He tried calling her, but Dr. Yonkeu had deliberately blocked her cell phone. Koffi immediately came to the conclusion that there must be something very wrong with Dr. Yonkeu.

"Maybe she was ill or something", Koffi wondered? "If she was indeed ill, he hoped it was nothing serious. He had lost his mother at a very early age; please God, he prayed, let him not lose the only person he really did care for at that moment." He was so worried.

With this thought in mind, he rushed to Dr. Yonkeu's room. He knocked on her door several times before Dr. Yonkeu came to the door and opened it. Her eyes were blood red from crying and she looked miserable. Seeing Dr. Yonkeu in such a terrible state, Koffi got so nervous and at the same time so anxious to find out what exactly had happened to her.

"What's the matter? Are you ill? What ..." Koffi asked? Dr. Yonkeu simply cut in and said she was quite well but that something terrible happened to her at school that she could not handle; and that was why she could not attend classes. Koffi became all the more anxious and impatient. He started thinking of all the terrible things that could have possibly happened to her. In fact, he could not just wait to hear what it was that had really happened to Dr. Yonkeu at school. He asked her once again and this time a little sharply.

"What really happened to you," he asked Dr. Yonkeu? After a pause, Dr. Yonkeu started narrating her story. "One of the Professors at the University," she said "had asked her to be his lover; and that he would buy her all the fancy dresses etc. However, when she turned down the offer, the Professor threatened her and said she was going to pay dearly for her actions."

Koffi was tongue-tied. He did not know what to do. He just simply kept on stirring at her and saying, "poor baby ..., poor baby, I should have told you all these things. It's really my fault, it's really my fault."

At that point, Dr. Yonkeu became very anxious and wanted to know more about what Koffi was saying. She then cut in.

"What in the world is all this business of being your fault? What have you been up to? Dr. Yonkeu asked Koffi, angrily.

She was now getting angrier and more impatient. Her imagination went wild and she thought perhaps Koffi was responsible for what had happened to her at school. With this thought on her mind, she once more asked Koffi to explain why he kept on saying that he was responsible for all that had happened to her. She could not just make any sense out of it all. It was all so strange for her to understand.

Finally, Koffi gently interrupted her and patting her on the back he said; "No Darling you do not understand. I should have told you all about university life. I feel so bad that I did not tell you all these things before. Perhaps if I had told you all that was going on here at the University, you may not have found yourself in such a mess."

He started telling her about some of the phony Professors at the University, especially some at Faculty of Law, which he knew better, and all their misdeeds. He told her that some of the girls at the Faculty do not always study, but that, they always passed their exams with flying colours simply by having sex or a love affair with one of the unscrupulous Professors. He said some of these Professors were oversexed. They changed girls just as people would change their underpants, so much so that they would have slept with most of the girls in their various classes by the end of each academic year. In fact they regard these girls as bitches, sex commodities, toilet tissue that one uses and discards as he pleases. It is a pity, because most of the girls never complain about it. Some of the lazy ones do actually enjoy the whole show.

Come to think of it, to whom could these girls complain? Remember we are living in a patriarchal, sexist society where men lord it over every woman. Men believe they own this world and women are just there at their disposal, to support them in whatever they do, and at whatever time. In fact, try saying no to your husband when he asks you for sex; sometimes even unprotected sex when he has the deadly AIDS Acquired Immune Deficiency Syndrome. Then, you will really see the animal in the man …He will beat the hell out of you; I mean, giving you a good beating. As far as he is concerned it is his right to have sex with his wife whenever he wants and however he wishes. As far as he is concerned she is just a sex object, a machine to bear and raise his children, a commodity he bought with his hard earned money (bride-price) - cleaning, washing, fetching water, cooking his food, etc. and slaving out on his farm; as it is still the case that men own most of the land in the country (see Goheen, 1996, 1988, 1984). In fact, we, with some knowledge on these things really feel helpless and sorry when we analyse man-woman relationship in this country. It is really the pits … These men really think they are "God's gift to women" as the famous Diva Tina Turner sings in one of her songs.

I tell you, sex abuse, sexual assault, rape and sexual harassment are real problems in this country. We still have a long way to go to bring things to order here. It is true there is sexual harassment all over the world, but here in Cameroon the situation is worse and more so, it goes unpunished here most of the time. It remains a major social issue in this country. In fact try complaining to any authority figure in and out of government that you have been sexually harassed; that is, touching, pinching, subjected to unwanted comments, fondling, groping, assault by men and you will see what will happen. To begin with, it is a very difficult issue to prove. Even the legal system in Cameroon is unable to do much about this issue for the courts are often over –burdened and there are fewer female lawyers who could better understand the position of female victims of sexual harassment, to handle those cases. Thus, in the end these men get away with it. More often than not these men go unpunished and you are stigmatized. However, the other day, I was really pleased when the Professor who had sexually harassed a female student at the other state University was suspended for four years by the Minister and Vice Chancellor. Things are beginning to change in the country as far as gender issues go. But we still have a long way to go. This case is more of an exception than the norm, but we are happy that at least something has been done in this case. In fact, today with the crushing economic downtown in the country when jobs are hard to come by, women are often pressured to exchange sex for jobs and job security just as these female students at the University of Roses exchange sex for a pass in exams and tests. I tell you it's terrible here. In fact sexual harassment is a reflection of a deeper broader issue: gender inequality in this country (See welsh 1999, 2000). Indeed, "throughout the world, women are treated as second-class citizens. They have less political power than men, have lower social status, earn less money and are not fully protected by the law. In short, almost every society in the world may be described as a patriarchy: a social arrangement in which men dominate women. This arrangement moreover, is supported by "sexism": an ideology that maintains that women are inherently inferior to men and therefore do not deserve as much power, prestige and wealth as men". (Tim Curry et al; 2002: 199). Also see Romaine; 1994: 100; Nana-Fabu S.; 2009:139).

"I tell you things are terrible for women in this country. They suffer a lot."

Dr. Yonkeu cut in and asked whether it did not matter that most of the Professors were married men?

Koffi just simply laughed and asked her what being married had to do with anything?

"Poor baby, I did not know you were so naïve. Most men married or not, do the same thing most of the time. I tell you, when it comes to liking or having sex with women, being a married man does not really seem to matter in a lot of instances. You would even be surprised to find that, married men are sometimes even worse than bachelors. A lot of them have mistresses or "deuxième bureau" as it is popularly known here in Cameroon; and you better believe it, these mistresses tend to be the ones who enjoy most. More often than not, the married men abandon their wives and children at home with not even enough money to buy food for the kids, not to mention clothes for themselves and the children. However, these men's mistresses are well taken care of. They buy them the latest of everything, latest designer dresses, latest cars, etc. etc. They pay their rents and furnish their apartments or villas with lavish expensive furniture, most likely, furniture from "Mbenge".

Dr. Yonkeu interrupted and asked what "Mbenge" was?

"Ah! Darling", Koffi said, "Mbenge is America, France or England, or any European country. Don't you know?"

"No I did not know," Dr. Yonkeu replied.

"In fact, you can see how expensive some of these University girls dress," Koffi went on. "Where in the world do you think they get their money from? From "sugar daddies", I mean those men who keep them as mistresses. They do not only buy the girls these expensive things, but every now and then they take them to some of the most expensive restaurants and night clubs in town. They can end up spending more than a hundred thousand francs CFA (100,000 Francs CFA) in a single night at one of these fancy night clubs. During the long summer vacations, these men would take the girls along with them to overseas to spend the holidays at their luxury holiday homes or expensive hotels. I tell you, some of these men do terrible things."

"I'll be damned! No wonder, some of these girls are the way they are," Dr. Yonkeu remarked.

"If you want to know all about this," Koffi went on, "just go by the University Campus at night. You will see all the "Mrs. Ndis', I mean the "Mercedes Benz" cars of all sorts, 4x4's of all calibre parked in front of the hostels waiting for their young mistresses. One often wonders if this country is a really "Highly Indebted Poor Country" like they say, the "bottom of the heap"? Gee, and when the girls do come out of the hostels, they look just like "mammy waters" ... I mean, mermaids. They are usually dressed to kill. It's simply amazing how these girls recognize their lover's cars even in the dark. They never seem to make mistakes. And you would be surprised what sort of men these men are. They are usually top men in society, that is, "la crème de la crème" in society. You may find this funny...but you may even find your father there".

"Oh! No," Dr. Yonkeu said laughing cynically. Aren't you exaggerating now? My father could not do that... He could not do such a thing." Koffi then asked Dr. Yonkeu if he is not a man. He is not a eunuch, mind you! And please Babe, don't be so naïve. It seems there is still a lot about this world you have yet to learn." "Yes", Dr. Yonkeu replied feeling very sad and disappointed. "Yes indeed, I think there is still a lot in this world I have yet to learn, poor pitiful me" like Linda Rondstadt would say, Dr. Yonkeu replied sadly.

At the back of her mind though, Dr. Yonkeu could still not understand why it is that, a lot of older men prefer having love affairs with girls; and why a lot of people or society generally does not seem to mind! However, when it is the other way round, when an older woman dares to do the same with a younger man, society vehemently condemns it. Take the case of Mrs. Bobinga who had dare defy the odds and had an affair with a young guy. And believe you me this guy was not even all that young relative to Mrs. Bobinga's age. But because she was a woman, a married one at that who had dare gone against the so called norms of society, norms that only women are supposed to adhere to at all cost and not men; the whole society, the terribly hypocritical and unfair society we now live in, was ever so quick to make a lot big deal out of it. When you talk of making a mountain out of a mole hill, this sure was it. No one even bothered to find out why and under what circumstances Mrs. Bobinga did what she did; but everybody was ever so quick to pass judgment on her to condemn her, finding her guilty even before she was tried. The poor woman was so scandalized. She had become the talk of the town and everywhere she went, people were talking about her and pointing fingers at her even some of those pretentious, hypocritical men and women with very questionable reputations. Mrs. Bobinga just happened to be a scapegoat whom everybody was quick to condemn. Funny how people are ever so quick to "remove specks from other people's eyes when they have logs in their own eyes". This was exactly the fate Mrs. Bobinga suffered. Mrs. Bobinga was just so scandalized, so shamed, so sick of being talked about and pointed fingers at, so despised by the unjust, sexist society, ironically a society, she herself happens to be a creation of and a creator of. She found it really impossible to live in it anymore, she had been pushed to the limit; and with her back against the wall she tried an unsuccessful suicide attempt by jumping from the third floor of her office building that left her paralyzed from her waist down. What an absolute loss to society! How unfair how inhumane! How cruel society was to her. When Dr. Yonkeu wondered, would society actually going to be so less prejudiced to its fellow human beings? Just imagine the total sadness and hardships this whole incident brought to bear on Mrs. Bobinga's family, her young children for that matter who still depend on her physical and emotional assistance for their well-being; and who now have to deal with a handicapped mother for the rest of their lives, all these, because society refuses to be humane, tolerant and above all forgiving especially in relation to women. How terribly selfish and unfeeling we have all become! Some societies even stone women to death because of adultery. How sad! How cruel! Similarly Beauvoir (1972, in Kimmel D.C. 1974: 167) draws our attention to the "double standard of aging-which may have more impact than simply living longer. She notes that insofar as women receive considerable esteem for their physical appearance, when advancing age reduces their attractiveness, in our "youth oriented" society, their self-concept and self-esteem are diminished in ways that do not occur for men, especially "successful" men. In the same way, while older men receive social approval for marrying or dating younger women, older women are seldom likely to date younger men; although in some countries older women are deemed to be appropriate initial sexual partners for young men since they are said to have more experience. One wonders if this is not sexual exploitation of these older women since they are only used for a purpose after which they are in a way discarded, Dr. Yonkeu wondered. However as the popular female writer further states, older women generally who divorce or are widowed are usually less able to find suitable marriage partners than in the case for older men.

"Now, that business aside," Koffi went on; "the problem at hand is trying to find out what one could possibly do about the situation between the Professor and yourself. You know Babe," Koffi said, "I haven't told you this, but I am repeating my second year, and if I fail my exams again, I will be kicked out of the University."

For a while, Dr. Yonkeu could not believe what she was hearing.

"What do you mean by that? How could you be repeating your second year when you work so hard; and besides, you are such an intelligent man?" Dr. Yonkeu asked angrily? "My darling", Koffi said chuckling, "you really do not know what is happening here at the University, do you? Guys, that is, men like us, really suffer here at the University. Listen, this may sound strange, but it's the truth. Women can always use their "bottom power", I mean sleep with Professors and be able to get away with so many things. At least, they will be sure to pass their exams and have their Bachelor of Arts or (LLB) degree in law, even though they may know little or nothing for that matter, about Law.

In fact, why do you think the Universities in Cameroon are often referred to by many a critics as a "glorified secondary school"? This is so because, the University is suffering from serious moral decadence – atrocities ranging from ethnicism, examination fraud and leakages, plagiarism, fraudulent diplomas;

to sexual harassment by some of those unscrupulous Professors; the result of which is the ever falling academic standards at Universities. Little wonder, qualifiers such as "chicken- parlour" intellectuals, "polycop peddlers", "skirt chasers" et cetera have all been used to describe the University Professors. Thus because a good number of these Professors are often preoccupied by these vices, they usually turn out to be so inefficient, unprofessional in carrying out their duties. Their intellectual ability is for the large part questionable. Even some of their diplomas are fraudulent. As such, most of the time, they find they are unable to effectively dispense worthwhile knowledge to the students, to enable them acquire the necessary skills and methodology in seeking out things for themselves. Given these circumstances, Universities, for the most part, end up graduating quite a number of men and women who are at best, intellectually mediocre or barely literate and unable to find work. It's rather unfortunate! Thank God, they have recently introduced the (BMD) Bachelor's Master Doctorate program in the University system. We hope this will make professors sit-up and prepare students like they should instead of messing around with little girls. In fact, check this out. When these little girls who have just had their A' Levels are freshly admitted at the university they look so happy, radiant, young, and ready to start the challenge of University life. However, by the time they spend just a few months or a year at the university, they change dramatically, physically, and there is no more radiance and youthfulness on their faces; emotionally, they are the "pits" quite literarily because of sexual harassment from teachers, fellow male students and older men known as "sugar daddies". Many of these girls become sad "little mammies". It's a pity!

Indeed, a lot of the girls use this same "bottom power" method even after they graduate from the University to acquire jobs; and they live comfortably for the rest of their lives even though they remain mediocre in their jobs. Come to think of it, who can blame them for this? It seems to be about the only skill they acquire from the university. But with us men, things are not in the least easy here at the University. Unlike our female counterparts, we cannot even count on having sex with the female Professors, so as to be able to make it here at the University. This option is completely closed to us, since in the first place, there are fewer female Professors here; and second, the few who are here do not really engage in such activities. If anything it is rare. So, all that we rely on here at the University is hard work and luck, a lot of it, and hoping that we do well in our exams, and that the Professors would be merciful enough to pass us. Mind you hard work alone is no guarantee that one would pass one's exams. Luck is also necessary. And "woe betide you" should you a male student, be caught fooling around with one of the Professor's girls! Then you could be rest assured you would never make it at the University.

So you see, Koffi resumed, that is why many male University students look for girl-friends in some of the local Secondary Schools and High Schools; and most of the time, these girls are even so childish and so naïve that they may end up putting one in big trouble. For example, most of these girls know very little about contraceptives and before you know it, they are already pregnant. Then their parents come along and force you to marry their pregnant daughters, even though they know you are still a student and as such, you cannot afford financially of course, to take care of a wife and a child. Sometimes, some of the girls are so naïve that when the baby does come, they do not even know how to take care of it. Some do not even know how to change the baby's nappies. It is just like the blind leading the blind. Worse still, some of these girls even go as far as having back street abortions with some "quack" doctors when they do realize they are pregnant since abortions are still not really legal in this country, except on specific circumstances; e.g. when a woman's life is at stake. Many of them die as a result of it; and others ruin their reproductive systems so badly that, they may end up unable to have children in the future when they want to."

"Thank God they have started teaching some sex education at both Secondary and High Schools, Dr. Yonkeu said. Thanks in large part to the AIDS pandemic. That would help a great deal," Dr. Yonkeu remarked.

"So you see", Koffi continued, "We the male University students have a real problem in our hands. All things considered, I only pray that you darling, won't find yourself in similar circumstances now that you have refused going out with the Professor. That Professor could make sure that you fail in all your exams and eventually, you will be kicked out of the University. The sad thing about it all is that, there would be absolutely nothing you could do about it. The system is so corrupt and the courts over-burdened that it would be simply impossible to administer any real justice. If you do not have enough money to bribe here and there, chances are that, your case may never come up for a court hearing even if you do sue the Professor. It is a very frustrating business whatever way you look at it. However, we remain hopeful with the recent case of the professor who was suspended for four years for sexually harassing a female student. Things seem to be on the right track.

At that moment, Dr. Yonkeu knew she was going to be in real trouble at the University. She realized she had to do something about it, and fast too. Why on earth, she wondered, should such atrocities be tolerated at a University, a place for acquiring knowledge; or a "temple dusavoir" as the French call it, which should be the epitome of decency and justice? Little surprise, in a recent (2013) UNESCO evaluation of Universities in Africa, none of the Universities in Cameroon figured among the top one hundred (100) Universities; Dr. Yonkeu thought. All things considered, she figured this was not the time for questions to be raised or even for crying. Indeed, she thought to herself, this sexual harassment is a real problem in this country. For instance every day in this country women experience some form of harassment or another.

Fancy this young lady – Endale who was seen making love to a University Professor on a staircase the other day at about 7 P.M. It is true Endale is not a very bright student, but really making love to someone in a public place such as a staircase to be able to pass one's exam, is really demeaning, degrading, dehumanizing and the lowest of the low. Imagine her, pants pulled down and bending over like a cat for that heartless, mean Professor to have sex with her. This mean Professor was thrusting between her thighs into her vagina so mercilessly without any feelings of love and tenderness as if she was a piece of meat; this creature is there only to satisfy the lust of this "beastly man." Of course, the man was pleased to assert this dominance both as a male who demands and has sex with a woman, wherever and whenever he wants to with her and hierarchically as teacher of this little naïve student girl, who has to submit to him at all times, without any qualms. This is awful: How low can human beings fall? A real aberration in every sense of the word!

This is similar to the case of young Yerima, a first year student at the university who was seen having sex with a Professor at another faculty in broad day light; a professor who could very well be a grand-father. You see, the other day, he was seen having sex with Yerima on the sofa in his office. Little Yerima was there lying helpless like a sacrificial lamb enduring the beastly thrusts of this man into her vagina. Again, it was obvious that the old man wanted to reassure himself by proving his dominance and virility on top of this "little" girl. He was there sweating like hell: and growling like a dog fighting with a bone; on top of Yerima not realizing that his window curtain was half open. Indeed, it was free pornographic viewing for all passers-by. How shameful and disgusting it all was! The indiscretions of these professors are incredible. Worse still he was totally oblivious of the fact that he could easily have had a heart attack from all the excitement of an "older" man having sex with a younger woman. In fact, this has recently been the cause of many deaths in the country. Many of these older men died of heart attacks "AVCs" as the French call it. In spite of this, men still take the risk. As a man once said "it is better to die making love to a woman than dying anyway else". This shows how worthless life has become to many men, even married men, with children who are prepared to risk their lives for pleasure that only lasts a few minutes. This world is really upside down, Dr. Yonkeu said.

In fact, we often blame some of these unscrupulous male professors for having sex with young vulnerable female students but sometimes it is also the fault of these girls who are always looking for the easy way out. Many of these young people, both boys and girls, are no longer willing to work and earn an honest living. Most of them want to harvest what they did not sow; and that is why mean old men like these professors take advantage of them. In any case, I believe these men should know better and should leave these young girls grow up the "normal" way. What they are doing is sexual exploitation of these young vulnerable girls living in a society that is increasingly becoming devoid of any morality. No wonder, the other day, there was a conference on morality in Yaounde, the political capital, organized by education authorities in the country to seek ways of instilling some morality in young people through the reinstitution of civic education in schools (Equinox News, July 2013). It is about time this is done for things have really got out of control in the country. Moral socialization of Cameroonians is a must today. There is about total moral decadence in the country, Dr. Yonkeu said. Also violence of all sorts resulting from massive unemployment, frustration and moral decay are especially rife in big cities like Yaounde and Douala. Things such as drug abuse, alcohol, and hard drugs such as marijuana, cocaine, are now on the increase. Wife battering, rape, murder, suicide, have become every day events. Fay mania, bribery and corruption are also very common. There is almost total chaos in cities in Cameroon. On the social front, we have many children who do not respect their parents or the elderly/aged. There is also a high rate of child abuse too- child battering, child trafficking, rape of children, even, boys and girls below eight years, homeless children, child prostitutes, adult prostitution and other such vices.

For the most part, people live in fear. People do not trust one another anymore as it used to be the case. Everybody seems to be a potential threat or criminal to everybody else, in these increasingly "Geselschaft" type societies (Tonnies F., 1887); Wirth (1938), Simmel Georg (1950); Milgram (1970). For example, a woman alone in her house or apartment in the city of Douala does not open the door to a man she does not know. One avoids going out at nights or very early in the morning because of fear of being attacked by robbers, raped or even murdered, especially in poor neighbourhoods. One shuns eye contact or casual conversation with another because one feels constantly under threat. For instance, a taxi or motorcycle taxi driver who in the past assumed that strangers entering in his taxi did so for legitimate purpose of being transported to their destinations (a well-structured situation); no longer makes such an assumption without some reservation today. This is after there have been many robberies and murders of taxi drivers. Sometimes, taxi drivers too are themselves the criminals, murderers and robbers.

Also parks such as that at the Douala seaport have become places where people are murdered or hang outs for drug addicts and robbers. Even the Urban Delegate of Douala was attacked by armed robbers herein 2007. These places of relaxation and leisure have now become places of crime and violence. Of course, robberies or hold up men in banks, microfinance institutions, supermarkets, corner shops, clothing stores, cyber cafe's where people go to for internet services etc., have become very frequent. So it is not surprising that many shop keepers now see potential customers as potential criminals. Today urban crime rates and violence have risen significantly and urban awareness of crime and violence has become more and more pronounced. Thus, many urban dwellers like here in Douala, now feel the institutional structure of Cameroon, especially institutions of Law and Order are breaking down. Cities and towns seem continuously unmanageable as the majority of city dwellers have become increasingly alienated. Many city dwellers do not seem willing to pursue their ends within the constraints of institutionalized politics. For instance, many people don't recognize the importance of judicial decisions to the success of their cause. They feel lawyers and judges and the police or the forces of Law and Order are generally corrupt. In fact, the last report from Transparency International (July, 2013) put the police as the most corrupt institution in Cameroon followed by the Judiciary. This explains why jungle justice or mob violence is on the rise in the country.

Similarly many urban dwellers in particular and Cameroonians as a whole have lost confidence in political parties as an institution that can help them in their plight; or help in their socio-economic and political empowerment. The poor in particular, in cities, especially here in the city of Douala place little faith in the efficiency of working within the established political parties. They think politicians are there just for their personal gain, and the well-being of their families and friends. No wonder some people feel politics in Cameroon is "belly politics" or "ventrocracie" (See Bayart J.F, 1989, Mbembe A., 2005, and Ngadjifna C. 2009). So many Cameroonians, especially city dwellers have turned to violence, crime and other radical means to confront their problems (see Lewis M., 1973:181-202). The escalation of crime and violence in towns and cities of Cameroon have peaked in recent times. Also, most of these crimes and violence are often committed by young people; men and women between ages 15 to 34 years old; often with these socio-economic profiles –being single or single parenthood, low educational achievement or status, low income, drop out of school, physical and psychological problems, unemployed, or doing a low pay job at the informal sector, living with parents, a parent or a family member, or homeless, deviant and drug abuser (alcohol, marijuana), petty theft, recidivist etc.

For instance, recently in Buea in the South-West Region and Suza in the Littoral Region, people with some of the above attributes (single, unemployed, drug abusers, age 15 to 34) committed such hideous homicides. They actually slit the throat of their fathers because their fathers had refused to give them the share of the money they had demanded after the father had sold his property; a house he had built with his hard earned money (Equinox Radio News, August 2013). How terribly sad! Did these children have to kill their father just for money? This is a real abomination, a moral dilemma to face day in day out in recent times. One need not mention the many babies thrown in pit latrines and trash-cans every now and then in cities and towns such as Douala, Bamenda, by young unwed mothers.

These problems are really formidable for city authorities to handle. There does not seem to be any respect for human life whatsoever nowadays. People are ready to kill even their own parents, brothers and sisters for money and other material things. Everyone, especially young people want to be rich overnight without little or no effort at all. Come to think of it, who can really blame them when more often than not; they have "Fay men" embezzlers of massive public funds, cheats, and other unscrupulous persons as role models? The socio-economic situation in the country is really dire.

It's all terrible … this sexual harassment and morality problems are major social issues in this country. Solutions have to be sought and fast too, Dr. Yonkeu concluded. She then decided to start by applying for as many Overseas Scholarships as possible. "Who knows, maybe her luck has not quite run out. As soon as she got the scholarship, she would get the hell out of this jungle they call the place of higher learning", The University of Roses, Dr. Yonkeu thought.

She went on working as hard as always, although she knew very well that she would not make it with that Professor "screwing" things up for her at the University.

It was again the end of the year, and every student was anxiously waiting for his or her results. Then "Dee" day arrived at long last. As was predicted, in spite of all the hard work, Dr. Yonkeu and even Koffi flunked. Although they were both disappointed, they were however, not surprised because down deep in their hearts, they had expected such an outcome, given the circumstance. Koffi and Dr. Yonkeu had worked ever so hard only to fail their exams in the end. They were certain; the mean Professor who tried to have an affair with Dr. Yonkeu had blackmailed them to the other Professors at the Faculty. Of course those girls who hardly did any studying at all, passed as usual, and it was all smiles on their faces. "It is ludicrous" Dr. Yonkeu said.

"Poor Koffi, he failed his exams because he happened to be dating the wrong person", Dr. Yonkeu thought.

Dr. Yonkeu felt so sorry for Koffi, even more than for herself. It's a pity, she thought, that such a nice, decent and hard-working young man should go through such hell, through no fault of his. How cruel! How terribly cruel! She said sadly.

At least, she thought, she had a decent and comfortable home to go to. Koffi on the other hand, him being the orphan that he was, had literarily nowhere to go to. He could not go back to the only thing he had inherited from his parents; the old crumbing shack in one the slum areas of the city of Douala. He really did not know what to do or where to go to.

Koffi did have some uncles and aunts of course, but they have never had time for Koffi. In these parts of the world, they often talk about social solidarity, the extended family that is always working hand in hand, taking care and helping each other especially in times of trouble. If this had been the case before, this seems to be more theory today. In practice, this is hardly the case in most situations. Most aunties and uncles and other relatives generally, only pretend to care for nieces and nephews and other family members they could get something out of. Most often than not, as soon as they milk you of all you have got so much so that you have nothing left to offer, they just abandon you. No one cares if you live or die.

If you happen to have a well-to-do father and uncles who only burn their own money on women and booze, then you are really in trouble. Stories abound of such uncles who go as far as killing their 'rich' brothers in order to inherit the latter's wealth. In some traditions, one inherits not only his brother's wealth, but his widow and children too. This is not all. It also entails a great deal of responsibilities on the part of the brother toward his late brother's wife and children. For example, he would have to see to it that, they are well taken care of and also well provided for.

However, the so-called uncles inherit their brother's property and wealth and spend it on mistresses, booze and of course, their own immediate family, while the widow and her children are left to fend for themselves in whatever way they think fit. Most of the children end up as beggars, or worse still, as pick pockets on the streets. The widow, if she happens to be in good health and had some money saved up somewhere in a "njangi" or so, she may start some petty trade business just to have some food to eat for her children and herself. It is always, a very painful experience. The hypocrisy involved in some of these traditions is indeed appalling. In fact nowadays, the extended family concept is in most cases more of a myth than reality.

Poor Koffi found himself in this miserable condition. He was in such difficulties, yet none of his so-called uncles and aunts came to his assistance. In the end, he had no choice but to go and squat with one of his friend's downtown. He also planned to look for a job and try to save some money so that he could go somewhere, most likely to a neighbouring country where he could afford the University tuition and continue with his education.

As for Dr. Yonkeu, she was so aggrieved by Koffi's situation but there was very little she could do at that moment. She only hoped that someday, she may be able to help Koffi in one way or another. Dr. Yonkeu and Koffi spent their last night at the University together. The following morning, they parted with plenty of tears in their eyes, both trying to console each other that everything would be all right even though they were well aware things were not going to be at all   easy, for them, Koffi in particular with no socio-economic support-whatsoever. They had a real mountain to climb.

Dr. Yonkeu went home to her parents and Koffi went to live with his friend in one of those rough neighbourhoods downtown, doing petty jobs here and there to keep going. Sometimes, he worked at building sites, other times, as a porter or loading man at Douala Seaport. Things were rough for him as he had no capital to start up his own business in the informal sector as many unemployed persons do. As a matter of fact, he did apply to the government organization that gives loans to young people to start up small and medium size enterprises, to no avail. It is certainly a good initiative to help young people go into some business to help reduce the high unemployment rate in the country. However, there are so many intrigues involved in accessing loans such as bribery, ethnic factor, nepotism, favouritism or "man know man" in common parlance; that many young people simply give up or stop trying to access loans from the organization.

Poor Koffi! Someday, probably when as I am planning to do, I may have gone and come back from the United States, God willing; I will do all I can to help people who find themselves in a similar situation as Koffi. In fact, why not create something like the Gramean Cooperative Bank in Bangladesh, created by Professor Mohammed Young in 1978 with only 27 dollars. This is a people's cantered business that has markedly reduced poverty especially among women and has been an engine of growth and development in Bangladesh. Studies on the Bank have shown that borrowers generally and female borrowers in particular, have improved their incomes, widened their asset base and crossed the poverty line to a life of honour and dignity. This could be seen in the tremendous improvement in the nutrition level in families, the lower child and maternal mortality rates and the adoption of family planning by families using the Gramean Bank. In all it has resulted in the visible empowerment of many rural and grassroots people, especially women in Bangladesh. This has been made possible by the fact that access to credits at the Gramean Bank is considered as a human right. For instance people do not need collateral security to access loans. Instead this is done by peer group co-guarantee. Similarly, when, a customer cannot pay his or her loan, the Gramean Staff quickly acknowledge that the customer has a problem and therefore needs help. Sometimes, they even grant a defaulter another loan if need be and reschedule his or her former loan as a long-term loan under concessional terms (see Rishal A. et al., 2010).

This is the spirit, Dr. Yonkeu thought. She vowed to emulate the way the Gramean Bank does business to help many poor Cameroonians, both in urban and rural areas get out of the extreme poverty many of them now find themselves in when she has the opportunity to do so (see Bangladesh Micro Credit and Development Journal, 1981).

Dr. Yonkeu's parents were so shocked when she came home and told them she had failed her exams and that she was not going back to the university. We could not understand how an intelligent and hard working girl as Dr. Yonkeu could fail her exams. We, my wife and I, tried to convince her to go back to the university and give it one more try, but she was determined not to go back there. She however did not tell us why she did not want to go back to the university because she felt we would not take the whole matter lightly. She knew we were going to follow up the matter until that Professor responsible for our daughter's failure was kicked out of the University. Mr. Tchuente said. As for Dr. Yonkeu, she was not ready to start fighting for her rights as yet. Besides she felt fighting such a system where corruption was so ingrained would be such a very difficult thing to do. It needed a lot of time, planning and certainly a lot of money, and Dr. Yonkeu was not ready for such a fight as yet. She did however hope that someday, she would be able to do just that.

Some months had passed by and Dr. Yonkeu was already getting used to staying at home; such a humdrum life. She spent most of her time reading and flower gardening. She simply adored flowers, and she found flower gardening so soothing to her worried mind. Then, one bright sunny afternoon, whilst she was outside weeding one of her favourite flower beds, a 'Zinia' flower bed, in full bloom, her mother called her and told her she had some mails. She said they looked like mails from the United States of America.

'Unbelievable', Dr. Yonkeu exclaimed! Could it be the replies from the universities she had applied to, she wondered?

She rushed out of the flower garden and went straight to a nearby tap, washed her hands quickly and ran to the sitting room. She took the letters with her hands trembling and quickly tore open the envelope, and then she quickly browsed through the contents of both letters.

'Mai' she exclaimed! 'They both contain letter of admission to the University of Orange, New York, USA. The university has offered me free tuition, but I will have to work for my room and board. What an offer!' It's simply wonderful. She screamed and hugged her mum and dad and everybody was so happy about the good news. In fact, there were tears of joy on everybody's cheeks. Dr. Yonkeu was just so happy that she became so confused. She did not know what to do. She then decided she needed some time to be alone. She went off to her room and lay down on her bed. She started trying to imagine what life would be like in the great country –The United States of America. She could not believe what had happened to her. It seemed to have happened so fast. She read and re-read the letters over and over again.

'This cannot be true', she said to herself. 'So I will be really going to the United States; what a dream come true! She tried mimicking the American accent, those she had probably heard in the movies.

'Hey man, what's up...?' as Eddy Murphy would say. She laughed at herself. It was really a dream come true for Dr. Yonkeu.

'God', she thought, 'really moves in the mysterious way. It's true they say, every disappointment is a blessing. 'Imagine', she said, 'she had taken such a great risk by not submitting to her Professor's dirty ideas as some other girls at the University did, so as to be successful at their exams. In the end, she was kicked out of the University; and now, just by the stroke of luck, she would be going to that dream country of hers, the United States of America. It is really true that when one knows and one is convinced that one is doing the right thing, God always comes to one's rescue sooner or later even though the going seems to be rough for some time, Dr. Yonkeu thought.

She started fantasizing about what life would really be like for her in the United States. She first thought of all the good side of things. She had read in some books that the United States is land of plenty, of freedom, and opportunity; and that it is a country where anybody could be anything they wanted to become provided they worked hard at it. First she thought she would go to Hollywood where stars are made; take a few acting lessons and become just like some of those Hollywood super stars, stars like Betty Davies, Marilyn Monroe, Grace Kelly, Liz Taylor, whose movies, those old movies, she absolutely adores; Jane Fonda, Sally Field, Isabel Sanford, Joan Van Ark, Linda Evans, Julia Roberts, Linda Grey, Felicia Allen, Joan Collins, Fay Donaway, Cecily Tyson, Mary Tyler Moore, Meryl Streep and many others; or why not, take some singing lessons and become just like Aretha Franklin- the Queen of Soul, Albertina Walker my favourite gospel singer, Tracy Chapman, one of the very inspiring singer of all times, Tina Turner - the queen of Rock and Roll, Gladys Knight and the Pips, late Donna Summer, Barbara Streisand, Millie Jackson, Dionne Wawrick, late Whitney Houston, Candi Staton, Linda Ronstadt, Dolly Parton –her favourite country artists, Janet Jackson, Jennifer Lopez, Shakira, Lady Gaga, Beyoncé, Madonna the 'Material Girl', Diana Ross and many others. Ah talk shows! Why not? She may just as well start her own "talk show" and become just like Joan Rivers, yeh, funny Joan; or Oprah Winfrey, sweet insightful Oprah. That would be just swell! Real cool! Of course, while in Hollywood, she would live the most sophisticated lifestyle Hollywood had ever seen. She would buy the hottest and fastest sports car, live in one of those exquisitely furnished Victorian mansions with all the trimmings of luxury money could buy, such as a swimming pool, manicured lawns, a private Lawn Tennis Court, et cetera; and she would look for a Billy Dee Williams or a Denzel Washington and make the best out of life; just like the "crème de la crème" do. Oh! What a life that would be, she thought smiling broadly.

Of course, how can I forget …she carried on? My favourite sport, Lawn tennis! I would do all in my power to meet my sport idols, the William sisters. They are simply adorable! How beautiful! How talented! Would do all I can, just to be friends with them. Maybe when I make friends with them, they would teach me a thing or two about lawn tennis. Who knows? May be with time I too, would also become a super star in tennis. There are also the prolific world renowned, American writers Maya Angelou and Alice Walker, Dr. Yonkeu thought. I have always admired these great ladies; just like my favourite jazz singer of all times, the talented Louis Armstrong, the superstar. I would do all in my power to meet them; and why not, learn a thing or two of how to become a novelist or a poet. Then, I would be able to write books and poetry on gender discrimination in Cameroon; more precisely, on woes of womanhood. This will really be exciting, Dr. Yonkeu whispered to herself, smiling reassuringly.

Oh! Yes, am...am... may be, just maybe I could also even come near to being like my all-time role models: these illustrious ladies, Hillary Clinton, Condoleezza Rice and Michelle Obama, the First Lady of the United States of America, the great country. These ladies are all so majestic, so intelligent and so very successful; with such stunning beauty that just happens to be the icing on the cake. Oh how I wish I could achieve even a third of what these great women have achieved! They are simply out of this world, she concluded.

Then a thought suddenly came to her mind. Her dream, yes indeed her dream – how easily people so often forget of those they left down below when things start going good for them ! I no, she thought, I would not let that happen to me. When she would have made all those monies, she would take a trip back to Cameroon, start a project whereby, decent housing could be built for those less fortunate as the former president, Jimmy Carter is currently doing in some sub Saharan African countries. Remember, those whom time seemed to have passed by; those "nobodies"; create more job training programs in which people could be trained to have skills that would enable them earn a decent living so as to be able to at least buy enough food so that no man, woman or child for that matter, would go to bed hungry again, ever. It sounded so good and easy to implement, but in reality, such projects would be difficult to implement in Cameroon where there was so much bureaucracy and red tape involved. What the heck; she thought, it would be worth the try.

Being carried away in such deep thought Dr. Yonkeu was suddenly aroused by a wrap on her bedroom door. It was her mother. She said they had something very important to discuss with Dr. Yonkeu. Still elated, she pulled herself together, came out of her room, and followed her mother to the sitting room. Dr. Yonkeu's father was sitting comfortably in his favourite armchair and drinking his favourite beer. He started off by saying that he hoped they had all calmed down from the great joy that had filled the house, although he did admit it was a difficult thing to do. However, he said without wasting any more time, they had to get down to serious business to see how things could be arranged for Dr. Yonkeu's quick departure to the United States. He went on that Dr. Yonkeu had already wasted one year at home and that it would be just great if she could start school in the U.S. the next semester, that is, in the spring, which was just two months away. He said the following day, they should start moving on with preparations to obtain her passport and visa. In these parts of the world, he added, one needs to do a lot of pushing and of course spend a lot of money to obtain such things as passports. They estimated that it would take about two months to get that done. When everything would have been obtained, the passport, the visa, etc, etc, they would then go to the village, Bangoulap in the West Region of Cameroon, so that Dr. Yonkeu would bid farewell to her grandparents, who in fact were already getting very old. After that, she would spend the rest of the week at their home in the city before she finally would leave for the United States.

The following day, Dr. Yonkeu and her father went to the passport office and saw everybody whom they had to see. It took them a lot of time, patience and money to do so. However, in the end it all paid off. Before they left the passport office, the guy in charge of issuing out passports assured them that everything would be alright, and that they should come in a month's time to collect Dr. Yonkeu's passport. Things went by so fast as preparations were going on for Dr. Yonkeu's departure. Just as the boss at the passport office had promised, in a month's time Dr. Yonkeu went to his office and collected her passport. When she held the passport in her hands for the first time, it finally dawned on her that she would indeed soon be leaving for the dream land, the United States of America. She was just overwhelmed by it all.

The following two weeks were spent in the village as planned. On the one hand, Dr. Yonkeu's Grand Parents were happy that their grand-daughter would soon be leaving for the United States, the White man's country, as they called it; but on the other hand, they were sad that she would soon be leaving them. A special farewell ceremony was held at her grandparents' compound and all the family members around showed up. Each and every one of them brought along some sort of a gift, either a big bag of maize or groundnuts, chickens, palm wine, goats, and so on and so forth. They also gave Dr. Yonkeu their blessings of good luck, success; and they all prayed that God would take her to the United States and bring her back to Cameroon safely after her studies. They also performed some traditional rites for her safety by calling upon her ancestors to pray for her. They did so by pouring wine on their graves or libation and reciting prayers in the dialect. They all said they would really miss her. It was all so emotional for Dr. Yonkeu so much so that she could not hold back the tears that continuously rolled down her cheeks throughout the ceremony.

After spending two weeks in the village, Dr. Yonkeu and her parents returned to their home in the city. A farewell party was also arranged for Dr. Yonkeu's friends in the city, two days after they had arrived from the village. Everybody at the party wished her well, and they all said they hoped the good Lord would guide Dr. Yonkeu throughout her stay in the United States and that He would bring her safely back to Cameroon after she had finished with her studies. They of course could not help feeling they could be in Dr. Yonkeu's shoes. In fact here in Cameroon, it was every young man or woman's dream to go to this great country – the U.S. of A.

The day for Dr. Yonkeu's departure was fast approaching. Before they knew it, it was already the eve of her departure. She could hardly believe it herself. It was so surreal. It was now time for her dad and mum to give her their final advice and blessings as the tradition was, before she left for the United States, the following day. Her father and mother gave her all the motherly and fatherly advice they could give, and it all ended up by them telling her to study real hard and to also try to be as good and as kind and as respectful as possible to everybody. Her mother of course advised her to eat the right foods and be careful about her health generally. She had heard it was very cold in the United States especially during the winter months and so she warned Dr. Yonkeu to always try to keep warm during those months. They also told her to work hard and to always pray to God for help.

Finally, it was time to go to bed. As soon as the old Grand Father's clock sounded eight (8 P.M.), they decided to go to bed because they had to wake up early the next morning since Dr. Yonkeu's flight was the early morning flight. They kissed each other good night with tears in everybody's eyes. Mother led us in prayer. It was a very emotional moment. We then went to our respective rooms.

When Dr. Yonkeu went to bed that night, she could hardly sleep. She was in Cameroon in person only. Her mind and soul were already somewhere in the United States. She did however have mixed feelings about leaving-fear of the unknown on the one hand, and on the other hand, anxiousness to see this country she had only read and seen so much about in films; had only imagined how things would be like there. However, her desire to actually go to the United States superseded the former by far.

Then it finally dawned on her. Her English, the way she spoke English! You know, the English that people spoke in these parts of the world was quite different from that of Americans at least in intonation and slangs. In fact if anything, it was closest to the English spoken in England than in the United States. She had read so many American novels and she had watched so many American movies and she felt she won't be too lost. Whatever the case, she felt she was a quick learner, and she resolved that it would not be too long before she would become a real 'Américain' as they say here in Cameroon.

She left no stones unturned. She thought of all that might possibly happen to her. She thought of the Blacks in the United States. How would they receive her? Would they be friendly to an African knowing that their ancestors were "sold" to the Americas by their African brothers? 'What a pity, she thought, that such an awful thing ever happened. Anyway, she hoped that many African Americans would want to know something about the land their forefathers were brought from, and then she would be more than pleased to tell them all about Africa. These thoughts occupied her mind the whole night. She could not sleep a wink. Before she realized what was happening, it was almost day break.

She had just fallen asleep for less than an hour, when her mother awoke her by a knock on her door. 'It was time to get up, take your bath and get dressed' she said.

Dr. Yonkeu jumped out of bed, feeling so tired from the thoughts and sleeplessness the night before. She rushed into the bathroom, took a quick shower and got dressed.

An hour later, they were on their way to the airport. Everybody was somewhat nervous, except for Dr. Yonkeu's father who managed to 'keep his cool'. They arrived at the airport on time. They checked in Dr. Yonkeu's luggage and after all the formalities with the airport authorities, it was finally time for her to board the plane. Dr. Yonkeu and her parents hugged, kissed each other good bye and Dr. Yonkeu walked away, tears in her eyes, and boarded the plane. As the plane took off for Paris France, it was then that it really dawned on Dr. Yonkeu that she was really leaving Cameroon for the country she had so often dreamed of, the United States.

She had a pleasant but tiring flight to Paris. Early the next morning, she boarded the Trans World Airways from Charles De Gaulle Airport to Kennedy Airport, New York. It was a very, very, long tiring flight. When she arrived at the 'Big Apple', - New York Kennedy Airport, she did not need anyone to tell her they had arrived in the United States of America, the 'wonderland'. It was all reality now. Yes, she thought, this was really a country worth coming to. Everything seemed so different; so fairy-tale-like, yet so real. Planes were taking off and landing every minute, it seemed. It was a complete contrast to the Douala International Airport where one would be very lucky indeed to see a plane land and another one take-off on the same day. Just for the numerous activities at the Kennedy International Airport, she knew she was in a completely different world with different everything. Her first impression was that, everything seemed so big, the people, not to mention the cars. 'This', she said to herself, 'is really the greatest country in the world, as she had read in some books. They sure do things in a big way! So big, yet so beautiful, and so orderly. What a place!

After about an hour of checking and re-checking her luggage, and all the formalities with the immigration officers at the Airport, she boarded another plane for Orange city, New York, which was about thirty minutes flight away from New York City. She arrived at Orange City on time. It was a very small airport, compared to Kennedy International Airport; but all the same, it was as busy as ever, with passengers here and there and planes taking off and landing. When she got out of the Airport, she took a taxi to the University of Orange campus. When she got there, she went straight to the Foreign Students Office as they had advised her to do in their letter.

The Foreign Students' Advisor was a tall, pleasant African American lady with an Afro hairdo and lovely dark brown eyes that beamed with so much love and kindness. She welcomed Dr. Yonkeu very warmly; and after a quick chat on how her flight was and how she felt, the Foreign Students' Advisor gave her a map of the school Campus and she directed her to her flat; which she was to share with one Jewish American woman, a pretty lady with beautiful black curly hair, about shoulder length, and a tender smile. Her other roommate was a charming middle-aged Chinese lady with a very distinct accent, which was like sing song to the ears, so unspoilt. She had also just arrived from the People's Republic of China. They were indeed very pleased to have Dr. Yonkeu as their roommate. They both welcomed Dr. Yonkeu very warmly and after a brief chat about her flight and what her major field of study was going to be at the University; and a couple of friendly jokes and laughs, they offered her dinner. Dr. Yonkeu told them she was indeed very grateful for the offer, but that she was too tired to even eat. All she needed at that moment, she said, was to take a good shower and go off to bed right away, which she did.

CHAPTER FOUR:
WOES OF WOMANHOOD: DR. YONKEU'SLIFE IN THE UNITED STATES

It was only two days before classes would start. Dr. Yonkeu had to undergo the drudgery of signing up for the courses she wanted to take. Fortunately, an Adviser at the Political Science Department had been assigned her; so he helped her a lot in deciding on what courses to take. However, she also had to see the various Professors she would be taking their courses to sign her form and if possible have a brief chat with each of them about the nature of the courses they were offering. It was such a long day and by the time she had finished seeing all the Professors, and signing up for the various courses, she was pooped; and it was already getting dark.

When she returned to her flat, she went straight to the bathroom and took a shower. She had a quick dinner and immediately after, she 'hit the sack'. She slept so soundly that she did not even hear a thing when her roommates returned to the flat.

The following morning, she had to report at the Foreign Student's Office at 8A.M. where she would be assigned a guide who would show her around campus.

At 8 A.M. exactly, Dr. Yonkeu was at the Foreign Students' Adviser, she introduced Dr. Yonkeu to her guide. Her guide was Jenny, a beautiful tall blue eyed blonde Anglo-American probably in her early twenties. She was ever so nice to Dr. Yonkeu and she wanted to know all there was to know about Africa, and of course, about Dr. Yonkeu, and Dr. Yonkeu obliged.

The first place she took Dr. Yonkeu to was the University Library. It was an old building. Jenny said it had been built long ago. It should be so because Dr. Yonkeu had noticed it sure looked different from most of the other buildings on campus which were not so much Victorian. The Library was dedicated to one of those great 'wise' men, a Jewish American, himself an alumnus of the University, who had made tremendous financial contributions to the building of the Library, a rather old fashioned but so very majestic with neat, beautiful, solid, red brick walls that had sure stood the test of time. I tell you, 'they don't build them like that anymore! Such magnificent craftsmanship! Ah the "good" old days" Dr. Yonkeu thought. She then took Dr. Yonkeu into the Library. Dr. Yonkeu could not believe her eyes when she walked into the Library. It was nothing like Dr. Yonkeu had seen before. They had all types of books on all kinds of subjects one could possibly think of. Dr. Yonkeu was simply dumbfounded.

Jenny asked Dr. Yonkeu what she would be studying at the university so that she could take her where she could find books on the subject. Dr. Yonkeu told her she would be studying Political Science. Jenny then smiled broadly and told Dr. Yonkeu that she came to just the right Institution. She said the University of Orange was one of the top Political Science Schools in the nation and as such the University Library was well stocked with all kinds of books and journals one could imagine on Politics. Jenny then took Dr. Yonkeu to the Political Science section of the Library. It was indeed well stocked with books and journals. While she was in Cameroon, Dr. Yonkeu's problem was not having enough books to read. Now it seemed she would run out of time to read all the books she would want to read.

Dr. Yonkeu asked Jenny if some books were not censored in the United States as it was the case in Cameroon. Jenny just laughed.

'Censorship', Jenny said, 'was unheard of in the United States[13]. Our forebears had sacrificed their lives so that, we, the future generations could enjoy these liberties. In the United

---

[13] However, it should be noted that recently (2013), President Obama has been accused of some press censorship and for having some security officials listen to people's phone conversations for fear of terrorism in the U.S. This was revealed by Edward Snowden.

States, she went on, press freedom happens to be one of those freedoms that Americans hold so dearly at heart'.

'No wonder', Dr. Yonkeu just thought to herself, 'the United States is such a great country! How many countries in the world would allow freedom of speech and freedom of the press', she wondered? Very few indeed! No wonder these Americans, she thought, are able to send people to the moon, and make many scientific inventions and other useful discoveries so often! They have access to books of all kinds and their freedom of expression allows them to be able to think freely which in turn allows for creativity on the part of individuals and groups. Oh! How she wished countries in those parts of the world where she came from, would emulate such constructive 'Western' ways!

Jenny then took her to the Newspaper and Journal section of the Library, where she said, time and again, Dr. Yonkeu could come and relax while reading her favourite newspaper or magazine or whatever she wanted to read. Yes, once again, it was well stocked with all the Journals and Newspapers of the world imaginable. Dr. Yonkeu was even surprised to find the 'West Africa' and "Jeune Afrique"; some magazines she used to read back in Cameroon from time to time. Dr. Yonkeu was so overwhelmed with joy. She finally had found what she had been looking for. Her thirst for knowledge, she thought, would indeed be quenched in this library. She was so sure about that. At the spur of the moment, she decided that half of her days would be spent at the library. She would 'devour' as many books as possible.

Her mind suddenly flashed back to Cameroon and she thought of Koffi. Poor Koffi, she thought, if only he could be here now! All his dreams of acquiring knowledge would really be fulfilled. She wondered what Koffi could possibly be doing at that moment. She then resolved to do all in her power so that Koffi could join her in the United States someday.

Just at that moment of deep thought, Jenny said they should move on to something else. She took Dr. Yonkeu to the School Restaurant, and showed her how she could obtain food. On their way out, she even bought two popcorn; and two sodas from the soda machine for both of them. She said popcorn was a favourite American snack. She said now, some clever fellow had even come up with a new brand of popcorn – the low calorie popcorn, which had become most women's favourite, even some overweight men's. Many women in the United States; she went on were trying to slim down, and why not; to be just like the late Princess Diana of Britain. You see, she said, many Americans are just fascinated by Royalty, the British Royal family, in particular. However, in spite of all this talk of slimming, she went on, one needs to see how a lot of Americans still do 'pig out' on popcorn and soda or beer when they are watching some of their favourite football or basketball matches on television. She then asked Dr. Yonkeu if they do play 'football' back in Cameroon.

'Yes' Dr. Yonkeu said naively 'they do play football back in Cameroon. In fact, Cameroon has one of the best soccer team in Africa. The team is just indomitable! with that son of a gun, that "super black man", Roger Milla, who dazzled in 1990, World Cup spectators in Italy by scoring more goals than any black man his age had ever done since the fabulous, world renowned soccer player- Pele of Brazil. Roger Milla even had a wriggle dance he performed, wriggling his buttocks whenever he scored a goal, it was such fun. Now we have Eto'o Fils who is another famous Cameroon soccer player, another super star. In fact if only the Cameroon politicians had not been constantly interfering in the management of the team in such negative ways, the Indomitable Lions would have been one of the best soccer teams in the World. Politicians should generally let technicians do their job and only interfere when it is absolutely necessary to do so. Jenny just said "no kidding" and burst out laughing; and Dr. Yonkeu was wondering what the fun was in what she had just said. She just couldn't understand it. Jenny then explained to Dr. Yonkeu that soccer was quite a different game from football in the United States. She said football is one of America's favourite sports. She said the University of Orange even has its own football team but that it was nothing as great as the professional teams. People, she went on, make a fortune just from playing football; even basketball another popular sport in the United States. Some of the top basket teams in the U.S. NBA are the Los Angeles Lakers, the Boston Celtics and the Milwaukee Bucks.

'Nothing' Dr. Yonkeu said to herself, 'is small in the United States. One could make a fortune just from doing about anything. All one has to do, is to make sure that one does whatever one has to do, well; and chances would be that, one would most likely make it. 'This', she went on, must certainly be the 'Promised land' she had read about in the Bible.

Jenny then took Dr. Yonkeu to the Recreation Hall where there were all sorts of fun games and even a couple of television sets, and television games. She said she was not really a television freak, but a great number of Americans were. She said there were numerous television channels to cater for a variety of tastes and interests.

When she said that, Dr. Yonkeu wondered why many Americans wouldn't become television freaks when they have such a wide variety of programs (from educative to fun) programs and channels to choose from. One need not mention the Computer Hall. Boy!, it was stocked with all sorts of computer sets imaginable with numerous computer programs and games. Students were all over the place doing research on the computers while others were playing games and so on and so forth. "Wow" Dr. Yonkeu said, this is really the place to be! She would also pass a lot of her time here to get all the latest information and news of the world as many of these computers have free internet services", she thought. This certainly explains why America has produced so many great scientists in the world and why the standard of living in America is generally so high. This sure is a great country" she said. How many people in Cameroon have access to computer sets, let alone access to internet connections? Not that many. Even State Universities like the University of Roses in Cameroon are in dire need of computers and internet connections. Students would usually cue or wait for a long time to have access to the Internet in the few "cyber cafés" around University campuses. Moreover it costs a lot of money to do so. So generally students and even University teachers do not go to the "cyber cafés" that often, except when it is absolutely necessary for them to do so. Even "I phones" remain a luxury to both teachers and students. Oh how I wish Cameroon students could have access to computer and the internet like these American students! Things would really change for the better in Cameroon and we too could produce great scientists, improve the standards of living and why not go even to Mars as the

Americans have done. With knowledge everything is possible. Knowledge like my father always used to say, is power. 'These Americans', Dr. Yonkeu thought to herself, 'are really blest'. She wondered if they are aware of the fact that they are a blest people. They just need to go to other countries to see how other people live to really appreciate what they have.

Jenny then asked Dr. Yonkeu how television in Cameroon was like. Dr. Yonkeu laughed.

'It is not even one third of what you guys have', Dr. Yonkeu said. There are only a few stations and the programs are very selective. Some people never even watch television because they find the programs so boring; and some even go as far as saying it was more a television for kids than for adults; because of the many dance programs. Anyway, Dr. Yonkeu said she hoped the television would improve with time given that television in Cameroon had not too long ago been installed. In fact, it is one of Dr. Yonkeu's least worries because there were still a lot of more important things to be done in Cameroon in terms of improving people's standard of living. Left to her, television could wait. That money could be used to provide decent housing for the poor or other necessities of life to people who could not afford them. Besides, few people in Cameroon could afford good television sets. Many people have second hand T.V. sets.

They then went to all the various classrooms where classes are held every morning. Jenny then showed Dr. Yonkeu all the various offices, such as the bursar's office, one of the most 'unpopular' offices for students as far as paying debts to the University goes. By the time they had gone through everything, she then gave her phone number to Dr. Yonkeu and asked her to call her whenever she needed help, or wanted to find out about something both on or off campus; or just for a chat. Dr. Yonkeu then told Jenny how much she did appreciate her help and that she wished and hoped that their friendship continues. They then said goodbye to each other and parted.

Dr. Yonkeu then walked to her flat overwhelmed by everything she had seen and heard. After a quick shower and a quick dinner, as usual, she went to bed. Although she was really exhausted, she could not sleep. Her mind kept wondering back to the day's events. She just marvelled at the many opportunities Americans have; such as their tremendous access to knowledge, not to mention their freedoms- freedom of speech, freedom of press, all sorts of freedom; even freedom to demonstrate peacefully. If only Cameroon was like this, she thought, maybe they too would be able to manufacture most of their own goods instead of importing from Americans, Chinese and other developed countries; who knows, maybe they could even build their own cars and planes. Access to knowledge, to technology, she thought was a vital key to success. Just look at how great the United States has turned out to be! It is all because the people can think freely, and express themselves freely without fear of persecution. No wonder Black brothers like Charles Drew and others were able to make great scientific inventions which are now used all over the world. Fancy that it was Charles Drew who invented Traffic lights, and another black brother who made possible the use of plasma in blood transfusions! Boy those black brothers were something, considering that their access to education materials was very limited in those days due to racism! Bless their souls! Oh! How she hoped one day most countries in the world could be like that. With that thought in mind, she slowly dozed off.

The following day was her first day of class. She got up very early, took her shower, ate some breakfast, got dressed and then she went off to the Bus Stop. She had to catch the 7 A.M. bus in order to be on time for her first class at 8 A.M. The school bus was on time. She boarded it and after a few stops at various school residences, they arrived at the school campus. All the students disembarked and rushed off to various directions. However, most of the students had early morning classes to go to.

Dr. Yonkeu then went to her first class in the United States. She was about ten minutes early. She just sat there and while she was waiting for the Professor to come, she felt a little nervous not knowing how the course on Political Theory would be. It was five minutes to time, and nearly all the students who had signed up for the course were there.

Her first surprise was that, there were only two Blacks in her class. She wondered where all the other Blacks were and what had happened to 'Affirmative Action'. However, later, she learnt that the University of Orange was one of those schools they called 'white school'. There was no law forbidding blacks to attend the university, but few blacks attended the university. Some said the tuition was very prohibitive to most Blacks; while others said there was subtle racism at the University that made it uncomfortable for Black students to attend. Dr. Yonkeu would not know, nor could she understand all these things since she was just new in the country; as they say in Cameroon, 'Jonny just come'. The only thing she knew about racism in the United States was what she had read in some of the only few books she came across in Cameroon. All she knew was that after the Great Civil Rights Movement in the sixties when Great Americans like President J.F. Kennedy, the Rev. Dr. Martin Luther King Jr., Rosa Parks, Angela Davis, Rev. Jesse Louis Jackson, Andrew Young, Malcolm X and many others, had fought against racism in the United States, the Government had passed laws against racism; and that, since then, Blacks and Whites lived in harmony.

However, later on in some of her Sociology and History classes at the University, she learnt about what some scholars call 'Institutional Racism', which they claimed still existed in the United States. Some prominent Scholars like S. Carmichael and Charles Hamilton for example, described racism as consisting not merely in the form of overt discriminatory acts and attitudes by some whites against Blacks, but as something that is subtly embedded in the normal operation of established social institutions. These institutions do have rules that appear fair and unbiased on the surface but they do have penalizing effects on Blacks.

Dr. Yonkeu realized that not all was roses in the great country after all. They still did have some serious social problems that have yet to be completely done away with. That hideous thing 'racism' was still alive and well in the United States after all, she thought sadly.

All things considered, Dr. Yonkeu's first experience in her first class in the United States was very exciting, very eye opening indeed. Her Political Theory Professor did arrive just a little after 8 A.M. He was a tall handsome middle aged Jewish American man, with a full head of hair; and wearing some very prominent eye glasses with thick black frames tightly hugging his nose. It was just a perfect fit, one would say. He introduced himself to the students and then, talked a little about what the course would be like. It sounded interesting. As time went by, Dr. Yonkeu found out that his classes were really fun to be at. He made everybody feel at home. He always tried to relate every day's happenings to his lectures. Dr. Yonkeu also found out that he had fought in World War II as a young man. In many ways, he made it known to his students that he was against all forms of discrimination, be it sexism, racism, fascism, etc. etc. He encouraged his students to participate in rallies against racism, and other forms of discriminatory acts. Any student who had racist or sexist feelings, could not seat through his classes. He or she would feel very uncomfortable indeed. He was just the kind of Professor that Dr. Yonkeu had hoped for. They seemed to be on the same wave length. He was not uptight or too formal as most professors in Cameroon Universities had been. One felt so relaxed in his classes, and as such, one participated fully in class discussions. Sometimes he even went as far as joking and even swearing in class; saying things such as; 'goddam place', 'son of a b…', etc. 'Where on earth could one hear a Professor swear in class but the United States', Dr. Yonkeu thought? With time, Dr. Yonkeu really looked forward to attending her Political Theory classes. She wished all her Professors would be that way; simple, very knowledgeable but very respectful.

As a matter of fact, most of her Professors turned out to be very nice, pleasant and very understanding indeed. You would think such very learned and very knowledgeable people would be snobbish, and condescending, right? A lot of these professors were real down to earth people. Amazing, isn't it? As such, although at first Dr. Yonkeu felt so very inadequate whenever she was with them, they soon made her feel so worthwhile, to the extent that she completely lost the 'inferiority complex' she had as far as the professor/Student relationship went. She indeed felt she too was really somebody. It was such a great feeling and such a new experience for her. The Professors often would allow one to express one's viewpoint about certain issues in class discussions. They never made one feel out of place or stupid. Sometimes, some students would say things that were really incorrect, but the Professors never made them feel bad or even silly. Rather, they encouraged the students to go do some more reading and some more fact finding on that particular subject. In all, classes in the United States were a real learning experience and Dr. Yonkeu thoroughly enjoyed every one of them. The Professors also had office hours when students could go and see them with their problems, or even just for a chat. This was a totally new experience for Dr. Yonkeu. She thought of some of those Professors at her Cameroon University who were almost unapproachable and most of the time, unwilling to help students with their problems. Instead, they always tried to put students down; and they felt so all powerful and all knowledgeable. They tend to forget that no one person was capable of knowing everything. Dr. Yonkeu wished they could come to the United States and learn a thing or two about what a student/Professor relationship should be like. This is not to downplay the great job some of those conscientious devoted and patriotic University teachers back in Cameroon do considering the limited finance and infrastructure they have to put up with. For example simple sanitation measures such as the provision of clean water and toilets at schools, universities, workplaces and the public generally remains a huge problem in Cameroon. This usually has very negative socioeconomic consequences on girls, women, female teachers/professors and female pupils/students in particular. For instance many women would often be late at workplaces, schools, colleges, universities because they would have to quite literarily want to empty their bowels and urinate well before leaving their homes in order to avoid wanting to go to toilets that are often not there or that are so very unsanitary for use, during work or school hours.

Often this impacts negatively on women's work performances and academically, blocking their upward social mobility in society. On the other hand, men/boys generally are not under such pressure as women when they have to urinate because they could easily do so beside parked cars, and even at walls. Women find it so difficult to do the same. It is so terrible, such a disregard for basic human dignity and that of women in particular.

All the same, this does not mean university professors should be so condescending to students; most of them poor students, who are also trying to better their lives and contribute to the development of the nation.

Dr. Yonkeu did also have her on campus job since foreign students were not allowed to work off campus. She worked as a Library Assistant. Although she did not earn a fortune doing that, she earned enough for her general upkeep. Besides, she really enjoyed her job. She was where she had hoped to be – at the Library. By working in the Library, she got to read so many books and she broadened her knowledge about so many things, both about the United States and other parts of the world. All her co-workers, students as herself, were so friendly to her and they always tried to make her feel at home. As a matter of fact, at the end of every semester, they always made sure they had a beer and pizza party. It was real fun at those parties and Dr. Yonkeu thoroughly enjoyed every one of them. Even Mr. Billman, their supervisor, this average height, medium built, bespectacled middle-aged guy did also attend those ends of semester beer and pizza parties. Mr. Billman, you see, turned out to be a real darling. He was in no way your typical supervisor; you know those stern and almost unapproachable supervisors. Thorough, conscientious and hardworking he was, but not over-bearing. He was such a gentle person, very patient and very respectful of everybody.

Believe you me, Library work is no way easy, -you know, picking out small oblong shaped cards, typing and filling these cards is no easy task. It is indeed tedious. However, the students' managed to keep up with their work, thanks in large part to Mr. Billman's understanding and gentle ways. Who said men could not be gentle creatures? Boy! These people and their gender business! Mr. Billman sure proved them all wrong. This sure helped keep up the student's moral. Come to think of it, Mr. Billman was always ready to help anyone out with whatever difficulty one encountered in his or her work. Being the thorough person that he was, he did not mind going over something, as many times as need be just so as to enable one do one's job correctly and properly too. You know what it could be like working with a bunch of impatient young men and women. But Mr. Billman managed to 'keep his cool' at all times, never letting things get out of control. He sure turned out to be the right man at the right place. He was such an extraordinary fellow, a rare breed indeed.

Rumour has it that Mr. Billman was "gay." "Gee", Dr. Yonkeu thought, if this was how "gay" people were then she did not understand all the force about them! In fact, in this world of ours, where a lot seem to be going wrong, maybe, these so called "gay" people may just be the ones to put things right after all; Dr. Yonkeu thought. She certainly was for social inclusion, not social exclusion. As far as these "gay" people are not paedophiles, they should be left alone to do their thing in the Privacy of their homes. This applies to Cameroonians, a deeply conservative and homophobic people. It will be a very long time indeed before Cameroonians could accept homosexuality. So gays in Cameroon are advised to be sensitive to this and not flaunt their homosexuality until such times that it is acceptable there. This is to avoid physical and verbal violence against them.

Her extra-curricular activities were also hectic. She met quite a few African students and she got to learn quite a lot about other African countries from these students. She also made some African American friends at school, some of whom lived in the City of Orange. One of the girls, Tammy became particularly close to Dr. Yonkeu. She wanted to know all there was to know about Africa and Dr. Yonkeu was ever so happy and more than willing to tell her all she knew about mother Africa. Dr. Yonkeu also learnt a great deal from her about African Americans.

Tammy the African American did talk to her parents about Dr. Yonkeu a lot and her parents became ever so anxious to meet Dr. Yonkeu – 'a true African in flesh and blood', as they said. Tammy told Dr. Yonkeu how anxious her parents were to meet her, and they both agreed on a day when they could all get together. Tammy and her family were such staunch Christians that they never missed a day of church. Tammy did ask Dr. Yonkeu if she would come and visit her family on a Sunday. It was arranged in such a way that Tammy and her family would come and pick up Dr. Yonkeu on a Sunday morning and take her along to church; after which they would all go to their home, and have lunch together. It sounded all nice and fair to Dr. Yonkeu. At least, it was a welcomed diversion from reading the many books she had borrowed from the Library. Besides she had never been to a real 'Black' Church before. She had only heard about them.

Somehow, she had come to realize, rather painfully too though, that, most things in the United States seemed to be separated on the basis of colour, race and ethnicity- Black, White, Native American, Jewish, Hispanic, etc, etc. They tend to have Black neighbourhoods, White neighbourhoods, White schools, Black schools and even Black Churches and White Churches. Funny, isn't it? "Thank God, that this is de facto, not de jure, Dr. Yonkeu said.

She even did find out that the University of Orange was a Jewish College. "It was a Jewish College", she thought, "then the Jews sure know what they are doing for this university happens to be one of the top University in the country."

But she wondered what the 'melting pot' concept was all about since there were still so many colours and ethnic barriers existing in the United States. She wondered if all the great people like the late Presidents John F. Kennedy, Roosevelt E.; Martin Luther King Jr., Mariane Anderson, Rosa Parks, Maya Angelou, Coretta Scott King, Jesse Jackson, Marcus Garvey, Asa Philip Randolph, Paul Robeson, Fannie Lou Hammer, Edgar Wiley Evers, Malcolm X and many others had all fought and died in vain. True, racism was now illegal in the United States, but it seemed that everyone still understood or knew exactly where the 'free zone' so to speak ended. It was more of 'equal but separate society', at least in terms of people's basic human rights which were guaranteed by the law of the land. This worried Dr. Yonkeu a lot. After all these years! Yes after all these years, she kept repeating, feeling so totally sad and helpless, 'one would have thought'... all God's children, Black men and white men, Jews and Gentiles ...would have now learnt to live together in peace and harmony. But that certainly did not seem to be the case in this her beloved "adopted" country- the United States. Instead, every now and then, that ugly monster- racism does show up its head in one way or another, one form or another, one shape or another, poisoning the air with such terrible hate among God's children resulting in such violence and untold pain, and suffering, mental anguish on a whole race of people just because they happen to be born Black! How sad! The picture perfect image she had of this great country was beginning to fade away. It was no more such a perfect country after all. There was still a lot of work yet to be done to make the picture perfect.

In any case, on Sunday morning, as was arranged, Tammy and her family did arrive on time to collect Dr. Yonkeu. They all seemed so perfectly dressed for church. Surprisingly enough, Tammy was in the Church Choir. She wore her choir robe. Her mother had on a beautiful white dress and a black hat; and her father had his black suit on. There was also a little girl in the car, Amy; her name was Dr. Yonkeu later found out. She had on a pretty pink dress. She also had a white satin ribbon tied at the end of her pony tail hairdo. She looked ever so cute. Dr. Yonkeu went into the car, cheerfully greeted them; and after all the introductions, they drove off to church. The church service was more or less a normal church service, except for the fact that the congregation was all Black. There was also a lot of singing and the preacher preached in a very powerful voice; while the congregation was always saying 'Amen' or 'Hallelujah' from time to time. Dr. Yonkeu was visibly delighted.

What Dr. Yonkeu found very different about the service however, was when it was confession time and everybody who had something to confess or some favour he or she wanted to ask from God, would walk up in front of the Alter and start praying in a loud voice. Most of the women were even in tears praying with their hands raised high up in the air. Some of them even started speaking in tongues; and one of them even went into a trance as she was praying, and collapsed right there. Some ladies quickly rushed to her aid, and they started fanning her. After she had recovered a little, they walked her very slowly back to her seat. It was really remarkable. Never had Dr. Yonkeu witnessed such as scene before[14].

After the church service was over, Dr. Yonkeu and her friends had a chat with some of their friends; after which they all walked to the car at the church parking lot; they then entered into

---

[14] However today in Cameroon cities in particular, churches similar to this one have mushroomed. These churches are usually designed to lure many people with socio - economic problems such as the unemployed people, especially women with marital and poverty problems who are offered small loans, comfort, etc.; a sort of social solidarity as strategies of survival, during these difficult times of financial hardship.

the car and drove home. A few minutes after they had arrived home, food was served. Dr. Yonkeu was just about to start eating, when Tammy's father said they should all say 'Grace before the meal'. Dr. Yonkeu was so embarrassed. You see, she just couldn't remember when last she did 'say Grace before the meal'. That must be way back in Cameroon. How people take things for granted, she thought to herself. It's good, she felt, that people such as Tammy's Dad were around to remind one to at least thank God for one's meals. After they had all said Grace, they then started eating. 'Boy!, that was some good home cooking', Dr. Yonkeu remarked. As a matter of fact, she had never eaten such good food since she left Cameroon. She certainly missed her mother's good cooking. There were some black-eyed peas cooked in rice, some greens, baked chicken, Apple pie of course, and other delicious foods. Tammy told Dr. Yonkeu it was a typical African American meal. Dr. Yonkeu really enjoyed the food. She also noticed that, Tammy's parents were living quite well. In fact, they had a lovely home in a very nice neighbourhood. They must be the "Black Middle Class', she had read about in some of her Sociology Text Books. They sure have overcome", she thought to herself. 'The Civil Rights Movement' and President Johnson's "Civil Rights Act" of 1964 she felt were not in vain after all. Thank God for it! she whispered. Dreams do really come true in the United States. The essence is to carry on with the struggle for even more freedom and equal opportunity for all; and not to despair. Look now we even have a black president, President Obama. Who would have thought a black family would ever occupy the "White House"? Only in the United States could this happen. It would be quite some time before any European country has a Black President", see how the black female Ministers in France and Italy are being denigrated and called names such as "Arangatang" because of their skin colour. This is unbelievable in the 21st century", she concluded.

After they done eating, everybody rested a while, and conversation started. Tammy's father asked Dr. Yonkeu how she had been enjoying her stay in the United States so far, just to break the ice. A little after that, Tammy's father and mother asked her so many other questions about Africa. They wanted to know how Africa was like, what the climate was like, and how the people were like, what foods they ate etc. and Dr. Yonkeu happily obliged. They were very pleased to learn about all these things.

Then, the little girl, Amy who was in the pretty pink dress, came up to Dr. Yonkeu and asked her whether it was true that people in Africa lived on trees? Tammy had just started telling her to be quiet when Dr. Yonkeu cut in and told her to allow the little girl ask her question. Dr. Yonkeu told Tammy that it was better for Amy to learn the truth than to live in such ignorance. Dr. Yonkeu then asked little Amy where she had heard such a thing? She said some white kids at her school once told her that where her ancestors came from, Africa that is, people lived on trees. She said the White kids were sort of making fun of her.

Dr. Yonkeu then sat the little Amy on her laps, and started explaining the facts to her. She told her that, what the kids said about Africans living on trees was not true. It is true, Dr. Yonkeu went on, that there is a lot of poverty in Africa and that most people do not live in well –built houses with indoor toilets and electricity or even indoor water supply, etc; but that people in Africa do not live on trees. Smiling patiently, Dr. Yonkeu then asked her if she had any more questions she would like to ask about Africa. But the little girl already obviously embarrassed; said no.

But Dr. Yonkeu smiled at her reassuringly and she smiled back shyly and said "OK I have just one more question."

"OK Amy and what is your question" Dr. Yonkeu asked?

"Aunty, tell me; is it really true that Africans do not have enough food to eat and that they often die of starvation? In fact Aunty, I often see starving African children on television. Is it for real? The children look so emaciated. It is really pathetic."

"Actually Amy, I wouldn't say you are wrong about that. True many African children do not really have enough food to eat. However I think there are some things you should know as to why this happens. You see Amyit's always good to put things, in perspective, in context.

"Yes Aunty, tell me why this awful thing is happening."

"Once upon a time Amy", Dr. Yonkeu retorted; that is before the Whiteman came to the African continent, I don't think things were nearly as bad especially in this domain. There is no way to actually say how things really were back then given that we were not there. Nonetheless, from the stories our old folks told us and from the few books written on Africa during this period, one would think the situation back then could not have been that hopeless. On the contrary, one could deduce from, these facts that, had there been cases of starvation, the old African was well equipped in his own way to handle it. He knew exactly how to manage it, and sometimes, how to solve the problem. You see Amy back then the African was to a large extent, self-sufficient. The land was vast and plentiful. Moreover the African was one with nature. Therefore when faced with such a natural disaster or calamity such as draught, or threatened with food insecurity, he was in a better position to deal with the crisis. For example, since Africa was a vast continent with no artificial national boundaries as it is the case today, the African would simply migrate to another virgin area where there was plenty of food when faced with the problem of starvation; "hunting and gathering societies". At least, as one could imagine, there was usually plenty of food for everyone.

However, one day something unimaginable happened that was to change the fate of the African continent forever. In fact from that time on, Africa and Africans have never been the same again; and from the looks of things, they will never be the same again, ever.

"Boy! Aunty, what is it that really happened? I can't wait to hear it."

"Sure Amy, I'll tell it to you. You see Amy, what happened was that the Whiteman had come to Africa; at first maybe for purely exploratory motives; or like the learned Ali Masrui put it, "to find out what lay beyond the horizon", for curiosity sake pure and simple. However, you could bet your life on it Amy, this adventurism was soon transformed into purely commercial motives designed to get the maximum at least in terms of natural resources, out of Africa at a very low cost. All they now had in mind was to make profits, profits, profits, maximum profits all the way. This Amy is what the Great

African President Kwame Nkrumah(1972: 17) called colonialism. This is basically an unequal relationship between developed and rich countries, usually those of Europe and America and the "poor" undeveloped countries of Africa and other parts of the world. These wealthy countries imposed their civilization in these "poor" countries that is a sort of "deculturation" in terms of values, religion, morality, language, equipment and technology (See ELA J.M., 1990), in order to exploit these "poor" undeveloped countries economically. To facilitate their fundamental objectives of control and exploitation, the colonialists made sure the colonies remained underdeveloped socially and culturally. This is crucial because a people without a culture are a lost people. The colonialists installed and maintained archaic forms of social relations in the colonies, and then they embarked on the propagation of capitalist modes of production and social relations in these colonies; sometimes through the use of force or violence.

With time Amy, this system evolved into "neo-colonialism" another subtle institutionalized and "legalized" form of domination and the exploitation of Africa's socio-economic and natural wealth which is now the order of the day in post Independent Africa. In fact, colonialism had prepared the "bed" quite literarily or the way for the installation of neo-colonialism or re-colonization "recolonisation" as (Ela J., 1990) calls it, in Mother Africa. This Amy was of course after many of these African countries had gained their independence from their colonial masters: England, France, America etc. This is now a new form of socio-economic and cultural domination and exploitation by these former colonial powers on their former colonies. They often do this by joining forces with the post-colonial governments and the African "elites", the local "bourgeoisie" (Ziegler J. 1980, Bourdieu P. 1986, Smith S. 2010, Eteki M.L. 2001) whose main goal is to exploit their own people, the suffering African masses, the disparately poor Africans, the "wretched of the earth"; and maintain social order in the African society for the socio-economic interests and benefits of these neo-colonial powers. In fact, these neo-colonialists and their African "partners" are often more interested in maintaining social order in the African continent than social justice or the guarantee and respect of human rights. They are also "homo economicus," persons whose actions are well calculated and who always put their interests first before those of other people. No wonder the educational system in Cameroon for example, a fundamental cultural aspect, remains largely colonial today. (See Nug B.2009; 2014; Mboa Massok, 2014; Equinox Radio 10/08/2014).

Another strategy which the neo-colonial powers use to carry out their exploitation mission is to paralyze or render ineffective governments and institutions of these so called independent African countries in a way that these governments and their people are in effect run by remote control, by their former colonial masters; so infantile. Often, with little or no input from these African governments and their leaders, decisions are taken in New York, Washington D.C., London, Paris etc. for issues that concern Africans by people who have sometimes never even been to Africa and who know little or nothing on the reality on the ground there. Other times, the donor-led model of sustainable development with key players like the International Monetary Fund (IMF) and the World Bank have always had some perverse incentives such as privatization, massive salary cuts, reduction of government employees and redundancies in the few industries in Africa (see Sama Nwama H. 2007). These are some of the reasons why the western driven donor-led model of sustainable development, and even to some extent those of new powers such as China, well-meaning as they have been, have to a large extent failed woefully on the African continent; and why many Sub-Saharan African countries in particular remain underdeveloped leaving many Africans poor, miserable, vulnerable, disillusioned and of course hungry. These development projects and programs to a large extent remain alien to Africans as they are for the most part not grassroots-based. This also reveals that Africa is not only a victim of Western capitalism or neo-colonialism (The "victim paradigm"); but that Africans too also contribute immensely to their subjugation, underdevelopment and misery by allowing these Western powers to dominate in many aspects of African life. (Nyamsi F., 2014, Equinox Radio, 10/08/2014).

Like I was saying, these colonialists had found the bountiful natural resources and minerals in Africa – such as gold, diamonds, silver etc.; animals of all sorts, timber, elephant tusks, hides and skins etc.; and worse still human beings in the form of cheap slave labour. In fact according to Anyangue C. (1987: 51) forced labour was a French colonial policy in Cameroon. Often the French would talk in rather glowing terms about their so-called "mise en valeur du Cameroun" or "l'oeuvre de la France au Cameroun", conveniently forgetting that they had inherited an impressive infrastructure from the Germans. They of course added improvements here and there, but their methods were not that very different from the German's.

> *"Fettered to each other requisitioned persons, (chiefs were required under pain of destoolment and harsh penalties, to supply quotas of men to the French administration, planters and concessionaries) were marched to go and work on private plantations (the notorious one at dizangue) and mines especially at Betare-Oya) as well as on projects of a public nature such as the completion of the half-finished German railway to Yaounde"*

In addition, these workers

> "Worked *under slave conditions and were to say the least, quasi-slaves. They were flogged at will, paid starvation wages, poorly fed and lived under extremely poor sanitary conditions. Hundreds died. The tribulations shocked the World.France however continued to issue categorical denials claiming that the situation had been grossly exaggerated by people envious of her."*

Thus during this period;

> *"The legal framework of the policy of forced labour was the ignominious system known as the "idigénat".The term forced labor (travail force) was itself a blanket term. It covered several different legal categories of compulsory work: "travail public obligatoire, prestation" or tax in labor for public works, generally levied through the chiefs and redeemable in cash, and military conscripted labor or the "deuxième contingent" of the colonial army, used to carry on public works.*

There were two systems of forced labor, one to achieve certain economic objectives, the other as a means of coercion. Both were combined in the "indigenat" which was a decree of 8th August 1924 introduced in Cameroon and allowed for imprisonment for up to ten years." (See Le Vine, 1964: 108; Morgenthau, 1964: 1-2)

You see Amy this was the tragedy that had befallen "mother Africa." This drastically changed this self-sufficient continent for good; the ravages of which are still plaguing this "Garden of Eden" of long ago; when Africa was Africa" (Ali Mazrui)

"But tell me Aunty, I still don't understand it. What has all this got to do with starving in Africa?"

"Oh! Amy, you don't understand, do you? I am getting there. You see Amy, like I was saying, when the white man came to Africa, he immediately realized he could make tremendous profits from the abundant natural resources on the continent by way of trade. He imagined he could extract the raw materials from the continent take then to his continent, either to Europe or North America, manufacture luxury and durable goods from them, and then resell them to other European, Asian and other components of the world, even to Africa itself making tremendous profits. This was so because countries of the world did not yet have the technology to transform raw materials into durable finished goods. This way, these white folks were sure to make maximum profits from this trade given their sole monopoly of technology to transform raw materials into goods on a massive scale.

"But really Aunty, I still cannot see how this brought starvation on the African continent on such a massive scale.

"Oh! Little Amy, I know you are still too young to figure out all this; and just how impatient you are to know exactly what happened. Oh the impatience of youth! You know Amy; I used to be like you when I was your age. I remember when my mum used to explain things to me, or even when she told me those children's stories, fairy tales; I often could not wait to hear what happened in the end. For example I was anxious to know whether in the end, Cinderella did actually get married to the lovely prince and live happily ever after..., rather than listen to all those minute details that were so boring to me. Funny how children are all the same all over the world! I can really see myself in you when I was your age. Anyway Amy, you've got to bear with me. You see, I've got to get the facts right so that Tammy, Grandpa and Grandma would also see how things had evolved on the African continent. Don't worry Amy; I will make things real simple for you to understand.

So like I was saying Amy, only the white folks had the technology to transform raw materials into finished goods on a massive scale, (the industrial revolution of 18th century Europe), making tremendous profits. You see, the African people who were self-sufficient and without the demographic boom like it is, did not see the need, the necessity in such industrialization and commercialization on such a large scale for profits. At least, during this period, they seemed satisfied with their very simple and natural way of life; with the plentiful fish from the numerous lakes, streams, rivers, seas and oceans as well as the abundant fruits and foods from the very fertile lands and forests. So there was really no need for big manufacturing industries yet. They preferred their natural way of life. For instance they did not realize what an immense touristic attraction it would be, building five star hotels along some of those beautiful sandy beaches or along the wonderful rolling hills. This attitude, as you could imagine, posed a real problem to these white people when they came to Africa to exploit the immense natural resources of African lands. They realized they had to change the mentalities, the attitudes the tastes and appetites of Africans to carry out their exploitation and commercial goals. Thus, they were determined to use whatever means necessary even force (guns) if they had to get their message across to Africans. They had to make their profits and profits it would be no matter what. They had realized Africa was not only a source of vital natural resources but also its potential as a vital market for their finished products. So when the moment was right, they embarked on a vigorous "civilization" campaign on a massive scale on these "backward – bush" people of Africa, these "savages" as they called Africans. Mind you they were very careful to make Africans not to be very "civilized", but just "civilized" enough to enable them see the need for and develop the tastes for the white man's finished goods and products- the manufactured goods; the white man's way of life. These white folks even went as far as creating a small "middle class" of people popularly known in Africa as the African elite; which was at best a very poor imitation of the white middle classes in Europe with little or no initiative of their own. This African "middle class" would be the propagators and consumers of this "imported opulence" on the African continent. This class of people was the ones to set the pace or the standards for the rest of the African masses. In this way, the white folks would be guaranteed a steady and profitable market for their manufactured goods-clothes, cars, luxury household items, furniture and food and even arms. In other words, this could be seen as brainwashing- making Africans to despise and look down on their own cultures and way of life, even their languages; while embracing everything that was white as the best, the ultimate.

For instance writing on French rule in Cameroon before the 1960 period, (Anyangwe C. 1917: 48-49) makes clear the process of the creation of the small elite group or "assimilation" in Cameroon. He states that the French accomplished their "civilizing mission" in the colonies by pursuing two basic colonial policies. There was civilization in politico-cultural terms which meant assimilation and thus, direct rule. In socio-economic terms, it meant resorting to forced labour as a justifiable means to an end-the much vaunted advancement of natives. Assimilation was the cornerstone and substratum of French colonial policy. It fostered the concept of the "évolués". This was a distinction made between citizens "citoyens" and subjects "sujets", a kind of separating the sheep from the goats. The "citoyen" was a French man or a native who had evolved and attained such standard of French culture as qualified him to be assimilated to a Frenchman. A "sujet" was a native who had not yet been assimilated.

> *"In theory, assimilation was only a transition through an evolutionary process by which the entire native population was to acquire French citizenship. In reality however, only few Cameroonians ever became "citoyens". There was really no desire and ...wisdom in assimilating every Cameroonian, making them "citoyens". France still needed "sujets" to do the dirty work, to*

*dig the mines, and cultivate the plantations for her.
And since "citoyens" were by law exempted from
such labors, there was no sense making every
"sujet" a "citoyen". The policy of assimilation
served France very well because it fostered in the
colonized people a subservient attitude and enabled
France to adopt a paternalistic attitude toward
them."*

Furthermore, Anyangwe C. points out that:

*"The policy of assimilation was a political trojam
horse by which natives were made to depend upon
the metropole for virtually everything. It
engendered in them the belief that they were
incapable of ruling themselves and managing their
own affairs and that their destinies and fate were
by some divine Providence bound to that of
France."*

So you see Amy, therein lies the fundamental answers to
your questions about starving African peoples. Like I said Amy,
the white folks had now designed a valuable system that would
guarantee them maximum profits from the African Continent in
terms of the raw materials they would exploit at a very low cost
and a steady and reliable market for their manufactured goods
(Ela J. M., 1983). This way, they were sure to maintain their
acquired wealth and prosperity. Many of the African elite became
middlemen in the trade of African resources; thus in a way,
making some profits too from the cheap labour of their African
brothers and sisters –the labourers. To make things even easier
for them, the white man embarked on a crude unnatural
geopolitical system based on a "divide and rule strategy, which
would forever guarantee the white man's hegemony over African
lands and African peoples. Africa was then divided into little
"banana Republics" in ways that would facilitate the maximum
exploitation of African vast natural resources and control over the
African people. This, Amy, was to transform the face of the
African continent forever. This gave rise to some ruthless, often
meaningless fratricidal wars which, as a matter of fact, are still
plaguing a lot of African nations today, with often devastating
consequences, on the well-being of many African peoples.

This, Amy, is one of the main causes of the starvation problem in Africa today. You see, when people are engaged in these senseless, brutal wars, there is just no way they could cultivate food for their subsistence. The whole place is usually in chaos and nothing good, worthwhile, gets done; only death and unnecessary suffering all the way. Believe you me, it is women and children who suffer most as they usually end up in some refugee camp; with very little food, medicines, water and other necessities of life to survive on. It's terrible, awful. Isn't it Amy?"

"Sure is Aunty, terrible indeed!"

"So you see Amy, after the white folks had partitioned Africa in such unnatural and inhumane manner, the coast was now clear for maximum exploitation of Africa's abundant natural resources and their complete control over African peoples. Before long these whites were exploiting more and more raw materials from Africa from which they manufactured more and more goods for sale to African countries at cut throat prices and other continents. Mind you, they were still very careful not to reveal their manufacturing technology to Africans; just the minimum deemed necessary, such as extractive industries, so as to avoid any future competition that may arise should some Africans decide to engage in the manufacturing business; and to facilitate transportation of raw materials to Europe. Moreover the socio-economic and political structures that developed on the African continent were so damned inefficient, such that such manufacturing activities could never have thrived there had some people even wanted to do so. Thus by and large the African was doomed to a perpetual life of dependence on white people for their socioeconomic, political and even cultural survival and well-being. It was White Cultural imperialism all the way.

"How terrible Amy said sighing."

"Yes Amy, but you have not heard the last of it. Just listen. Like I pointed out earlier; white people were now extracting a lot of natural materials from Africa among which was timber- for the manufacture of wood furniture and other wood products, both for sale in Europe; other continents and Africa too. Remember I had told you white people had now introduced their culture and "way of life" to Africa and they had made sure that many Africans looked upon everything European American – their culture, their civilization as superior to theirs. Thus, as one would imagine, many Africans were now trying to be as European/American as possible by consuming many European and American goods, while looking down on their own goods and culture. You won't believe this but to many Africans white people had become almost "God-like" and these Africans were determined to do all in their power to become just like whites even today. So as one could imagine many African people's ambitions then and even now are for example, to dress, talk, and even eat as white people do. They furnish their homes like whites and in short, live like whites. As such, instead of using their bamboo houses and bamboo furniture – chairs, beds etc. as they did before the advent of colonialism, they all now want wood furniture as their white masters. Other wood related industries such as the paper industry are all over Europe and Africa.

To make matters worse, many ordinary Africans continue to use wood as a main source of fuel, for housebuilding, canoe building and a lot of other things. This led to the indiscriminate cutting down of a lot of forest trees; trees that had stood majestically for centuries, having withstood the test of nature – volcanic eruption, strong winds, floods and the lot, protecting the precious African soils and providing food and shelter to both humans and wildlife; all for timber exploitation for the different industries both in Africa and abroad as well as for local consumption. They also would clear whole forests for agriculture plantations- growing cash crops like tea, cocoa, coffee and bananas.

Moreover, with the population boom in recent times, especially on the African continent, it became necessary to grow more and more food to feed the ever growing population. This has led to the acquisition of forest lands for food cultivation. A lot of forests have been destroyed to provide farm lands for the growing population, most of whom are farmers. Large plots of forests were cut down for the cultivation of cash crops for the badly needed foreign currency which a lot of African governments need for their functioning and survival. Today on the African continent, whole lands lay bare; a real rape of the forest in every sense of the word. This has led to a serious ecological imbalance, resulting in draughts and even desertification in many parts of Africa.

You see Amy, after so many forests have been destroyed; the soil is now exposed to strong winds and very heavy rainfall which results in soil erosion. The fertile top soil is eroded leaving the land barren. Plant, aquatic and animal life, vital sources of food for a lot of Africans have become extinct, since their natural habitats have been destroyed. This poses a serious threat to the survival of mankind as a lot of people are unable to find food to eat. Starvation and starvation related diseases are now rife in many African countries. Also with the global climatic changes caused by massive air and water, pollution from industries, cars and desertification, the problems of hunger, starvation, misery and socio-economic instability have worsened in many African countries. In fact draughts and floods all over the world and particularly in Africa are now regular events, with often dramatic consequences on food production in Africa in particular.

So you see Amy, this explains why you have been seeing those pathetic pictures of starving African children and even adults, regularly on your T.V. screens. I tell you, unless immediate steps are taken to restore the ecological balance all over the world and in Africa especially, you will continue to see such terrible pictures, of starving African people on your T.V. screens. In fact, it would not only be an African problem but other countries in the world, especially the less developed countries would also soon be facing similar problems if nothing serious is done to resolve these environmental problems. This is a real challenge to mankind which can seriously compromise the survival of humans and wildlife."

"But Aunty, can't something be done about this problem? Grandpa, Grandma, can't we send some of our hamburgers to these starving children in Africa? They are really suffering", Amy asked; feeling so worried?"

"Sure Amy", Dr. Yonkeu retorted. "There is a lot you and other Americans and other people of the developed countries could do to resolve this problem. You see Amy, it would be very kind and generous of you and other Americans to send some of your hamburgers to these starving people in Africa. However, I am afraid it's just a very short term solution to this immense problem. In fact, what Africa needs now is to seek long lasting solutions to this problem. Socio-economic, political, scientific and natural solutions are necessary to combat the global environmental problems and the problems of the ever advancing deserts, deforestation; as well as the preservation of the little forests and forest resources left on the African continent. These solutions should be sought and implemented within a short delay if these problems are to be resolved. The environmental problems in Africa should be treated as an emergency. People are suffering, people are dying. There is not much time left for these people. This is the only way to prevent Africa becoming one vast desert land.

First, there must be effective mass education and sensitization campaigns on the African continent to educate Africans on the necessity of preserving the forests and of restoring the forests by re-afforestation. This is not to say that the forest resources should not be exploited but that it should be exploited in a wise and rational way so as to preserve the ecological balance. Timber industries should be made to do the same. They should be made to replace or replant trees as they cut them for timber exploitation. When they replant these trees, they should be cared for so that they could grow healthily. The companies should be made to contribute financially for the whole afforestation project. By all means, the rape of our forests should stop.

African farmers who for the most part are women, who use rudimentary tools and methods to farm, should be helped and made to use better tools and methods so as to be more productive. They should be provided with agricultural inputs- expertise, tools, fertilizers, seeds and capital by African governments, local organizations and Non-Governmental Organizations, to make them stop using the slash and burn method of farming for example, which also contributes to the destruction of the forests. For sustainable management of the soil on hill slopes, farmers should be advised to make horizontal rather than vertical rows to prevent soil erosion. They should also be encouraged to farm on small plots of land (intensive farming). This could be done by furnishing them with appropriate farming inputs, techniques and expertise such as safe and natural or organic fertilizers (cow dung) improved seeds to enable them have better yields from small plots of land. There should also be the provision of sufficient safe water for irrigation. Furthermore, subsistence farmers in general should be provided with the necessary technology and capital to transform and package their agricultural produce in ways that they could be preserved and sold in the local and world markets. This will not only improve their socio-economic status in terms of the money they would make from it, but it will also help improve food security for Africans all year round and help them compete better in the world marketplace.

At the moment a lot of the food stuff these farmers produce rots in bushes as they lack good farm to market roads to transport the food and effective ways to preserve them. So the technologies to transform and preserve these foods would go a long way to reduce starvation in Africa. Similarly, the old ways of farming in Africa should not be totally discarded. There are many important traditional African agricultural technologies that are still viable. Instead, modern agricultural technology should be integrated into local or traditional agricultural systems to enhance agricultural production in Africa. If these things are done, and there is more investment in agriculture generally, this sector could also absorb many unemployed persons, thus reducing the very high unemployment rates in Sub-Saharan Africa.

You see Amy, these are some of the most effective ways of arresting the fast advancing deserts in Africa and help reduce or eradicate starvation in Africa. If the whole world join hands, by supplying the technical know-how and financial assistance in the fight against desertification and starvation in Africa, I honestly believe, it won't be too long before starvation in Africa becomes history. Also African leaders should do all in their power, and be encouraged by European and American governments to put in place democratic humane governments in Africa that could reduce the gap between the rich and poor and ensure social justice in society to avoid socio-economic instabilities and the dreaded fratricidal wars which have greatly contributed to starvation and misery all over Africa; such as in South Sudan, the Central African Republic, the Democratic Republic of Congo and Rwanda (2013, 2014). Also the developed countries which are the worst polluters of the world's waters, air and lands should be made to reduce considerably, or why not, stop their massive pollution of the environment through the emission of pollutants and other dangerous substances from their numerous cars and industries. This will go a long way to reduce starvation and massive suffering in Africa.

As far as the demographic solution to the problems of starvation and misery in Africa go, I think caution should be exercised here; Dr. Yonkeu said "Birth control aimed at limiting births should only be used for a short time until such times that the ecological balance is restored. Therefore men and women should be educated to use birth control during the implementation stages of these projects so as to prevent starvation and death. However as soon as things are back in order, I believe the African population (men/women) should be allowed to have reasonable numbers of children each family can provide with optimum care. This would ensure their children's health and well-being; and it will not put the restored ecological balance in jeopardy. This way, the survival of the human, animal, bird and aquatic life would be guaranteed forever as God, our father in Heaven had intended. "Wow, that's some story" Amy said. "I must have to tell my friends at school about it. This way, everybody would know why there is starvation in Africa. I am sure they would tell their parents and friends about it too. That way, the word could go around fast and I am sure a lot of people would want to help out. Really Aunty, I never knew all this stuff. Thanks Aunty for telling me about the starvation problem in Africa."

"It was my pleasure Amy…" Dr. Yonkeu said as she gave the little girl a peck on her cheek. Amy then smiled back sweetly to Dr. Yonkeu as she quickly slipped down from her laps, and anxiously walked away, as a bird freed from its cage. "Oh, isn't she lovely, simply adorable," Dr. Yonkeu remarked as she watched the little girl walk out of the sitting room to the porch. Everybody in the sitting room smiled and nodded in agreement with Dr. Yonkeu.

"Poor Amy, she had probably had enough of all the serious talking and she must have wanted to relax and to refresh her mind with something less serious, light; as she could not just wait to start playing with her toys and dolls the moment she was out on the porch.

Later, Dr. Yonkeu learnt that the little girl. Amy was Tammy's daughter. Tammy had her when she was in high School. Tammy said she did obviously not plan on having a child at High School but peer pressure and sexual adventurism made her do so. It seemed, she said, a lot of her friends at High School had kids, and they seemed to be doing well; so she just followed suit, just like that not knowing what an immense task it was, raising a child. The guy she had the child with did not want Tammy to have the child. He had even asked Tammy to have an abortion, but being the Christian that Tammy is, she had refused to have an abortion. So when Tammy gave birth to the baby girl, the guy simply left town, and since then, Tammy had not seen nor heard from him. However, Tammy's parents help her out a lot with caring for the little Amy.

It is even better that abortion is legal in the United States, Dr. Yonkeu thought. Although nobody wishes that people just keep getting pregnant and having abortions irresponsibly, and better still without genuine health reasons, it is worthwhile that women have the option of a legal and medically 'safe' abortion. In countries such as in Cameroon where abortion is illegal, it is the case that quite often a lot of terrible things do happen. More often than not, quite a number of girls as well as women still do have abortion anyway; and most of the time, it is some back street abortion with a quack doctor or with some crude native medicines they buy at the local market; which either end up ruining their reproductive systems for life, or worse still, causes death in some cases.

Tammy's parents told Dr. Yonkeu that the number of single parent families had tremendously increased in recent years in the United States with the young people. The situation, they went on, was largely caused by the relatively higher rate of unemployment, the relative lack of knowledge about and access to adequate family planning methods among young African Americans generally; and the high rate of drug abuse among Americans generally. They said these were some of the crucial socio-economic problems the American society was still trying to grapple with.

It was then that Dr. Yonkeu truly realized that the United States still had its problems in spite of the freedom and very relatively high standard of living the people have. However, she was still very optimistic about the future of the country. She hoped the Democratic System, time and the goodwill of the American people generally would prevail and would help solve these problems.

It was already getting dark and everybody seemed to be exhausted. So many questions about Africa and the United States had already been raised and answered. In all; it had been quite a learning experience for everybody. Dr. Yonkeu and Tammy had to prepare for classes the following day; and of course, Tammy's father and mother also had to prepare for work on Monday. They all agreed it was a day well spent and Tammy's parents told Dr. Yonkeu they hoped she would come over to see them more often. Tammy and her father then took Dr. Yonkeu back to her place and after biding Dr. Yonkeu good night, they drove back to their home. Dr. Yonkeu went off to her flat, made a cup of hot chocolate and after drinking, she went to bed. It had really been a hectic day for her.

The following day, it was school as usual. She seemed to be doing so well at school generally except for some problems she was having with Statistics. She started devoting a lot of time on Statistics. Her Statistics Professor was very understanding and helpful. She was ever ready to help Dr. Yonkeu with any problems she had on Statistics.

Meanwhile, Dr. Yonkeu had joined some of the clubs on campus. She belonged to the 'Coalition for the Promotion of Human Rights' club and the 'African Students Union.' It was just amazing the number of students' clubs there were at the University. There were clubs for every single thing one could think of –from political to just fun clubs. Students indeed had a wide range of clubs to choose from. If one were to follow all the club activities on campus, one would never make it academically. This indeed; was quite a new experience for Dr. Yonkeu. In fact, she thought it was really great! It was a marked contrast to the University of Cameroon where there had been only a few students' clubs.

The Clubs at the University of Orange were also very active. Some of the most interesting Club activities, Dr. Yonkeu thought, were those that had to do with inviting guest speakers to the University campus. One of such memorable speakers that Dr. Yonkeu's club – the 'Coalition For the Promotion Of Human Rights' invited, was a representative of the then African national congress' (ANC) to the United Nations. This was really an eye opener for her. He gave the whole history of the ANC, and he went as far as explaining how the ANC had no choice but to embark on an armed struggle in 1961. He said that, they had tried all sorts of peaceful ways and means of solving the apartheid problem in South Africa to no avail. In fact, he went on; all they got back in return, was often, a violent suppression of their efforts by the then racist South African Government. He said the massacre of Sharpsville in 1976, of, innocent children who were demonstrating peacefully against to learn in the "Africans" language in schools in South Africa, by the racist Pretoria Government force, was just the last straw that did break the camel's back. It was then that the ANC had no other alternative left but to fully embark on an armed struggle against the Pretoria Government. Chief Luthuli, one of the Black Nationalist Leaders in South Africa, he said, puts the trend of events, leading up to the armed struggle into a better perspective:

'...who will deny that thirty years of my life have been spent knocking in vain, patiently, moderately and modestly at a closed and barred door? What have been the fruits of moderation? The past thirty years have seen the greatest number of laws restricting our rights and progress, until today we have reached a stage where we have no rights at all.'

'Late Nelson Mandela, the giant of African politics, the very prominent, courageous, visionary and charismatic Black nationalist leader in the then South Africa, and who actually became President of South Africa, the ANC Representative at the United Nations; said, sheds even more light as to why the ANC had decided to fight rather than talk or negotiate for Black people's freedom in South Africa.

'...the old methods', Nelson Mandela had said, 'of bringing about mass actions through public meetings, press statements and leaflets... have become difficult to use effectively...We require the development of new forms of struggle...on a higher level... there is no easy walk to freedom anywhere.'

Really, how better can one put it, Dr. Yonkeu said to herself. It was such a very moving story; and the ANC Representative's oration so sad and yet so mesmerizing Dr. Yonkeu was indeed so happy to have found out the truth about the purpose and the activities of the ANC Organization. Now, more than ever before, she was determined to work even harder toward the dismantling of remnants of apartheid in South Africa. Like the French would say, she thought, "la vérité finit toujours par triompher" How so true, she murmured to herself.

The ANC representative went on that, they had been labelled as a communist terrorist group, but that it was a false accusation and a tactic used by neo-Nazi Organizations to distort the truth from people and other Organizations who were interested in helping in the fight against 'apartheid' in South Africa.

'Heaven help the young generation of South Africans to follow in Mandela's footsteps, and give them more strength and courage to carry on with the struggle for Black freedom in South Africa and the world; and may God receive those valiant liberation fighters like the Great Mandela, Steve Biko, Oliver Tambo, Walter Sisulu, Lilian Ngoyi, Ida Antwana and many others who have departed from this earth. These men and women are for sure our modern day heroes and heroines', Dr. Yonkeu said to herself.

Of course, while the ANC representative to the U.N. was speaking, there were neo-Conservative groups outside with their anti-Communist banners discouraging people from going to listen to what the African National Congress had to say. They said he was a communist.

In fact, what annoyed Dr. Yonkeu about these neo-Conservative groups was not their existence as groups. After all in the United States, there is freedom of speech and freedom to assemble peacefully. However, the false allegations by some of these groups are what are terrible about it all. You see, they tend to label anybody or group advocating for people's basic rights as communists. This somehow distorts the truth and stifles many genuine reform measures that may have been taken either by Government or individuals to better people's lives.

However, that was the United States of America and every group has the right to exist. The good thing about it all is that, whenever a neo-Nazi speaker comes to speak on campus, the anti-Nazi groups such as Dr. Yonkeu's would also have the right to demonstrate peacefully against such a speaker, and to make people well aware of the pain and suffering activities of such groups may bring to bear on the innocent. This, Dr. Yonkeu felt, was true Democracy in action. This was far better than in those parts of the world where Governments to a large extent; tend to allow people to know only what they want them to know and nothing else. This indeed, stifles a lot of progress and development in those countries. It also impedes the growth of human potentialities. In fact, access to information is so vital a factor for achieving and guaranteeing freedom; freedom to think, freedom to choose, freedom to decide etc., which are all, absolutely necessary for achievement, development and progress. As Alfred Sauvy rightly puts it: '… to be free today, is to be informed'. How true, Dr. Yonkeu thought.

In any case, University life in the Unites States seemed to be so full of excitement; except of course for the fact that one also had to work very hard as well. One found out that one was busy round the clock doing one thing or another. One had to plan or organize one's schedule so as to be able to allocate some time for fun. It was hard work indeed, but when one had set one's mind at what one wanted to do, and worked hard at it, one's chances of succeeding were very high indeed. Hardly one would not make it under these circumstances.

Dr. Yonkeu continued working so hard and she continued doing so well academically. It all paid off in the end. Dr. Yonkeu did graduate in the end. She had her (BA) Bachelor of Arts Degree in Politics. She was immediately admitted into the Masters Political Science Program. Her dream was really coming true. She was really overwhelmed with joy. Time and again, her parents would write letters of encouragement to her. 'Everything was really possible in the United States,' she thought. She was more than ever determined to make it to the top. This would make some of those Professors at the University of Cameroon ashamed when she returned home with her degrees. She resolved to work even harder, until she would have her Doctorate Degree. 'After all', she thought, 'this was the United States of America. A little luck and hard work would always pay off as it had just happened to her.'

At this point, her mind drifted back to Cameroon. She thought of Koffi. She wondered where he was and what he could be doing. She had not heard from him for quite some time. Poor Koffi, she said to herself. She would try and write to some of those scholarship boards to find out if Koffi could be awarded some scholarship to come and study in the United States. She then wrote to Koffi using his friend's address.

Koffi wrote back to her as soon as he got her letter. He said he was still struggling working at a construction site; and that, he was still unable to save any money for his schooling. They work hard, he said, but in the end, they are paid peanuts. When Dr. Yonkeu read Koffi's letter, tears rolled down from her eyes. 'Poor Koffi, she kept saying. She decided to write to Koffi immediately and ask him to send all his certificates to her so that she could try to see if she could get some scholarship for Koffi in the United States.

As luck would have it, the scholarships Board wrote back to Dr. Yonkeu and told her they had sent a lot of scholarships for different fields of study to Cameroon. All they said Koffi had to do was to go to the Ministry of Education in Cameroon and apply for a scholarship. The Scholarship Board assured Dr. Yonkeu that Koffi was just the sort of candidate they were looking for. Dr. Yonkeu immediately wrote back to Koffi and told him to apply for some of those scholarships at the Ministry of Education in Cameroon. She assured him that he would most likely be given a scholarship to come to the United States.

Koffi did as Dr. Yonkeu had advised him to do. He forwarded all his certificates to the Ministry of Education in Cameroon. However, later when the list for those persons who had been awarded scholarships came out, Koffi's name was not among them. People who did not even have one third of Koffi's qualifications, but who either had godfathers or brothers or sisters working at the Ministry of Education; or those who bribed heavily; those from some ethnic group, or those who knew some big 'shot' in Government to intervene on their behalf, all had scholarships even though they did not have the right qualifications, except Koffi and other unfortunate persons, the "wretched of the earth".

When Koffi wrote and told Dr. Yonkeu the story, she cried for days. She could hardly sleep at nights. She wondered why people were so unfair and wicked in those parts of the world. It is true, she thought that there is unfairness everywhere in the world, but somehow, she thought, the unfairness in those parts of the world where she is from by far surpasses those in countries like the United States of America. Had she applied for scholarship now, she thought, she would have never had it. She would have been in a similar situation as Koffi. Thank God!, she said, she had applied for her own scholarship at a time when the United States Government and other European Governments awarded scholarships directly to qualified individuals by passing all the 'isms', ethnicism, nepotism, "clientelisme", sexism etc., you just name it now, plaguing the Government. Dammit, she thought, life is just so impossible in Cameroon. Bribery and corruption are so deep rooted in the system, to the extent that, even patients have to bribe some of those corrupt unscrupulous medical officials before they could even be attended to in public hospitals even in emergency situations. And even when they do get attended to, or get admitted at the hospital, they soon find out that, it has all been a waste of time and effort on their part if they don't have money. Their chances of getting proper treatment are for the most part non-existent.

To begin with, being able to see the Doctor is one thing; and getting proper treatment is another. The problem is that, most of the time, Doctors at these hospitals do not even have the basic medical equipment or medicines for that matter, to work with; even simple things such as cotton and alcohol, especially in remote areas. As such, if the patient does not have money to buy these things and other medicines, from the nearest Drug Store, the Doctor often finds there is very little or nothing at all he/she could possibly do to help the patient. To make matters worse, the prices of drugs are so high that, more often than not, patients find they just cannot afford to buy even the simplest medicines. Under such circumstances, all the Doctor finds he could possibly do is to stand there helpless, unable to do anything as he watches the patient struggling in pain, gasping for breath as he/she slowly dies. It is often a traumatic experience for both doctors and patients.

Even the sanitation conditions in some of these hospitals leave little to be desired. The odour and filth in some of these hospitals are beyond description, just deplorable. In spite of all these, the hospital wards are often full to capacity. As such, a lot of times, patients have to make do with beds with no mattresses on them. Worse still, a lot of patients often have to lie on the floor. Many a times, Doctors find themselves operating on patients on bare tables, you know, wooden tables; not to mention the many women who often find themselves giving birth on beds with no mattresses on them, sometimes, even on the floor. If one could only imagine the pain a lot of women have to put up with during delivery under normal circumstances, then and only then could one fully understand the hell these women go through, when in addition to that, they have to give birth lying on very hard surfaces. In fact, only then can one fully grasp the magnitude of the appalling state of medical conditions in the country. As a Doctor once puts it, 'it is a very sad situation. What can we do? We see these things every day; for example, patients just lying there on the floor helpless, bleeding to death, yet there is virtually nothing in this 'godam' world we could do about it all, since we have neither the medicines nor the appropriate medical equipment to work with. It is really terrible, but I guess we've gotten used to it". "How could one put it any better? This sums it all". Dr. Yonkeu thought. Sometimes, it is also some unscrupulous Doctors who cause the suffering of patients as they try to make their money on the side as they prescribe unnecessary medicines and medical operations to patients. It's so terrible! These Doctors have become "commerçants" business people, rather than medical Doctors. How sad," Dr. Yonkeu concluded.

Even the public school system is not the exception to the rule. Quite often, a lot of parents find they have to bribe corrupt school officials in order to have their children admitted at school. And even after these parents, as it is often the case, have scrapped the little money they have or borrowed money to bribe those corrupt school officials to have their children admitted at some of these schools, they soon realize that their effort has all been in vain. This is so because, the education the children receive from some of these schools is nothing to be desired. Moreover, the very low pay of teachers makes them less motivated or less willing to do their work properly. Standards are so low that, these children often end up failing all the national and international Examinations. The children are doomed for failure the moment they step foot into those classrooms. Instead of the schools preparing them for success, they seem to be preparing them for mediocrity and failure. It is all such a sad situation. 'Maudite Afrique' or 'damned Africa' indeed as some put it Dr. Yonkeu concluded.

Another academic year has just begun, and Dr. Yonkeu was well aware of the fact that, she would have to try and forget about Koffi's problems so as to be able to concentrate on her studies. She did find out that one could have one's Masters' Degree in a period of one year that is of course, if one really worked hard at it. Given her very limited finances, Dr. Yonkeu decided she was going to do just that. She resolved to devote a lot more of her time on her studies so as to be able to have her Masters' Degree in one year. She also came to the decision to cut down on some of her extra-curricular activities, so as to able to achieve her goals. She was well aware this was not in any way going to be an easy task to accomplish. But what was she to do? It seemed to be the only way out, considering her financial circumstances. Sometimes, she figured, one has got to make the best out of the little one has, she either had to make do with the little money available to her and continue with her studies, or return home, to Cameroon, that is, with only her Bachelor of Arts Degree. That she felt, would be self-defeating, considering the enormous opportunities there were for her in the United States to pursue further studies; if only she were able to make some sacrifices on certain things time and again; such as working harder than usual and cutting down on certain 'luxuries'. Moreover, working hard, and as such, keeping herself busy most of the time, would, she hoped, help, take her mind off Koffi's problems at least, for the time being.

She then embarked on a rigorous work schedule. Her time was divided between her school work and her on the campus job. All the time, she hoped and prayed she would be able to make it in the end. She worked so hard, so much so that, she did not realize it was nearly the end of the Academic Year; and that she was almost through with her course work. From time to time, her mind sort of drifted back to Cameroon. She wondered how Koffi was getting along with his plans. One day, she found she could hardly do anything. She kept thinking about Koffi. She could not understand why there was this sudden surge in her to contact Koffi. She finally decided to write to Koffi and find out how he was doing. Then a thought suddenly came to her mind. What if, she thought, she asked Koffi to contact her parents to help him pay his fare to the United States? Then she would use the little amount of money she had saved up, to pay for Koffi's tuition in one of those Technical College where Koffi could come and study something like Computer Sciences. This would enable him find a job in one of the many companies in the city as a Computer Technician in the United States, she thought. This would enable him earn enough money to continue with his studies. After all, the Computer Technician course only took six months; and knowing Koffi, there would be no way he wouldn't make it in six months' time. He was a very hard working and intelligent young man.

She immediately wrote to Koffi giving him all the necessary information that would enable him to obtain all the necessary documents to come to the United States. She got so excited about the idea and she kept imagining how happy Koffi would feel when he received her letter. She had posted the letter she wrote to Koffi by express mail, and so she was expecting a reply from Koffi in about two weeks' time, the latest.

Two weeks elapsed and the third week came and passed, and the fourth was almost coming to an end, and she had not had a reply from Koffi. She became really worried. 'What the hell, she wondered may have gone wrong with her letter to Koffi? Her imagination went wild. Maybe, she thought, Koffi had succeeded to leave the country as he had planned. At this thought, a faint smile came to her face. The smile just lasted for a while. She remained so worried. Something must have gone wrong with her letter, probably in Cameroon, she thought. After all, she had heard awful stories about some of the Post Office Workers in

Cameroon. It is alleged that, when some of these Post Office Workers saw mails from abroad, they would open it to see if there was money order in it which they would go and cash. If there was no money order in it, they would simply throw it in the waste paper basket or if one was lucky he or she would receive a letter in an opened envelope. The thought of such a thing happening to the letter she wrote to Koffi only infuriated her all the more. How wicked some people could be, she thought. After all, these Post Office Workers are being paid monthly. She wondered why they could engage in such awful practices. If they were not satisfied with their pay, they should demand higher pay from the Government, rather than make innocent people suffer, Dr. Yonkeu said aloud. However, after one month had passed, and she had still not heard from Koffi, she became convinced that Koffi never did receive her letter. She then wrote another letter to Koffi and posted it that same day by express mail again.

Some weeks had passed, when one early morning, she went to check the mails in her mail box, and found a letter from Cameroon in it. It was none of her parent's handwriting, neither was it Koffi's. She wondered who else would have written to her from Cameroon since most of her other friends did not know her address. She became nervous. Her heart started beating so fast. She wondered why she was feeling the way she did. After all, it was only a strange letter from Cameroon, she tried to console herself. She then mustered all the courage she could at that moment, and pulled out the letter from the mailbox; and with her hands shaking, she did at last tear the envelop open. She quickly browsed through the letter and she found out that it was from Koffi's friend. She wondered why Koffi's friend would be the one to reply to her letter. That was pretty unusual, very strange indeed, she thought. Could Koffi have been so ill that he could not write, and had asked his friend to write for him, or had Koffi already left the country before her letter arrived, Dr. Yonkeu wondered? She was visually worried. She then began reading the letter. It read thus:

Elimbi Martins
P.O. Box 201 Douala
Cameroon, Central Africa
April 20.

Dear Miss Yonkeu,
    We did receive your letter dated 6th March. I am indeed very sorry to inform you that, your friend Koffi passed away on the 21st of March. He did commit suicide by taking an overdose of assorted drugs.

    I found a note beside his body which said that I should write to you as soon as possible, telling you that he decided to take away his own life because it seemed his greatest fear, was slowly but steadily coming true. The way things were going for him, he stated, showed that he would probably end up a pauper. He said you should forgive him, but he would rather die than live in poverty again. That was probably why he decided to take away his own life.

    It is a pity!, Miss Yonkeu because when Koffi died, none of his relatives came forward to claim his body. It seemed they were all afraid to spend money on the burial formalities. So Koffi was given a pauper's burial ceremony and buried in a pauper's grave-yard.

    So Miss Yonkeu, you see, that's the sorrowful situation. It's a pity, because your letter to Koffi would have made all the difference in the world. But you see Miss Yonkeu, your letter arrived here a little too late, just two days after Koffi had committed suicide. Poor Koffi, I think it's God's will that things had to happen this way. So Miss Yonkeu, let us all pray that Koffi's soul will rest in perfect peace with God our Father in Heaven.

    Bye for now Miss Yonkeu and God bless you! Your Friend
Elimbi.

After Dr. Yonkeu had finished reading the letter, her first reaction was shock and utter disbelief. She could not imagine, not even in her wildest dreams that she would never see Koffi again. 'No', she screamed, 'he can't be dead!' Dr. Yonkeu rushed into her room, shut the door and burst out crying. 'Poor Koffi, Poor Koffi!' she kept repeating. 'Just look at the pain and suffering the social injustice in some of these parts of the world could bring to bear on a young harmless man like Koffi. They would not let him realize his dreams. And her letter, she thought, yes, her letter. Indeed, she repeated. Eddy was right. It really did come a little too late. Fancy what difference that little piece of paper would have made to Koffi's life. Society had pushed him to his limits. He had no hopes left and there was no one he could turn to for help. Poor Koffi! If only he had received her letter two days before!' Dr. Yonkeu kept on saying and weeping at the same time. 'His so-called relatives, why did none of them come to Koffi's aid before things got out of hand? Even after they learnt he was dead, none of them came to even give Koffi a decent burial! Ah! She thought, 'the extended family' concept, the African solidarity, the warmth and strength of the extended family, "mechanical solidarity" (see Durkheim E.) had really become a real myth in Africa. When you have money, you are everybody's aunty, uncle, sister, brother, cousin, nephew or niece, not to talk of the numerous friends you would have. When you go broke however, nobody wants to even hear your name being mentioned. What a sad world this is!' Dr. Yonkeu thought.

For quite some time, Koffi's death kept on worrying Dr. Yonkeu. The effects could be seen even on her class performance. Her Professors became so worried. They did not know what the matter suddenly was with Dr. Yonkeu. She had been such a good and outgoing student, they thought, but her performance had suddenly dropped and she had become somewhat of a loner; a recluse. She seemed preoccupied by something that nobody could really figure out.

It got to a point that, one day the Foreign Students' Adviser had to intervene. She called Dr. Yonkeu to her office and told her that she was worried because she had been having a lot of complaints about her poor work performance both in class and on the job. She asked Dr. Yonkeu whether the pressure of school and work was beginning to take its toll on her. Dr. Yonkeu said no. She then said there was already some speculations that Dr. Yonkeu had started taking drugs to help take away some of the pressure from all the work she had to do. She said drug-taking was always accompanied by the supposedly withdrawal syndrome Dr. Yonkeu seemed to be suffering from. She said it was fast becoming a common practice among some young people to take drugs whenever they were under a lot of stress or pressure to succeed, either at school or at work, or even when they had love problems and so on and so forth.

Dr. Yonkeu just sighed and told the Foreign Students' adviser that she had never taken drugs in her life and that she did not intend to start doing so now. She said she did appreciate the Foreign Students' Adviser's concern for her well-being, but that she should not worry. She lied that she was just having a few family problems, but that everything would be all right shortly. The Foreign Students' Adviser also said she hoped that Dr. Yonkeu would get over whatever it is that was troubling her soon because her work was already suffering a great deal. She also assured Dr. Yonkeu that, her door was always open should she need any help. 'How thoughtful and kind!', Dr. Yonkeu thought. 'If only her problem was that easy to resolve!' she murmured to herself.

Dr. Yonkeu did however; manage to carry on with her work till it was the end of the academic year. She wrote a brilliant Master's Thesis on 'democracy'. The thesis examined a problem that had for long troubled Dr. Yonkeu. It examined the issue as to whether 'Democracy' should solely be based on majority rule. If so, she questioned what would become of minority interests? 'Should majority rule be at the expense of minority interests?' She came to the conclusion that whenever there was majority rule, there should be certain socio-economic mechanisms such as affirmative action for some period of time of course, within the system to guarantee and protect minority interests. Her adviser, who was also the professor she worked with, really liked the logical way in which she developed her arguments. He said Dr. Yonkeu did have some brilliant ideas, and that she could go a long way with those ideas. These words of encouragement, simple as they may have been at the time, did in fact give Dr.

Yonkeu the confidence, the green lights to go ahead and do her (Ph. D) Doctorate Degree.

She did indeed take a year to do her Master's Degree as she had anticipated. Then, it was graduation day. She was not as happy as she would have been, had Koffi been alive. Koffi's death drastically changed her outlook on life. All she wanted at that moment was to accomplish her academic goals and then, return to Cameroon. Then she would see what she could do to ameliorate the lives of the less fortunate, remember, those that time seemed to have passed by; the forgotten, the disinherited , the down-trodden, the scums of the earth.

After graduation, she decided that the University of Orange had so far been so good to her; and that it was time to move on to other things, and experience what life was like in another University, most likely in some Mid-Western State. She had been up North for quite a while, and she had often wondered what life would be like in the Mid-West. Her experience in the North had really been an eye opener. She felt she had learnt quite a lot that she would not have ever learnt in Cameroon. She had also grown so mature and she felt she had a better grasp of what life was really all about. Nothing, she felt, could be beyond her reach. She had learnt to strife for whatever thing she wanted. She now realized that in the United States, things did not come as easily as some people would imagine. Like in any other country in the world, there are obstacles on the way. However, unlike in many other countries, the major difference with the United States is that the obstacles one encounters there are not as insurmountable as is the case in so many other countries in the world. In the United States, one often finds that, with a little luck on one's side and hard work, most, if not all of the barriers come crumbling down, and it is left for one to either grab the opportunity and make the best of it, or lie down on one's back and do nothing.

Dr. Yonkeu sent her applications to as many Universities as possible in the Mid-West; but she got the most favourable reply from the University of Olive. She was admitted into the Doctoral Program and she was awarded free tuition and an on campus job as a Project Assistant to a Professor at the History Department. She was indeed very happy with the offer. Her parents were also very pleased and thankful to God. She could see her dreams finally coming true. She could hardly believe it though; so surreal; 'only in America, only in America, 'she kept on repeating 'could one's dreams really come true. 'The books she had read while she was back in Cameroon about the good life in the United States of America may have exaggerated some, but they were not far from the truth, she thought. Now, she had to grab the opportunity before it slipped away from her.

She wrote back to the University of Olive accepting and thanking them for the offer. She then contacted all her friends, Professors and of course the Foreign Students' Adviser and told them that she was going to leave the university of Orange for the University of Olive to do her Doctorate in the Fall. She thanked them for all the help and kindness they had shown her, and told them that she hoped someday, she would be able to pay back in whatever way possible. They were all so pleased for her success in gaining admission into the Doctorate program at the University of Olive. They were all unanimous about the fact that, it was a good university. However, their only regret was that she was leaving them. They all said they would really miss her. They nevertheless, wished her the best of luck with her future plans.

Dr. Yonkeu had never realized how attached she had become to the University of Orange and to her newly-found friends until a few days before she was to leave Orange city for good. The university had become like a home away from home for her; and friends and Professors had become one big family. It was very emotional indeed parting from people one had grown to love and cherish, she thought. How she wept as she boarded the plane for Olive city.

CHAPTER FIVE

WOES OF WOMANHOOD: DR. YONKEU'S LIFE AT THE UNIVERSITY OF OLIVE, MID-WEST, USA

When Dr. Yonkeu arrived at Olive city, she took a taxi straight to the University of Olive campus, and reported at the Foreign Students' Office. The Foreign Students' Adviser, a smart-looking, dark haired middle – aged White lady welcomed her with the usual Mid-Western warmness, as she would later find out. They chatted for a while, and she told Dr. Yonkeu she had been unable to find a permanent lodging for her at the moment. However, she said she had arranged for a temporary lodging for Dr. Yonkeu until she could find some place suitable for her needs. She took Dr. Yonkeu to the temporary lodging in one of the Undergraduate Dormitories. She then went with Dr. Yonkeu to the School Restaurant and showed her where she would be buying her food.

Most of the girls in the Undergraduate dormitory were very nice and pleasant. They wanted to know who Dr. Yonkeu was and where she came from. As it turned out, most of them had never really come into such close contact with an African before. They were all so excited about all what Dr. Yonkeu told them about herself and about Africa. After having found out a lot about what they wanted to know about Dr. Yonkeu at that time they all went about their respective businesses. Some of those who came in later, went and introduced themselves to Dr. Yonkeu and had a quick chat with her. Of course there were some who could not be bothered with Dr. Yonkeu. They just went about their usual business as if no stranger was in their dormitory.

Dr. Yonkeu tried and tidied up her little room. In the evening, she took a shower, got dressed, and went to the school Restaurant where she bought some dinner. She did not feel a total stranger anymore. Most of the Universities in the United States, she had noticed, were very similar in many ways. She just needed to know where all the various offices and classrooms were located. That was all it took to get around.

After dinner, she went back to her room in the dormitory. Being so exhausted from the flight and the day's events, she fell asleep so easily. When she actually did open her eyes, it was already daybreak. She quickly hurried off to the shower, took a nice long shower, got dressed and went off to the School restaurant where she had her breakfast. She then went to her Department to see the director of the Doctoral program, to arrange for her courses and discuss other matters concerning the program.

As it turned out, the director happened to be a she. She was a tall attractive grey haired lady. She had on a long black skirt that came all the way to her ankles and a well-tailored flowery blouse. She had that serious look about her but time and again she would smile at Dr. Yonkeu as if to say I am only human. Don't look too, surprised or afraid. That sure was reassuring to Dr. Yonkeu and made her feel somewhat at ease. 'Wow', Dr. Yonkeu thought, 'a lady Director! Women have really made great strides in integrating into mainstream America. Fancy having a female Director of a Doctoral Program! Dr. Yonkeu was really impressed. And it sure was not a case of tokenism either since there were many women like her in top positions in the country. 'Thumbs up she said, to Gloria Steinem, Flo Kennedy and many other feminists. They have done a great job for the advancement of Women's Rights in the United States.' She indeed hoped and prayed that, someday, the women's movement in Cameroon and other countries in that part of the world would be able to achieve such great successes for women as those of their United States counterparts.

Professor Phillips, an Anglo-American lady, as Dr. Yonkeu later found out was a very gentle soft-spoken pleasant and simple lady, in spite of her immense achievements in the academic domain. She had written quite an impressive number of books and numerous articles in some of the top Social Science Journals in the United States. Dr. Yonkeu could hardly wait to read some of her books and articles. She imagined they must be very informative. The director looked so very intelligent indeed. Dr. Yonkeu was so delighted.

After all the introductions, the Director, Dr. Philips, said, she was very pleased to meet Dr. Yonkeu as they shook hands. She then offered Dr. Yonkeu a seat. They talked about the Program for quite some time. After that, she said she hoped Dr. Yonkeu would enjoy her stay at the University. She then asked her secretary to take Dr. Yonkeu and introduce her to her Academic Adviser. The Secretary, a very pretty, and very nice young lady took Dr. Yonkeu to her Adviser's Office and introduced her to him. Dr. Yonkeu's Adviser, Professor Mark, was an African who had lived in the United States for a very long time. Dr. Yonkeu later found out that he was even married to a White American Lady, and that he had two beautiful children, a boy and a girl. He was a very warm and kind-hearted man. Dr. Yonkeu was very pleased she would be working with an African since she was going to specialize on 'African women and the Political Economy'. From what she later learnt, Dr. Mark was well informed on 'Minority' issues generally; and as far as the African situation was concerned, he was no stranger either. Not only had he lived it, he had also read and written a lot on African Politics. Dr. Yonkeu was ever so happy the way things had been going so far.

After having a pretty long chat with her Adviser, and having decided on what courses she would be taking, Dr. Yonkeu then went to the History Department where she was introduced to the Professor with whom she would be working, on a Project on Women Farmers in the Mid-West. Professor Edwards, as he told Dr. Yonkeu his name was, was an Anglo-American. He was a really nice, warm, and a very learned man, as Dr. Yonkeu realized as she chatted with him, about himself and the Project they would be working on together. It seemed the perfect project for Dr. Yonkeu. It was a project aimed at sensitizing the public about the plight of the female farmers and finding ways of ameliorating the status of the latter. She could very well relate to some of the issues involved in this Project to the situation of the African female farmers, to a large extent, she thought. In fact, this was a painful reminder to her of the terribly sad situation of female farmers in Africa. She thought of all the inconveniences and hardships they are often subjected to; such as their lack of finance, as well as their low status in society generally.

African female farmers, she figured, are really the 'backbones' of African societies, considering their crucial role in the economy, in terms of their money generating or entrepreneurial activities, (such as in petty trade in products ranging from household goods to farm produce); as well as in feeding the ever growing African population; thus keeping the latter, the labour force, healthy and active in the developmental processes of the nations. These women's workload are really immense, and for the most part, arduous. They are usually busy round the clock. They have the enormous task of taking care of the household chores, doing the 'back-breaking' farm work, as well as making the much needed financial contributions; or today with the high unemployment rate, take care of the general upkeep of the household, and the well-being of the family; thus subsidizing the meagre wages of their husbands if they work, who are usually victims of the crude and inhumane capitalist system operating in most of Africa, by of course, selling their farm produce. Yet they remain so marginalized in society. In fact, as a result of this tedious farm labour, a lot of these women end up with 'bent backs'. It is often so sad seeing a lot of these young women with their backs so bent, and already looking very old. And yet, time and again, they manage to keep a smile on their often tired, sun baked, and worn out faces. Oh, the dignity, the perseverance of these African women is just incredible. Their situation is indeed pathetic, both financially and physically. Take the palm of their hands for example. They are usually as rough as a grater, as calloused as ever and as hard as a stone from the never ending weeding and hoeing they have to do on the often rocky and hard lands; and pounding food in mortars with a pestle. One need not mention the terrible condition of their finger nails which are permanently blackened cracked and crooked, with layers upon layers of thick black soil stuck underneath as a result of the amount of weeding they do on their farms, as well as their husbands' farms year in year out. No wonder, they grow old so prematurely. This could be seen on their weather-beaten faces with rough skin from working on these farms for very long periods. Thank God for having given the African good teeth if not these women would be without teeth. It is indeed pitiful. And I tell you, you have not heard the end of it. After sweating it out on the farms toiling under the burning sun on almost barren farm lands they return to their homes late in the evening only to begin the tedious manual labour all over again (what the French would call "un éternel commencement". This notwithstanding though, they have to sweat it over a 'stone age' cooking fireplace in a suffocating smoke filled kitchen struggling to prepare a hot meal for their Lord and Master-their husbands and of course their families. Usually they would have to blow out their lungs at the fire to keep it going; leaving their eyes blood red and bulging and almost falling from their heads; and their noses running endlessly. Not to mention the terribly crippling and chronic back pain these women suffer from as a result of all the tedious manual labour they do day in day out. I tell you, whoever said the African woman is a "beast of burden" couldn't have put it better. You've got to see it to believe it, Dr. Yonkeu thought. They say hell is somewhere up there, but I tell you Dr. Yonkeu said, it is right here on earth for the African woman, especially this category of African women. Yet their condition never really improves. Everything basically remains the same, year in year out. In fact, the name 'African farm women' has become synonymous with 'chronic poverty' and 'misery'. Yet it is these women who really keep the wheels of society turning, by making sure everybody's stomach is full. How then is one to possibly justify the enormous discrepancy in the tremendously vital role these women perform in society, and their terribly impoverished state of living? As one woman succinctly puts it, "We are on our feet all day long working hard; and at nights, instead of having a good night's rest, 'ils, nos maris nous écrasent au lit'. Hope you get the meaning! This may sound funny in a way, but there is a lot of truth and reality in it. In fact, it shows us how women are oppressed in every way by men and of course capitalism; and how some women in Africa are becoming increasingly aware of their oppressed status in the African society; thanks in large part to the women's liberation movement. Like feminist therapists Ernst and Good is on put it: "the significance of the women's liberation movement, is that it enables us to see the ways in which capitalism invades and attempts to control all areas of our lives and this necessitates a response, a struggle, not just in the factory but also on the playground in schools, at home and in bed," (See Zaretsky E., 1976).

'Really, let's face it, Africa sure has her priorities all mixed up ', Dr. Yonkeu said to herself. 'It's high time', she went on, 'Africa starts putting her money where her mouth is; by actually taking concrete steps to redress the plight of her farm women. Thus far, Africa, that is, seems to be suffering from a conflict of interests where there should not be any whatsoever.'

Talk about misplaced priorities and colossal waste of money, check this out! This very 'rich' African guy, apparently trying to please the good Father in Heaven goes and builds a humongous luxury Cathedral, one that could only be compared to 'St Peter's Basilica' in Rome; worth millions and millions of dollars in the middle of nowhere, in the heart of the African jungle; while the majority of the people in his country barely have roofs over their heads. Not to mention the millions of people, women children and men all in his country and on the African Continent as a whole who die of starvation and malnutrition every day. How about that? And believe, you me, a lot of these projects are usually financed with loans from the notorious International Monetary Fund (FMI) and the World Bank, which then turns around and impose their terrible inhumane 'Structural Adjustment Plans' or better still their "Structural Destruction Plans" with often terrible debilitating consequences on the already suffering masses who never even gained a thing from these massive projects. Yet when it comes to paying back these humongous debts, it is done on the backs of the already suffering masses rather than the corrupt Government officials all over Black Africa who make tremendous financial gains from these often irrational projects.

If I do remember my Scriptures very well, Dr. Yonkeu thought, I guess the Good Lord ..., forgive me if I am wrong, abundantly made it clear that, '...where two or three people are gathered together in my name, there shall I be in their midst.' He did not say when two or three are gathered in a homogenous luxury Cathedral. Certainly not, and I can bet you, Dr. Yonkeu whispered to herself, that this luxury Cathedral this guy built provides shelter for the jungle creatures around; the snakes, the lizards, the monkeys...et cetera, for three hundred and sixty four days out of the three hundred and sixty five days in a year. Really, even the jungle creatures are better housed than human beings; I mean not just anywhere but in very expensive living quarters. How about that? For a change, top priority is being given to the protection and the well-being of wild life, at the expense of human beings. What a difference! I guess it has always been the other way round on the African continent, if my memory is not failing me, Dr. Yonkeu said sarcastically. It is nice alright, Dr. Yonkeu continued, to worship in a nice, decent environment, a decent Church House. But this, a luxury Cathedral in the middle of nowhere, she thought, is a real exaggeration! Really it's absurd!

In fact, examples of such misplaced priorities by top Public Officials abound on the African Continent. Take the case of some of these nations that can barely hold their own financially, yet the governments of these countries continue to embark on huge, sophisticated and very costly projects that are not viable on the African continent in terms of maintenance and suitability. Ironically in these countries the ordinary people lack basic healthcare, food, water, education, electricity etc. One need not mention the white elephant projects abandoned here and there. Indeed pray that you do not have an accident on the highways or roads in the rural areas. It is nothing less than a death sentence, for there would be no ambulance service or well-equipped hospitals to treat you. It's so unfortunate, Dr. Yonkeu said to herself. Social inclusion remains a myth in these countries.

You see, Dr. Yonkeu thought, as critical and as vital as these farm women's role may be in sustaining the population and the economy of these African nations, they are to begin with, not often compensated accordingly, that is, in terms of their financial rewards, and their access to financial resources, such as Bank loans (which they could use in improving their agricultural output). Secondly, they are neither often given enough consideration by Agricultural Experts to begin with, the Government Officials and the general public for that matter. These people just take everything for granted.

For example, as it has been amply documented by Scholars such as Boserup (1970), Mascia Lees (1984), in the case of Modern Agricultural Experts, and the modern agricultural practices, and equipment they introduce and promote in the region, they are often ineffective in either changing or improving the economic and physical conditions of female farmers. More often, than not, it is the male framers who benefit from these modern agricultural machinery and equipment because the social, physical and financial situations of the female farmers are not, it seems, generally taken into consideration, by the Agricultural Experts who design and manufacture them. Maybe they are unaware or they quite simply ignore the fact that a lot of the farmers in Africa and a lot of developing countries are women. You see, most of these Agricultural Experts who design and manufacture these modern agricultural machineries are for the most part, males and Europeans and Americans for that matter.

Thus, a lot of the time, the cost of the modern agricultural equipment and machinery imported from European and American countries tend to be prohibitive to most female farmers and sometimes, even to some male farmers as the ecology in Africa is not taken into account. The female farmers do not just have the financial resources to be able to afford them. Also, sometimes, the machinery and equipment are just too heavy for a lot of these women to operate conveniently. They just don't just have the physical strength to do so. When it comes to land ownerships, we find that most of the land is owned by men in traditional societies even though it is women who do most of the farming. To make matters worse, when women produce all the food stuff, there are no infrastructure to enable these women earn a good living from their work. For instance, there is a lack of farm to market roads to take their food products and sell at the markets; and since they don't have good storage facilities for this food stuff, most of their produce end up in garbage bins; they simply get bad. It is such a waste of time and energy. Little wonder the majority of poverty stricken people today in Africa are women, especially this "group" of women. It is about time these women organize in cooperatives and start helping themselves rather than counting on governments that have "more important" things to take care of; or on a public that can barely hold its own considering the terrible economic climate in most of these African countries. So women have got to create these organizations so as to make their food producing role not only highly regarded as it is beginning to be the case today but also financially rewarding.

In fact, Dr. Yonkeu felt, the project she would be working on with Professor Edwards was very timely indeed, considering the critical problem of poverty and starvation a lot of African countries now face. This, she hoped, would draw some attention to the plight of African female farmers who produce most of the food on the continent; which may in turn, bring about some positive socio-economic and cultural changes on their behalf. In fact, she thought, it was about time this happened. It was long overdue. She became so excited and she could not just wait to actually start working on the project.

During her discussion with Professor Edwards, she felt so much at home. In fact, it was just as if she had known him for a very long time. So far, all the people she had met were really nice people, she thought. She hoped the trend would continue like that.

After having signed up for various courses, and having finished with all the academic formalities, Dr. Yonkeu decided to start looking for accommodation, preferably, some place near the University Campus. That would just be perfect, she thought. She went and bought some of the local Newspapers, and she also picked up some of the most recent School Newspapers. It may sound a little farfetched, but some of the School Newspapers seem more informative than some of the National Newspapers in some parts of the world. She then went to the School Cafeteria, bought a cup of tea, and took it to one of the tables where she sat down. She would be looking for 'Ads' for apartments and rooms to let while sipping down her tea, she thought.

She quickly glanced through the papers for some news; and then she started going through the advertisement section very carefully. Some of the advertisements were so funny that she could not help chuckling, and drew a few eyes on her. Fancy someone putting an 'Ad' in the papers for a Marilyn Monroe or Dolly Parton look alike to accompany him to an all-night party! Dr. Yonkeu found that so funny. Where on earth, she wondered was one going to find ladies who looked either like Marilyn Monroe or Dolly Parton? These women are so unique. She continued looking through the 'Ads'; and she actually did take down a couple of phone numbers by the time she was through with all the papers. She then went to a nearby phone booth and called up a couple of those numbers and the landladies were all ever so anxious to have her come over to see if she would like the rooms they had available for rent. Dr. Yonkeu was so excited. Some of those places were just a couple of minutes ride by bus from the University campus.

She went to a couple of those places not knowing what was awaiting her there. She had heard of racism, but she had never encountered outright racism in her life. This was going to be her first real encounter with racism and it was going to remain with her for the rest of life. She went to a couple of those houses where they had rooms to let. Whenever she went and rang the door-bells of these houses, the landladies would peep through the peepholes, and as soon as they saw a Black face, they would not even bother to open the door. They would just simply ask her what she wanted. Dr. Yonkeu would explain to them that she saw their advertisements in the papers for rooms to let; and that, she had just called them up and they had asked her to come over to see if she liked the rooms. The Landladies would just cut Dr. Yonkeu short and they would tell her that the rooms had just been taken. Dr. Yonkeu would try to explain to them that she had just called a couple of minutes ago; and that the landladies had assured her that the rooms were still available, but the landladies were adamant. They just kept on insisting that they were sorry, but that the rooms had just been taken a few minutes before Dr. Yonkeu had arrived.

Dr. Yonkeu could not believe what she was hearing. She was astounded. Just a few minutes earlier, she thought, those very ladies had been ever so polite to her on the phone and they had even suggested over the phone that she should come and see if she would like the rooms they had to let out. And now the very ladies would not even have the decency to open their doors before talking to her, as if she was a thief or she had some contagious disease. Unbelievable!, she thought. She felt so sad and so frustrated. She wondered how blackness had become a contagious disease.

Just as these thoughts were going through her mind, it suddenly dawned on her that some people in the United States were still as racist as ever in spite of all the laws against racism. She stood for a while and looked around her. All the houses in the areas were well kept and the lawns were all clean-cut with beautiful flowers everywhere. Everybody she saw walking around was whites and they stirred at her with such bewilderment. Then it suddenly dawned on her that she was really in a white neighbourhood. So these things she had only read about in books in her Sociology classes were really true in real life, she thought. There were indeed black and white neighbourhoods! It was as if she was in a trance, the 'Great Revelation' as she had read in the Bible. She was indeed experiencing the other side of the great country, the United States of America, the dirty side, so to speak.

Remember, during all her years at the University of orange, Dr. Yonkeu had lived on the University campus; a very sheltered life indeed. She never really got to experience life in the real America, the one off campus. Only once in a while was she whisked in a car from her flat on campus to a friend's house off campus; and after some time, she was brought back to the University Campus. How could she have ever encountered such outright racism? Her chances of ever having such an encounter were very slim indeed, one in a million, one would say.

In fact, the nearest she had indeed come to experiencing such outright racism was in books mainly; and when she had heard about some racist remarks some white folks used on black folks; such as some whites referring to blacks as 'black sambos'; "darky", "soap dodgers", "niggers" and the lot. Other times, it was in the movies, when occasionally, some movies had been made on the subject of racism; such as the famous movie Sydney Poitier starred in called, 'Guess who is coming to dinner'. In fact she had thought it was all acting, an exaggeration, when she did see that movie. She never thought some people were still so racist in the United States. Moreover, never had she been, let alone imagine she could actually be an actual victim of racism, be it verbal or otherwise. Now it was really happening to her. At the rate in which things were going, she seriously wondered if she was ever going to find housing off the University campus. She felt absolutely so sad and disappointed about it all. What a pity! It is amazing how after all these years of living in the same country with Blacks, some Whites remain as racist as ever she thought. It's a shame that a great country such as the United States with so much good in it could be so marred by racism, one of the worst ills in the world that had ruined so many lives in the past, especially during the days of slavery and colonialism; and continues to destroy many lives in many European countries. She felt so bad and dejected. This was the other side of her 'dream land', the land that had so far been already so good, so marvellous to her in so many other ways, Dr. Yonkeu thought. She earnestly hoped and prayed that someday, racism would be wiped out of this great country, and why not the face of the earth? Only then, she thought, would the United States really assert itself as truly the greatest country in the world.

It suddenly occurred to her that she must leave that neighbourhood before it got dark. She had read in books how Black people were attacked and even shut when they were seen in White neighbourhoods, especially at nights. She was afraid that she could also be a victim of such an attack. She had already had one bitter experience, she thought, and it would be too much for her if that too happened to her on the same day. She then walked as fast as she could to the nearest bus stop. She then took a bus back to the university campus. It was already dinner time when she arrived on the university campus. She just went straight to the School Restaurant, bought some dinner, ate a little and then slowly walked back to her room in the dormitory. All along the way to the dormitory her mind kept on going back to the incident at the White neighbourhood. At night, she could hardly sleep. She kept having nightmares of the incident. She would see the white lady time and again peeping through the peephole on the door and saying, 'the room had already been let out; and she Dr. Yonkeu, standing there helplessly, wondering where on earth she went wrong. She would then wake up sweating. It was so terrible.

In any case, classes would soon begin in earnest, and it was very necessary that Dr. Yonkeu found somewhere to stay before then. The following day, Dr. Yonkeu got up early in the morning, took her usual shower, got dressed and went and bought some more local Newspapers which she took with her to the restaurant. She would be looking for the 'room to let' 'Ads' while she ate her breakfast, she said. She did indeed find a couple of 'Ads' for rooms and flats for rent. She took down the phone numbers and the addresses for the various places.

However, this time, an idea suddenly came to her mind. She would look for a white girl, pay her bus fare and ask her to go and pretend as though she was the one who wanted to rent the room or flat. After she had negotiated with the Landlady or Landlord and agreed on everything, she would then come and tell Dr. Yonkeu, who would be hiding not too far away, about two blocks away. After a little while, she would then go back and tell the Landlady/ Landlord that something had just come up, and she would no longer be able to take the room. A few minutes later, when she must have left the house, Dr. Yonkeu would then go to the very Landlady/Landlord and ask if he/she could rent the room to her? If the Landlady/Landlord then refused to rent the room to her, she would then be convinced that it was really her skin colour that was really the problem; and not that someone else had just taken the room. She would then decide on her next move. Who knows, maybe she and her white friend may even tumble on a Landlady or Landlord who did not care about what one's skin colour was, provided that one would be a good tenant. At the back of her mind, she also hoped that being with her White friend would enable her find a place quicker.

Dr. Yonkeu found a White girl who was willing to go along with her plan. Linda was a beautiful, tall and elegant American girl, of around twenty years of age with chestnut brown hair cut real short and striking blue eyes. She was a very nice and easy-going girl, whom as Dr. Yonkeu found out, couldn't care less about what skin colour people had. She was nice and friendly to everybody who was nice to her, irrespective of one's skin colour. Dr. Yonkeu and Linda agreed on the houses to go to, where they had rooms to let. They then took a bus to the neighbourhood. Linda went up to the first house and rang the doorbell. A White lady came, peeped through the peephole and saw Linda. She then quickly opened the door. Meanwhile, Dr. Yonkeu was two blocks away watching. 'Wow!' she whispered. 'The Landlady actually opened her door. That's something.' Linda told the Landlady that she was the one who just called on the telephone a while ago, and that the Landlady had asked her to come over and take a look at the room she was renting out. The Landlady was ever so nice, and she even invited Linda inside the house to take a look at the room. Before long, everything was settled between the landlady and Linda, and Linda left. After some time had elapsed, Linda went back to the very Landlady and told her she could not take the room as planned because something serious had just come up which made it impossible for her to rent the room. The landlady was disappointed, but she said that was all right. She said she hoped Linda would have her problem settled soon enough. Linda then left once again.

After some time had passed, Dr. Yonkeu went to the very house and rang the doorbell. The Landlady peeped through the peephole and when she saw a Black face, she did not even bother to open the door. She simply asked Dr. Yonkeu what she wanted. Dr. Yonkeu said she had come for the room the Landlady was letting out. The landlady just told her that she was very sorry, but that the room had just been taken. Dr. Yonkeu just shook her head, and sighed. Feeling so disappointed, sad and helpless, she slowly walked away contemplatively. She joined Linda who was watching two blocks away a few minutes later. Linda and Dr. Yonkeu were now convinced that racism was alive and well in the United States of America. Linda was very angry. She said Dr. Yonkeu could contact a lawyer and take the Landlady to court for there were laws against such acts of discrimination. Dr. Yonkeu just said it was a shame that the Landlady was such a racist. However she said she was not quite prepared to start fighting in court as yet. She said she only hoped that with time, such ladies would come to realize their ignorance and do something positive about it. In every society, Dr. Yonkeu went on, there will always be 'good' and 'bad' people, and that the Landlady just happened to be one of those 'bad' or rather, ignorant ones. All one could do, she said, was to pray that with time, there would be less and less of such people in the United States or better still, in the world.

As fate would have it, though Linda told Dr. Yonkeu that, it just occurred to her that, a friend of hers, a white girl lived in an apartment building just a few minutes' walk away from the University Campus. She said she was sure there were a couple of studios still available in the building. However, she said she would ring up her friend in the evening just to make sure there were still some vacant studios in the building. If there was one, she said she would contact Dr. Yonkeu and both of them would go and see the landlord early the following morning. Linda and Dr. Yonkeu caught a bus back to the University Campus. They ate dinner together at the School Restaurant; and after that, they wished each other goodnight as they both parted and went off to their respective dormitories.

At night, Dr. Yonkeu kept praying that there would be a vacant studio at the apartment building where Linda's friend lived. She could not wait for daybreak. As soon as it was daylight, she got up, rushed to the shower, took a quick shower, got dressed and walked to the School Restaurant where Linda had said she would meet her. Linda was on time. However, she said she could not get hold of her friend the night before, but that it did not matter. They would both just go to the apartment building and find out if they still had studios to rent. They both ate their breakfast and after that, they took a walk to the Apartment building. The landlord, a huge, dark haired, white guy was at his office. They knocked on his door and he asked them to come in. They both walked into his office. They asked the Landlord if there was any vacant apartment in the building. The landlord said all his two bed roomed apartments had been taken, thinking of course that it was Linda and Dr. Yonkeu who wanted to share an apartment. You see, it is a very common practice in the United States for students to share apartments. That makes apartments affordable. To rent an apartment by oneself is a very expensive business.

However, the Landlord said there was a vacant studio if they were interested? Oh! You won't believe it, but Dr. Yonkeu's face was all smiles the moment the Landlord said that. Even Linda's face lit up. They asked if they could take a look at it. The

Landlord led the way upstairs? It was on the second floor. He opened the door, and Dr. Yonkeu and Linda walked in. It was just perfect. The studio had just been recently renovated and everything seemed to be in good working order. Dr. Yonkeu and Linda walked out, and they accompanied the landlord to his office. They negotiated for the rents, and Dr. Yonkeu and Linda walked out of the office so delighted. They hugged each other so many times, and Linda promised to help Dr. Yonkeu move in the following day.

The following morning, Dr. Yonkeu and her friend Linda gathered her little belongings, called a cab and drove off to Dr. Yonkeu's new place of residence. They parked in her things, sat down and chatted for a while. At lunch time, they both decided to celebrate at a nearby Mc Donald's, just a couple of blocks away from Dr. Yonkeu's apartment. They each had a Big Mac, a large Coke and some French fries. They were both so happy. Dr. Yonkeu was so very grateful to Linda for having been so helpful to her. She even ran out of words to really express how grateful she was to Linda. On the other hand, Linda was so happy for Dr. Yonkeu and wished her a very pleasant stay in the United States. Linda gave Dr. Yonkeu her telephone number and told her to call whenever she needed help or whenever she felt like having a chat. Dr. Yonkeu was so overwhelmed by Linda's kindness. This was somebody she had barely known, and see how kind she had been to her, Dr. Yonkeu thought. Some tears of appreciation rolled down her cheeks as she waved goodbye to Linda who was then walking off to the University Campus. Dr. Yonkeu then walked back to her new studio apartment.

In about a week's time, classes began in earnest. Dr. Yonkeu quickly realized that the Doctorate Program was not going to be as anything she had done so far. The Doctorate Degree entailed a great deal of work. One had to read a lot and write a lot of essays. A good deal of research was also one of the key elements in a Doctorate Program. Dr. Yonkeu's schedule was so tight that she barely had time for her meals. It made no difference to her whether it was a weekend or a weekday. When she was not busy doing her class work, she was busy doing her on campus job-research for Professor Edwards. She seemed to be working round the clock. She however did not mind it too much because this tremendously broadened her scope of thought and imagination, and of course, her knowledge. She took nothing for granted. She learnt to analyse things more logically. In all, it was a great learning experience for her.

She did quite well in most of her courses, except for her Statistics course which was once again, giving her some problems. However, this time, she got a lot of help from other students who were good at Statistics, especially from Kenny. Kenny was a kind Jewish American with dark brownish hair and a somewhat protruded stomach from the beer he usually drank. He was always ready to help Dr. Yonkeu whenever she had problems with her Statistics homework.

One incident stands out in Dr. Yonkeu's mind. One afternoon just immediately after her Statistics class, Dr. Yonkeu had decided to spend only part of the afternoon to do her Statistics homework. She thought she had mastered that particular branch of Statistics. She had decided she would finish up with that particular assignment and move on to something else. She had started working on the homework when just after a few steps; she realized she could not go on with it. She was stuck in the middle of the Statistics problem. She felt so sad and so silly at the same time. They had just come from class where they had been taught how to solve a similar problem, she thought, and there she was, a couple of minutes later unable to solve a simple problem. She felt so terrible with herself and she started wondering as to whether she was even capable of doing a Doctorate Degree after all. She could see all her dreams crumbling right in front of her eyes. At that moment, she just burst out crying. She could not understand how she could be trying so hard but nothing seemed to be forthcoming.

As she was sobbing, Kenny walked into the Study Room from nowhere. He heard Dr. Yonkeu sobbing, and he immediately walked over to where she was sitting and asked her what the matter was? Dr. Yonkeu explained to him that she could not believe she could not solve a simple Statistics problem after having just come from a Statistics class where a similar problem had been solved. Kenny, being the patient and understanding person that he was, told Dr. Yonkeu not to cry anymore. He tried consoling Dr. Yonkeu that she may find it hard to believe, but that occasionally, even he himself does run into a similar problem. He said in the future whenever Dr. Yonkeu had such a problem, she should just stop doing whatever she was doing, relax a little and then go back to the problem. He said Dr. Yonkeu should then, patiently take one step at a time and try to solve the problem. He said one's brains need to relax time and again. Human brains, he said are not like machines. Even machines, he went on, do get tired time and again, for example, when they break down. He told Dr. Yonkeu not to feel bad about it all, for a lot of people do run into similar problems from time to time. He then sat down beside her and patiently went step by step, showing her how to solve the problem. He then allowed Dr. Yonkeu to solve the remaining problem on her own. She did quite well. She then realized that what Kenny had said was really right. One's brains really did need some time to rest before they could resume functioning normally again. From that day onwards, she also learnt to be patient with whatever she was doing, especially when she was doing her Statistics homework.

As time went by, she began to get used to her workload. She also really enjoyed doing research on Professor Edwards' project. She realized what major strides women in the United States had made in asserting their rights in mainstream America relative to the old days. There was a lot more though to be done in this area, but there was hope in the air given the sort of Democracy that exists in the United States. Women would at least, always have the right to demand their total emancipation which hopefully would come with time. So too, she hoped, would be the case with other minority groups such as African Americans, Native Americans, Hispanics and other such groups.

As far as her social life went, Dr. Yonkeu got to meet a lot of nice people, and she made a lot of friends at school. One of her very good friends was Susan, an Irish American lady in her early sixties with a heart of gold, so kind; who was also in the Doctorate Program. Susan did introduce Dr. Yonkeu to her husband Ray and her daughter, Emily; and with time, they became just like one big family. As a matter of fact, Dr. Yonkeu often spent New Year's Day with them and their two friends, Steve and Jane. They also would often invite Dr. Yonkeu for thanksgiving and to summer cook-outs and house parties.

Sometimes, they would take her along to some of those exclusive restaurants where only those who belong to a particular club, or 'la crème de la crème' of Olive Society so to speak, would go to for a meal time and again. Not to mention, the theatre, musicals and Jazz concerts they did take her to.

It was a real pleasure and honour for Dr. Yonkeu; and believe you me, she was ever so appreciative of it all.

Holidays in the United States generally, could be very lonely for foreign students; and as such, Susan and Ray's invitation to Dr. Yonkeu during most of these holidays, especially on New Year's Day, made all the difference in the world to her. She really looked forward to those getogethers at Susan and Ray's home. It was often great fun. It usually started off with a swim at their beautiful swimming pool which overlooked a screen porch where one could relax on one of those outdoor chairs either reading a newspaper or a good novel. After that, they would eat some really delicious shrimps cooked over a charcoal grill, some garlic bread and some vegetable salad, one of Ray's specialties; while of course, sipping down some good American wine or drinking some of the good old 'English Bitters', that is English beer Susan and Ray always brought along with them from their yearly summer vacations in 'good old England'. They usually ended up with some really delicious cheese cake, Dr. Yonkeu's favourite, for desert.

After everybody was stuffed so much so that they could hardly walk, they would then retire to the basement where Ray had a projector for showing slides. They would then watch the various slides Ray always took during some of those his exotic vacations around the world. Dr. Yonkeu particularly enjoyed some of the slides Ray had taken when he was once vacationing at Alaska. The slides were indeed beautiful. They showed the natural beauty of Alaska; all the beautiful birds and animals in their natural habitats, the wonderful hills standing tall and majestic, the rugged valleys daring you to come down if you have the guts to do so, and the sweet humming rivers. You could almost hear the sweet and gentle melodies coming from them. In all, it was such breath-taking scenery.

By the time they were through watching the slides, they would be all exhausted but very delighted indeed, and ready to leave for their various houses. Susan of course, always remembered to park a bag with all the goodies, cakes, cookies and so on, for each person to take along with them. How absolutely kind and thoughtful, Dr. Yonkeu would say to herself. Really, Susan and Ray were both like parents as well as friends to Dr. Yonkeu. She would never forget all the wonderful times she spent with them. They are really her cherished friends.

Dr. Yonkeu was also beginning to enjoy her classes so much so that, she actually looked forward to attending each and every one of them. She was also beginning to fully participate in some of the heated debates on some of the burning social issues of the time that took place in some of her classes. Mind you, at first, she was somewhat shy about expressing her feelings on certain issues but with time, she could not just wait to be called upon to say something or give her opinion on some of the issues she felt so strongly about. She found debates so stimulating, to the extent that, sometimes in class, she would actually imagine she was on the 'Phil Donahue Show' talking out her mind. You see, the 'Phil Donahue Show' was one of her favourite talk shows. In fact, as a rule, she made sure she never missed any of the talk show, the David Letterman Show, and most of all, the Oprah Winfrey Show. She did very well in most of her courses in spite of the material difficulties she was faced with time and again.

Even with her on campus job, she found that she still had a lot of difficulties making ends meet. It seemed as if as years progressed, books became more and more voluminous and more expensive too so much so that, there came a time when Dr. Yonkeu could not afford to buy all the required books for her various courses. Although the library was fully stocked with all kinds of books, she usually did not always have the time to be able to be at the Library all day long. Sometimes, she would rather stay at home and do her studies, especially on Sundays. So it was always better to own some of the essential books in her various courses. However, it was not always possible to buy all the books because of her limited finances. Nevertheless, thanks to some of her kind friends, she always made it through each semester;

Betty especially, a very kind-hearted beautiful; shapely, and somewhat petite German-American Lady with long flowing blonde hair, was very helpful to Dr. Yonkeu as far as books went. Another Anglo-American, Bruce, whom as she later found out was one of the top students in the Doctorate Program, was also very helpful to Dr. Yonkeu in obtaining certain vital books. At first, when Dr. Yonkeu first met Bruce, she thought he was one of those 'red-necked' White Americans who couldn't care less about Blacks. He was a huge auburn-haired man and he spoke with a distinct Southern accent. Dr. Yonkeu had heard so much about racism in the South, and when she heard Bruce speak in that Southern accent, she let her imagination take the best of her, by thinking that Bruce must be one of those Southern 'blueblood' Whites who only dealt with Blacks when it was absolutely necessary for them to do so; and that under no circumstances would they want to socialize with Blacks. However, Dr. Yonkeu was wrong. Bruce happened to be one of those Southern Whites who took people for what they are irrespective of one's skin colour; a true humanist indeed. As a matter of fact, Betty, Bruce and Dr. Yonkeu went to those beer parties time and again in Olive city, being the beer city of the USA. It was always such fun drinking beer together.

Dr. Yonkeu would always remember Bruce and Betty for their kind gestures to her, especially when she was preparing for her Comprehensive Examination. This Examination was very crucial since one had to pass it, or else, one would be automatically dropped from the Doctorate program. Dr. Yonkeu knew she had to give it her all and study real hard for the Examination. It was for her, 'a do or die' situation. She was well aware of the fact that, all the past three years she had spent on the program so far, would have been wasted if she failed the Comprehensive examination and was kicked out of the Doctorate program. In fact, the Examination determined whether one was to go on and write one's Dissertation or not. In a way, as the saying goes, it sure 'separated the men from the boys or the women from the girls' as she would like to put it. As such, Dr. Yonkeu knew she had to do a lot of reading if she was to make it in the end. To be able to do this, she needed all the necessary books in all her courses, but she did not have enough money to buy all the books.

She started looking for the books she could not buy at the Library. It was a very tiring and frustrating task especially when she was unable to find the books she needed at the Library.

One day, as she was going to the Library, she met Bruce and Betty on the way. They asked her how she was preparing for her Comprehensive Examination. Before she could even say anything, Bruce and Betty said if she needed books and articles, they could lend her some of the main books and articles in all the main courses. They said those particular books and articles had been very helpful to them when they did the Comprehensive Examination. Dr. Yonkeu was so overwhelmed with emotions that tears filled her eyes. She however, managed to hold them back; and told Bruce and Betty that, she would indeed really appreciate it if they could lend her all the necessary books and articles. They agreed and they even promised to deliver the books at Dr. Yonkeu's apartment the following morning. How kind! Dr. Yonkeu thought. She just could not believe her luck. It was a real miracle to her. Who says miracles don't happen anymore? She thought.

The following morning, as Bruce and Betty had promised, they were at Dr. Yonkeu's apartment with boxes of books and articles. She was overwhelmed with joy. Dr. Yonkeu could hardly find words to express how thankful she was to Bruce and Betty. She was ever so moved by their kindness to her. She could hardly believe her eyes. She was visibly happy with tears of joy and appreciation flowing down her cheeks. She held Bruce and Betty in one big embrace and thanked them for being so kind to her. She told them she would forever be indebted to them. They in turn, told her not to worry, and that whenever she needed any more help, she would just let them know. They then left and drove off to the University Campus.

Dr. Yonkeu was so pleased. She could not believe her luck so far in this her 'dream country', the United States, it seemed as though whenever she found herself in difficulties some Good Samaritan always came to her rescue. She was forever grateful to these kind people, and to God who sent them to her whenever she was in such difficulties. She resolved to study real hard and pass her Comprehensive after all the help she had received, especially from Bruce and Betty. That, she thought, would also make them Bruce and Betty, happy.

Her Comprehensive Examination had now started. She worked round the clock. Her hard work did indeed pay off in the end, when her results came out. She made it. She was so pleased; and of course, she owed much of her success to Bruce and Betty. Bruce, Betty and Dr. Yonkeu did go to the bar that night and celebrated with a couple of beers. Dr. Yonkeu once again told Bruce and Betty how she would be forever grateful to them for being so kind and helpful to her when she was most in need of help.

As of that time, Dr. Yonkeu started spending most of her time, working on her Dissertation. She had already collected a great deal of information on the subject. She was now also working in close collaboration with her Academic adviser, the Kenyan, professor mark, who also happened to be very knowledgeable on the subject of 'African Women and the Political Economy'. His ideas were very helpful and he also gave Dr. Yonkeu many books and articles on the subject. In fact, he always encouraged Dr. Yonkeu to work even harder at those times when she felt like giving it all up. Dr. Yonkeu will always cherish the help she got from him.

Occasionally, Professor Mark would have getogethers at his house and he would invite Dr. Yonkeu, a lot of Africans on and off Campus and many of his American friends. Dr. Yonkeu got to meet a lot of Africans that way and she made a lot of friends at these getogethers. One of the friends Dr. Yonkeu made at one of these getogethers was an African American lady Vicky. Vicky was a stunningly pretty, average height African American Lady. She had a smooth chess nut complexion and big sexy eyes. In fact, Dr. Yonkeu and Vicky got to be so close that they were almost like blood sisters. She learnt a lot more about African Americans from Vicky. Dr. Yonkeu did find out that Vicky was one of eight children. She also happened to be the only female who was married out of the five females in the family. The other four were however, single parents. They all had children with various men who either had left town, or who were in town, but could not possibly help much in raising the kids due to financial constraints. They were either unemployed or worked at a low paying job. Vicky's father, Dr. Yonkeu did find out, died when Vicky was about twelve years old. So the responsibility of bringing up eight children had solely been that of Vicky's mother. She did manage to raise all her children on her minimal income, working mainly as a cleaning lady in some of the offices downtown. Talk of 'superwomen'; she was indeed a real 'super woman', in every sense of the word; raising kids, handling her job, and managing the household, all single-handedly. What a lady!

In spite of everything, Vicky's mother looked real young and still pretty for her age. She was a very cheerful lady, kind and welcoming, and she always made sure she shared the tittle she had with her friends in need, whenever possible. Occasionally, she would invite Dr. Yonkeu over to her house, for some 'soul food' as she called it. Gee, did she cook well. Dr. Yonkeu did thoroughly enjoy those meals, especially when she did make some corn bread, baked chicken and some greens. She indeed was a very good cook. This reminded her of her mother in Cameroon who was also such a good cook. Dr. Yonkeu also did notice that, although they lived a relatively simple and sometimes, difficult life, in terms of finances, there was plenty of love and happiness in the family. Everybody seemed to care deeply for everybody's well-being. They all felt so bad whenever any of them had some sort of problem, or was in some financial difficulties. They would all rally to that person's aid, by contributing the little money each of them had to help out. They were indeed wonderful people.

Dr. Yonkeu did ask Vicky why many of her sisters were not married, but they all had children? She also asked Vicky why it was that most of the children's fathers were not at least helping out financially with the children's up-keep. Vicky said it was because a lot of young African American men never still make it at College, whereby they could graduate and be able to secure good paying jobs. Most of the men, she said, end up either on the dole, or doing some low paying jobs. The money they made was not even enough to take care of their own needs. She said that, racism, especially in the school system did play a crucial role in a lot of the problems the men were faced with. Some of the men end up as drug pushers because, she said, it was easy to make quick and sometimes big money doing it. Sooner or later, though, they get busted and sent to jail. Other times, she said, the men themselves get hooked on the drugs and end up as mental cases unable to function properly in society. She said the drug problem had become a very serious problem in the United States.

She also said that many African American men, do not find it financially wise to marry the mothers of their children because whenever they did get married to the women, the latter would no longer be eligible to receive, (mind you, often as a last resort, being unable to find a decent good-paying job), the often minimal allowances the States gives to mothers with dependent children. As such, the financial responsibility of raising the kids would then solely rest on, the husband; and if the husband was unemployed, or was making very little money, there would be no way he could possibly take care of his family. So most of the time, as hard a decision as this may be for these men, they end up with no other choice, than that of not marrying the mothers of their children. She said this was a very sad thing since it did make the realization of the concept of nuclear family-'husband, wife, children/child almost impossible in the African American Community. She said that, she hoped that something would be done in the very near future to do away with these socio-economic ills currently plaguing the African American Community.

Vicky and Dr. Yonkeu spent most of the summer vacations together. Usually, they would pack a picnic basket and go to the lake front where there was always some event going on there, among which was the famous 'Summer Fest' an event that every Olivian and even people outside the State of Olive always looked forward to during the summer months.

The opening ceremonies of the 'Summer Fest' were usually fantastic and spectacular. There was always so much pomp and pageantry. It was usually a great day for the Mayor of Olive in particular and other city Dignitaries. There was usually the grand march down the Grand Avenue, led by the various School Bands and Majorettes, all dressed in their splendid outfits. Then came the Victorian-looking or vintage cars- preceded by the Mayor and his wife, gracefully waving to crowds as they drove past them. They were followed by the horse-drawn carts with people in them dressed as they did in the old days, in those beautiful and elegant vintage clothes, at least from what one saw in the movies. It sure was reminiscent of that era of carriages and graceful living. This was followed by a flotilla of floats representing each and every major ethnic group in the city of Olive. This was where one saw real creativity. For example, there was the African American float. It was usually a replica depicting life in a typical African village. For example, one could see women cooking food in a three stoned fire-place, girls fetching water in little calabashes from the stream, little girls and boys, some half-naked, running around playing with each other, chickens and goats running about and a lot more. It all looked so real. There were a lot of other floats representing one thing or another.

The opening ceremonies often did culminate with brilliant fireworks in the evening period at the lake front. It was usually the highlight of the 'summer fest' and it was ever so beautiful, so virtually stunning, and so festive, with the Mayor declaring the Summer Festivals officially open. In all, it was usually one of the most colourful events and one of those rare occasions that brought people of all races and all ethnic and cultural backgrounds the old and the young together. One only wished it could be like that forever-true solidarity of the human race; where these wonderful differences in colour and culture among people are considered to be more enriching than threatening.

After the opening ceremonies, the lake front is often packed to capacity with the crowds of people enjoying the different ethnic foods and activities of the summer festival. It was really a fantastic event. Most ethnic groups that made up the Olive Community – German American, Jewish Americans, African Americans, Native Americans, Polish Americans, Italian Americans, Spanish Americans, would usually dress in their cultural gear, and they would both display and sell their ethnic foods or art works. There were also a lot of traditional dance groups, and some famous Jazz, Rock, Pop, and Soul music groups. In all, it was a really fun event. Those were some of the times Dr. Yonkeu really enjoyed during her stay at Olive city.

Summer months generally in Olive, were usually jammed parked with cultural activities. One of the other memorable events was the 'Juneteenth' day. This was a day that African Americans had set aside to commemorate the day slavery was abolished. Dr. Yonkeu really enjoyed this day because most of the activities displayed – dances, foods, art works etc. were so African in nature. This made her feel so much at home in such a faraway country.

There was also the German Festival. During those few days, the Germanic-Americans came out in full gear of their Germanic heritage. They would dance just as they did in the old country; and of course, there would be plenty of beer (Olive being the beer capital of America) and they would eat a lot 'Bratwurst' (sort of sausage like) which Dr. Yonkeu really liked. Dr. Yonkeu absolutely enjoyed every minute of these summer festivals. She wished the summers would never come to an end, but sooner or later, reality does hit, when summer is all over and it is back to winter time once again. And you better believe it; the winters in Olive are usually terribly cold. There are usually the huge piles of snow everywhere and the cold winds blowing from Chicago usually made life almost unbearable. It was one of those rare things that Dr. Yonkeu never did get used to during her entire stay at Olive. It just proved to be too overbearing for her.

In any case, School had started once again and Dr. Yonkeu was by then doing some finishing touches on her Dissertation. It had turned out to be a very huge Dissertation and things seemed to be moving on in the right direction. By the end of the academic year, everything was in order. She had finished and she had successfully defended her Dissertation. All seemed to have gone so well. She had made it. She was only waiting for graduation day, that great day when she would wear her cap and gown, proudly walk down the aisle and receive her Doctorate Diploma from the hands of nobody else but the Chancellor of the University. How Great!

She could hardly believe it. Five years ago, she could only dream of a Doctorate Degree. Now it was only two days to graduation day, she thought. It all sounded too good to be true, but it was really true. America, she thought, had really been good to her. It's true she did have some ups and downs, but all things considered, she had made it. 'All is well', she thought, 'that ends well.' Dreams, she said, really did come true in this great country. Look at her, a simple girl who had come to the United States a couple of years back, with virtually nothing, but a dream to one day have her Doctorate Degree. Now that dream had really come true. 'God bless America', she whispered with such deep feelings of gratitude and love. Graduation day did come; and it was amazing how all her friends, Whites and Blacks all did turn up to cheer her as she walked down the aisle and received her Diploma from the Chancellor of the University. She was so happy, and for the first time, she felt like patting herself on the back and saying 'yes girl, you really did it'. Her friends had organized a surprise party for Dr. Yonkeu. As soon as the graduation ceremony was over Bruce and Betty came up to her, and after a lot of hugging and hand shaking, they said she should come along with them so that they could take her back to her apartment. As they drove off, Dr. Yonkeu noticed that they were going to some other direction, not the one leading to her apartment. She did not think much of it anyway. She thought maybe they had to pick up something someplace before taking her back to her apartment. However, they kept driving on until they arrived at a certain hall. She saw a lot of cars parked all over the place. She wondered what could be going on inside the hall-probably one of those political meetings, she thought. Bruce then told Dr. Yonkeu and Betty to wait a little, while he went to the hall to see if somebody he was looking for was there. He walked into the hall, and as soon as the crowd saw him, they all rushed out shouting, 'congratulations, Dr. Yonkeu! Congratulations!' They came to the car and pulled out Dr. Yonkeu and they took her to the hall. Boy! It was amazing, the hall was so well decorated with signs all over the walls that read, 'congratulations Dr. Yonkeu; congratulations for a job well done! Dr. Yonkeu could not believe it. All her friends were there, even her Adviser and Professor Edwards, the History Professor she used to work for. She was so overwhelmed with joy so much so that for a while, tears of joy just rolled down her cheeks uncontrollably. She could not hold back the tears, no matter how hard she did try. Her emotions were so intense. There was plenty of booze and enough food for everybody. It was one of those very pleasant surprises that would live with Dr. Yonkeu for the rest of her life. She had never felt so happy before, not even when she was at home in Cameroon. America would have a special place in her heart as long as she lived, not to mention all her wonderful friends who really helped in one way or another to make her dreams come true. It turned out to be a wonderful party. People danced, drank and ate until it was about four in the morning. Dr. Yonkeu will always live to remember that day.

A few weeks later she started preparing for her return back to Cameroon. She had a lot of parking to do. She did not realize she had collected so much stuff during her stay in the United States until she actually started parking. She however managed to do all her parking and she was now only waiting for the day of her departure. She started having flashbacks on her life in the United States. She thought of all her experiences, both the good ones and the bad ones, but mostly the good ones of course for the latter sure did overshadow the former by far. She thought of all the wonderful people who had been so good to her and had helped her through those impossible times. Increasingly, she came to the realization that, those people were more than family to her. No extended family in Cameroon, she thought, would ever be as dear to her as the one in the United States. She said there was no way she could ever be able to pay back these people. It is true, she thought; the United States was not a perfect country as she used to think back in Cameroon, but it was by far the best in many ways as far as she was concerned. It was a country with a lot going for it, and a lot of hope for even better things to come.

At long last, it was the day of her departure. It was all surreal. Her friends, Susan and Ray, came very early in the morning and gave her a ride to Olive International Airport. When they arrived at the Airport, many of her friends were already there waiting to bid her farewell. When she saw them, she did no longer feel like boarding the plane anymore. She thought of simply how good these friends had been to her, and she indeed wondered if she could really cope with life in Cameroon without them. She would really miss them, she thought. However, it was soon time for her to really board the plane. She then kissed all of her friends goodbye with plenty of tears rolling down her cheeks. Many of the girls were also crying. It was really an emotional scene. She felt so sad leaving people she had absolutely come to love and cherish. However, that was life, or better still, as the

French would say, 'c'est la vie'. You meet and part; or as the French artist Mireille Mathieu sings in one of her records: on ne vit pas sans se dire adieu". She then went and boarded the plane.

As the plane cruised smoothly in the clear blue skies, she gradually got over the pain of having to part United States; and she became so excited about returning home after all; Cameroon and the city of Douala especially. "Home indeed!, she thought;" where at least one thing was certain- she wouldn't have to put up with racism in the United States anymore; the United States, where being black remains a huge social problem unlike in Cameroon where most people are as black as herself; where she wouldn't have to worry about being a potential suspect of theft and other crimes whenever she found herself in a grocery store or at a shopping mall as in the U.S. where little white old ladies would panic and grab hard on their purses or handbags as she walked past them for fear that she may be a thief or she may attack them, simply because of her black skin colour ; where simple things such as sitting beside Black people on the bus was problematic for some Whites as if blackness would rub onto them. At least, she carried on; she would be going back to Cameroon where the black skin colour is the norm and not a curse. This, she thought to herself, was the one thing she was sure about in Mother Africa, Cameroon, to be precise. Of course, she was well aware of the plethora of heart breaking socio-economic and cultural problems such as the heart breaking poverty problem, awaiting her in Cameroon, but she was damn certain, it would not be the race problem; that dreadful and shameful problem that has so bedevilled this great adoptive country of hers, the United States; and that won't just go away from this marvellous country; that cancer that seem to have eaten so deep into the fabric of the American society; that "albatross" that hangs around the necks of Americans as that of the "Ancient Mariner"; that "magic" word that to a large extent plays an incredibly important role as to whether one makes it in the American society or not; or whether one is accepted in the American society or not.

"Thank God", she said to herself once more, she would not have to put up with that hideous racism anymore; at least not for a very, very long time. That notwithstanding she smiled broadly and said, America had been so damn good to her! But like the adage goes: "East or West, home is best", she chuckled. "I am going back to my roots" she said, as the marvellous reggae singer, the late Lucky Dube sings. Therefore, in spite of everything, she could not wait to be back in Mother Africa, Cameroon and Douala to be precise. In many ways, she really did miss Cameroon, the land of her birth.

CHAPTER SIX

WOES OF WOMANHOOD: Dr. YONKEU BACK IN CAMEROON

At long last, the plane, Swiss Air Flight 121, landed at the Douala International Airport. Dr. Yonkeu took a look at her watch. It was 8pm. Boy, do these Swiss people keep to time. No wonder they are known for making the best watches in the world, she murmured to herself, smiling broadly. She and all other passengers then disembarked the airplane and walked to the airport building. However, with all the numerous checking at the Airport, it took Dr. Yonkeu another couple of hours before she could actually walk out of the Airport; where she met her family who were anxiously waiting to see her. They were ever so happy to be reunited with Dr. Yonkeu once again. It was all kisses, embraces, and plenty of tears and joy all the way. They said they had been worried sick, thinking that Dr. Yonkeu had not arrived as planned; for it took such a long time before she came out of the Airport. But thank God, they said, she was here. That, they said, was all that mattered to them. Dr. Yonkeu was also very happy to be with her family once again, after having not seen them for such a very long time.

However, with all the police, custom and "gendarmerie[15]" checking and delays at the Airport, Dr. Yonkeu realized she was really back in Cameroon, where nothing was done as it should, where everything was complicated and where nothing seemed to be working right. She thought of how she used to fly from one

---

[15] Gendarmerie is part of the forces of law and order in Cameroon.

city to another back in the United States with little or no questions at all being asked. All she did was, pick up her luggage at the luggage claim area whenever she arrived at her destination; and she was off to wherever she was going. Life, she thought, had really been made considerably easy for the people there. From now on, she figured, things were not going to be the same for her anymore. 'How funny', she thought, 'life is. One constantly finds oneself having to adjust to yet ever different situations and environments. It's all so strange. She knew she had to adjust to life in Cameroon, and fast too, if she was going to make it there. Somehow, she got the feeling things were not going to be easy for her in her 'beloved' country. What a feeling! She thought.

However, her family was very pleased to see her after a long time, and Dr. Yonkeu also felt pleased to be home once more. They collected her luggage and they all drove back home. Dr. Yonkeu was so exhausted from the long flight, the jet lag that she could not eat all the wonderful foods that her mother prepared for her. She only ate a piece of chicken, drank some soda and after a brief chat with her parents, she went to bed.

In the night, she kept on dreaming of the United States and the friends she had left behind. It still had not dawned on her that she was now in Cameroon. It would be a while before she actually got used to the idea that she was no longer in the United States; that blessed country, where all seemed possible. Oh! How she already missed it!

The following morning, she got up early, took a long warm bath before she went and joined her parents at the breakfast table. They ate and chatted for a long time about life in the United States and some of the changes that had taken place in Cameroon. For quite a few months, Dr. Yonkeu was trying to settle down. She had sent cards to all her friends in the United States promising each of them that she would write a longer letter as soon as she had settled down. At the moment, she said, she was in the process of trying to get used to her 'new' but 'old' environment.

It took quite some time for Dr. Yonkeu to be well rested, after which, she started compiling her dossiers for the various Government ministries, International and Private organizations to which she was going to apply for employment. She finally got all her Diplomas and Certificates together and mailed them off to the various ministries and Organizations. She was now waiting for their replies. She waited for a very long time but she heard nothing from any of the places she had sent her applications to. This was Dr. Yonkeu's first shock. She could not understand why the Ministries and Organizations to which she had sent her applications to could not at least have the decency to reply to her even if they did not have any vacancies, with one of those: 'I am sorry... letters.' That would have been understandable enough. This sort of a thing, she thought, was unheard of in the United States.

One day, she was chatting with some friends casually when they asked her if she had had any job offers as yet. She told them that it had been quite some time now since she did mail off her dossiers and application letters to various Government Ministries, Private and International Organizations, but that she had not heard a word from any of them. Things, she went on, tend to be very slow here in Cameroon. She wondered aloud what the reason could be for that. Her friends just started laughing. She wondered what it was that was funny about what she had just said. She thought her friends must either be sadists, crazy or simply heartless for laughing at such a serious matter. If anything, she thought, they should feel sorry for her for being without work. Her friends just carried on laughing, until they had thoroughly amused themselves. Then they said sarcastically, 'welcome to Cameroon'; and then, they told Dr. Yonkeu that things were not done in Cameroon that way. They said that, to begin with, she made a fatal mistake by sending her dossiers by mail. They added that, chances are that the dossiers would get missing somewhere at the Post office; or that if at all they were not missing there, they would take a very long time before they would actually reach their various destinations, because generally in Cameroon, mails took a very long time to reach where they had been posted to. Besides, they carried on, now with the internet and cell phones people no longer used the post office.

Secondly they said, if at all the mails did reach their various destinations, there was a very high possibility that they never reached the personal office or Ministers of the various

Ministries Dr. Yonkeu had mailed them to. In order to ensure that her dossiers would reach the right persons Dr. Yonkeu had intended them for, they said, she herself would have to go to each and every one of those Ministries she wanted to work with and demand audiences with each and every one of the ministers in charge. Of course she would have to bribe quite a few workers in each Ministry or ask someone who was a friend to the Minister of State to take her there before she would be able to see the Minister. If she did not do so, they said her dossiers would be left somewhere in some drawer or shelf at the various Ministries collecting dust. Worse still, they said, one of the workers may just decide to throw them away in the waste paper basket and they end up in somebody's toilet having been used as toilet paper; or with the "Mammy Makala" for bundling up "Makala" for her clients and then Dr. Yonkeu would have to start all over again from scratch trying to compile new dossiers. They hoped, they went on, that she did not send any of her original diplomas or Certificates because she would just have to consider them lost forever. Damn it! Dr. Yonkeu cursed.

Dr. Yonkeu then told them that fortunately she had not sent out any of her original Diplomas and Certificates. She said she had suspected that, generally things were not, being done like they normally should, and that she had kept her original diplomas with her, just in case those she had sent out got missing somewhere along the way. She went on that, she had noticed that in Cameroon, most people were trying to make quick and big money too one way or another, and as such the bribery, fraud and corruption had reached its peak in the country. Everybody wanted to be rich overnight. No one wanted to work honestly for their money. The misappropriation of public funds by some unscrupulous public workers had become a daily occurrence in spite of the fact that some of these people actually do end up in jail. There is high level corruption and impunity in the country. She wondered how there could be any genuine development in the nation given these circumstances. Most people tend to think only of the present, not the future of the nation. "That", she said, "was very sad indeed." Little wonder, the other day a little boy of twelve was heard applauding a public official who was accused of having stolen ten billion Francs CFA from the State coffers.

Fancy this little boy referring to this man as "tough guy". How ironic, Dr. Yonkeu thought some hero! She said aloud. This reminded her of what a famous African Scholar, Ali Mazrui once wrote about the misappropriation of public funds by Government officials in Africa. During Colonial times in Africa, he said, those Africans who often misappropriated public funds were quick to justify their actions when accused of doing so, on the grounds that, they were stealing from the White Masters who as most historical records would clearly show, were known to have exploited the Africans more than whatever amount of money the Africans could have possibly stolen from them during this period. In fact, like it is often said in Africa, even the "missionaries came for our goods, not for our good. They asked us to close our eyes and pray and then robed us blind in the process."

However, today in the post-independent Africa, misappropriation of public funds is still alive and well as ever. You see, some habits die hard. Nevertheless, the crux of the matter now is from whom exactly would these people who misappropriate public funds today, say they are stealing now that the 'White Masters' are no more? In the final analysis, they are only stealing from their own people. As such, they are largely responsible for the impoverishment and misery of the vast majority of the African peoples; and thus, causing unnecessary pain and hardships to often innocent struggling people. The contribution of these people to the debilitating 'economic crisis' now facing most of African nations is enormous. If only these people could just sit down for once, and think of the devastating socio-economic and often serious health consequences their avaricious acts do bring to bear on their fellow citizens, maybe they would just decide to stop doing what they do.

It is indeed ironical, Dr. Yonkeu thought, that these stolen monies, usually huge amounts of money, are often swindled into some European countries where they are either invested in real estate or some fantastic projects in these countries, (often, projects that are badly needed by people in their own countries). Thus in doing so, these people further enrich the very European Colonial Masters (they used to want to punish by stealing from them during Colonial times); while at the same time, reducing the vast majority of their own African Brothers and Sisters to abject poverty and misery; all sorts of undue hardships and of course, chronic underdevelopment. As one political analyst once put it people who were the 'vas-nu-pieds d'hier', have become billionaires overnight not through hard work, but often by fraudulent means.

How on earth, Dr. Yonkeu wondered, could there be any possible explanation for such grotesque, outrageous and inhumane behaviour? It sure runs contrary to the fantastic rhetoric of 'rigor and moralization' which some of these very people who milk dry the nation's financial institutions, often stress in the speeches they make aimed at encouraging the ordinary folks to be diligent or to work hard toward resolving the 'economic crisis' now plaguing the nation. You see, talk is really cheap. They often say one thing, but they are quick to do another, all for purely personal gains, greed. How terribly hypocritical and selfish! Really the problem with Cameroon, and a lot of other African countries, Dr. Yonkeu figured, is not the notorious 'economic crisis' as most people are led to believe. The problem could all be found in two words: 'moral crisis'; which in fact is the root cause of the 'economic crisis', stemming from corruption, impunity and fraud by unscrupulous public officials, ethnicism, favouritism, nepotism, sexism, misappropriation of public funds, et cetera. These have all contributed greatly to the crushing economic crisis in most of Africa today. It's a shame that things such as these should even happen. "Gee!" What a mess, Dr. Yonkeu exclaimed.

In any case, Dr. Yonkeu decided to take the advice of her friends and she started serious job hunting all over again a week later. She did manage to have a few appointments at various ministries and as it is often the case, and they did promise that they would contact her shortly. However, she waited for a long time but she never did hear a word from, any of them. At this point, she had become really frustrated. Days, weeks and even months passed by, but nothing seemed to be forthcoming.

One day however, a friend Ali came by to visit her; and Dr. Yonkeu told him she was having enormous difficulties trying to find work, and wondered what she could do next since she had done everything imaginable. The friend just laughed and asked her if she had not been following the news either on radio or on television? He said that things were rough out there in the nation. He said there was the notorious 'economic crisis'; and that with each new day, comes the sad news of one bank or another, one industry or another, one company or another either laying off workers or worse still, closing down completely.

The devaluation of the "Franc CFA", the drastic pay cuts in Government services and even in Private Companies has worsened the plight of the Cameroonian people. Food prices and prices of other commodities have skyrocketed to the extent that a lot of people are forced to go without some of the basic necessities of life. In fact, people were already having tremendous difficulties trying to make ends meet with their regular pay. Most workers, he went on, already leave on 'OD', that is, Bank Overdrafts. Cutting workers' pay has indeed been disastrous, he said. Already he continued, the unemployment situation in the country was just incredible; and the number of the unemployed keeps rising each year with more young people graduating from Colleges and Universities. There were already lots of jobless Degree holders in the country. He said he had recently heard over the radio that there was already a hiring freeze in the Government services; except of course, for those with parents, relatives or 'godfathers' in top Government positions. This, he said, has only worsened the unemployment situation in the country. Things, he added, were just impossible. Most jobless people, he went on, had now taken to alcohol and marijuana to help them forget their numerous problems. In fact, he said, someone had even come up with a joke about the beer brewing companies in Cameroon. The companies are officially known as "Brasseries du Cameroon". The fellow changed the name to 'Brasseries do Cameroon'; in Pidgin English; meaning that, the beer brewing companies have dealt with Cameroonians by making a lot of them alcoholics foolish; unassertive and helpless.

In fact, the beer brewing companies in the country, he said, seem to be some of the few companies still doing profitable business in the nation, at present. However, a lot of these companies too are also complaining about the 'economic crisis'; and rumour has it that they too would soon lay off a lot of workers. It's a shame, he said. Some companies, he went on, were just hiding under the cover of the 'economic crisis' so as to be able to lay off as many workers as possible, and as such, maximize their profits. A lot of companies and even some individuals, he said, would indeed build their fortunes on the backs of suffering people. It's a shame! And I tell you Dr. Yonkeu, he continued; when things get this bad in the country, you women really go through hell. I really feel sorry for 'women libbers' in times like these. It seems as though all their effort to liberate the Cameroon woman has all been in vain.

'How is that?' Dr. Yonkeu asked.

'Just think about this', Ali resumed. 'I tell you, a lot of the time, women; and mind you, when I say women, I mean both married and unmarried women, more often than not, find themselves not only in terrible economic hardships, but they are also subjected to many forms of social injustices and exploitation. A lot of the time, their male counterparts tend to use them as if they were mere commodities in the market place; or as means to an end. Mind you, I am not just only talking of the usual, the occasional maltreatment, in the form of 'beating' or disrespect from their male lovers or husbands. It's way beyond that. And believe you me; even parents are caught up in this viciousness.

Listen, this may come as a surprise to you, but the truth is that, a lot of parents now use their daughters to make money. You see, it seems this thing of paying bride price is now back in full force. It is now "en vogue". In fact, it had died down considerably or as the French would say, it had become 'démodé' or at best, just a symbolic gesture. However, it seems the economic crisis has brought back to life this ugly monster. And you can bet on it, some parents are having a bonanza. They are making big money out of the whole thing. Whenever they are confronted with this mean act, these parents are quick to say it is the African Tradition to demand the payment of brideprice for their daughters. But I tell you Dr. Yonkeu, even they themselves know that, tradition has very little to do with it nowadays. The whole business of tradition is simply a cover these parents use to make as much money as possible from the "sale" of their daughters. It's just terrible.

These days, as soon as a parent knows his daughter is 'mature' for marriage, he starts looking forward to marrying her off to some man. And you can be rest assured, it is not just to any man, but to a "man of means"; some man from whom he could get or rather extract a fabulous brideprice for his daughter. To people like these, having their daughters well educated before marriage can very well wait. It is certainly no longer top priority for them as it was the case in Cameroon not too long ago. It's awful.

In fact, don't be surprised to find even ten or thirteen year old girls being sent away to marriage these days. This way, fathers avoid the financial cost of raising their daughters to maturity before marriage. These parents just don't seem to care; or they pretend to be ignorant about the health risks a lot of these underage brides are more likely to be subjected to, especially during pregnancy and childbirth. All they seem to care about is the amount of money they make out of their often helpless daughters. In fact, a lot of studies have been done which show that, the risk of anaemia, eclampsia, and vasicovaginal fistula, all life threatening illnesses, are highest among teenage mothers. It's a pity that things such as these are least worrisome to a lot of these parents.

I tell you, just the other day, I was at a marriage ceremony, one of those traditional marriages, in which I actually saw a father, one of those mean fathers, bargaining away with his would be son-in-law for the appropriate bride price for his daughter; as if the daughter was just a piece of meat in the market. It was an awful experience. The father wanted a 'cool' 5.000.000 Francs CFA for the brideprice of his daughter. However, the would-be son-in-law managed to bargain it down to (3.000.000 Francs CFA). It was shocking the way the whole thing was being conducted. Forgive me, but if I may say so, it was a real 'slave market'. After they had settled for the (3.000.000 Francs CFA), bride price for the man's daughter, the would-be son-in-law paid in cash and the would-be father-in-law, wrote him a receipt for that amount of money; after which he handed over his daughter to the young man, just like that. I tell you, never had I witnessed such a humiliating scene before; a real aberration in every sense of the word. What people would do for money! I said to myself. It was so terrible, so very mean of this father. Boy!, they talk about 'African Tradition', but I can assure you that today; this particular one had a lot more to do with making quick money than tradition.

Just tell me Dr. Yonkeu, how are Cameroon women ever going to regain their self-respect when they are being sold away to men just as if they are articles in the market. I can bet you; any woman who has been sold off to a man in this manner would have to be just like a slave to him. She would be unable to do anything for herself without his authorization. On the other hand, she is bound to do whatever he asks of her, even if it is to her disadvantage; one need not mention the fact that, she is more likely to be subject to all forms of abuses imaginable, should her husband be a mean guy. Tell me, where does this leave the Cameroon woman, if not to make her further dependent on the Cameroon man, and as such, to be forever subordinate to the latter? It's appalling. I tell you; things on the whole, have certainly gone out of control in this country. One really does wonder when things would ever get better.

Hmm! you are here lamenting over the commoditization of female children by their "capitalistic" parents who charge exorbitant dowries from their daughter's suitors; but that is just the tip of the iceberg, Dr. Yonkeu said. Have you seen what has happened to the institution of marriage and the family as a whole in Cameroon lately? Dr. Yonkeu carried on. I tell you my friend, the terrible economic situation in Cameroon has not only led to the breakdown of the traditional African family but it has also led to the breakdown of traditional African norms regarding the institution of marriage. Today, because the vast majority of African men are unemployed or do not have a "respectable" profitable business, very few of them, do actually get married. However, these men do have to satisfy their lust "one time or another and because most of them do not have the money to do so by going to prostitutes" (the group of people society regards as "deviants"); they then resort to very unconventional and very sexist ways and means of doing so. For example, nowadays quite a number of young men do not hesitate to tell lies to women out rightly, that they would marry them if these women engage in sexual intercourse with them. Yet others use the pretext that they want to make sure that their young woman is capable of having children before they could marry her. All these are just some of the mean ways these men use, to quite literally "get under women's pants" or to satisfy their lust or better still to prove their virility or to make sure they too have children a cherished African thing to do; but all these of course without taking up the socio-economic and cultural responsibilities that go with bearing and raising children. And I tell you because most women in Cameroon have been conditioned to believe that marriage is the "be all and the end all" of womanhood, they become easy preys to these "suckers", these consciously irresponsible men who then leave the responsibility of raising the children completely in the hands of these women. This in fact accounts for the tremendous increase in single-parent households in Cameroon headed by women, which in turn is largely responsible for the feminization of poverty and all its ramifications in the country lately. One need not mention the many new born babies thrown in pit latrines and or in dust bins to die as was the case recently (2014) where twin babies were thrown in a waste depot in the Omnisport neighbourhood in Douala.

Indeed, Dr. Yonkeu, things do not seem to be getting any better here in Cameroon. In fact, things only get worse every day and believe you me, this economic downturn is gradually but steadily transforming people into irrational beings and overturning the established order of Cameroon. It's a pity the way things are. And some people too… They are just so mean, so avaricious, to the extent that, they would do just about anything for money. I just only hope and pray that there would be more people like you, who could dare speak up against such gross injustices and crimes against humanity perpetrated against women in this country. That sure would help a lot in improving women's lives.

'And boy, talk of colonialism! Who said it was a thing of the past? Wishful thinking hey...Ali carried on sarcastically. 'I tell you, 'as one late president of the U.S. would say, you ain't seen anything yet'. O.K. For the benefit of doubts he said; let's assume colonialism is no more. But let me tell you this, you can be rest assured, something else, an even more ruthless form of colonialism has replaced it...Neo-colonialism. "Like they say, the Whiteman may have left through the door but sure came back through the window. I tell you Dr. Yonkeu, the colonial masters may have gone, but their sons and daughters, even their grandsons and grand-daughters are back in full force. And boy, are they just like their fathers and mothers, or their grand-fathers and grand-mothers for that matter; especially as far as profit making goes. Really, you do not need too much brains to figure out, neither do you need lenses to see the enormous often negative, socio-economic and cultural impact of neo-colonialism upon the Cameroon citizens and Cameroon itself. Really, the whole thing is just an instant replay. Imagine, one only read about these things in history books and other similar documents. Never did one think one could actually see it happen, let alone, be victims of it in the 21st century. Just look at us. Everything about us is Europe or Western like they say. Our television and radios are bombarded with one Brazilian, European or American soap after the other. Everything about us; the way we dress, the language we communicate in and even the way we talk are all white. Boy! Before we know it, our staples – foo foo, garri and plantains would be replaced by "hamburgers" and god knows what. It's terrible! Only this time around, some of these neo-colonialists, these 'nouveaux arrives' so to speak, happen to be far more sophisticated, tactful, and sometimes even more careful about the feeling and desires of the indigenes in the way they go about things.

Moreover, what is even more perplexing about this whole business, Dr. Yonkeu cut in is the fact that, it is the Africans or rather the Cameroonians themselves, or even more precisely, the Cameroonian ruling clique, who have themselves asked for, and graciously received the services of these noble Europeans; and not the other way round, as it was in the past, when the latter's fathers and mothers, their grand-fathers and grand-mothers had considered it their duty or took it upon themselves to bring some 'civilization' to the 'darkest of continents'-Africa.

Today, however, we ourselves lure these Europeans to our shores; our country with guarantees of the exotic 'good life' and of course fabulous pay checks to come and 'develop' our beloved nation and 'civilize' our backward peoples. How tragic! To the ruling clique, the Cameroon intelligentsia' are just no good; and they are incapable of handling even the smallest tasks. Ironically, a lot of these very Cameroon intelligentsia' more often than not, happen to have received their training or formal education from European and American countries, the citizens of these very continents they are now hiring. Yet the ruling clique are often very quick to dismiss their own people, the Cameroon intelligentsia' as being incapable, mediocre and often claiming that they are left with no alternative but to look for Europeans to run the country's top corporations, financial and banking institutions; since most Cameroonians are incapable and at best, inefficient. These Europeans and Americans they claim are the best people to do the job. Everything a white man touches, to some of these corrupt, inhumane self-serving people; it does seem, turns into Gold; whereas, whatever their own brother a Black man touches turns into waste matter, 'shit you know to put it more bluntly' How terribly ridiculous and sad', Dr. Yonkeu said. "When would the Black man, Africans in particular, ever going to start thinking of themselves as capable as every other human being on this planet earth; and stop perpetrating their own supposedly, inferiority, and at the same time, reinforcing their own subjugation by being so totally dependent on the White race for their existence and survival, as it is now the case here in Cameroon and a lot of other similar African countries Dr. Yonkeu wondered?

The problem, Ali continued, "is not that there are no capable Cameroonians to do these jobs, but rather, it is just that, they, the ruling clique, for the most part are suffering from a terrible inferiority complex; and are often blinded by their own built in prejudices and selfishness to the extent that, they don't just take their time to look for capable Cameroonians to do these jobs. In fact there is the new "Chinese invasion"; Chinese business people, engineers and workers doing brisk business in the country and making fabulous profits which like the Europeans and Americans before them, end up in China instead of investing here in Cameroon. How Sad!

I tell you Dr. Yonkeu it's awful! Can you imagine this? Sometimes, they would rather have white people, even white football coaches come all the way to Cameroon, to do these jobs and pay them exorbitant salaries rather than have Cameroonians who do not meet their biased criteria to do the jobs. This is so absurd considering that a Western consultant or a white expatriate usually earns in a day what an average Cameroon worker earns in a year. It's ridiculous. Believe you me Dr. Yonkeu, there is so much wrong in this country."

"Really, I wonder what makes people to be so malicious to the extent that they would actually prevent one of their own countryman or woman to earn a decent living", Dr. Yonkeu reiterated. "I see why the unemployment situation in the country has surged so terribly. When we do not want to employ our own countrymen and women; and we go all the way to Europe, America and recently to Asia to look for White persons to come and do our jobs, why wouldn't the unemployment rate in the country be so high? It is only logical for this to happen. Boy!, I think it's high time we put our house in order. Things cannot just be allowed to go on like this indefinitely. We must all work toward genuine changes in the country before we find ourselves in deep water", Dr. Yonkeu concluded.

Ali then told Dr. Yonkeu that now in the country, nobody gets employed without the intervention of somebody who happens to know someone in a top position in a Private Organization or Government Institution. "It is not what you know, your Diploma" he said, "it is who you know, 'man know man' that counts, cronyism. Credentialism means nothing to these people." Ali did however promise he would take Dr. Yonkeu to one of his friends who happen to be the Director General in an International organization and find out if he could possibly employ her.

Dr. Yonkeu's friend Ali actually did arrange for a rendezvous with the Director General, Dr. Yonkeu and himself, some days later. On the day of the rendezvous, Dr. Yonkeu was so anxious. She woke up early that morning, took a quick shower, got dressed in her black skirt suit and white shirt, ate some breakfast and was anxiously waiting for her friend to come along and take her to meet the Director General. He did arrive on time. By 8 A.M., they were at the Director's general's office.

Dr. Yonkeu's first encounter with this 'big shot', the Director General, was really awful. He happened to be not only sexist, but a very rude man. He was just like he looked. He was a thickset, bespectacled guy with a very condescending look, a bushy greyish black moustache and a vicious smile. He had asked

Dr. Yonkeu for her dossiers. When Dr. Yonkeu gave him her Diplomas, he just took them, quickly glanced at them, and told her very rudely that they were worth nothing; and that he was more interested in seeing her Dissertation. Dr. Yonkeu got real mad at that stage. She resented people to treat her so rudely as if she had done something wrong, or as if she was nothing. 'Being a human being, "she thought it was enough". She did not have to be some Director or something like that to be respected" Even in the United States where she was a foreigner, she was never treated this way, the man was very condescending indeed. She was so furious and she was just about to tell the Director General that he could stuff his job in his…, you know what, when her friend suddenly discretely gave her a pinch on her leg and whispered to her to keep her cool. He said he would explain things to her later. Dr. Yonkeu could not believe such rudeness. 'Who the hell, she thought, does this 'ass…think he is'? Anyway, she managed to calm down, just for her friend's sake. She then pulled out her Dissertation from her bag, and gave it to the Director General. He just glanced at it and told Dr. Yonkeu that he would go over it detailly and that he would send it back to Dr. Yonkeu in a week's time. Dr. Yonkeu did insist that he returned it to her as promised because it happened to be the original and the only copy of her Dissertation she had with her at Cameroon. He said not to worry and that she could rest assured he would return it to Dr. Yonkeu as promised. As Dr. Yonkeu later found out from her friend Ali who had introduced her to the Director General, the man, resented the fact he should be under pressure to employ Dr. Yonkeu at the Organization a woman, and more so, a 'Doctor', when there were so many men out there with lesser qualifications too, to do the job. Dr. Yonkeu would be a drain on the budget he had planned for one of those luxury vacations in Paris-France with one of his many mistresses.

You see, this Director General like many African men, still do feel a woman's place is, and should be at the household, more precisely in the kitchen. According to these male chauvinists, these somewhat misogynists, women should be also solely responsible for bearing and raising children; doing their household chores and taking care of their husbands or "Masters". Top jobs in politics, business and government must be exclusively for men. These men like the Director General feel it is the women's Liberation Movement that has brought disorder in society. It has made women grow horns quite literarily. Many women now believe they can do whatever a man can do.

Like the director General put it: "it is the late Goldameir, Margaret Thatcher, Indira Gandhi and Benazir Bhutto who started all this. Now we have others like Angela Merkel in Germany, Christina Krushna of Argentina, Michelle Bachelet of Chilli, Dilma Russef of Brazil, and still others in South America, and the lot. Even our "good" African sisters like Ellen Johnson Sirleaf in Liberia and Joyce Banda in Malawi have joined the bandwagon. I don't know what these women want. The disorder is too much. They are becoming a nuisance to society. They want to be everything and everywhere in society. This is not right.

Imagine, now I am under such pressure to hire Dr. Yonkeu for a job I have been preserving for my brother-in-law, Mbella, my ethnic brother too; who would soon be graduating from the University of Champagne in France with a Bachelor Degree in Sociology. I don't know how I am ever going to explain to my brother-in-law, Mbella that I had to hire a woman at a job he could have had; all this because women like Dr. Yonkeu refuse to accept their "rightful" place in society. Now we are forced to put up with women Ph. Ds, women bus drivers, women motorcycle taxi and cab drivers, female engineers, female fire fighters, female pilots and what have you? Left to me, these women should never be employed or allowed to do these jobs. That way, it would be a lesson to young girls not to aspire to such jobs and top positions in society; something which runs contrary to nature. I mean, these jobs are just not appropriate for their god given role as bearers and nurturers of children. They spend all their time struggling and before they know it, it is too late for them to have kids. These women should be put in their "right" places in society; the household and other petty jobs in the informal sector of the economy. Even if they have to go to school, they should be made to study in disciplines to prepare them for such female jobs or nurturing jobs like being primary or secondary school teachers, secretaries, nurses, telephone or "call box operators", hair dressers, etc. This way they could better organize their time to do the chores in the household and their jobs outside of the household.

Already, a lot of these women wear trousers most of the time like men. I swear, we haven't heard the last of this. Soon these women like this "Mrs Man"-Dr. Yonkeu, would want to marry men; rather than men marrying them. God forbids!!! After struggling with his sexist thoughts, the Director General reluctantly called in one of his Directors, introduced him to Dr. Yonkeu and asked to see if he could find a job at his Department for Dr. Yonkeu.

The Director seemed to be a nice guy; tall, dark, handsome and gentle; although a little more flesh on his somewhat thin frame wouldn't hurt. After having had a brief chat with Dr. Yonkeu, he asked her to come and see him the following day since he had some urgent business to take care of at that moment. Dr. Yonkeu said that was no problem and that, she would come and see him the following day. In every way, the Director was more of a gentleman than the Director General who gave the impression that one had to bow down to him. 'Hell no! Not I', Dr. Yonkeu said. He was even lucky her friend intervened just on time before she told him what exactly she thought of him, Dr. Yonkeu thought. The culture of impunity had eaten so deep into the fabric of this society that people just do as they please and behave like tin gods in their small offices. How sad," Dr. Yonkeu concluded.

When Dr. Yonkeu and her friend had left the Director General's office, the friend started explaining to Dr. Yonkeu that, he would have informed her before, that it was just the Director General's habit to say things so rudely, but that in all, he was not that bad a man. Dr. Yonkeu then said 'she was sorry', but that, if the guy continued that way, sooner or later, someone who did not know that rudeness was part of his nature, was going to beat the hell out of him." In fact, after this episode with the Director General, Dr. Yonkeu wondered when gender parity would ever be the norm in Cameroon. She thought of the capitalist transformation of the economy which has resulted in "class" divisions with often devastating implications on women's status. In fact, the proletarianization process in Cameroon has led to the further exploitation of women's labour power leaving the vast majority of them poorer. The capitalist enterprise in Cameroon is dominated by foreign capital with a small indigenous capitalist class made up of predominantly males who serve as intermediaries in the economy and state institutions to mainly maximize profits for foreign capitalists. The social stratification in this country is abominable. In an ambiguous system where capitalist enterprise often coexists with non-capitalist forms of production, the vast majority of Cameroon women find themselves at the lowest levels in the occupational hierarchy mainly in areas of subsistence agriculture (farm women) petty commodity production, petty commerce mainly in foodstuff (known here as "buyam sellams") call box operators, commercial sex work and mainly low level clerical jobs. These women who mainly work in the informal sector of the economy are usually the working poor, the vulnerable. For example, it is not uncommon here in Cameroon to hear people making fun of a man who works as a secretary in an office. Often they would say things like "eh...tu fais les métiers des femmes" or "you are doing a woman's job". It is terrible! The Cameroon economy should be restructured to enable women, especially poor women to have control over conditions of their production in subsistence agriculture or in artisan activities as well as other activities in the public and private domains so as to make these activities more appreciated and more profitable for their general well-being; Dr. Yonkeu thought. In short, Cameroonians generally and women in particular must have access to productive education and modern technology to improve their socio-economic status.

"Right now, in the economic domain", she continued, "Women are very marginalized and given the least chances of advancement even though increasingly numbers of women are breadwinners of their families. This is because of the chronic economic crisis in the nation which has left many males unemployed; resulting from the shutdown of the few factories and industries that existed, redundancies and the massive salary cuts. In fact, the minimum wage is about 36.270 Francs CFA today which is very low indeed. In spite of this women continue to dominate in the low pay, low prestige and low status jobs in the informal sector of the economy. It is clear that "gender apartheid" is alive and well in Cameroon, which makes women one of the most disadvantaged groups in the country, socially, culturally, politically and of course economically. This is wrong" Dr. Yonkeu thought. "An enabling socio-economic environment should be provided to help women excel in this country.

However with people like the Director General in positions of power, this seems to be more of a dream than reality. They will make sure the gender status quo remains intact in this country. How sad" she thought' however, she said aloud, "I will not let this be I will fight this unjust system to the very end. I cannot put up with this institutionalized sexism. In fact, if more respect were given to girls as equals of boys from infancy; and if they were educated on their shared responsibility in all aspects of a safe secure and harmonious family life, the system would be rid of most, if not all gender discrimination practices. The socialization process in Cameroon has to be changed to bring about social inclusion in the country. Women have to be more aggressive in overcoming their oppression in the private and public domains with or without the help of their male counterparts. In fact like Harriet Martineau (1802-1976) the "mother of sociology" who translated the work of Auguste Comte, the "father of sociology" and laid down the ideas that have become a cornerstone of modern sociology in her research entitled "In Society in America" (see Lipset 1962; in: Curry T.et al., 2002:10), Dr. Yonkeu refused to accept the notion that women were appendages to their husbands, fathers, brothers or other responsible men, and that they were expected to fill domestic roles and bear children like this Director General says. Instead Dr. Yonkeu felt like Martineau that the emphasis should be on core values that concern "human equality" as it is to a larger extent in the United States. Social strains, Martineau explained are created when people behave in ways that are contrary to these core values. In time, these strains become the principal cause of social change. Women must therefore stop being comfortable with their current debased status. Women must wake up from their slumber" Dr. Yonkeu concluded.

Weeks had passed, and Dr. Yonkeu had still not heard from the Director. She started getting worried. She hoped the Director was not just playing games with her. Months then came and passed, and she still had heard nothing. She then decided to go and see the Director once more. She did go to see him, and he said he was really sorry, but that he had been out of town for some time. However, now, he said everything was going to be all right. He then asked Dr. Yonkeu to come and see him again in about two weeks' time. In two weeks' time, Dr. Yonkeu was there, but the Director was nowhere to be found. His Secretary, a pleasant middle-aged lady, told her to come in a week's time. She said something just came up and the Director had to leave town. Dr. Yonkeu felt so disappointed. She wondered what sort of organization this was that things never seemed to go as planned. However, she just kept hoping for the best, and in a week's time, Dr. Yonkeu was back at the Director's office again. This time she met the Director. He did tell her that she would soon start working with him, and that she should be patient. Things went on like that for quite some time. It was all promises, promises, and promises. Dr. Yonkeu kept on going back and forth like that for about five months. She was so furious each time but she managed to calm down and be patient. Things, she thought, had become so hard in the country, and to find a job, she was told, one had to be really patient and try to "keep one's cool", although time and again, this proved to be so difficult to do. Dr. Yonkeu however was cautiously optimistic that she may just have the job at the organization.

Finally, after eight months had passed, she was in the end given, not even a full time job, but a Consultancy job, that would only last a week. She could not believe what was happening to her. After all the waiting, she thought, that was all they could do for her? Nevertheless, she decided things were hard, and she accepted the Consultancy job. After the contract was over, she went back home again; and the same back and forth movement started all over again. She waited for another six months again, before the Director gave her another Consultancy job, this time for four months; and he promised her another long-term contract as soon as she had finished her four months consultancy contract. He even went as far as promising that, after the long-term contract, she would become a full member of staff at the organization. Dr. Yonkeu thought that was not a bad deal after all, considering how difficult it had become to find work in the country. She signed the contract. After some time, she moved out of her parents' house to a small apartment she had found not too far away from where she worked. All seemed to be going on well. At least, she seemed happy with her job for a while.

However, it was not too long after before she started having some problems with some of the male members of staff. She later found out that some of the male members of staff thought 'they were God's gift to women,' as Tina Turner would say. They thought they could have an affair with just about any woman at the Organization they wanted to. At any rate, Dr. Yonkeu was not worried since she was not attracted to any of her male colleagues in that way. However, what annoyed Dr. Yonkeu most was not even that one of them had wanted to have sexual intercourse with her to no avail but that the 'clown' was a so-called married man. What shocked Dr. Yonkeu even more was when after she had clearly but politely told this particular fellow that under no circumstances would she engage in sexual intercourse with him; but he kept insisting. And one day, he even actually tried to force himself on to her. That did it. At that point, Dr. Yonkeu got so furious and pushed him off her. When Dr. Yonkeu asked him why the hell he was behaving the way he was; just like an animal with no self-control whatsoever; he had the cheek to tell her that it was the way he normally handled women, because it is his experience that, most of the time, when a woman says 'no' to a man, she really means 'yes'. And so, that was why he said, he was trying to force himself on to Dr. Yonkeu, thinking that she of course meant 'yes' when she said 'no'. Granted, Dr. Yonkeu was no prude, but neither was she a bitch either. As such, she resented the way this guy was trying to treat her just as if she was dirt; a child who does not know what she wants, so patronizing. She was mad as hell.

"How sexist and ridiculous", Dr. Yonkeu thought. "The guy's ideas seemed so absolutely preposterous." She could hardly believe it. She could not just hold back her anger anymore, and she let it all out on him. She told him off; and she demanded that at all times, she be respected and be treated as a colleague at work and nothing less. She said she was not anybody's sex object, and that moreover, she was at the Organization to work and not to play dirty games with 'sexist pigs'. In fact, Dr. Yonkeu had heard how generally sex harassment was a common occurrence at that institution. She had heard that some of the male staff members would ask the Secretaries and even some of the female students who came there from time to time for some practical training courses in Development, to have sex with them. If the Secretary refuses, the male staff members concerned would make sure that Secretary gets fired sooner or later. As for the female students who refused to have sexual intercourse with a particular male member of staff, she is doomed. She could be rest assured she would never make it at that institution. She would end up failing her Examinations.

Anyway, when some of the male staff members had realized they would not have their way with Dr. Yonkeu, they started blackmailing her with all sorts of false accusations. They made up stories that Dr. Yonkeu must have had her job by sleeping with the Director – 'boyfriend'. When Dr. Yonkeu heard all these lies, she was furious at first, but she later decided to brush them aside for she felt that, as long as her conscience was clear, and that as long as she never did any such thing with the Director, she would just simply ignore the gossip and go about her work. She couldn't help though not thinking how petty some of the male staff members were. She also wondered why some men often think that a woman could never make it on her own or without a man behind her, who in most instances would only be helping her as payment for having had sexual intercourse with him? What a pity!, she thought.

Meanwhile, she carried on with her job as usual. She was a month away from finishing her four months contract and hopefully, begin her long-term contract, as the Director had promised her, when it seemed her luck suddenly ran out. She never knew the Director General and the Director were having a lot of problems. She later found out that there had been a power struggle between the two for quite some time. It finally came to a crunch when the Director General decided to fire the Director.

It all happened so unexpectedly, one day when the Director had gone out of town. It was a bright and sunny Monday morning, and everybody was busy doing their work when the Director General arrived. He called all the Secretaries and asked them to assemble all the staff members in the Conference Room, because he said he had something very important to tell them. The Secretaries did as they were told.

When every staff member had arrived, the Director General told them that, as from that day on, the Director would no longer be their Director. He said he was the one who had brought him to the Organization, and that, he had the right to also kick him out whenever he was not satisfied with his services. The Director General then appointed an acting Director to replace the old one; who as a matter of fact, did become the real Director after the former Director had left.

Every staff member was so shocked. Nobody could figure out what had gone wrong between the Director and the Director General. After the meeting was over, everybody just quietly walked back to their various places of business. One could read the shock and bewilderment on everybody's face. It was as if they have just heard that, one of their close friends had passed away.

The following day however, supporters of the fired Director typed out leaflets and pasted them on all the Notice Boards, stating that: 'things were done at the Organization as if it was a Dictatorship type of Government operating there; a real abuse of power. The Staff members were asked to stay calm and go about their daily businesses; and that, they, the former Director's supporters were going to see the end of it all. They had vowed to reinstate the former Director in his rightful place, or have the Director General eventually kicked out of office.

After Dr. Yonkeu had read the notices, she could not help but imagine how the whole situation was so similar to one of those 'coup d'Etats' that had just taken place in one of the neighbouring African countries; whereby supporters of the overthrown Head of State had written back home, advising the population to stay calm, and assuring them that everything would return to normal, that is, as soon as the former Head of State would be returned to power. What a drama! Dr. Yonkeu thought.

However, confusion broke out at the organization. Staff members were split into two camps, one supporting the Director who had been fired, and the other, supporting the Director General. Dr. Yonkeu found herself in the middle of nowhere. Before long, some of the staff members who supported the

Director who had been fired resigned from their jobs and found different jobs in other Organizations; having of course made connections with top members of those Organizations over the years. The other staff members who supported the former Director, but had not resigned from their jobs, were forcefully terminate from their jobs, some of them, even before their contracts had expired. The Director who had been fired started doing all in his power to see to it that the Director General was also removed from office. A real battle now ensued between the former Director and the Director General. The matter became so serious that even the Presidency of the Republic had to intervene to see how the matter could be settled. The Director General and the former Director were in disagreement as to the payment due members of staff who had resigned and the payment due the former Director himself.

Meanwhile, at this juncture, Dr. Yonkeu had already sensed that she was going to be in a great deal of trouble. She quite literarily smelt a rat. Her four month contract had ended and in all, she felt she had done an excellent job. However, she had the feeling that somehow, things were not going to work out right for her. From her intuitions, she knew the long-term contract the Director who had been fired out promised her, would never come to be. She was right because most of the staff members that remained at the Organization were opposed to the former Director; and they were determined to see to it that anybody whom they felt or even suspected was somehow close to, or sympathetic to the former Director was sacked. These vicious friends of the Director General were already having a great deal of influence on the way the organization was being run. These friends of his, Dr. Yonkeu thought, would make sure that he never renewed her contract.

And so it happened that, when Dr. Yonkeu went to see the Director General about her contract, he promised that he would first of all evaluate Dr. Yonkeu's work before he would be able to take any decisions. He did promise though to get back to her as soon as possible. He said, if they found out that they liked her work, she would be recalled; if not, she would have to go. Dr. Yonkeu thought that would be fair enough. She was confident she had done an excellent job, and if they went by her work, there would be no way she would not be recalled. "However, the Director General's vicious friends, would they not tell him not to recall her", Dr. Yonkeu wondered? However, she kept hoping for the best.

When next she went to check on the Director General to find out if he had finished evaluating her work, her greatest fears came true. Things had sure changed. First of all, from the way in which the Director General received her, she could tell things were not going to work out right. He was so cold to her. He started off by telling her how things were now so difficult in the country generally; and that even the Organization could no longer afford to hire any more persons. He said they were having enormous financial problems. Dr. Yonkeu asked him whether it was because they did not like her work. He said, 'certainly not, he did like her work. However, he said the problem was that the Organization was currently having a lot of financial difficulties. He told Dr. Yonkeu to just be patient and go and wait. He said as soon as they had some money, they would have her recalled to her job.

At the back of her mind, Dr. Yonkeu knew that, it was all talk. Her gut feeling was that, someone must have said something bad or blackmailed her to the Director General which in fact must have had a lot of influence on the Director General's decisions. She suspected it must have been the 'son of a bitch'; the guy who had tried to be fresh with her but had not succeeded, who was behind it all.

As a matter of fact, Dr. Yonkeu's suspicions couldn't have been more right. As it turned out, Dr. Yonkeu did hear from some very reliable sources that the 'clown' who had indeed tried to go to bed with her but had been unable to do so, had indeed said some really terrible things about her, all lies of course, to the Director General, that had made it absolutely impossible for her to be recalled to her job at the Organization.

'Yes', Dr. Yonkeu thought. 'Go ahead. Give a dog a bad name and hang it. After all, this is your world, a man's world. You are in control, of everything, sometimes even our bodies. We women are just like reserves in a team, waiting on the side-line for those rare occasions when our help or expertise may be required. As soon as we are through with whatever we are supposed to do, we are once again, pushed back on to the side-line, sometimes, without even a word of thanks or appreciation; that is, if we are lucky. Otherwise, we are simply 'discarded' and forgotten as if we never did exist; just as one would throw away groundnut shells without any thought or feeling whatsoever, after of course, having extracted and eaten the delicious nuts within, how sad!'

It's a shame though, because Dr. Yonkeu had thought the Director General could not have been so easily misled. But boy was she wrong about that! She had thought he was a reasonable man, and a man of honour, whom she had hoped would handle the whole matter very objectively. But that was not the case. He was like them all; back stabbers. They all pretend they do care for you when you happen to be with them. But the moment you turn your back, they all wish you would drop dead. "Stinking hypocrites" (Song by Jimmy Cliff). They would one day pay very dearly for their diabolic acts', Dr. Yonkeu said aloud.

'Besides', she thought, 'isn't it up to a woman to decide whether to, or not to have sex with a man', he wondered? Why in the world, she thought, should she then be subjected to such base and inhumane treatment? Using any form of coercive tactic to make a woman go to bed with a man, even if the man happens to be the woman's husband is nothing less than rape. It is cruel and a total abuse of her rights both as a human being as well as a woman. It's a shame! She has to go through all this hell just because she is a woman', she thought.

She also did find out that, a close relative of hers; in fact her uncle; remember, the mean uncle with whom she was constantly in disagreement on so many family matters, had indeed also used this opportunity to blackmail her to the Director General of the Organization. He had gone and told him every lie imaginable, terrible things that Dr. Yonkeu had supposedly said about the Director General; all so that, the Director General would not have Dr. Yonkeu re-employed. Dr. Yonkeu could not just believe such viciousness. 'Can you imagine your own real blood relative doing such a diabolical thing to you? Really, whom can one really trust in this world', she wondered?

Come to think of it, she thought, this shouldn't come as a total surprise to her considering that since time immemorial there has always been bitter antagonisms between people and their closest friends and worst still, between blood relatives, even among brothers and sisters resulting in violence and terrible bloodshed. Just take the case of Arabs and Jews in the Middle East who are supposed to be blood relatives; yet they have always quarrelled, fought and killed each other so mercilessly. One need not mention the fratricidal wars that have for so long plagued the African Continent.

For instance, there are the ethnic wars or better the genocides in Rwanda, Burundi, Angola, South Sudan, Central African Republic, and the Democratic Republic of Congo and so on. How terribly sad, "I guess like the old African adage goes "it's really one's brother who kills one", "na manyi brother di kill yi." How so true! In fact, what Dr. Yonkeu's uncle had done to her was another way of killing her considering how difficult it had become finding work at the time. Like they say, "there are many ways of killing a rat". This sure was so true in Dr. Yonkeu's situation.

This as a matter of fact was the beginning of such bitter antagonism between Dr. Yonkeu and her uncle that it did seem only death could resolve. "I mean" Dr. Yonkeu thought, "some things; one would forgive but not this one". It was all just too much for her to handle.

So you see, Dr. Yonkeu's chances of being re-hired, had indeed been blocked on all fronts – the Director's and the Director General's. She couldn't just believe her ill-luck, her misfortune. She indeed wondered how it is that, some people could be so mean that they would go at all lengths, just so as to build their own happiness on the unhappiness of others. These people, she felt, were nothing less than devils in human form. As the famous writer, Shakespeare once wrote: 'There is really no art to find the mind's construction in the face...' This couldn't have been well thought of, and better said, especially when it comes to dealing with such devilish people, she said to herself.

Given the circumstances, she was now convinced that, all that the Director General was telling her were simply stories, just to buy time and cover up his vicious plans. She was quite aware of the fact that the Organization was indeed having some financial difficulties, but hell, she figured that could not by any means, have prevented them from hiring one more staff member. Besides, which Organization in the entire country wasn't having some form of financial difficulties, she wondered? It was all a conspiracy against her and a vicious one too, she thought. As a matter of fact, she had just learnt that two women had been employed on the very Project she used to work on. 'How unfair the world is', she thought. 'One person works, and others reap the benefits. Like they say "monkey work baboon chop" how true! Imagine, she thought, she had proven she could do a good job; yet, when they had to hire people, they chose two other women whom they hardly knew anything about, either personality wise, or of their work ability for that matter. 'Doesn't the word 'meritocracy' exist in their vocabulary and if it does, does it not mean anything to them?' Dr. Yonkeu wondered. The whole thing is just so unfair, she thought. Oh how tears flowed form her eyes as she suddenly had a flashback of all the indignities and hardships she had had to put up with in the United States only to return home, in Cameroon and be treated as an outcast, a worthless object, dirt…this really made her sad.

She particularly remembered the terribly cold winter night in December 2008, when she was almost frozen to death. You see, Dr. Yonkeu was terribly broke and she did not have money for heating. She suddenly came up with this deadly idea to put on the gas cooker to heat up the room. She did not realize she was falling asleep as the room started warming up. Before long, she was deep asleep and was only miraculously awoken some time later by the choking gas fumes from the cooker which made her cough a lot as she was grasping for breath. She immediately rushed to the gas cooker and turned it off. Then she opened all the windows of her studio apartment for a while to let out the deadly fumes. This has been a real close call with death, she thought.

By the time she closed the windows, the room was once more cold as ice. She could feel it right in her bones. She quickly slipped on two thick woollen sweaters; then she put on her big winter coat and went back to bed. In fact, she could hardly sleep a wink. She kept on thinking of how disastrous things would have been had she not gotten up the moment she did. She would have choked to death and the whole apartment building reduced to ashes. The thought of it all brought chill to her spine and made her shiver with fear. Thank God, she thought, things did not get to that stage Mai! What it means to be a poor student there in the White man's land, she exclaimed sadly. "Imagine those days I used to go to bed hungry because of lack of money to buy food; and my stomach growling continuously as if to say hungry! Hungry! Hungry! But there was nothing I could do about it; since I had to save up money to buy two expensive text books for two of my core courses. In fact, had my kind American friends not come to my rescue so many times and lend me books, I really don't think I would have had my degrees. "Bless their hearts!" she whispered to herself as tears of appreciation rolled down her cheeks uncontrollably.

"No" she said determined, "I won't let these "bastards", these male chauvinists get me down anymore. I will have to fight for my rights as a woman and as a human being no matter what it takes; no, no way, so help me God!"

"Being a woman in this country is no easy business. Let no one fool you," she said to herself. "Look at me; I have really been through thick and thin, just because I am a woman first and foremost. Just see, I was the last to be hired and the first to be fired. I swear, being a woman in this country is the pits; a life of constant struggles and hardships. No one could possibly tell me any different. For I came, I saw and I am actually living it all now; the real woes of womanhood in my own country, How sad!"

And "ethnicism", yes indeed, "ethnicism", that hideous word that other form of racism, African style, that terribly nauseating word, that age-old disease that has ravaged Africa. It sure had its own fair share of contribution to Dr. Yonkeu's misfortunes. Boy, has it been catastrophic for a lot of Cameroonians and Africans as a whole for so long. As one social analyst succinctly puts it, "ethnicism" is only next to kleptocracy among the numerous ills that has bedevilled post-independent Africa. How true Dr. Yonkeu thought. How absolutely true!

One often wonders why there should be so much hate among citizens of the same country – Cameroon, the most important and must powerful element of identification of all Cameroonians; based solely on ethnic lines. It is indeed a shame that things like this should even happen. In fact, one only needs to look into past history and even fairly recent happenings in Cameroon as well as the continent as a whole to be able to see and indeed assess the tremendous injustices, pain, and suffering that "ethnicism" in all its shapes and forms has brought to bear on a lot of peoples. One need not mention the ruthless ways in which it often stifles a great deal of individual and human potentials, and thus, quite literarily strangling progress and National Development in African countries. It is indeed unfortunate.

The problem is that, each and every one has to belong to a specific group or ethnic group. One cannot simply be a citizen of the nation. That's just impossible. If this be the case, how then could one possibly be judged, rewarded and classified for that matter? You see, there are certain specific characteristic traits, stereotypes, clichés that have largely and for so long, been associated with members of each and every ethnic group or groups for that matter; and as such, one is always expected to act and behave along the lines of his or her own ethnic group. Any deviation from that is often construed by many in Cameroon as somewhat 'abnormal'; deviant and it indeed poses a real problem as to the distribution of various national resources, which is often along ethnic lines. For example Kamdem E (2002) explains that the ethnic-tribal culture has become an important dimension or factor in the management of organizations and seems to constitute the basis of the logic of power in Africa. This is so because, chances are that, some ethnic groups or groups may just be able to acquire far more than what they were supposed to have gotten; either through hard work and more creativity on their part, or simply, through sheer numbers. This is considered very dangerous indeed for national stability and cohesion by many people in Government; since they believe, this may lead to the offset of the status quo as it now exists in the nation; in the political as well as the social and economic domains. You see, it is widely believed that, this would not be too good for the national well-being, national unity, since things have supposedly been meticulously programmed in a certain way so as to produce these desired results, and thus maintaining the present organization of society; which according to them, is the best that there is, and that could ever be. Little wonder, any mention of changes in the way the country is currently run, sends shivers down the spines of the ruling clique, and those privileged few, who benefit enormously from the current social organization. The way things are at present, the ethnic factor has by far, most certainly surpassed the work ethic and the degree of the development of human capital as critical and vital factors that determine one's degree of success or failure in life. Under these circumstances, the correlation between the degree of the development of one's human resources and the differential rewards one often is supposed to receive has been rendered so very insignificant. More often than not, it is the case that, one is employed, appointed to a post; promoted or even dismissed from his or her job, not necessarily on the basis of one's talent or lack of talent, one's academic achievements or non-achievements, one's hard work or poor work performance, or even one's work experience or non-experience, but on the basis of one's ethnic affiliation. How terribly regressive and sad," Dr. Yonkeu thought.

"And God help you, should you be a member of a certain ethnic group the one that, often, many people do not even want to hear the mention of its name. This is so mainly as a result of maybe, some past event or some mainly unfounded 'negative traits' or cliché that have for long been associated with people of that particular ethnic group. Other times, it is due to jealousy, pure and simple, perhaps as a result of the economic successes and dynamism of the ethnic group. As one observer points out, "this ethnic group is more often hated for possessing qualities which have made cities such as Paris, London, New York, Tokyo, Bonn etc. leading economic Capitals of the world today. These people, he went on, 'display an economic and intellectual aggressiveness…' in a country where these qualities especially the first, are frowned upon." "This", Dr. Yonkeu thought, "is not unlike the abominable anti-Semitism that prevailed in Nazi-Germany, culminating in the dreadful holocaust there. Is this what Cameroonians want?" Dr. Yonkeu wondered.

In fact, this was a painful reminder to Dr. Yonkeu of how only recently she had been a victim of the above circumstance, being a member of the ethnic group that few people have any regard for. In her own case, a top Administrative Official at the organization where she had worked would have clearly been of tremendous help to her. Clearly, he would have helped re-instate her at her job at the Organization, were it not of the fact that she was from "that" particular ethnic group, the one that many people in Cameroon couldn't bear the mention of its name. "He could have liked to help her, he found he just couldn't. "How could he possibly help her," he wondered, "given that she was from "that" ethnic group? He obviously found himself in an almost impossible situation which in fact, could even jeopardize his entire career. "How" he wondered, "would he possibly explain the whole situation to his fellow ethnic group? Could he really make them understand why he did what he did? It would not even matter to his ethnic group that, Dr. Yonkeu happened to have been born and raised in their region although she was of "that" ethnic group, the one a lot of people love to hate; not the less, the fact that, she is above all, a citizen of Cameroon. It was all so very overwhelming for this top official that, after trying a few moves to help re-instate Dr. Yonkeu at her job, to no avail, he quite simply bowed out of it all.

You see, the ethnic problem as it is, is very closely linked to the language problem which has brought about tremendous discontent and has caused a lot of suffering to large numbers of people in the country. Even Dr. Yonkeu sure had her own fair share of suffering and hardship derived from this problem.

You see, she was born in the "Anglophone" region of the country, and she was educated and raised as an 'Anglophone'; although she was 'francophone' by biology. Her parents were of "that" 'francophone', ethnic group. However, they too have lived most of their lives in the 'Anglophone' region of the country; and had, as a matter of fact, received their education in the English system. In fact, they were now so 'Anglophonized' in their way of life, so much so that, one could hardly even know they were of 'Francophone' origin. As a matter of fact, they all considered themselves to be Anglophones.

Cameroon, you see, happens to be a bilingual country in which, English and French are the two official languages. As such, people who speak English are officially known as 'Anglophones'; whereas, those who are French speaking are officially known as 'Francophones'. However, it is worth nothing that, this division was brought about by the "Colonial"[16]masters, mainly the British and the French, who had come after the Portuguese and the Germans. As such, during this period, they partitioned the nation into two sections, the French and the British sections, and imposed their languages on the various peoples under their rule, respectively. Thus, the part that was under British rule spoke English; while people under French rule spoke French. As such, the various ethnic groups that found themselves under these two "colonial" masters were divided into two basic groups and regions along these language lines, that is, the French and the English respectively. However, after obtaining their independence, they "opted" for reunification, and became one nation, thanks to the Union des Populations du Cameroun, UPC, movement that had fought bravely and tirelessly for the independence and reunification of Cameroon before 1961.

As most scholars of African History would clearly recognize though, a lot of times, these "colonial" divisions did not often take into consideration certain vital ethnic, cultural and traditional factors unique or specific to the African peoples; and certainly, those of the Cameroon people during this period. As such, often, they would draw up ethnic or even regional boundaries that clearly divided say, one ethnic group into two groups, each under a separate "colonial" power; thus separating whole families and groups of people into two separate and often distinct cultural camps; as in the case of the Cameroon people whereby; part of an ethnic group could be under British rule, while the other would be under French rule. The case of Muyuka in both the "English" and "French" region in Cameroon is a case in point. This caused a lot of chaos and disruption in society, not to mention the enormous psychological and emotional pain it brought to bear on the people.

Another crucial factor that was often overlooked by the "colonialists" was the immense inter-ethnic dealings and relationships among these people, mainly by way of trade for the

---

16 Note should be taken that Cameroon has never really been a colony under the British and the French but a trust territory; that is being governed by country, countries chosen by the United Nations. However, being a trust territory was in many ways like being a colony such as in terms of cultural and socio economic discrimination and exploitation of these powers.

most part, marriages and sometimes, even wars and defeats of course. So as it did often happen, there was a great deal of migrations of people from one ethnic region to another; which sometimes, even led to some people actually adopting the culture and dialects of the ethnic group and thus, actually becoming members of other ethnic groups. Other times, people simply migrated to other regions, without actually giving up their original identities. For example, they originally may have come from an ethnic region in the 'Francophone' region, but they may have migrated and lived in the 'Anglophone' region, perhaps to work, or even to escape war, forced labour imposed upon them by colonialists, political strife or even political persecution in their region of origin. As a result, they may end up becoming so 'Anglophonized' in terms of both culture and language that one could hardly tell they had originally come from the 'Francophone' part of the country. However, often, they could make sure; they go back time and again to their villages or towns of origin to visit their other family members who may still be living there. As such, they never really server ties with their original ethnic groups or regions of origin; although they would now be officially classified as 'Anglophones'; given that English would be now, their official language in both school and workplace. However, in a lot of their informal dealings, such as in the market place or so, 'Pidgin English' is widely used, or as most Linguists would say, it is the 'Lingua Franca'. At their homes, however, they usually would speak in their native dialects and in "Pidgin English". This form of migration was typical during "colonial" times and it became even more popular during the period immediately following "colonial" rule in Cameroon.

One may compare it to something like this. Someone may have been born and raised, say at some city in the South of the United States, for example, Atlanta, Georgia. However, later on in life, he decides to move on to another city in another State for job hunting, or maybe as a result of a job offer, say to Rochester, New York. However, during his stay at Rochester, he would go time and again back to visit at Atlanta, Georgia where some of his family may still be living. He may later, even decide to return to Atlanta for good, probably for his retirement that is after his contract at the job at Rochester must have expired.

This may not be a very good comparison to the situation in Cameroon given the sort of almost ethnic fanaticism that often characterizes the situation in most of Black Africa. Nevertheless, it does provide an idea of what the migration pattern is like in Cameroon; and of what may be involved in being labelled either as an 'Anglophone' or 'Francophone' in Cameroon. However, the major difference is that, the guy who migrated from his 'francophone' village to say a town in the 'Anglophone' region would now have to learn and be able to communicate fluently in English, and of course put up with some of the :negative consequences, mainly in the social and political domains on the part of some of the natives or indigenous people[17]of the region, or areas, that usually comes with this sort of migration; that is you are never considered as one of them. You are always an outsider; unlike say the case of a guy who simply moves from one city to another or one State to another in a relatively more monolithic country in terms of language and culture such as the man in the United States. In his and other similar cases, one does not necessarily have to put up with the above negative consequences. He simply remains an American first and foremost.

However, given that Cameroon is a Bilingual country, being able to speak either French or English should not in any way be either debilitating, detrimental or beneficial for that matter for one's degree of success or failure in life. They are in this case, two equally important and official languages, and should be seen as such, no more no less. However, this seems to be the case only on paper in black and white. In real life though, this is hardly the case. A lot of factors do often come into play that makes the realization of this, absolutely impossible. In the final analysis, as usually is the case in many other similar situations in the world, one group often ends up being dominant over the other in a lot of ways. This may be brought about either as a result of numerical superiority, population wise, the degree of development of human capital such a in terms of education or availability of financial or natural resources in a region and of course, the ethnic factor in Africa.

---

[17] Note should be taken that the real indigenous people in the whole of Cameroon are the "Pigmées".

In the Cameroon situation, the Francophones happen to be the dominant group, mainly in terms of demographic superiority, and financial superiority and boy, have they abused it!!! As a result, one's chances of making it is often higher, should one be 'Francophone', that is, should one be able to speak and write French; and better still, should one be of some ethnic groups in the 'francophone' region; but mind you, not just from any ethnic group there. You must be of some specific ethnic group depending on who is in power, people of "pays organisateur" like Ateba Eyene puts it. Note should be taken that this behaviour is not the monopoly of Francophones only. Anglophones do the same. For example, when Anglophones occupy top high-profile positions in Government, the tendency is also for them to favour people of their own ethnic groups in matters of employment, "concours" (competitive exams) for admission to top professional and academic schools such as the Administrative school "ENAM" Medical and Law Schools etc., appointments to top posts and the award of scholarships to study abroad etc. So we see that both Language groups behave in similar ways although the impact of Anglophones in the polity of the nation is relatively negligible as there are few of them who occupy positions of power in Cameroon. Thus, generally, it is often the case that, only those 'Francophone people who either through personal interest or occupation, may want to, or feel obliged to learn to speak and write English. Thus, most of the time, it is always the 'Anglophones' who often find themselves in positions whereby if they are to make it in the society they have to learn to speak and write French; whereas the 'Francophones' do not generally feel the need to learn to speak and write the English Language. In fact, it is generally the case that, whatever is French is better, superior, whereas anything English is rejected outright as being inferior. In short, the francophone attitude toward the Anglophone is downright condescending and patronizing. The latter is a sort of second class citizen.

Given these circumstances, a lot of Francophones tend to be more "successful" and more in control of many key positions in society, than are the 'Anglophones'. The 'Anglophone response to, this has been understandably very bitter and sometimes, confrontational[18]. Some of them, mainly those of the separatist movement have been demanding cessation and the establishment of their own nation. This is very unfortunate. At a time when there is the talk of globalization and when many countries are in the process of uniting in various groups or camps in the World so as to achieve more effective development, Cameroonians who have always been and lived as one Nation and one People before the advent of European colonialism in Africa are now demanding separation. It is really sad! For example, there is this name calling whereby Anglophones refer to Francophones as "frogs" while Francophones refer to Anglophones as "Anglofools" and "Biafrais". A lot of times, Anglophones they feel so left out in the running of the country and in determining their own life chances (see Mbangwana P., Mpoche K. and Mbuh T., 2006). For example they feel the union of the Francophone and Anglophone Cameroons has never been on an equal basis. The tendency, they feel is that they are continuously being assimilated into the Francophone culture and system; and that very little has been taken from the Anglophone system and culture. For instance recently in April 24, 2014, the plan to regularize and harmonize the judicial system in Cameroon raised a storm of protest among Anglophone lawyers in the nation's capital, Yaoundé, as they feared the "Common law" an Anglophone cultural heritage risked being thrown out of the judicial system. (Equinox Radio News, April 24/ 2014).

It is worth noting that the Cameroon Government has been trying so hard to reduce or completely do away with this language[19] and ethnic barriers and antagonisms in the country, in words and in actions; but they persist. For example, the President recently appointed the second in line in the nation from "that" ethnic group; and the Prime Minister from the Anglophone Region together with some Cabinet Ministers from many of the ethnic regions in Cameroon to diffuse the ethnic and language

---

[18] For more on the Francophone/Anglophone problem in Cameroon, see Mbangwana P., Mpoche K. and Mbuh T. (2006) Language, Literature and Identity in Multicultural Societies.

[19] For instance, around the first week of February of every year has been set aside as a bilingual week in Cameroon where people are sensitized of the necessity of being bilingual, but this is yet to yield fruits.

tension in the country; and prioritize national unity instead[20]. However, not much has changed. Persons and groups are still suspicious of one another. One wonders when meritocracy would ever become the norm again in this part of the world as it was to some extent, during and immediately following the post-colonial period in Cameroon. One cannot understand the mentality of many Cameroonians today as far as the ethnic factor is concerned. They refuse to see the richness and dignity in diversity as they stick to their egocentric and biased behaviours. Others blame the polity of the Cameroon Government as the root cause of the ethnic divide or ethnicity in the country as it prioritizes "regional and ethnic balance, a sort of favouritism" in many aspects of life in the society. These critics feel this is tantamount to the divide and rule strategy and that it reinforce poor governance and the ethnic factor resulting in mediocrity and general underdevelopment in the country. This is all so mind-boggling and regrettable.

When we even have some members of the Cameroon "intelligentsia" involved in this ethnic-bashing, the situation then becomes real dangerous. Instead of helping to improve the understanding of ethnic and cultural diversity in the country, they are the ones inciting ethnic hatred and even cultural supremacy of the Francophones over the Anglophones in the country. Ironically many of these intellectuals have their children studying in, the US of A and England. Whom do they think they are fooling, only themselves.

Fancy this intellectual in a public discourse, referring to the Bamilékés as "migrants, people who migrate a lot"; and that they are people who want to occupy all the top positions in the country. Even if they are competent, they do not have to occupy these posts. She carried on that other people of other ethnic groups have to occupy these posts even if they are incompetent. This she said was ethnic equilibrium. What arrogance! True Dr. Yonkeu thought there must be quotas for some ethnic and even gender groups in the country until such times that all regions of the country have achieved a similar development status especially

---

[20] One only hopes these appointments are not window dressings; but that these people are competent enough and have real power to effect worthwhile changes in the country that would promote social justice and national development.

in the education sector. However, caution must be exercised here to have only capable persons of these minority groups to govern the country. As a matter of fact people in minority groups need competent role models, not just anybody.

Secondly it is unacceptable to consider persons of the same country, the same nation as "migrants". In fact people of the same country have the right to settle anywhere in the country and feel at home there as the President of the Republic has always insisted in his speeches. Also, ironically this same intellectual had also moved from her region of origin to work in another region. The discourse of this intellectual and others like her is testimony of the mediocrity that characterizes some of the intellectuals in the nation. Indeed, Cameroonians should be constantly reminded of the fact that the first and only real indigenous peoples in Cameroon are the "pygmies/ pigmées" who unfortunately today, happen to be one of the marginalized and exploited groups in the country. So intellectuals should try to have their facts right before they make such dangerous statements in public; fuelling so much hate among citizens of the same country (see song on migration-Talla André Marie).

Cameroon, known as "Africa in miniature" enjoys a rich and diverse cultural life. We do not need bigots and egocentrics who risk throwing this country of peace loving people into a senseless civil war that may reduce this country into pieces of dysfunctional "micro States" where lawlessness and hate reign supreme like it is currently the case in the neighbouring Central African Republic, South Soudan, Somalia and Rwanda some years ago. We have to give peace, love and progress a chance like the very prolific songwriter and popular British Musician, the late John Lennon sings in one of his songs. Similarly Cameroonians in general and the Bamilékés in particular should all rise up as one people, one nation and say no to such divisive tendencies by insisting on the fact that they are not "migrants" but that they are all Cameroonians and that they want their rights in this their land; like the famous Jamaican and legendary reggae star artists Jimmy Cliff and late Bob Marley sing.

Therefore this intellectual should know that when the Bamilekés leave their regions of origin to settle elsewhere in Cameroon, it is a normal human thing that has been going on since time immemorial all over the world. People would always move to other areas or regions in a country or even migrate to other countries to look for employment opportunities or a better life. Therefore the Bamilekés should not be the exception. So this intellectual should bear in mind that when Bamilekés and other members of other ethnic groups for that matter leave their regions of origin to settle elsewhere in Cameroon, especially in Yaoundé the political capital and Douala, the economic capital, it is because like every human being, they are looking for employment and a better life, especially during these times of very high unemployment rates in the country. Therefore it is not because the "Bamilékés" like to migrate as she puts it, it is because to begin with, industrialization in Cameroon is not decentralized but centralized in Douala and Yaoundé in particular. Secondly like most people would admit in Cameroon and as some studies have even shown, the Bamilékés happen to be a relatively more dynamic and out-going people. What is bad in this? After all like Frej Soumaya et Al., (2003) explain, it is not only financial resources that are necessary for the development of a locality or a country, but the individual actors, the people themselves, determined and dynamic individuals alone or in groups who are also very vital for development.

Therefore, instead of accusing the Bamilékés for migrating, the authorities that be should reinforce their capacities, that is the knowledge, skills and competences, the "état d'esprit" of these dynamic people for the good of all Cameroonians and the good of the world.

In fact, as Freund J. (1965) makes clear, the State-Nation is not the property of any individual, any social group, any political party, any religion etc. except in absolute monarchies, in totalitarian systems where the "Monarch is the State" or the "Political party is the State respectively". Therefore, Cameroon is for all Cameroonians, to live in and to work wherever they wish all over the national territory; and be able to hold whatever position (appointed or elective) in and out of government that they are qualified for and capable to hold. Of course, this is the humane and democratic way to go which could be achieved only if we all respect each other's human rights and dignity.

In fact all these completely debunk the intellectual's unfounded explanations on why many Bamilékés move from their regions to other regions or areas in Cameroon. Her analysis is certainly blurred by her narrow mindedness and her egocentricity. We do not need another holocaust in Cameroon as it was the case in Nazi Germany, Fascist Italy or more recently the genocide in Rwanda. As a social scientist, she has to ship in or ship out, instead of spreading false information with her biased and dangerous analysis of social issues. We do not need such stereotyping in the 21st century. It is dangerous Dr. Yonkeu said. Also one only hopes that when Cameroon would become a well-developed country to a point that the unemployment and poverty rates are considerably reduced, this sort of arrogance, egotism, and ethnicity would also reduce considerably or why not disappear from the Cameroonian socio-economic landscape. What is happening today in Cameroun is a sort of auto-destruction which should not be tolerated.

Back to the Anglophone problem in Cameroon, ironically, even the Anglophones who often complain about being marginalized also discriminate against each other. For example, there is a fierce antagonism and in fighting between the Anglophones of the South West Region and those of the North West Region and among Anglophones generally. This has worsened in recent times fostered by egoistic individuals of both regions who increasingly want everything just for themselves their families, their friends and a few lucky people who slip through the net time and again.

Why all these divisions and antagonisms in a country so blessed with immense natural and human resources, one would ask? All this because a few selfish materialistic persons and groups want everything for themselves and nobody else, Karl Marx, Max Weber and Durkheim were really right when they criticized the bourgeoisie in industrial capitalist Europe for maximizing profits on the backs of the suffering masses- the proletariat; and deliberate calculation in a society characterized by anomie and alienation. Many of these characteristics are found in the Cameroon and many African societies today. The "divide and rule" strategy of the colonial masters is alive and well today in Cameroon and many African countries. Who said colonialism is a thing of the past? The situation in Africa is really pathetic. "Indeed it will take a really long time before Cameroonians do away with these meaningless divisions, antagonisms, and selfishness that have eaten so deep into the fabric of the Cameroon society." Dr. Yonkeu said sadly.

Meanwhile, some of those Anglophones and members of some ethnic groups who happen to have crossed the various barriers and have made it in society so to speak, either by holding top Government and Political positions, do often tend to protect only their own personal gains and interests, often enriching themselves, their families and friends; and often ignoring or forgetting to represent and foster the general interests of their fellow 'Anglophones ' and ethnic groups who are often in so many ways, discriminated against in the Cameroon society.

Similarly, some other 'Anglophone' guys who have made it, often sometimes tend to resent being associated with the 'Anglophones.' They in a way develop a sort of inferiority complex; a sort of self-hate. Therefore they do all in their power to be acculturated or better still, assimilated into the 'Francophone' system and ways. How ironic. They end up refusing to even speak English-the number one language in the world; when they happen to meet fellow 'Anglophones'. For example, one may go for some official business to an 'Anglophone' official's office. When one however, speaks in English to the 'Anglophone' official, the latter would make sure he replies to that person in the French language, often in awful French, with mixed up tenses and phrases, having not actually mastered the language himself; thus making a total fool of himself, in the process of trying to show how "francophonized" he has become; a big deal hey! You see, that is one thing about being 'bilingual'. You never are perfect in both languages. Such individuals however, only help to perpetuate "Anglophobia" in the country and to further strengthen the already disadvantaged and often lower social status assigned to "Anglophones" by their 'francophone' brothers. It's such a shame! Dr. Yonkeu thought. As a matter of fact, Cameroon happens to be one, if not the only country in the world where the English language, the most spoken language in the world is shunned. How ironic!

Dr. Yonkeu did find herself in an even worse situation. You see, as mentioned earlier, she happens to have been born and raised as an 'Anglophone' although she was 'francophone'; although, some narrow minded Anglophones and Francophones would insist on referring to people such as her as "francanglais"; pity! However, in spite of everything, she considered herself to be first and foremost Cameroonian, then 'Anglophone' by language and culture and 'francophone' by ethnicity. In fact, she was strongly of the opinion that, labels such as 'Anglophone' or 'francophone' are simply vestiges of the "colonial" past which should be of no significance today. To her, they are highly divisive; and as such, present a real threat to national integration. They do nothing but create more hatred among people and as such diverting national attention to petty squabbles when, there are a lot of more important and more serious national issues such as unemployment, poverty etc; to be taken care of. So she tried as much as possible not to be associated with either being 'Anglophone' or 'francophone'. To her, she was Cameroonian and that was all that mattered. After all, when Anglophones decided to join Francophones, they did so on the grounds that they are all Cameroonians, nothing else. It is as simple as that, Dr. Yonkeu said to herself.

However, in spite of her open mindedness with regard to the whole issue, things did not often work out for her. Somewhere along the way, Dr. Yonkeu discovered that, the 'anglophone/francophone' phenomenon was just so complex and so powerful a phenomenon; and that, it was also so alive and well to the extent that, one could not just simply ignore it as a non-issue. These labels, she found out, have a very crucial role to play in the distribution of goods and services in the country, just as it is the case with 'ethnicity'. The two sort of complement each other so well. Even one's social and personal ties are greatly affected by this division. For example, one would often get married to a person not purely for the sake of 'love' but quite often, on the basis of ethnic and language affiliations. Even friendships are very often along language lines. The divisions in this society are just incredible, weighing down national development.

For people like Dr. Yonkeu who are of a double affiliation, that is, 'francophones' by ethnicity and 'anglophone' by language and culture; or those with one parent who is 'anglophone' by language and culture; or those with one parent who is 'anglophone' and the other 'francophone', things get even more complicated and frustrating. As mentioned earlier, given these circumstances, people like Dr. Yonkeu should officially be considered as 'Anglophones', in Cameroon. However, quite often, they find they are rejected by both camps, that is the 'Anglophone' camp and the 'francophone' camp. They often feel so lost in their own country. Being Cameroonian does not seem to be enough. One has got to belong exclusively to one of the ethnic as well as the language groups. As it is, more often, when they meet a 'Francophone', they find they are rejected by him/her. They are told they are not 'Francophones' but 'Anglophones'. When they often meet an 'anglophone', they are rejected as well on the grounds that they are not 'anglophones' but 'francophones'. It is so terrible, such a confusion. As such, when for example, 'Anglophone' quotas have to be filled, say for some scholarship to study abroad, admission into the Cameroon University, or even for employment in a Government service, people like Dr. Yonkeu stand very little chance in getting one of these, that is, either the scholarship to study abroad being admitted into the university or even being employed at the Government service. You could be rest assured, some 'anglophones' on the various committees would make sure they seldom get selected for any of these things. This would also be the case for them when there are 'francophone' quotas to be filled. It is often such a traumatic experience for people like Dr. Yonkeu. Where, one would ask, do they really belong in the country? Nowhere, it would seem. It is often real hard for them. They often feel like 'children of lesser God', children no one wants, abandoned children, rejects of society who are often scorned by the public at large. They, their children to come, and their children's children, it does seem, are doomed never to hold any of those top Government and political positions that are often reserved for members of specific ethnic as well as language groups, except of course they are really lucky as it occasionally happens. What could they possibly do about it; and where could they possibly go to for help? It is a real dilemma.

Usually, each ethnic group or groups[21] as well as language group has its own Region as well as its own minister of State, Senator and member of parliament; where persons of the ethnic group or groups as well as language group, could go to for help. However, because the language groups and ethnic affiliations are often so closely linked together, this is also reflected in the persons being appointed or elected to be Ministers of State, Senator and Members of parliament respectively. As such, people in Dr. Yonkeu's situation often would find themselves in a similar position as the one when various ethnic and language quota are to be filled say in employment and other such things. When they go to 'Francophone' Ministers of State or Members of Parliament (who are of the same ethnic group as they are but not of the same language group), with their problems, the 'francophone' Minister of State or member of parliament, is often unable to help them because they consider them as 'Anglophones'. When they then go to the 'Anglophone' Ministers of State or members of Parliament, (with whom they are of the same language and cultural group, but of different ethnic origin), with their problems and ask for help, they are likewise unable to have any help from them on the grounds that they are 'Francophones' by ethnicity. Things are often so impossible for them. Where, they would wonder, does this really leave them?

Now, the crux of the matter is, where do people such as Dr. Yonkeu really do fit into, in the Cameroon society? Nobody seems to want to have anything whatsoever to do with them. They are just like out casts. Yet, when their parents or they themselves pay taxes, they do not do so based on any ethnic or language affiliations for that matter; neither do they pay taxes to any one specific ethnic group or language group, but to the Cameroon government. It's such cruel injustice; people like Dr.

---

[21] The ethnic factor is also visible in Government Ministries. For example it is not uncommon to find that when a minister or top government official is of a certain ethnic group, many workers in that ministry or public corporation would be members of the minister's ethnic group and often they communicate in the ministers dialect during office hours.

Yonkeu often have to put up with. The terrible irony of it all is that, it is the very taxes that people such as Dr. Yonkeu's parents and other citizens pay that are used to keep the country going. Why then one may ask, should their children often be denied their basic rights as Cameroonians? It is all so unjust and so inhumane.

Little wonder, some people in this group are now beginning to ask for an 'eleventh region' for people such as them, since there are currently ten regions in the country that do represent the rights and interests of the various ethnic groups and the two language groups. As such, these groups are asking for their own region, 'the eleventh region' with its own Minister or Ministers of State, Senators and its own member or members of Parliament etc. who would represent their interests at the national level, just like all the other ethnic groups and language groups; and to whom they would be able to take their problems to. This, they feel, would only be fair and proper, given the current social organization in the country. They see no reason why they should be denied their rights as Cameroonians which other Cameroonians enjoy. Why should they suffer just because they happen to be of a dual affiliation? After all, they had not asked to be born into these circumstances. It is all so unfortunate that, things have to be this way, Dr. Yonkeu thought because this should promote national integration and not the other way round.

Remember when the top official at the Organization where Dr. Yonkeu had worked, found he could not possibly help reinstate her at her job at the Organization? Yes indeed, he couldn't no matter how strongly he did feel Dr. Yonkeu ought to be reinstated at her job.. He just found he just could not do otherwise given the ethnic and language divisions in the country. These are what one would call very 'soft spots' which would require a great deal of skill, tact, and of course courage and a strong sense of justice when dealing with them. In the end, he found he could not just help Dr. Yonkeu, not just because she happened to be of "that" "ethnic group", the one some people would not even bear to hear the mention of its name; but because she was also considered to be 'Francophone', ethnic-wise, while he was 'Anglophone' by ethnicity. This Dr. Yonkeu thought, was indeed sad. She was so full of self-pity. Didn't it matter, she wondered, that at least officially; they were both 'Anglophones'? It was just all too much for her to make any sense out of it. "But what happened to the Anglophone society of yesteryears where a high sense of social justice and morality reigned supreme" Dr. Yonkeu wondered? Back then nobody seemed to care whether one was Francophone or "Bami" as the Bamilekes are often denigratingly referred to today in Cameroon where morality and social justice are almost non-existent; and where the ethnic factor is now the order of the day. In fact, Dr. Yonkeu remembered her father telling her how back then, that is in the 1950's 60's and even the 1970 period, they had absolutely no problem in the former Anglophone territory either with the people or the Government in the Region. First one was recruited in government or appointed to a post purely on the basis of merit, nothing else. For example after British rule in the former West Cameroon or Southern Cameroons, he was appointed Accountant General for the whole of the English speaking Cameroon. Quite a number of other persons of ethnic groups in French Cameroon were also appointed to top posts of responsibility purely on merit and as Cameroonians of course. Similarly one was accepted as a full fletched member of the Anglophone community on the basis of one's language-English, individual merit and of course by the fact that one was a Cameroonian. Also exogamy was common. Those sure were the "good old days", Dr. Yonkeu thought. In fact, that was national integration; not what we call national integration today marked by all the "isms" imaginable – "ethnicism", sexism, nepotism, favouritism, clientelism…you just name it. In fact, some of those who are preaching national integration today are just those same people who are actually promoting national "disintegration"! What hypocrisy! Fancy one being denigratingly referred to as "not being the daughter or son of the soil", in one's own country of birth, as a "settler", "deracinated" or "lose country" by some of these "ethnocentrists", these "ethnicists"; some of them with even doubtful origins. In fact, similar pronouncements had led to the holocaust or genocide of Jews in Nazi Germany, Fascist State and other similar countries in Europe between the 1933 and 1945 period. What a pity! Dr. Yonkeu thought.

You see, all along, during her studies in the United States of America, Dr. Yonkeu had had to do quite a number of case studies on certain 'burning' socio-economic and political issues that were said to be affecting the American society. You know, Americans are some people! They often want to be pretty certain about the claims they make, especially in 'Academia'. As such, just 'theory' on its own, is not often enough for them especially when it has to do with issues in the Social Sciences. More often than not, one has got to back up one's claims not only by theorizing, but by providing substantial, first-hand, empirical evidence for one's claims or findings to be acceptable by the general public and scholars alike as being worthwhile and scientific. As Grawitz M. (2001:62) puts it, « la nécessité de l'expérience est saisie par la théorie avant d'être découverte par l'observation». How so true in Dr. Yonkeu's case.

However, this time around, Dr. Yonkeu felt she would be just the perfect candidate for a case study, given her own real life experiences on some of the critical and burning socio-economic and political problems in Cameroon. There could be just no way, she thought, the person doing the study on her could run out of concrete evidence to back up or support his/her claims. What has she not really been through, she wondered? She has seen it all, she thought. She has not only been discriminated against for simply being herself, but for being a woman, for being born into a certain ethnic group and for speaking a particular official language, real sad! She said.

Dr. Yonkeu felt so lost, just like a stranger in her own country. In fact, she felt, even strangers were given better treatment than herself. It was all so unbearable, so painful for her. Could she really be in her own country, the land of her birth of her ancestors or was it all a dream? She wondered. She felt so disconnected from the Cameroon society.

As these thoughts were going through her mind, the story of the African American who was so anxious to return to his roots in Africa came to mind. He then saved up all the money he had and made arrangements to do just that. However, when he got to Africa, he was faced with the shock of his life; culture shock. It soon became apparent to him that, he was not only considered by a lot of Africans as a non-African, an American and treated as such, but worse still, he was unjustly put into prison. Poor fellow, Dr. Yonkeu thought. How terribly demoralizing this all must have been for him! This Dr. Yonkeu said to herself, was no different from how she felt in her own country; where she is constantly a victim of hate and sometimes, outright rejection. At least she thought, no matter how terribly heartbroken or disappointed the African American might have felt with the cruel treatment he got from his African brothers, he still had somewhere he could go to, some refuge, although not the best, the United States of America. However, she Dr. Yonkeu had absolutely nowhere to go to, but Cameroon. Cameroon was where she was born; and where she had always considered as home. Now she has been rejected by her own people and left in the cold with nowhere to go to, and no one to turn to for help. How terribly disappointing and sad, Dr. Yonkeu thought. She could now really understand and feel the enormous pain and suffering, even the trauma that people who have been discriminated against, go through; whether it be racial, sexual, ethnic or language discrimination for that matter. It was really such a terrible and inhumane experience for her. As Bernice Brown Cronkite once wrote, she felt just like 'the Child Without a Country.'

At that moment of deep thought and confusion, her mind suddenly drifted to Koffi. He must have been in a similar predicament, she thought, when he had decided to take away his own life. With all the ethnicism and other injustices in the country, he probably stood no chance of having a scholarship. He could not really understand how people less qualified than him could have been given scholarships while he was rejected, even though the criteria for the award of scholarships was solely based on one's academic merit. She thought of the whole situation, and tears rolled down her cheeks. She then said to herself, 'well, Koffi did end up taking away his own life, but she was not going to let that happen to her'. At that point, she vowed to fight back, to fight the battle to the very end. As far as she was concerned, it has to be inclusive feminism all the way, nothing less.

Months came and passed, but Dr. Yonkeu was never recalled at the Organization. Meanwhile, her rent payments had been accumulating a great deal. She had even had numerous eviction notices. Life was really becoming impossible for her. She did not even have money to buy food anymore. Hard as the decision may have been for her at that particular point in time, she decided all the same, to move back in with her parents. In fact, given the almost impossible circumstances in which she did find herself, moving in back with her parents seemed to be the only possible thing she could do. That, she thought, was it for her.

In retrospect what Dr. Yonkeu did find even more shocking about the whole incident, was the almost total lack of consciousness on the part of a lot of Cameroon women of their oppression. Imagine, when Dr. Yonkeu did tell some of her women friends about some of the sex discrimination problems, the sexual harassment problem in particular, that she did encounter when she worked at that Organization, she was really shocked and surprised at the way in which these women took the whole matter so very lightly. To them, what did happen to Dr. Yonkeu was not considered as being sexual harassment. To them and to Adama in particular, it was purely a natural, if not, a 'normal' everyday occurrence between two adults of the opposite sexes.

One could not help but assume that, women here must have been subjected to sexual harassment for so long; and that, it is so widespread that, it has not even dawned on them that they are being abused; a very serious abuse for that matter, of women's rights. They are not conscious of it. It had become what they now consider as 'normal'; something they expect to occur under certain circumstances such as the one Dr. Yonkeu found herself in. It is all so very predictable. For instance, in many instances, if a woman is seeking employment; or if she happens to have already been employed, she is in a way, expected to submit to whatever her often male bosses or employees demand of her; whatever that may be, even if it means having sex with them, or something of the sort, should the occasion arise. They've been conditioned to see things in this light especially now with the high unemployment rate in the country. What a pity.

As a matter of fact, even women who are self-employed, such as petty traders and business women generally often are not free from this problem of sexual harassment. Many a times, these women find they cannot sell their products to some male customers without having to give in to their sexual demands. Even young girls who often go about with trays of say 'groundnuts', fruits and other such things for sale, often find that, a lot of the time, they have to put up with tremendous sexual harassment or even rape from male customers. For example, they sometimes have to submit to having sex with a male customer, just say for a mere two hundred francs (200 Francs CFA) worth or so of 'groundnuts' the latter may have bought from them.

You see, a lot of these girls happen to come from homes and families that are often hard pressed for money. As such, they often feel obliged to sell all the 'groundnuts' or bananas they've got to sell on a particular day, in order to make their parents happy with them, as well as help out with the families' financial needs. However, sometimes, the problem is even made worse, because a lot of these girls do end up getting pregnant. Thus instead of helping out with the families' problems, they end up bringing an extra burden on their respective families; and creating a climate of even more deprivation at their homes. This would mean their parents would eventually have one more extra mouth to feed when the baby does come; thus compounding their already miserable state of living. It is often a very sad situation.

For some other women traders, they find they often have to have sex with men in order to buy goods (such as the freshest fish from fishermen at "Youpé" Douala) from them, at reasonable prices which they would then sell and make some profits especially when they are just starting out as entrepreneurs. This is often the case, since they do not usually have the capital or access to Bank loans to start off with; or the money for that matter to buy the goods and foods in the first place. So in a way, they become commodities; their bodies become the money they would now use to buy the goods. It is really terrible!

For yet some other women, mainly married women, who happen to have acquired some little capital from their husbands to start some form of petty trade, they soon find out the hard way, that their efforts have all been in vain. Usually, they end up giving all the money they make to their husbands; with the belief that, he would use the money for the benefit of the family.

However though, some of these men end up spending most of the money on booze and on other women they have affairs with. This is also the case with some working women, sometimes very well educated women with very good pay, who have joint bank accounts with their husbands. Talk of 'female solidarity'! This seems to be a real joke under such circumstances. We are talking survival here now, matters of bread and butter. How so sad! How so unfair! But life goes on.

In the case of some of the well-to-do business women, sometimes married too, who usually travel from country to country buying goods to come and sell in Cameroon, the situation is not all that different from the afore-mentioned. Sometimes, they also use this opportunity to have sex with male entrepreneurs, on the side, using their 'bottom power' mainly as a means of making more money by buying the goods cheaply from these men which they then sell in Cameroon and make good profits. Money is indeed the root of all evil. In all, whichever way one looks at each and every one of these situations, one finds that, they are all ways of exploiting women and keeping them forever dependent on, and subordinate to men. It is all such a very sad state of affairs, Dr. Yonkeu's said to herself.

Given these circumstances, although Dr. Yonkeu's female friends did feel sorry that she had lost her job, especially at such times of economic hardships, when jobs were so hard to come by, they just considered it to be one of those mishaps in life. They were all unanimous about the fact that, Dr. Yonkeu had lost her job simply because she happened not to have come to grip with the system in Cameroon as yet; having returned from Abroad, and having acquired what they called 'the White man's ways and ideas.' They all agreed that, it was just a matter of time before Dr. Yonkeu would learn, understand and get used to the system, the way of life in Cameroon. As such, they said, only then would she know what exactly would be expected of her should she find herself in a similar situation. Some sexual intercourse with those men at the Organization would not have killed her. Now see, she has lost her job, they concluded in astonishment.

Back then, Dr. Yonkeu was shocked at what these women were saying. How could they?, she wondered. They seemed to be trivializing the whole matter. If they only knew how she felt about it, she thought, they wouldn't dare say such ridiculous things. Dr. Yonkeu did not believe it all. They did not seem to consider what happened to Dr. Yonkeu so serious a problem, or as something quite out of the ordinary.

At first, Dr. Yonkeu was so angry at the manner in which the women had reacted to her problem and what they had said to that effect. However, she soon realized it was indeed no use being angry with them. If she did, she felt she would be doing exactly what the famous American Social Scientist William Ryan warned against – 'Blaming the Victim.' She was of the opinion that, this in a way must have been how Cameroon women have lived their lives; and that, they must have grown so accustomed to it all. They have so internalized their oppression to the extent that such things in a way have become 'normal' and part of their existence as women in a male-dominated or patriarchal society. The problem, Dr. Yonkeu concluded, was not only that, many Cameroon women were not conscious of the abuse of 'women's rights' in the country, but that, they did not even seem to know what their rights, are in the first place. It was all a very sad situation. It would indeed be quite some time before Cameroon women would really become conscious of their plight; and as such, be able to redress some of these ills, now plaguing the society. It was indeed sad the way quite a number of things having to do with the fostering of women's rights in the country, were generally being handled by some public officials as well as some private individuals.

To some Cameroon women, 'Women's Liberation' is seen in terms of emulation of some of those often negative and self-destructive practices that have for long been associated with the men folk; things such as smoking, heavy consumption of alcoholic beverage, cheating on their male partners and other such things. This is particularly so on March 8th, International Women's Day.

To those who seem to be conscious of their plight, and are of the opinion that, practices such as sexual harassment is a very serious problem in society and an abuse of women's rights; they often find it very difficult to make their grievances known and be accepted by the general public as an urgent social problem that needs to be redressed. More often than not, they find they are so powerless and they are often faced with tremendous obstacles of all sorts in trying to bring about positive changes with regard to women's rights in a society where sex discrimination practices in general and sexual harassment in particular are rife, so deep-rooted. It is all too often a very frustrating business for these women.

For example, one would quite often find that, one would indeed be making a complete fool of oneself should one go complaining either to some of one's peers, or even to some law enforcement officials for that matter about problems such as sexual harassment. To a lot of them, it is no serious problem. In fact, it is nothing an adult woman couldn't handle. To Dr. Yonkeu, it was all a very unfortunate situation.

All these made Dr. Yonkeu feel so left out, so alienated from her own people, the Cameroon people. In retrospect, she could not help but be of the feeling that the American people had relatively speaking been more accepting of her than her own people here in Cameroon. True, she thought, like the saying goes, "A prophet is never accepted in his own country; how sad!" In fact, in the United States, she was for the most part treated fairly; and thus, she always got out what she had put into whatever it was that she undertook.

This however was the complete opposite of her experience in Cameroon where conformity reigned supreme. Nearly everybody she met tried to change something about her; be it her ideas, the way she talked, the way she dressed, the manner in which she wore her hair, Dr. Yonkeu could not understand it all. To a lot of people, she was too strange, too foreign and as such, she did not fit into the Cameroon way of life. To them, her appearance, her mannerisms, her comportment and worse of all, her ideas especially on women's issues were so alien and so threatening to the gender status quo. She was not like the 'normal' Cameroon woman, the stereotypical Cameroon woman, who is supposed to be submissive, passive, never questioning of anything but accepting of all and above all, deferential to men. Dr. Yonkeu was certainly not this way. Sure, as much as she accepted and respected a lot of her African tradition, she certainly found some aspects of the African tradition and culture, especially those in relation to the treatment of women, such as female circumcision, "breast ironing", to stop girls developing breasts at an early age which could attract men to them, very repressive, self-negating, subjugating and at best obsolete. To her, they were totally unacceptable. As a result, she never hesitated, wherever and whenever possible to make her feelings known, her resentment of what she considered to be an outright violation of human as well as women's rights. This only alienated her further from her own people, her own women folk, the Cameroon people who happen to be 'die hearts' when it comes to maintaining the status quo as is, between men and women. Even some of her fellow women colleagues accused her of preaching "Western feminism" whatever that is. Dr. Yonkeu just couldn't believe it when she thought she was preaching "humanism." Dr. Yonkeu soon found out that she was indeed fighting a losing battle. This repressive attitude toward women was so deep rooted in the Cameroon society so much so that, it had now become a way of life for the people both men and women. As such, no amount of talking, it seemed, could possibly help change the situation. It was like 'spilling water on a duck's back! Like Nisbert R. A. (1984: 328) writing on alienated individuals explains in French, Dr YONKEU also actually felt « déraciné, isolé, coupé de sa communauté, dépourvu de tout statut sûr et de toute visée morale claire... et incapable de doter des résistances qui lui sont nécessaires pour vivre avec le monde et avec lui-même. » (also see Marx K., 1963 : in :C. Wright Mills).

But what the heck! Hard as things were, Dr. Yonkeu however, never gave up trying to help change people's mind-set and ideas about these things. It has to start somewhere. A strong stubborn streak continued to make her speak up against the unfair treatment of women and about other similar social issues in the society. It would be worthwhile, she figured, if by doing what she did could help bring about some changes, no matter how small, in the amelioration of women's condition. In all she was like a lone voice preaching in the wilderness. However, she just couldn't sit there arms crossed and do nothing about such gross injustices that were being perpetrated against her fellow women folk. Her conscience just would not let her do so, even if she wanted to. She was of the opinion that it was better to try and fail, than never try at all. Better sorry, she thought, than never. So she just carried on doing what she felt was right and humane and continued hoping for the better. After all, she concluded, 'freedom' like the famous African American Civil Rights leader, Asa Philip Randolf once said, 'is never granted; it is won…' As such, she was prepared to do just that, no matter what it took to do so; fight and win the battle against women's oppression in Cameroon. Thank God, she said, "Cameroon now has a Ministry of Women's Affairs and a well-educated and dynamic Minister. She hopes this Minister would do all in her power to reduce sexism in the country.

It was now only two months to go before it would be exactly one year since Dr. Yonkeu would have been jobless. She then decided she would go and see the Director General and at least, ask him to give back her Dissertation and other documents so that she could start looking for work somewhere else. She had heard that some staff members at the Organization had told the Director General and the new Director that she, Dr. Yonkeu supported the former Director. That only made matters worse. From then on, she knew she was never going to be re-hired at that Organization even though she was so innocent. However, she figured nobody at that 'goddam' Organization was ever going to believe her if she tried to argue she was innocent. She felt she was just the sacrificial lamb; her only crime, being born a woman. It was so unbelievable. True, the former Director had sometimes treated her kindly, and she appreciated that; but as far as what was happening at the Organization was concerned, that is the fight between the former Director and the Director General, she never took sides. She stayed out of it all and only minded her work. 'After all', she thought, 'she was only there for a couple of months, four months to be precise, and there was no way she could get involved in something she hardly knew anything about. Now they had come up with such lies, such big lies, just to make her suffer. 'She became all the more sad and at the same time, very determined indeed to fight the battle to the very end. After all, she has always been a fighter, she thought, and she would not let anybody "mess around" with her 'God given' rights. She would not let that happen.

It was exactly one year two days now, since Dr. Yonkeu had been out of work. So many people had promised to help her find work, but most of them turned out to be only empty promises. Only one or two people did honestly try to help her find work in some Organizations, although things did not quite work out. Some others even insisted that Dr. Yonkeu have sexual intercourse with them before they could help her find a job. Dr. Yonkeu just told them loud and clear, that if that was what they wanted, they might as well keep their jobs. She was not going to sink so low just so as to have a job. She wondered why these people saw her only as a sex object instead of as someone who had brains as they have and willing to put her brains to use in a constructive way to help in nation building.

As for the International Organizations to which Dr. Yonkeu had applied for employment, things were no better. She soon discovered that, nearly all of those Organizations had written back to her saying that they just couldn't employ her because she lacked work experience, although she had all the appropriate academic qualifications.

"Hey!" Dr. Yonkeu said sarcastically, "that sounds cool… But how on earth "she wondered, "was she supposed to have had work experience, when no one wants to give her the chance to have it. There is massive unemployment in Cameroon; and as such, the Government service which would have been a venue for acquiring such work skills, either by employing people or by granting subventions for work training problems, has itself issued a hiring freeze. Thanks in large part to the very policies of International Organizations such as the International Monetary Fund and the World Bank. These International Organizations impose such crippling austerity measures on a lot of Third World Governments by way of their notorious 'Structural Adjustment Plans' which often result in massive redundancies, retirements and unemployment in both public and private sectors in these countries. Yet, Dr. Yonkeu thought, when one applies for employment, even for volunteers work at these very International Organizations, they are quick to say one lacks the necessary work experience? Thus far, she has not seen anything positive coming out of these 'Structural Adjustments Plans' that these Organizations have imposed on these developing countries, other than undue suffering and hardships on the ordinary people. It is certainly not enough to just say one lacks work experience. What do they really expect one to do when all the venues for acquiring such experiences and skills have all been blocked on both the home and the international fronts? This, Dr. Yonkeu figured, is a classic case of a 'catch 22' problem. They should not just say these things. It would be more humane to find effective and workable solutions to these problems, rather than demanding the impossible.

The situation proved to be all too overwhelming for Dr. Yonkeu. She did not just know what to do about it all. Of course, most of her friends had by now abandoned her, knowing there was nothing they could gain by being friends with her; except for Fru and Kamga, who time and again, would take her out for a drink, or to some fine French or Italian Restaurants. She was ever so appreciative of this. These two guys, she felt, were really her true friends. Their friendship to her was indeed unconditional. This really helped keep up her moral and her faith in humanity in spite of all the emotional strain and other hardships she was now undergoing. At this stage, the job situation in the country had indeed become impossible. A lot of people were jobless and hungry in the country. People were finding it ever so hard trying to make ends meet. As a matter of fact, things steadily got worse with each passing day; yet nobody could do anything about it.

Really like the saying goes, "all men are equal but some are more equal than others. For example, whereas the rest of the country's people are suffering from the pangs of the economic crisis through massive retirements and redundancies, and by the terribly high rate of unemployment, the people in the National Security are in a way, having a ball. The economic downtown does not seem to have any effect on them one bit. Life goes on as usual for them, if not even better. They continue to have their recruitments, promotions and appointments as if nothing was happening. Thanks to the terrorist threats and civil wars in neighbouring countries such as Nigeria and the Central African Republic respectively. And boy, do some of them enjoy it, - booze, women and all the lot. It's just so unfortunate and so terrible, Dr. Yonkeu thought.

At this particular point in time, things had gotten so bad to the extent that even many directors of various organizations started refusing to grant audiences to people for fear that, a lot of these people would simply be seeking employment. They also made sure that they never advertise job openings in the papers or the radio, should there be any such openings at their Organizations. If at all some of them did advertise for these vacancies, it was purely for formality sake, because they made sure they often reserved the jobs for their own people; either for their relatives, or for children of their close friends, usually friends in high Government or political positions; even when these children may still be studying overseas. So by the time one sends out one's application there, the position would have already been filled or reserved for these 'chosen few'. One would be even lucky, should one even receive one of those: 'I am sorry but the post has been filled…' letters.

When occasionally, some of these Directors did grant audiences to certain people, they would become ever so rude to them as soon as they found out that the people had come looking for jobs. The situation had indeed gone out of control. If only, Dr. Yonkeu thought, these Directors knew how terrible and helpless unemployed persons felt when they were so rude to them, maybe; just maybe, they could try and change such bad and inhumane habits. One only wished they could be in these unemployed people's shoes to be able to actually experience the hardships, mental torture and suffering people who are unemployed undergo. In fact, even if a Director finds that he/she cannot employ someone, it wouldn't hurt in the least for him/her to politely explain or tell the unemployed person that he/she was sorry there were no vacancies at the organization. That does help a great deal instead of being so rude to often helpless people.

Dr. Yonkeu vividly remembers one of such incidents that happened to her. She had gone to see one of her father's old time friends, Dr. Njoh who was then the Regional Director of one of those top International organizations, to find out if he could possibly employ her at the Organization. Dr. Yonkeu's father had even written a letter to the Director explaining Dr. Yonkeu's situation to him, hoping that he may be able to help somewhat since in Cameroon now what matters is no longer what one knows but whom one knows sad isn't it?

When the Director, Dr. Njoh came to town, one of Dr. Yonkeu's friend Abu, who also worked at that Organization, and who had been helping her a great deal to find work in one of those organizations, informed Dr. Yonkeu that the Director was in town; and that he had also arranged for Dr. Yonkeu to come and see the man. When Dr. Yonkeu went to see the director to find out what the possibilities were for him to employ her at the Organization, the man was very rude to her. First of all, he did not even want to receive Dr. Yonkeu and he pretended he did not know who Dr. Yonkeu was, when in fact, Dr. Yonkeu's friend who worked at the organization had clearly told him who Dr. Yonkeu was. When he saw Dr. Yonkeu, his exact words to her were, 'and who are you again?' Dr. Yonkeu was so shocked. She could not believe the guy given that her friend had only a few minutes ago, told him who she was. The man just carried on and he did not even allow Dr. Yonkeu to introduce herself properly. He just picked up his brief case, and as he walked out of his office, he just rudely told Dr. Yonkeu that he had no job for her, and that she should better try somewhere else.

Dr. Yonkeu could hardly believe the rudeness from such an educated and respectable man whom she had hoped would at least know better. Besides, he was supposed to be her father's long-time friend. She felt so bad and so worthless and she barely struggled to hold back the tears that were about to flow from her eyes. She wondered what sort of a place the world had become. When people were up there, enjoying the big time, she thought, they had the tendency to forget the little people who had been their friends when they were down the social ladder, the ordinary folks, so to speak. When Dr. Yonkeu went back home, she went straight into her room and bolted the door. She could not hold back the tears anymore, she just burst out crying. Boy, did she cry her eyes out! She decided she would not tell her father about what had happened because he would be so shocked, and that would be too much for the old man. She however prayed and hoped that whenever she did become a 'rich' or an influential person in society; she would not forget those she had left down below. If anything, she would be polite and respectful to them even if she was not in a position to help them. It makes all the difference in the world when one is polite to people; especially to those seeking help of some sort, she thought. This Director too, was certainly one of those who discriminated against people of 'that' ethnic group many love to hate. How sad!

As these thoughts went through her mind, she indeed wondered when in fact, all these problems in the country would come to an end. 'For how much longer', she said to herself, 'could she possibly go on living the nightmare or living on the 'charity' of her parents; not to mention the many others who have to use all sorts of unpopular ways such as prostitution, just to survive?' In fact, the mere thought of living on the benevolence of others, or on depending on others for one's livelihood, was quite literarily killing her. She could now understand what the famous adage; 'he who goes a begging, goes a sorrowing' really meant. She was indeed living it. She just could not remember when last she had found herself in such a state of total misery and dependence. It was certainly not her style sponging, so to speaking on people. 'Things have got to change', she said to herself with such determination. Even her extended family had now turned their backs on her. She felt so alone in her suffering. 'Things just can't stay the same. Change is bound to come one way or another', she cried aloud. At this point, she was at her lowest. Never had she felt so frustrated, so helpless and so angry, all at once before.

She started soliloquizing. As far as the socio-economic problems in Cameroon are concerned, she thought, no amount of 'Structural Adjustment plans', overhauling, or tidying up, could resolve the present crippling economic crisis in the nation. Thank God! that the socio-economic problems in Africa as a whole, did become so acute at a crucial point in time, when the long-term effects of the major contemporary economic systems; that of "Communism" of Eastern Europe, and that of the Free Market Economy countries of Western Europe and America are as evident and as visible as ever. Thanks in large part to Mr. Gorbachev's 'perestroika' or his reform policy. It is a real mixed blessing for African countries. "Imagine" she went on, "one could now be as objective as ever in judging what aspects exactly, in both systems are worthwhile, implementing, workable and humane; and which are not. This way, one is likely to come up with a more balanced and realistic system, one would imagine, a 'mixed economic system of some sort, by combining those humane; economically sound and workable aspects of these systems, (the Communist and the Free Market economic systems), for African countries. Of course debts to developing and underdeveloped countries should be written off by the rich developed countries.

Given this reality, Dr. Yonkeu felt a complete change of the present socio-economic structures of the Cameroon society is an absolute must. To do this effectively, Cameroon she figures, should better opt for a basic 'Free Market Economic system; with of course, effective, comprehensive welfare programs, for the poor, the aged, the handicapped; something similar to the British welfare system, especially in the health domain. The access of the poor to effective health care facilities is so vital and necessary in a continent where ignorance about health care is rife and poverty so widespread; where for example maternal mortality and infant mortality run at a very high rate; and where poor adults die every day from often very simple and very treatable diseases, due to the lack of money to buy even the cheapest medicines. If anything, there should be only a very minimal medical fee charged for those who can pay. However, for those who absolutely cannot just afford to pay even this minimal medical fee, they should be allowed free medical care, thanks to Government and other philanthropic, private and international subventions.

Another problem of serious concern is the appalling and often deplorable state of housing conditions for the poor in Cameroon. Dr. Yonkeu felt there should be substantial Government investment in and proper management of low-cost housing for the poor in Cameroon. This seems to be the only way out, to resolve this problem. For example houses built for the poor should in the future be tailored to the social and cultural needs of the poor; not as it is now the case when housing supposedly meant to house the poor are so costly and are now occupied by the well-to-do. This well-meaning government policy to provide decent housing for the poor has failed woefully. (See projects in Yaoundé and Douala for example).

As far as the unemployment problem which by the way, currently tops the list of socio-economic problems, particularly among young adults, and females generally, Dr. Yonkeu figured it could be resolved, first, by encouraging the establishment of as many small business enterprises as possible. This she felt, could be achieved by giving more access to Bank Loans with low or manageable interest rates to genuine and capable individuals who already have or want to establish such businesses. They should also not be over taxed to the extent that they are unable to carry on with the business; thus defeating the very raison d'être of the establishment of such institutions in the first place. In fact, Dr. Yonkeu thought, past history, our present day experiences, and of course, extensive research and documentation on the project, all clearly show that, unlike the big and all powerful multi-national corporations, small and medium-size businesses, do actually boost a nation's economy, which in turn reduces the unemployment problem considerably. Thus given this reality, the Cameroon Government should by all means, encourage the establishment of small businesses in the country. It should also ensure that there are enough jobs for all those who want to work; by subsidizing job creating programs and projects in the public as well as the private sectors, such as in building the country's infrastructure, for example, roads, bridges, and the like, which the country is very badly in need of. Secondly, there should be effective, job training programs (training for decent paying jobs), financed by the Government, and other philanthropic private and international Organizations, to train the unemployed persons so that they could be active in the job market, even as technological and other changes occur in the system. This would not only curb unemployment, but it would also guarantee job security in any given country and an efficient and capable manpower. Of course there should also be the building of many industries as possible to absorb job seekers as they transform the country's many raw materials into finished goods that can sell locally and compete in the world marketplace.

Many Day Care Centres as seemed necessary to meet the demand in the country should be built to help mothers, especially single mothers who want to work, but are unable to do so simply because they do not have anyone responsible or anywhere safe to leave their children while they are at work. However, it is also necessary that these Day Care Centres be affordable for everybody who may want to use them, thanks in large part, to Government subsidies. Of course, sex discrimination must stop.

By the way have you noticed that most of the employers and people who run most of the top businesses in Cameroon are men, Dr. Yonkeu wondered?

Thus, rather than the "rich developed countries" simply dishing out financial assistance to poor, African countries; most of which is embezzled by corrupt public officials and as such perpetuating rather than doing away with poverty among the masses, Africa should itself create effective job-training programs, as well as provide sufficient decent and good- paying jobs and other concomitant programs and projects, for the masses. Low paying jobs at the informal sector of the economy must stop being the norm. Thus, the vast majority of the people would become income-generating, tax-paying adults, which would all be tremendously beneficial to the economies and finance situations of African nations.

Last but not least, is the terribly worrisome problem of Cameroon's neo-Colonial monetary or fiscal policy. Playing the devil's advocate, Dr. Yonkeu thought, if at all, at any one time or another, the monetary policy did work, the policy is not worth a dime today. It is as obsolete as ever. All the policy does, is to maintain Cameroon in an ever dependent state on the wealthy industrialized nations of the West. As such, Cameroon would be forever doomed begging for food and other basic necessities of life from her 'rich cousins' in the West; should Cameroon hold on to this defunct and at best, exploitative monetary policy. This, Dr. Yonkeu figured, would be absolutely suicidal and demeaning for the country. It all means, Cameroon would never grow up to maturity. She would forever be a baby to the Western world. How ironic that would be to think that, some time ago, Africa was for the most part, a relatively more independent and self-reliant continent; that is of course, before she was virtually reduced to her current state of dependency and beggardom by Colonialists.

To regain their relative self-reliance, it is imperative that African countries; have their own independent currencies; not currencies based on those of the West as it is the situation now. In this way, not only would Africa regain her socio political independence from neo-colonial forces, but each and every one of the African countries would regain her economic independence and be able to solve many of her economic problems, especially the unemployment problem with very little or no help at all from the industrialized nations which recently, have also been suffering from the economic crisis. In fact, each country would be in a position to be able to say, employ as many if not all of her able unemployed citizens; given that, each and every one of them would be able to determine and make available whatever amount of money that would be deemed necessary to do this; as well as manage other matters of the nation. After all, they would now be printing their own money and as such they would be able to make available the required amount of money they may need at any given point in time; a sort of "Quantitative Easing" policy like the Obama Government did recently to combat the economic recession in the U.S. Yes, there may be the problem of inflation. Yes so what about it? What is important is that Africa would regain her authority.

In the same way, the unequal global market that now dominate; in terms of economic relations between the rich developed world and the poor underdeveloped and developing countries, especially those of the African continent should be transformed to an equal global market where all nations, great and small, powerful and not powerful, rich and poor could compete on a fair and just basis. Currently, some nations are perpetually locked into the "proletarian" or "slave" category (e.g.: African countries South of the Sahara), and others into the "bourgeois" or "slave master" category (e.g.: the rich western countries). For instance, the rich countries of the West continue to dictate the terms of trade in the world market and they even subsidize their agricultural products sold on the global market, making fabulous profits. On the other hand, agricultural products from Africa sold on the global market receive very little or no subsides whatsoever. For example, Cameroon's external trade is currently estimated at about 100 million Francs CFA compared to those of Western countries estimated at Billions of Francs CFA (Equinox Radio News, 13/7/2014)   .

Such unfair world trade policies leave the majority of Africans who still work in the agriculture sector in a chronic state of poverty and misery. Indeed, this master slave relationship that Africa continues to have with the "God-like" West must stop. We all, black and white, red and yellow etc. have to take our destinies into our own hands. Things must change, Dr. Yonkeu thought to herself.

And the Western Nations, Dr. Yonkeu warns, should by all means not sabotage these policies by say, contributing to weaken the various currencies, no matter the inconveniences this may bring to bear upon some of their economies and their day to day activities; for it would only be in the short term. Instead they should in any way possible, encourage and help Africans help themselves to regain their independence and self-reliance. In the long term, they would find it was all worthwhile since they would no longer have to play 'big daddy' or be patronizing to Africans as they now do, by dishing out huge financial hand-outs to the latter every now and then. In this way, the West would be able to use their own monies to run worthwhile projects in their own countries and as such, help their own needy citizens.

On the other hand, Africans would just have to learn to do things efficiently for themselves rather than wait for others to do things for them. Similarly, the relationship between Africa and the West would most certainly be transformed into one of mutual help and respect for one another rather than the domination of one over the other, which is the West over Africa of course. Similarly, they would both if at all, be dependent on one another in a just way mutual for their well-being. Only in this way, Dr. Yonkeu thought, could African countries be able to compete freely and as equal partners with the West in a free world market. (Interview with Nana-Fabu Jacob Sunday, 2009).

In all, this new socio-economic and political order, would work and flourish, Dr. Yonkeu warps, only if Africa gets rid of all forms of discrimination; and other corrupt practices.

One very bright and sunny Wednesday morning, however, Dr. Yonkeu suddenly decided she had had enough with the run around she was getting from everybody; and she went to see the Director General of the Organization where she had worked before. She told him that, since his Organization had said they were unable to employ her due to financial constraints, he should simply give back her dissertation and other documents he had taken from her so that she could go and look for employment at some other Organization. The Director General simply said the

Dissertation was somewhere, and that he would look for it. Dr. Yonkeu asked him whether they did not have a filing system at the Organization whereby, people's dossiers are filed and kept in alphabetical order? That way, she said, it would be easier to retrieve people's dossiers and things. Dr. Yonkeu then told him she would give him two weeks to look for her Dissertation so as to be able to start job-hunting as soon as possible. She said the Director General was the one who had insisted on taking her Dissertation the first day they had met, and that, ever since then, she had been asking for it, but he kept on saying that he was busy, and that he would look for it. It was almost two years now, Dr. Yonkeu went on, and he had not yet found her Dissertation. However, she said she needed her Dissertation and that, he should very well give it to her the next time she would come to see him. The Director General just smiled at her viciously. She then stood up, and walked out of his office feeling so angry and disappointed. She was also worried because she had heard how some Cameroonians were copying other people's works, dissertations and presenting them as their works. "How dishonest", Dr. Yonkeu thought.

Two weeks had passed, and she was at the Director General's office as she had promised. She asked him for her Dissertation, but once again, he said he had not yet looked for it. This time, Dr. Yonkeu said nothing, although she was as mad as hell. She just simply shook her head, got up from her seat, and walked out of his office.

She allowed him a whole month before she decided to go back to see the Director General and ask him for the Dissertation. When she arrived at the Director General's office, he was not in. She enquired from the Secretary if the Director General had left her Dissertation with her? The Secretary said no, Dr. Yonkeu said nothing. She just walked away furious.

They had now pushed her to her limits. She was as mad as hell! She just went straight to her room, looked through her things, and she found exactly what she had been looking for- a hand gun. You know, she had bought that hand gun at a flea market some time ago. In fact, the day she bought the hand gun, she had not given it much thought. She had just bought it just as a mother just buys a toy for her child even though she had no plans of buying one on that particular day.

She found the hand gun, wiped the dust off it, loaded it, and put it in her hand-bag. She had never thought of killing anyone before in her life, not even when someone had hurt her so badly. However, she seemed not to care so much this time around. It seemed like the only alternative she had left. As a matter of fact, she had meticulously figured everything out, and it seemed whichever way she went, she was bound to end up in jail sooner or later.

Some friends of hers had even suggested that she should go and grab some of the computers from the Director General's office and keep them until they produced her Dissertation. She had seriously thought of doing so, but she had doubts as to whether that would produce any positive results. Maybe, she thought, the Director General would simply go and arrange with the police to have her arrested and locked up for stealing. Besides, she wondered what effects some missing computers could possibly have on such a rich Organization with plenty of foreign AID from Europe and America. The Director General, she thought, might simply decide to write it off as one of those unforeseen loses; and in that case, Dr. Yonkeu would be the looser, since she would end up never getting back her Dissertation again.

She thought of all the work and effort she had put into writing her Dissertation; the sleepless nights, the writing and the re-writing of various parts, and she became really furious. 'No', damn it, she said, she had had enough of the merry go round. She could not take any more of the nonsense. She decided she would go to the so-called Director General and ask him for her Dissertation one last time; and if he was unable to reproduce it, she would not argue with him, she would just "blow his brains out." She wouldn't careless if she was put in jail. After all, she thought, whichever way she went, she was doomed to end up in jail anyway. If she even sued him, chances are that, the case may never come up for trial, since she had been told one had to pay bribes, and big ones too, to some of those corrupt court officials before one's case could even get a hearing at court. Where would she get that sort of huge sum of money from? Besides, these big

Organizations such as the one she would be suing could afford some of the best lawyers in Cameroon who would argue their cases and make it seem as though they were on the right, even though they know perfectly well that they are at fault. She came to the conclusion that she had 'nothing to lose but her chains' whichever way things went. Being unemployed, she thought, was one of worst things that could possibly happen to anyone. It is so humiliating. One feels so worthless, a good for nothing; and chances are that, one would end up depending on hand-outs, or on some charity Organization for food and shelter. And there comes a time, when there is no 'Good Samaritan' anymore to provide one with these basic necessities of life, and one ends up somewhere on the streets helpless and desperate.

For most females, the next best thing they find they could do would be to become sex workers, whereas most males would most likely end up as thieves, bandits or pick pockets just to survive. In fact, unemployment does have such tremendous dehumanizing effects on people. As a matter of fact, Dr. Yonkeu was not ready; neither did she have the guts to do either of these. Had the financial institutions been carrying on well, she would have asked for a loan (if it were at all possible given the fact that one had to have substantial guarantee before one was given any loan), and start up a private business a consultancy on development etc. Unfortunately though, it seemed most of the banks in the country were in serious financial difficulties. They were all in the red and charged very high interests for loans. As for the Government Services, things had still not changed. The so-called 'hiring' freeze was still in effect. So you see, Dr. Yonkeu found herself in an impossible situation that she could absolutely do nothing about. It had now become for her, 'a do or die' situation so to speak. The country's myriad problems were literarily killing her. In the evening, around 7 P.M. when it was getting a little dark, Dr. Yonkeu decided to go and visit Koffi's grave in the Pauper's Grave-yard. She had bought a fresh bunch of pretty flowers which she took along with her. When she arrived at the spot where Koffi's friend had indicated Koffi had been buried, she said a couple of prayers and when she had decided it was time for her to leave, she started talking as though she was talking to Koffi in person. She said "she was so sure

Koffi was now, if not with God, in Heaven, he would be somewhere or somehow nearer to the Father in Heaven than she was. She said she is well aware of the fact that, what she had planned to do the following day was wrong before God and man, and that, it was not what Koffi would have liked her to do. All the same, she asked Koffi to forgive her. She said she was really in an impossible situation and there seemed to be no turning back. As she said these last words, tears poured down her cheeks uncontrollably as the world collapsed around her. She then slowly turned around and walked back home without looking back. "Life" she continued was a constant struggle; or as the French would say, "la vie est un combat" and that she was not giving up; at least not as yet. She would fight to the very end. In the night, she could hardly sleep. She kept on having nightmares in which there was a lot of shooting and blood involved. The following day, she got up really early feeling so tired, so exhausted from the sleeplessness the night before. She then took a shower, got dressed, ate a slice of bread and butter and drank some tea. She now regained some of her strength.

It was indeed a cool Monday morning. In fact, one could see the sun still trying to force its way through the thick dark clouds that had brought the heavy rains the night before. Dr. Yonkeu had asked her father if he could give her a ride to the Director General's office? She lied that she had an important appointment with him; and that maybe he could have even found some work for her as he did promise the last time she saw him. Dr. Yonkeu's father was so pleased and got all excited. He said 'of course he would take Dr. Yonkeu there.' Dr. Yonkeu's father was always willing to help when it had to do with helping Dr. Yonkeu find work. He said he felt so sorry about Dr. Yonkeu's situation; and he felt nostalgic about the good old days. During his time, he went on; just having a First School Leaving Certificate was a guarantee for employment and a good life, let alone a Bachelor's Degree. That was a sure key to success. He said he didn't think he would ever live to see the day, when people with Bachelor's Degrees would be jobless, not to even mention Doctorate Degrees. That, he said, was scandalous; and that, it would have been unheard of in their time. "Mai!" he exclaimed, 'how things had changed'!

'Indeed, things have really changed. Even your little girl', Dr. Yonkeu whispered to herself, "it has changed too; and she is going to commit murder, yes, a real murder.' They both went into the car, and drove off to where the Director General's office was. Dr. Yonkeu took a quick glance around and saw the Director General's imposing car at the parking lot. 'Thank God', she said to herself, "he was in. As soon as Dr. Yonkeu's father stopped the car, she came out of the car and walked toward the Director General's office. She seemed so calm, cool and collected, that nobody would have ever guessed or suspected what was going through her mind at that particular moment.

When she reached the Director General's office and saw his door open, she just walked right in. The Director General was somehow surprised to see her. He said good morning to her and asked her to have a seat. She did not seat, neither did she say a word. She just looked right straight into his eyes, and asked him for her Dissertation. The Director General, who as usual was sipping his coffee, said he still had not found it. Dr. Yonkeu said nothing. She just opened her hand-bag, pulled out the hand-gun, and fired two shots straight at the Director General's forehead. In a daze, she immediately walked right out of his office as though nothing had happened. She by passed the Director General's Secretary who had also heard the strange sounds but still could not figure out what had happened; considering that gunshot sounds were not sounds that one heard every day. As soon as Dr. Yonkeu had walked out of the building into the open space, she collapsed, gun in hand.

So many people in the surrounding area had also heard the strange sounds of shooting and before too long, a huge crowd had gathered around Dr. Yonkeu. Others ran into the Director General's office. The whole place was in absolute chaos, with people going back and forth. The Director General's Secretary had by then discovered what had happened to her Boss, and she had rang up the police and the Ambulance Service, who both arrived shortly afterwards. The Ambulance crew had rushed into the Director General's office and they had managed to carry the Director General, who was by then lost so much blood from the gunshot wounds on his head, away to the nearest hospital. After the Police had taken a few statements from the Director General's

Secretary, they then came and took Dr. Yonkeu into custody, and later brought her here, to court, for trial.

The big-tommied judge just sat there dumbfounded from hearing all what had happened to Dr. Yonkeu, and why exactly she had shut the Director General. After he had somewhat recovered from his shock, he just kept on repeating, 'what a pity! What a pity! What had become of the world, and the young people these days", he wondered? Why did she have to shoot the man? Why didn't she even try to sue him, 'he went on, knowing fully well that no action would have ever been taken, since in the first place, it would have taken so long for a court hearing. He however decided that since Dr. Yonkeu had shut a man who they were not even sure would live, he could do very little or nothing, but to give Dr. Yonkeu a life sentence in prison. "It was a pity", he said, "putting such an intelligent young lady into jail, but that he could do absolutely nothing about it. "Rules are rules" "la loi c'est la loi", he concluded.

Dr. Yonkeu who had by then fully recovered, from her ordeal, showed no sign of fright. She simply said 'she was also sorry about what had happened, but that she could really not help doing what she did. She said she found herself back against the wall; in an impossible situation, a do or die situation, sort of; and it was just a little too late for anyone to have stopped her, or for anything to have been done for that matter, which could have prevented her from doing what she did. "She then was handcuffed and taken off to jail. Her parents then left the court room feeling so sad and helpless. Her mother was weeping so hard.

A year had barely passed by, when the Judge who had sentenced Dr. Yonkeu, Judge Edu, was transferred to be Judge in another city. As for the Director General, thank God, he did not die although he was in a wheel chair and was still recovering from his head injuries. There were serious doubts as to whether he would be able to walk upright again.

Meanwhile, Dr. Yonkeu's parents had appealed her case and they had granted her another trial. The new Judge, Judge Manga had granted a hearing and a date was set for the trial. On the first day of the trial, it was a real circus. The court room was jammed parked with people who either had come to witness it, or who had simply come to see 'the' woman who had shut a man. To these people, that was such a big deal. Shooting itself was somewhat rare in Cameroon except by bandits and if anything, it would have been more understandable if it were a man rather than a woman who had done the shooting. That simply was unthinkable to these people.

The new Judge seemed to be very understanding about the whole situation. After all the days of court hearings, the Judge finally decided to release Dr. Yonkeu. He said, "really, Dr. Yonkeu did find herself in an impossible and very unfortunate situation. "However", he added, "she had overreacted by shooting the Director General". Nevertheless, he went on, 'he realized it was a little too late for her to have been able to react any differently, given all what she had been through. All the same, he insisted, "she shouldn't have shut the Director General" "Thank God"; he said the Director Generalis alive". He nevertheless released her on condition that Dr. Yonkeu never kept a hand gun, ever, again.

Dr. Yonkeu was indeed very pleased with the Judge's decision. It was one of those rare occasions that she felt she had received a fair treatment since her return to Cameroon. Dr. Yonkeu's parents were particularly pleased and grateful. The wardress who had brought Dr. Yonkeu to court for the trial undid her handcuffs; after which Dr. Yonkeu thanked the Judge and rushed to where her parents were standing. They all hugged each other with plenty of tears of joy running down their cheeks.

They all then thanked the Judge, walked out of the court room and drove home. Dr. Yonkeu just could not wait to take a long warm bath and put on some fresh clean clothes. They all had dinner together that evening after which they all expressed their hearty thanks to God Almighty for once more bringing the family back together again.

Some days did pass; and after having given a great deal of thought to the way her life was going, Dr. Yonkeu told her parents that she was going to start a school for orphans, in memory of her friend Koffi. She said she would name the school after Koffi. Her father said that was a very good and honourable idea, and he wished her well. He also promised to help her in whatever way possible. Her mother also felt that the idea of starting a school for orphans in Koffi's memory was a very noble and worthwhile idea.

Within a month's time, Dr. Yonkeu had already started some fund raising efforts. She wrote to as many Charity Organizations as possible in Switzerland, England and the United States of America explaining her project to them; and she asked them if they could help in financing the project? She got a lot of financial help for the project from these Organizations. They all felt it was a worthwhile project, in Cameroon where the street children phenomenon was fast becoming the norm. Of course, her friends in the United States once more came to her aid financially and morally when she wrote and told them of her project. In all, the fund-raising effort turned out to be a very huge success.

Within a year's time, the school had been built, and a month later, the school started in earnest, with its first enrolment of fifty orphan children from all the ten regions of the nation. The school was officially known as 'Koffi's School', and the children were called 'Koffi's children'. Dr. Yonkeu's parents were very proud of her. Time and again, her friends from the United States of America would pay a visit to 'Koffi's School' and they would bring along with them, a lot of presents, computers and books of course, for 'Koffi's Children'. Meanwhile, funds kept pouring in from all corners of the world. As for Dr. Yonkeu, she only hoped and prayed that all ' Koffi's Children', would grow up to be responsible and considerate men and women; and above all, that, whenever possible, they would always lend a helping hand to whoever was in need, before it was too late for them to do so. At this point, 6 A.M. to be exact, Dr. Yonkeu's alarm clock went off as she was still dreaming. At first she thought the alarm clock ringing was all in her dream. However, she soon gained some consciousness and woke up suddenly, feeling tired and shaken from her long, long, dream... She quickly wiped her eyes, slowly bent over, stretched out her right hand and stopped the alarm clock. Now fully awoken, she looked at the time on the clock. It was a few minutes past 6 A.M. Mai, what a dream she said to herself. "Thank God it was only a dream. How could I have ever shut anybody? I have never thought of doing such a thing in my whole life. It's awful! Come to think of it, why would it not be only a long, long, empty dream, when as late Pa Jacob Sunday Nana-Fabu used to say, "life just happens to be a long, long dream; an empty dream." From the time one is born one enters into this long, long, empty dream. When one dies, one sleeps forever, an everlasting sleep. This is when all of one's sorrows, struggles, illnesses, pains and toils all disappear for good, a never ending sleep. In fact, he said, in life when one sleeps and wakes up, one is simply preparing for that long, long, never ending sleep; the final sleep or death. How simply ingenious, Dr. Yonkeu thought. Nothing can be so true she concluded. With this thought, Dr. Yonkeu slipped out of her warm bed and walked straight to the bathroom[22].

---

[22] The author is proud to say that this book was influenced by the "African writers' series" which she read at her father's home library. At an early age the author was introduced by her father to the "African Writers' series" which he was a big fan of and which he had read every single one of the books. The author has also read most of these books and they continue to influence her writing in many ways, in content and form. Special tribute goes to the illustrious novelist Chinua Achebe, who recently (2013) passed on.

REFFERENCES

Books

Abdou Touré, 1985, *Les petits métiers à Abidjan : l'imagination au secours de la conjoncture,* Paris, Karthala

Abega S.C., 1999, *Société Civile et réduction de la pauvreté,* Yaoundé, Editions Clé.

Adepoju A., 1997, Family, *Population and Development,* London, Zed Books Ltd.

AFDB African Development Bank, 2000, *l'effet de la crise financière mondiale sur l'Afrique,* Working Paper series, 96, AFDB, Tunis, Tunisia.

Amin S., 1973, *La faillite du développement en Afrique et dans le Tiers-Monde, Une analyse politique,* Paris, L'Harmattan.

_ _ _., 1973, *Le développement inégal, Essai sur les formes sociales du Capitalisme périphérique,* Paris, Editions de Minuit.

_ _ _, 1973, *Neo-colonialism in West Africa,* Harmondsworth, Peguin.

Amselle J. L., et M'bokolo E., 2000, *Au cœur de l'ethnie. Ethnie, tribalisme et Etat en Afrique,* Paris, La découverte/Poche

Armelle C., 1999, "African Cities: Colonial Cities", In: *Revue Noire: African Urbis,* Montréal, Contemporary Art, Canada Press.

Atenga T., 2007, *La presse en sursis,* Paris, Muntu.

Ateba Eyene C., 2007, *Les paradoxes du pays organisateur : Elites productrices ou prédatrices : Le cas de la province du Sud à L'ère Biya (1982-2007),* Yaoundé, Editions Saint Paul.

_ _ _., 2012, *Le Cameroun sous la dictature des loges, des sectes du magico-anal et des réseaux maffieux. De véritables freins contre l'émergence en 2035 (La logique du cœur de la performance),* Yaoundé, Editions Saint Paul.

Anyangwe C., 1987, *The Cameroon Judicial System*, Yde, CEPER.

Babissakana and Abissama Onana, In : *Les débats économiques du Cameroun et d'Afrique*, Yaoundé, Prescriptor.

Balandier G., 1971/1997, *Senset Puissance: Les Dynamiques Sociales*, Paris, PUF.

Banfield, E., 1974, *The Unheavenly City Revisited*. Boston Little: Brown & Co.

Banque Mondiale, 2003, *Enquêtes sur les ménages au Cameroun*, Yaoundé, Presses de la Banque Mondiale.

Batten T. R., 1960, *Problems of African Development*, London, Oxford University Press.

Baulch, B., 2011, *Why Poverty persists: Poverty Dynamics in Asia and Africa*, Massachusetts, Edward Elgar Publishing.

Bayart J. F., 1989, *l'Etat en Afrique, la politique du ventre*, Paris, Foyard.

_ _ _., 1992, *La politique par le bas en Afrique noire*, Paris, Karthala

Beauvoir, Simone de, 1953. *The Second Sex* (Translated by H.M. Parshley), New York, Alfred Knoph.

_ _ _., 1968, *The Second Sex*, Bentan Books Chartton S.E.M., 1984. Women in Third World Development London, Boulder, Westerview Press.

_ _ _., 1972. *The Coming of Age*. (Translated by Patrick O'Brian), New York, G. P. Putnam and Sons.

Bekolo Ebe B. et al. 2002, *Intermédiation financière et financement de développement en Afrique*, Yaoundé, Presse Universitaire de Yaoundé.

Bergel E., 1955, *Urban Sociology*, London, McGraw Hill.

Berger Elena, 1974, *Labour, Race and Colonial Rule*, Oxford, Oxford University Press.

Berger P. et Luckmann T., 2003, *La construction sociale de la réalité*, Paris, Seuil .

Beryl Hintz, 2004, Shadows of Doubt. Milwaukee, Terrace Productions, Ltd.

Betts, R., 1977, *Imperialism and Colonialism in African Society, Culture and Politics*, New York, University Press of America.

Birhr A. and Pffepperkon R., 1996, *Hommes/Femmes l'introuvable égalité: école, travail, couples espace public*, Paris, ed. ouvrière.

Biya P., 1986, *Pour le libéralisme communautaire*, Paris, ABC

Boserup E., 1970, *Women'sRole in Economic Development*, London, Allen and Urwin.

Bourdieu P., 1984, *Questions de Sociologie*, Paris, Minuit.

_ _ _., 1986, *Sens et Puissance*, Paris, Minuit.

_ _ _., 1987, *Espace et pouvoir,* choses dites, Paris, Minuit.

_ _ _., 1998, *La domination masculine,* Paris, Minuit.

Braun, T., 2003, *Employment for Poverty Reduction and Food Security*, Washington D.C., International Food Policy Research Institute.

Bruntland G. H., 1987, *Our Common Future: Report of the World Commission on Environment and Development,* Oxford, Oxford University

Cantor et al., 1992, *Women in Power*, New York, Houghton Company

Carnoy M., 1974, *Education as cultural Imperialism*, New York, Longmann

Césaire A., 1955, *Discours sur le colonialisme*, Paris, Présence Africaine.

_ _ _., 1963, *La tragédie du Roi Christophe*, Paris, Présence Africaine

Chindji-Kouleu F., 2013, *Seule la mort dépasse l'argent. 500 pourquoi*, Yaoundé, Edition Espoir

_ _ _.2012, *Le pouvoir est sucré*, Yaoundé, Edition Espoir

_ _ _. 1990, *Etre Pygmée et citoyen*, Yaoundé, Le Flambeau

_ _ _., 2002, *Négritude, philosophie et Mondialisation*, Yaoundé, CLE

_ _ _. 2004, *Communiquer est un art*, Yaoundé, Editions Saagraph

_ _ _. 2005, *Initiation à la sociologie rurale*, Yaoundé, Saagraph

Chodorow N., 1995, *Feminism and Psycho-analytic Theory*, New-York, New York University Press

_ _ _. 1979, "Mothering Male-Dominance and Capitalism" In: Eisentein Z. R., *Capitalist Patriarchy and the Case for Social Feminism*, New York, Monthly Review Press

_ _ _. 1995, *Feminism and Psycho-analytic Theory*, New York, New York University

Claire Robertson and Iris Berger, 1986, *Women and class in Africa*, New York, Africana Publishing Company

Cohen D., 2004, *La mondialisation et ses ennemis*, Paris, Grasset et Fasquelle.

Cohen-Bracie B., 2006, *Communiquer efficacement sur le développement durable*, Paris, Démos

Combessie J. C., 2001, *La méthode en Sociologie,* Paris, La Découverte

Coquery Vidrovitch C., 1990, *Société paysanne du Tiers-Monde*, Paris, L'Harmattan

_ _ _. 1994, *Les Africains : Histoire des femmes d'Afrique noire du XIX au XXè siècle*, Paris, Desjouquères

_ _ _. 1991, *Tiers-monde: l'informel en question*, Paris, L'Harmattan

Cordonier R., 1987, *Femmes africaines et commerce : les revendeuses de tissu de la ville de Lomé*, Paris, L'Harmattan

Coretta Scott King, 1969, *My Life with Martin Luther King Jr.*, New York, Hott Rinchart and Winston Inc.

Courade R. B. et al., 1991, *Levillage camerounais à l'heure de l'ajustement structurel,* Paris, Karthala

Crozier M. and Friedberg E., 1977, *L'acteur et le système*, Paris, Seuil

Cutrufelli R., 1983, *Womenof Africa: Roots of Oppression*, London, Zed Press.

Curry T., JiobuR. and Schwirian K., *Sociology,* 2002, New Jersey, Upper Saddle River.

De Lancey V., 1988, *The political Economy of Cameroon: The Impact of credit Union Movement on the Production and Accumulation in the Agricultural Sector of Cameroon*, African Studies Center Leiden

Diarra J. T., *Christianisme et excision. Repères pour une prise de décision*, Bamako, Mali, Centre Djoliba

Diop G.A., 1960, *Le fondement culturel, technique et industriel d'un futur Etat fédéral d'Afrique Noire,* Paris, Présence Africaine

Droy I., 1990, *Femmes et Développement rural*, Paris, Karthala

Dubar C., 1991, *La socialisation : construction des identités sociales et professionnelles*, Paris, Armand Colin

Dugast I., 1954, *People of Central Cameroon*, London, International African Institute

Durkheim E., 1947, 1986, *Les règles de la Méthode Sociologique*, Paris, Quadridge, PUF, 5è Edition.

_ _ _., 1966 (orig. 1893), *The Division of Labour in Society*, New York, Free Press

_ _ _., 1966 (orig. 1897), *Suicide, A study in Sociology*, Translated by John A. Spantding and George Simpson, New York, Free Press

Eboussi Boulaga F., 1997, *La Démocratie de transit au Cameroun*, Paris, L'Harmattan.

Edari R., 1980, *Dependent Development and Urbanization in Kenya*, Paris, Berget-Levrault.

Essombe Edimo Nya banabebe J.R., 2007, Spécialité et développementéconomique à Douala, entre le hasard et la nécessité, Paris, L'Harmattan.

Edward I., 1980, *Contested Terrain*, New York, Basic Books.

Egerton F. C.C., 1938, *African Majesty: A Record of Refuge at the Court of the King of Bangangte in French Cameroons*, London, George Routledge & Sons Ltd

Ela J. M., 1998, *Innovations sociales et renaissance de l'Afrique Noire. Les défis du monde d'en bas.* Montréal, L'Harmattan.

_ _ _. 2006, *Travail et entreprises en Afrique. Les fondements sociaux de la réussite économique,* Paris, Karthala.

_ _ _. 1983, *La ville en Afrique Noire,* Paris, Karthala.

_ _ _. 1990, *Quand l'Etat pénètre en Brousse. Les ripostes Paysannes à la crise,* Paris, Karthala.

_ _ _. 1994, *L'irruption des pauvres. Société contre l'ingérence, pouvoir et argent*, Paris, L'Harmattan.

Eteki M.L., 2001, Le totalitarisme des Etats africains : le cas du Cameroun, Paris, L'Harmattan.

Eleanor Leacock et al., 1986, *Women's work: Development and the Division of labour,* by Gender Bergin and Garvey, published M.A.

Elias Norbert, 1991, *Qu'est-ce que la sociologie?*, Paris, Ed. de l'Aube, Paris.

Elstein J. B., 1981, *Public Man, Private Woman*, New Jersey, Princeton University Press

Elsthtain J. B., 1938, *Public Man, Private Woman*, Boston, Princeton University Press

Ernst S. and Goodison L., 1981, *In Our Own Hands, A Book of Self Help Therapy*, London, the Women's Press Ltd. Great Sutton Street.

Essè Amouzou, 2013, *Pauvreté, chômage et émigration des jeunes africains, Quelles alternatives ?*, Paris, Harmattan.

Fame Ndongo J., 1996, *Un regard africain sur la communication*, Yaoundé, St Paul

Fanon F., 1968, *Les Damnés de la Terre*, Paris, Maspéro

_ _ _. 1963, *The Wretched of the Earth*, New York, Grove Press

Ferone G., 2003, *Ce que développement durable veut dire*, Paris, Karthala

Foster et al., 2003, *Accounting for Poverty in Infrastructure Reform*, Washington DC, the World Bank.

Fox Piven et al., 1983, *Punishing the Poor Again, the Fraud of Workforce,* New York, the Nation Press.

Freund J., 1965, l'essence du politique, Paris, Sirey.

Garfinkel H., 1967/1984, *Studies in Ethnomethodology*, Englewoods Cliffs, Prentice-Hall.

_ _ _. 2007, *Recherches en ethnométhodologie*, Paris, PUF

Geschiere P. et Konings P., 1993, *Itinéraires d'accumulation au Cameroun*, Paris, Karthala

_ _ _. and Binsbergen W. V., 1984, *Old Modes of production and capitalist Encroachment: Anthropological Exploration in Africa,* London, African studies center

Giddens A., 2000, *Les conséquences de la modernité,* Paris, L'Harmattan.

Gilder, G., 1981, *Wealth and Poverty*, New York, Batam Book.

Goffman E., 1956, *La mise en scène de la vie quotidienne*, Paris, Minuit.

_ _ _. 1973, *La mise en scène de la vie quotidienne*, 2 vol, trad française, Paris, Minuit

_ _ _. 1975, *Stigmate. Les usages sociaux des handicaps,* Paris, Edition Minuit.

2002, *l'arrangement des sexes*, Paris, La Dispute.

Graff J., 2003, *Introduction to Sociology: Poverty and Development,* Cape Town, Oxford University Press.

Grafmeyer Y., 1997, *Sociologie Urbaine,* Paris, Nathan.

Gralbraith J. K., 1984, *La voix des pauvres,* Paris, Gallimard
_ _ _. 1984, *Théorie de la pauvreté de masse,* Paris, Gallimard

Grawitz M., 2001, *Méthodes des Sciences Sociales,* 2ème édition, Paris, Minuit

Grimes P. et al., 2000, *Economics of Social Issues,* 14th Edition, Boston, BunRidge: Irwin MC Grans Hills.

Gugler et al., 1994, *Cities, Poverty and Development Urbanization in the 3rd World,* 2nd Edition, New York, Oxford University Press, Walton Street.

Harrison Graham, 2005, *The World Bank, Governance and Theories of political Action in Africa.* The British Journal of Politics and International Relations Vol 7 n°2

Hess B-B, Markson E. W. and Stein P. J., 1988, *Sociology,* New York, MacMillan Publishing Company

Hilfilker D., 2002, *Urban Injustice: How Ghettos Happen,* New York, Seven Stories Press.

Huston C., 1994, *Children in Poverty,* New York, edited by Aletha Cambridge University Press.

Holborn B. et al., 1991, *Sociology. Themes and perspectives,* London, Harper Collins Publishers.

Isaac L., 1996, *Reading in Social Problems,* New York, The McGraw-Hill Companies Inc.

Isabel et al., 2012, *When the Global Crisis and Youth Bulge Collide,* Double the Jobs Trouble for Youth, Social Economic Working Paper. UNICEF

Institut National de la Statistique (INS), 2009, 2010, 2013, Yaoundé-Cameroun.

Jack Lang, 2013, *Vaincre le chômage,* Paris, La Découverte.

Jean J. et al., 2000, *L'Economie Camerounaise un espoir évanoui,* Boulevard Arago Paris, Editions Karthala.

Jordan B., 1996, *A Theory of Poverty and Social Exclusion,* 65 Bridge Street, Cambridge polity Press.

Joseph A., 2000, *Le rationnement du crédit dans les pays en développement. Le cas du Cameroun et Madagascar,* Paris, L'Harmattan

Kamdem E., 2002, *Le temps différencié, Management et interculturalité en Afrique : expérience Camerounaise*, Québec, les Presses de l'Université Laval et Paris l'Harmattan

Keller B. and Bary E. G., 1977, *African Women and Problems of Modernization: African Society, Culture and Politics*, New York, University Press of America

Kengne Fodouop et Metton, 2000, *L'économie informelle et développement dans les pays du Sud à l'ère de la mondialisation,* Yaounde CLE

_ _ _. 1991, *Lespetits métiers de la rue et l'emploi. Le cas de Yaoundé*, Yaoundé, Editions Sopecam.

Kessler Harris-Harris A., 1981, *Women Have Always Worked*, New York, McGraw Hill Book and Co.

Kimmel D.C., 1974, Adulthood and Aging. Now York, John Wiley and sons Inc.

Koh Bela A. J., 2006, *La prostitution Africaine en Occident*, Editions CCINIA Paris, communication.

Kottak C, 1991, *Cultural Anthropology*, 5th Edition, New York, McGraw Hill Inc.

_ _ _. 1991, *Cultural Anthropology*, 5th Edition, New York, Mc Graw Hill Inc.

Lautier B., 1994, *L'économie informelle dans le tiers-monde,* Paris, Editions la Découverte.

Kwame Nkrumah, 1972, La lutte de classes en Afrique, Paris, Présence Africaine.

Le Vine T., 1964, *The Cameroons from Mandate to Independence*, Berkeley, University of California Press.

Leacock Eleanor, 1972, *Introduction to Engels F., The Origin of the Family, Private property and the State,* ed. E Leacock, New York, New York World Press

Lewis M., 1973, *Urban America: Institutions and Experience,* New York, John Wiley & sons Inc.

Lewis V.H., 1965, *French Speaking Africa: The Search for Identity*, Washington D.C., Georgetown University Press.

Lipton J., 2002, *Including the Poor,* Proceeding of a Symposium Organised by the World Bank, Washington.

Little K., 1970, *West African Urbanization: Associations in Social Change,* Cambridge, Cambridge University Press

Long N., 2005, *Development Sociology, Actor Perspectives*, London and New York, Routledge

Lowy I. M. C., 2007, *Pour en finir avec la domination masculine*, Paris, Editions Seuil.

Mahammad Yunsus, 1978, Greamean, Village Bank, In: *Bangladesh Micro Credit Pioneer*, 3[rd]ed.

Mair L., 1974, *African societies*, Cambridge, Cambridge University Press

Morgenthau, 1964, Political Parties in French Speaking West Africa, Oxford, Clarendon Press.

Marie J. et al., 2002, *African Atlasses Cameroon*, Paris, les Editions du Jaguar Sifijer.

Marx K., 1963, (orig.1844), Estranged Labour- Economic and Philosophical Manuscripts of 1844. In: C.Wright Mills (ed.) Images of Man, New York, Goerge Braziller.

_ _ _, 1972, Manuscripts of 1844. Paris, Editions sociales.

_ _ _,1949, *The German Ideology*, New York, International Publishers.

_ _ _,and Friedrich Engels, 1967 (orig. 1848) *Th eCommunist Manifesto*, London, Peguin

Mascia Lees F. E., 1984, *Toward a model of Women's Status*, New York, Peter Lang Publishing Company.

Mbangwana P., Mpoche K. and Mbuh T., 2006, *Language, Literature and Identity in Multicultural Societies*, cuvilier-vertag: Giottingen.

Mbembé A., 1986, *Les jeunes et l'ordre politique en Afrique noire*, Paris, Le Harmattan.

_ _ _,1989, *Ecrire l'Afrique à partir d'une faille*, Politique Africaine, N°18

_ _ _,2005, *De la postcolonie,* Paris, Karthala.

_ _ _,2010, *Sortir de la grande nuit - Essai sur l'Afrique,* Paris, La Découverte.

Mbonji Edjenguèlè, 2009, *Santé; maladies et médecine africaine, plaidoyer pour l'autre tradi-pratique*, Yaoundé, les presses universitaires de Yaoundé.

Mead George Herbert, 1934, *Mind, Self and Society*, Chicago, University of Chicago Press

Merton Robert K., 1957, *Social Theory and Social Structure*, New York, Free Press

Mills C. Wright, 1956, *The Power Elite*, New York, Oxford University Press

Mills J. S., 1911, *The Subjugation of Women*, New York, Frederick A. Stokes

Monimat M. K. 1989, *Femme du Sahel, désertification au quotidien*, Paris, Karthala

Moore K., 2005, *Thinking about Youth Poverty Through the Lenses of Chronic Poverty, life-Course poverty and Intergenerational Poverty*, Institute for Development Policy and Management (IDPM), School of Environment and Development, University of Manchester, Chronic Poverty Research Centre (CPRC) working paper 57.

Muchielli A., 2004, *Dictionnaire des méthodes qualitatives en sciences humaines*, Paris, Armand Colin

Nana-Fabu J. S. and Azamo F., 1983, *Rapport de mission de contrôle de la perception auprès de l'ambassade du Cameroun à Londres*, Yaoundé, Ministère des Finances

Nana-Fabu S., 1987, *The status of Womenin Cameroon*, Ph.D. Dissertation, the University of Wisconsin Milwaukee, USA.

_ _ _, 2009, *The Feminization of poverty in Cameroon*, Yaounde, Clé

Nisbert R.A., 1984, *La tradition sociologique*, Paris, PUF.

Ndongmo J. L., 1981, *Le Dynamisme Bamiléké : la maitrise de l'espace agraire* (suivi de) *Lamaitrise de l'espace urbain*, Yaoundé, CEPER.

Nga Ndongo V. et Kamdem E., 2010, *La sociologie aujourd'hui, une perspective africaine*, Paris, l'Harmattan

_ _ _, 1993, *Les médias au Cameroun, Mythes et délires d'une société en crise*, Paris, l'Harmattan

_ _ _, 2003, *Plaidoyerpour la sociologie africaine*, Yaoundé, PUY

Nkrumah K., 1965, *Neo-colonialism, The Last Stage of Imperialism*, New York, International

Nkrumah K., 1970, *Class Struggle in Africa*, London, Panaf Books

Nug B., 2009, L'Hymne Nationale du Cameroun, un poème-chant à décolonialiser, Ydé, Clé.

Nyamnjoh F., 1991, *Mind Searching*, Kucena Damian Nigeria Limited, Anamba State.

Okonjo K., 1977, *Women in Contemporary Africa*, New York, University Press of America

Randall V., 1982, *Women and Politics*, London, MacMillan Press Ltd

Rey P., 1971, *Colonialisme, Neo-colonialisme et Transition au Capitalisme*, Paris, Maspero

Reynaud J. D., 1982, *Sociologie des conflits de travail*, Paris, PUF

Ridgeway C. *The Dynamics of Small Groups,* New York, St. Martin's Press

Rist co, 2001, *Le développement : historique d'une croyance occidentale*, Paris, PUF

Robertson C. and Berger I., 1986, women and class in Africa, New York, Africana Publishing Company.

Rodney W., 1974, *How Europe Underdeveloped Africa*, Washington, Howard University Press

Romaine S., 1994, *Language in Society. An Introduction to Sociolinguistics*, Oxford, Oxford University Press

Rosaldo M. and Lamphere L. eds, 1974, *Women Culture and Society*, Stanford, Stanford University Press

Rosaldo R. L., 1974, *Culture and Society*, Stanford, Stanford University Press.

Roulleau Berger L., 1999, *Le travail en friche. Le monde de la petite production urbaine,* Paris, Editions de l'Aube

_ _ _, 2004, *La rue, miroir des peurs et des solidarités*, Paris, PUF

Ryan W., 1971, *Blaming the Victim*, New York, Vintage Books.

Schaefer R. T., 1986, *Sociology*, Second Ed. New York, Mc Graw Hill Inc.

Schehr S., 1999, *La vie quotidienne des jeunes chômeurs*, Paris, PUF.

Smith S., 2010, Voyage en postcolonie, Paris,Grasset.

Simmel Georg, 1950. The Sociology of Georg Simmel. Kurt H. Wolf (trans) New York, Free Press.

Sinjoun Luc, 2003, *Sociologie des relations internationales africaines*, Paris, Karthala.

Sommers M., 2003, *Urbanization, war and Africa's Youth at Risk. Towards Understanding and Addressing Future Challenges,* BEPS, Washington DC.

Songuè P. B., 1990, *La prostitution en Afrique, l'exemple de Yaoundé,* Paris, Karthala

The American Psychological Association, 2012, *The Effects of Poverty, Hunger and Homeless on Children and Youth.*

Tim Curry, Robert Jiobu, Kent Schwirian, 2002, *Sociology for the Twenty-first Century,* 3rd Edition, New Jersey, Prentice Hall.

Tonnies F. 1887/1957, Community and Society, First Ed. East Lansing, Mishigan University Press.

Touré A., 1985, *Lespetits métiers à Abidjan. L'imagination au secours de la conjoncture,* Paris, Karthala.

Velden Thorstein, 1999, *The Theory of the leisure Class,* New York, Viking Press

Waquant L., 2008, *Urban Outcast. A Comparative Sociology of Advanced Marginality,* Cambridge, Polity Press, 65 Bridge Street.

Weber Max, 1922, *Economy and society* Translated by Ephraim Fischoff et al., New York, Bedminster Press

Weber Max, 1946, from H. H. Gerth and C. Wright Mills (eds), Max Weber, *Essays in Sociology,* New York, Oxford University Press

Weber Max, 1958, (orig. 1904), *The Protestant Ethic and the Spirit of Capitalism,* Tranlated by Talcolt Parsons, New York Scribner's

Wilson W.J., 1980, The Declining Significance of Race: Blacks and Changing American Institution, Chicago University Press.

Wirth J.A., 1967, *Urban sociology,* Eurasia Publishing House Ltd, New Delhi

Work Bank. 1991, Making Adjustments Works For the Poor: A frame for Policy Reform in Africa,

Zaretsky Eli, 1976, Capitalism, the Family and Personal Life, London, Harper and Row.

Ziegler J., 1980, Main basse sur l'Afrique, La recolonisation, Paris, Seuil.

Articles

Afonja A., 1986, "Land control: A critical Factor in Yoruba Gender Stratification". In: *Women and Class in Africa*, New York, Africana Publishing Company

Afonja S., 1981, "Current Explanations of Sex Inequality: A Reconsideration", In: *Nigerian Journal of Economics and Social Studies*, vol 21, N°2

_ _ _, 1983, "Women, Power and Authority in Traditional Yoruba society" In: *Visibility and Power: Essays on Women in society and Development* ed. Leela Dube,

Agih Isaac A., 2007, "Perspectives of youth Empowerment and sustainable Development in Nigeria". In: *Journal of Research and Contemporary Issues*, Vol 3 n°1&2, Makundi Aboki Publishers.

Amin Ajah, 2001, « Rural Poverty and Agricultural Development in Cameroon », Pauvreté et développement durable, colloque réorganisé par la Chaire UNESCO (Université Montesquieu-Bordeaux IV- UNESCO paris.

Babissakana, 2003, « Crise énergie électrique au Cameroun, la Banque Mondiale et le FMI devraient assumer leur abus d'ingérence économique » Yaounde

Bankole A. and Ndongo Y.F.O., 2007, "Globalization and the challenges of Industrial Development in Sub-Sahara African Countries: A study of Nigeria and Cameroon" in: *African Sociology Association Congress*, 15-18 July, South Africa

Beinstein H., 1997, "Notes on Capital and Peasantry", In: *Women and Class in Africa*, London, ed. Robertson C. and Berger, Sage Publication

Beneria L., 1981, "Conceptualizing the Labour Force: the Underestimation of Women's Economic Activities", In: *Africa women in the Development Process*, ed. N. Nelson, London Cass

Boyomo Assala L. C., 2006, « Ségrégation administrative et fragmentation sociale : éléments de dépassement », In : Simo D. *Construction identitaires en Afrique. Enjeux, stratégies et conséquences,* Yaoundé, CLE

Brenner M., 1982, « Unemployment in America » In: Hess B.B. et al., *Sociology*, New York, MacMillan Publishing Company.

Bujra Janet M., 1978, *Proletarianization and the "Informal Economy" a case study from Nairobi,* African Urban Studies, 47: 47-66.

Bujra Janet M., 1978, "Female Solidarity and the Sexual Division of Labour", In: *Women united, women divided* ed. P. Captan and J. Bujra, London Tavistock

Burvinic Magra and Nadia Yussef, 1978, "Women Headed Households: The ignored Factor in Development". Monograph prepared for the Office of women in Development, USAID

Burnley R., 1990, "Mobilising Savings in Cameroon" In: *Salford Papers in Economics*, Salford

Bruno da Ponta, 1974, Portuguese Colonialism in Africa, London, International Defence and Aid Fund.

Charmes J., 1998, « Le secteur informel, un concept contesté, des modèles d'évolution inadaptés, une réalité inconnue », In : *Tiers-monde*, octobre, décembre, vol 57.

Christansen C., 2011, *Youth Religiousity and Moral Critique: God, Government and Generations in Time of AIDS in Uganda,* African Development Volume XXXVI n°3&4. Council for the Development of Social Research in Africa.

Chodorow N., 1979, "Mothering, Male Dominance and Capitalism", In: Eisenstein Z. R., *Capitalist Patriarchy and the Case for Social Feminism,* New York, Monthly Review Press

Ciancanelli P., 1980, "Exchange, reproduction and sex subordination among the Kikuyu of East Africa", In: *Review of Radical Political Economy*, vol 12, N°2

Clignet R. A., 1977, Women, Education and Labour Force Participation: Social Change and Social Differentiation in Cameroon, In: *The Journal of Women, Culture and Society*, Chicago, the University of Chicago Press.

Commerton J. M., 1982, « Homophobia and social work » In Weick A and Vandiver S. T., *Women Power and Change,*

National Association of Social Workers Inc., Washington D. C.

Connor W., 1977, "Nation Building or Nation Destroying" In: *World Politics*, vol 24

Duignan P. & L. H Grann, 1975, Colonialism in Africa, In: *The Economics of Colonialism*, vol 4, Cambridge, Cambridge University Press

Duignan P. and Grann L. H., 1975, colonialism in Africa, In: *Journal the Economics of colonialism,* vol 4, Cambridge, Cambridge University Press

Durkheim E., 1998, « Représentation individuelle et représentations collectives » In : *Sociologie et Philosophie*, Paris, PUF.

Edari R., 1980, Dependent Development and Urbanization in Africa", In *La Dépendance de l'Afrique et les moyens d'y Remédier,* Paris, Berger Levrault.

Ekomo Engolo C. and Nana-Fabu S., 2008, « Une socio-anthropologie de l'économie souterraine, cas des petits métiers de la rue » In : *Revue Internationale des Sciences Humaines et Sociales,* vol 2 N°2, Paris, l'Harmattan.

Freud Sigmund, 1965, Feminity In: *New Introductory Lectures in Psycho-analysis*, New York, ed. J. Strachey, Norton

Gans, J., (1994), "Positive Functions of the Underserving Poor; Uses of the underclass in America", In: *Politics and society,* vol 22, n° 3 (September 1994), sage Publication.

Gittinger P. et al., 1990, "Household Food Security and the Role of women" In: *World Bank Discussion Papers,* The World Bank, Washington D-C

Goheen, M., 1996, "Men own the fields, women own the crops", In: *Journal of Social Science*, University of Wisconsin Press USA

Gramean Village-Bank, 1981, In: *Bangladesh Micro Credit and Development Journal*, N°007

Granovetter M. 1985, "Economic Action and Social Structure: The problem of Embeddedness", In*American Journal of Sociology,* 201- 225.

Guimapi C., 1995, « Les réactions de suivie des femmes à Yaoundé », In: Cahiers d'OSCICA, N°16, ORSTOM

International Labour Organiezation (ILO), 2011, Global Employment Trends, Geneva.

International Monetary Fund (IMF), 2003, Cameroon: Poverty Reduction Strategy Paper., IMF country Report N°03/249

Kabeer N., 1995, « Targetting Women in Transforming Institutions, Policy lessons from NGO Anti-Poverty Efforts » In *Development In Practice*, vol 5, Oxfam, Oxford

Kakou A., 2008, « Les dimensions centrales de la gouvernance et les priorités pour l'altérité des objectifs du Millénaire pour le développement », In : Grégoire L. J., Kane A. R. and Kakou A., *l'Afrique et les défis de la gouvernance*, Paris, Maisonneure et Larose.

Kalu W. J., (1993), "Battered Spouses as a social concern in work with families in two semi-rural communities of Nigeria" In: *Journal of Family and Violence*, vol 8

Keller B. and Bay E. G., 1977, "African Women and Problems of Modernisation" In: *African Society*, Culture and Politics, University Press of America.

Kettel B., 1986, The commodization of women in Tugen (Kenya) social organization, In: Robertson C. and Berger I., 1986, In: *women and class in Africa,* New York, Africana Company.

Landa J. T., 1993, « Culture et activité entrepreneuriale dans les pays en développement : le réseau ethnique organisation économique », In : *Berger B. esprit d'entreprise, cultures et société*, Paris, Editions Maxima

Leacock E., 1981, in Stamp P., 1986, "Kikuyu women self-help Groups" In: Robertson C. and Berger L. 1986, *Women and class in Africa*, New York, Africana Publishing Company.

Leacock E., 1981, In Stamp P., 1986, "Kikuyu Women's Self-Help Groups: Toward an Understanding of the Relation between Sex-Gender System and Mode of Production in Africa", In Robertson C. and Berger I., *Women and Class in Africa*, New York, Africana Publishing Company.

Lelay S., 2007, « Précarisation salariale et souffrance sociale », In : *Revue pluridisciplinaire en science de l'homme et de la société*, Formes et figures de la précarité

Longman T., 1999, "Nation, Race or Class? Defining the Hutu and Tutsi of East Africa", In: *Research in Politics and Society*, vol 6

Maldono C., 1988, « Les petits producteurs urbains d'Afrique Francophone » In : *Le courrier*, N°110

Marx Karl, 1963, (orig. 1844), "Estranged Labour Economic and Philosophic Manuscripts of 1884" In C. Wright Mills (ed) *Images of Man*, New York, George Brazillar

Mayoux L., 2001, "Tackling the Down Side: Social Capital, Women's Empowerment and Micro-Finance in Cameroon", In*Development and Change*, World Bank, June

Mazrui A. A., 1994, "Le développement dans un contexte multi culturel / orientations et tensions" In: Serageldin I. and Taboroff J., *culture et développement en Afrique*, Washington D/C, Banque Mondiale

Milgram S. 1970, In Schaefer 1986. Sociology, 2nd Ed. New York, McGraw Hill Inc.

MINFI, 2002, « Tableau de Bord sur la situation des Enfants et des Femmes au Cameroun », Yaoundé.

Mboumbou P., 2010. « Pour un renouvellement théorique de la Sociologie Urbaine ». In : La Sociologie aujourd'hui. Une perspective Africaine, Paris, Harmattan.

Moore J. & B., 1982, Social Problems, New York, Prentice Hall.

Nana-Fabu S. and Ekomo Engolo C., 2008, "An Analysis of the Political Status of women in Cameroon" In: *Journal of Research and Contemporary Issues*, Vol 3 n° 1&2, Makundi, Aboki, publishers.

_ _ _, 2006, *"An* Analysis of the Economic Status of Women in Cameroon"* In: *Journal of International Women's Studies*, Boston, Vol 8 N°1.

_ _ _, 2010, "An Analysis of Some Critical Urban Problems in Cameroon" In: *International Review of Human and Social Sciences (IRHSS)* Vol. 3 n° 3, Yaoundé, Presses de L'UCAC.

_ _ _, 2012, "An Analysis of the Link between Rapid Urbanization and Unemployment in the city of Douala" in *Mutibe*, revue pluridisciplinaire et bi-annuelle, FLSH University of Douala.

Ndongo Lebogo, 2002, « Automobile: le boom des congelés », Cameroun Tribune.

Ngandjeu J., 2005, « La Chine, 6ème Puissance Economique », Cameroun Tribune, N°8501/4700.

Nkohkwo A. and Tanyi R., 2007, "Sustainable Financing of projects in Africa: a diaspora perspective (Part II)" In: *Proceedings of the African diaspora Workshops on sustainable Development,* London, T.M.G. Registered Foundation Charity N°1114694, Edited by Nwana H.S. and Burnley R., Oxford Street

Nouihe Kante, 2002, « Les contraintes de la privatisation des entreprises publiques et parapubliques au Cameroun », In : *Revue Internationale de Droit économique,* vol XVI, N°4.

Okojié C., 2003, "Employment Creation for Youth in Africa. The Gender Dimension", Department of Economics and Statistics, The University of Benin, Nigeria.

Ondogo Fouda M., 2009, « Performance, financement et microcrédit dans les activités génératrices de revenus : une étude empirique auprès des marchés de Douala au Cameroun », colloque international : la vulnérabilité TPE des PME dans un environnement mondialisé. IMPME-AUF-AIREPME.

Obbo C., 1986, "stratification and the lives of women in Uganda",In: Robertson C. and Berger I. (1986), women and class in Africa, New York, Africana Publishing Company.

Poverty and Famine. An essay on Entitlement and Deprivation, 1992, Oxford University Press, New York.

Republic of Cameroon (August 2009) Growth and Employment Strategy Paper. Reference Framework for Government Action over the Period 2010-2020., Yaounde, Office of the Prime Minister, Head of Government.

Richal A. et al., 2010, Women's Credit Program and Family Planning in Rural Bangladesh, University of Dhaka, Bangladesh.

Robaud F., 1994, « Le Marché du travail à Yaoundé 1983-1993 : la décennie perdue », *Revue du Tiers-Monde,* tome XXXV n°140 page 751-778.

Robertson C. and Berger I., 1986, "Women's Education and Class Formation in Africa" In: *Women and class in Africa*, Africana Publishing Company.

Rwengue, 2003, "Poverty and Sexual Risk Behaviour Among Young People in Bamenda Cameroon", In: *AfricanPopulation Studies/Etudes de la Population Africaine*, vol 18, N°2. PP 91-104.

Sacks K., 1974, "Engels Revisited: Women, the Organization of Production and Private Property" In: *Woman, Culture and Society*, Ed. Michelle R. and Lamphere L., Standford University Press

Sama Nwana H., 2007, "Sustainable development: Africa Needs Another Model" In: *Proceedings of the African Diaspora Workshops on sustainable Development*, London, T.M.G. Registered Foundation Charity, N°1114694, Edited by Nwana H.S. and Burnley R. Oxford Street

Stamp P., 1986, « Kikuyu Women's Self-help Group: Toward an Understanding of the Relation Between Sex-Gender System and Mode of Production in Africa » In :Roberson C. and Berger I., *Woman and Class in Africa*, New York, Africana Publishing Company.

United Nations, 1995, Report on the Fourth World Conference on Women, Beijing, China, UN; New York.

United Nations Economic and Social Council (Economic and social Commission for Asia and Pacific committee on poverty Reduction 4th session) on Urban poverty and the working poor: facing the challenges of Urbanization and Urban Poverty in Asia and the Pacific (2007).

Vakunta P., 2011, "Music, Language and Human Rights in Cameroon: The Voice of Elwood, Valsero and Lapiro". Pambawuka News: Pan Africa Voices for Freedom and Justice.

UNICEF Report, 2011, "Poverty in Africa", Washington D.C.

Wirth Louis, 1938, "Urbanism as a way of life", In: *America Journal of Sociology*, vol 44: 8-20, n°7, University of Chicago Press.

World Bank, 1995, "Cameroon : Diversity, Growth and Poverty Reduction. Population and Human Resources Division", Report N° 13167-CM

_ _ _, 2012, Cameroon Economic Udate: Unlocking the Labour Force, Washington D.C..

Zambo B., 2002, « *Démocratisation, exacerbation, régime identitaire et rivalités ethniques : le cas du Sud Cameroun* », Afrique et Développement, Vol. XXXVII, N° 1&2.

Zolty A., 1990, "Cameroon: Agriculture, élevage, Pêche et forêt", In: *Afrique-Agriculture,* Etude speciale, vol 7, N°175.

Dissertations and "Memoires"

Boyomo A., 2012, Ph.D. Seminar: Methodology-Sociology, Douala, The University of Douala.

Daouda M., 2012, "Action des ONG pour le développement en zone rurale : cas de la COPRESSA, unpublished Master II mémoire en sociologie, Douala, The University of Douala.

Goheen, M., 1984, "Ideology and political Symbols: The Commoditization of Land, labour and Symbolic Capital in Nso", Ph. D Dissertation, Harvard University

Guebou T. F., 2007, "Formation du collectif et processus de construction du lien social dans les activités économiques spontanées : une approche sociologique des opératrices du poteau Elf à Douala », Unpublished Master II mémoire in Sociology, Douala, The University of Douala.

Moutombi A. T., 2013, "Action collective et comportements opportunistes dans les activités d'une entreprise : cas du contrôle au Port Autonome de Douala », Unpublished Master II Mémoire in Sociology, Douala, The University of Douala

Nanche R., "Youth Poverty in the City of Douala", Ongoing Ph.D Thesis in Sociology, Douala, The University of Douala.

Ndondock A. C., 2013, "Le vécu socioprofessionnel des agents de propreté urbaine de la société HYSACAM à Douala », Unpublished Master II Mémoire in Sociology, Douala, The University of Douala.

Ndongmo M., 2012, "l'Eglise Catholique et le processus démocratique au Cameroun: une analyse de la participation politique des archidiocèses de Douala et

Yaoundé », Unpublished Master II Mémoire in Sociology, Douala, The University of Douala.

Nga Ndongo V., 1975, "Ethnosociologie du bar à Yaoundé », Mémoire de DEES en sociologie, Yaoundé, Université de Yaoundé.

_ _ _., 1999, L'opinion Camerounaise : problématique de l'opinion en Afrique noire : Thèse de doctorat d'Etat ès Lettres et sciences humaines, Tome I, Université de Paris X, Novembre.

_ _ _., 2013, Ph.D. Seminar: Methodology-Sociology, Douala, The University of Douala.

Ngadjifna, 2009, "Structures lamidales et pouvoir moderne au Nord-Cameroun », Ph. D Sociology, The University of Yaounde I.

Nobouk Bessi M., 2013, « La régulation organisationnelle des risques de travail en entreprise : les Aciéries du Cameroun » Mémoire de Master de Sociologie, Université de Douala.

Retibe Y., 2013, "Vulnérabilité des institutions et travail des enfants dans la ville de Douala au Cameroun », Unpublished Master II Mémoire in Sociology, Douala, The University of Douala.

Segnou E., La gestion publique et privée de la mémoire du nationalisme camerounais : réalités, impacts et enjeux et perspectives, ongoing Ph.D. thesis in sociology, Douala, the University of Douala.

Tefe Tagne R., 2010, "Les marchés alternatifs : Pour une sociologie Economique des petits métiers Urbains », Thèse Doctorat in Sociology Douala, the University of Douala.

Tokam W., 2013, "Champ Politique Camerounais : Contribution à l'analyse de la volatilité électorale dans les départements du Haut-Nkam, de la Ménoua et du Noun », Unpublished Master II Mémoire in Sociology, Douala, The University of Douala.

Webography

What is poverty www.fightpoverty.mmbrico. Doors to Diplomacy, 2006, sponsored by US State Department and Global Schoolnet.

Fight Poverty www.fightpoverty.mmbrico. Doors to Diplomacy 2006, Sponsored by US State Department and Global Schoolnet.

The American Psychological Association, 2012, the effects of poverty, hunger and Homelessness on Children and Youth.

Dimensions of rural poverty. Html, (updated, 13th February, 2007). Rural poverty in Africa.html.

Poverty Threhold, 2010, Wikipedia, the free encyclopedia Wikipedia, Wikimedia Foundation, Inc.

Gender Equality, 2010, unesco.org.

Frej Souamaya et al. 2003, La construction sociale des localités par des acteurs locaux: conceptualisation et base théorique des outils de développement <http/intervention économique:revue.org, 1966/Octobre 2013.

Mass Media
Afrique Media, 2014.

Biya P., 2014, End of year speech to the nation – Cameroon, Yaounde, *CRTV and Cameroon Tribune*.

Equinox Radio News, (2010, 2011, 2012, 2013, 2014), Cameroon.

British Broadcasting Company (2012, 2014), London, U.K.

Cameroon Tribune Newspaper (2012, 2013, 2014), Cameroon.

La Nouvelle Expression Newspaper (2012, 2013, 2014), Cameroon.

Mutations Newspaper (2012, 2013, 2014), Cameroon.

Aurore Plus Newspaper(2014), Cameroon.

Le Messager Newspaper (2012, 2013, 2014), Cameroon.

Ouest Littoral Newspaper(2014), Cameroon.

Transparency International Cameroon (2012, 2013, 2014) Yaounde-Cameroon.

Radio Balafond(2010,2011, 2012, 2013, 2014). Cameroon.

KORI FM., (2014), Cameroon

NOSTALGIE Radio (2013, 2014), Douala-Cameroon.

Sweet FM 2013, (2014), Cameroon.

L'oeil du Sahel, (2013, 2014), Newspaper, Cameroon.
STV, (2013-2014), Cameroon.
Canal 2 International, (2013-2014), Cameroon.

INDEX

Fouda M, iv, 58, 61, 368

Freund J., 312, 356

Garfinkel H., 74, 76, 356

gender, x, 20, 33, 40, 41, 42, 44, 45, 46, 49, 52, 53, 61, 67, 68, 70, 71, 72, 79, 85, 102, 161, 180, 198, 288, 289, 310, 327

Government, 18, 21, 22, 24, 30, 31, 40, 50, 55, 62, 74, 76, 80, 84, 85, 86, 89, 122, 127, 135, 195, 221, 223, 225, 226, 230, 243, 244, 272, 274, 276, 284, 294, 301, 307, 309, 314, 316, 317, 319, 330, 332, 335, 336, 337, 338, 343, 364, 369

HIPC, 62, 127

HIV/AIDS, 19, 43, 86, 107, 119, 134

Holborn B., 78, 357

infrastructure, 20, 33, 52, 53, 67, 89, 197, 207, 245, 336

insecurity, 19, 53, 62, 107, 112, 130, 204

Kah Wallah, 43

Kamdem E, iv, 17, 61, 74, 80, 301, 357, 360

Ketcha C, 43

Kettel B, 39, 366

Lamphere L, 71, 361, 369

Lewis M, 17, 93, 99, 172, 358

Luckmann T, 76, 352

Mahatma Gandhi, 27

Mascia–Lees, 40

Mascia-Lees F. E., 70, 74

Maurice Kamto, iv, 21

Mbonji Edjenguèlè, 111, 359

Millennium Development Goals, 85

motorcycle taxis, 26, 80, 93

Nana-Fabu S, 19, 35, 36, 41, 56, 58, 60, 64, 69, 70, 73, 74, 78, 79, 80, 90, 94, 107, 108, 114, 129, 156, 162, 365, 367

Ndam Njoya, 21, 22

Ndondock A. C, v, 94, 371

Ndongo F, 18

Nga Ndongo, iv, vi, 31, 75, 76, 360, 371

Ngadjifna C., iv, 172

Nkwame Nkrumah, 27

Non-Governmental Organizations, 55, 76, 216

Okojie C, 20, 25

Ottou D, 18

patriarchy, 40, 53, 68, 131, 157, 162

petty traders, 43, 50, 51, 95, 106, 323

poverty, xi, xii, 17, 18, 22, 23, 43, 44, 46, 47, 53, 55, 58, 61, 62, 63, 65, 66, 74, 75, 77, 78, 83, 85, 87, 88, 89, 94, 96, 97, 105, 107, 108, 109,